W9-BXC-554

Mom,

Merry Christmas 2001!

Love,

Bob, Mary, Bobby, Mary K.

VOLUME III

COLLECTOR'S REFERENCE & VALUE GUIDE

FEATURING THE

FINDERS KEEPERS SECTION AND 3 VOLUME INDEX

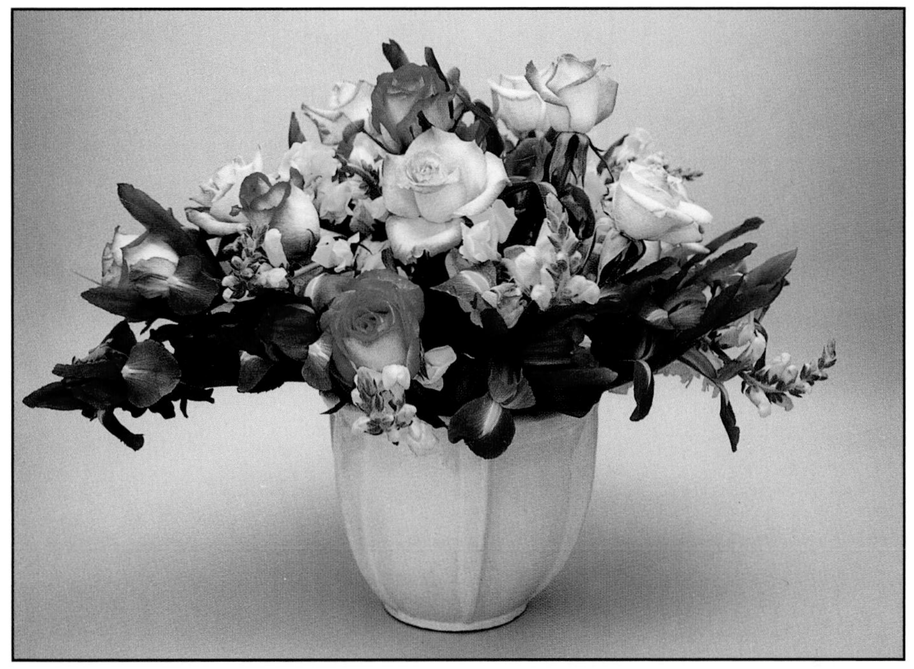

Floral arrangement in ribbed jardiniere, 7". No mark. $80.00 – 100.00.

COLLECTOR BOOKS

A Division of Schroeder Publishing Co., Inc.

The current values in this book should be used only as a guide. They are not intended to set prices, which vary from one section of the country to another. Auction prices as well as dealer prices vary greatly and are affected by condition as well as demand. Neither the authors nor the publisher assumes responsibility for any losses that might be incurred as a result of consulting this guide.

On the front cover:

Floraline Model 475, 14" tall vase, page 258
Floraline Caterpillar Planter, page 235
Butterfly Flower Holder, page 147
Large Pedestal & Jardiniere, page 112
Planter with Applied Birds, page 155
Cat Vase, page 123
Basketweave Pedestal & Jardiniere, page 42
Brown Drip Plate and Cup, page 224

On the back cover:

No. 50 Vase, page 119
Cat, page 117
Rabbit, page 117
Tall Vase, page 125
Small Vase with Handles, page 121
Fish, page 117

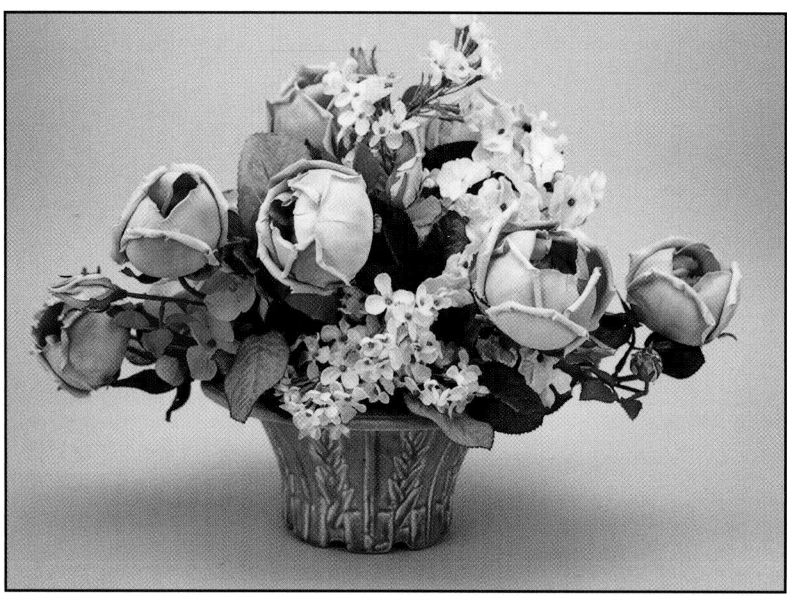

Floral arrangement in decorative bowl. 5" height. No mark. $45.00 – 60.00.

Book layout: Holly Long
Cover design: Beth Summers

Searching for
A Publisher?

We are always looking for people knowledgeable within their fields. If you feel there is a real need for a book on your collectible subject and have a large comprehensive collection, contact Collector Books.

COLLECTOR BOOKS
P.O. Box 3009
Paducah, KY 42002–3009
or
www.collectorbooks.com

Contents

About the Authors

Bob, Craig, and Margaret are long-time collectors of Nelson McCoy Pottery. Their collecting began when McCoy was usually the pottery on the floor at an antique show or in the grass at a flea market. It was one of the "other" potteries. However, part of the attraction to McCoy then was that you could find it as well as afford it. These factors are major reasons that the collections of the Hansons and Nissens have grown to a combined total of more than 5,000 pieces.

Bob and Margaret are interested in a variety of collections in addition to McCoy, including Brush-McCoy, and J.W. McCoy as well as many pieces from the "Arts & Crafts Era." In addition to pottery, they collect reverse paintings and trays, silhouette pictures, vintage whimsical plastic pins, and electric novelty clocks. Bob and Margaret have four children and live in the Seattle, Washington, area.

Craig, and his wife Pat, also enjoy collecting a number of other things in addition to the Nelson McCoy pottery. They have a modest collection of Van Briggle and Roseville pottery. They also collect Aladdin electric lamps, beaded "sugar" shade lamps from the '20s, cupid photos, rug and pillow beaters, "Chandler" pastels, and fruit and vegetable wall pockets. Craig and Pat have one daughter and are located in the greater Milwaukee area of Wisconsin.

Vintage items included in many photographs throughout the book are used to enhance a piece or to demonstrate a particular way of displaying pieces and are part of the authors' collections. Both the Hansons and the Nissens have a primary "obsession" of collecting McCoy pottery.

Margaret Hanson (holding Fergie), Craig Nissen, and Bob Hanson

Dedication

We would like to dedicate Volume III not only to all collectors past, present, and future as we have for our previous Volumes, but especially to all the long-time collectors of whom so many are responsible for establishing McCoy Pottery collecting we all love!

Preface

Our third reference book is again exclusively about the pottery made by the Nelson McCoy Pottery Company from 1910 to the mid-1980s when it was finally sold to Designer Accents.

We again have presented the content of the pottery information from the perspective of the collector. The order of the pieces are generally chronological as in the other two Volumes. We have continued the practice of including brief facts and/or opinions we have picked up during our collecting experiences or have received from other collectors.

A new addition to Volume III is an Index, 20 pages in length, covering pieces contained in all three Volumes. We hope you find this a valuable tool for reference and for locating information in any of the Volumes. We wish you the best of luck with your collecting and may Volume III be enjoyable as well as helpful in referencing some of the individual pieces you may find.

Acknowledgments

We again have numerous people to acknowledge and thank for their assistance. We said it previously, but it is so appropriate to say again, it is only with all of the generosity and caring of these people that we could accomplish this project. The type of contributions covered all the areas of need, frequently offered without even asking. To all of you, we cannot really say in words the magnitude of gratitude we feel; it has been another true labor of love for McCoy Pottery completed with your help.

The collectors pictured on the following pages as well as those listed below are the people responsible for all of this assistance. We are pleased to be able to include them in this book of Nelson McCoy Pottery as a small token of our significant appreciation. Again, thank you!

Kathy & Dominick Maloney, New York
Billie & Nelson McCoy, Ohio
Roy & Nancy Demory, Virginia
Jamie Nance, Tennessee
Lillian Conesa, Florida
Pat Nissen, Wisconsin
Randy & Karel Kimbrough, Texas
Diane & Warren Sadler, Tennessee
Harper Hanson, Washington
John (Jack) Hauseman, Ontario
Gerald Donaldson, Ohio
Basil & Dianna Adkins, Ohio
Linda & Mark Gilson, Michigan
Hallie Hanson, Washington
Dan & Marge Prater, Ohio
Fred & Sarah Wolfe, North Carolina
Mike & Mo White, Virginia
Paul & Debbie Moody, Virginia
Jeff Koehler – Koehler Auctions, Roseville, Ohio
Jean Bushnell, Colorado
Nicole Nissen, Wisconsin
David & Dee Lorberbaum, New Jersey
Bob & Debbie Morris, Virginia
Dan & Becky Snyder, North Carolina
Fred Tabler, Ohio
Ken & Julia McDaneld, Illinois
Pat & Royal Ritchey, Alabama
Bobbi Jo Waniger, Wisconsin
Bill Cook, Minnesota
Joan Bertsch, Georgia
Theron Hanson, Washington
Lee & Linda Padberg, Oregon
Scott & Heidi Whaley, Washington
John Geleski, Ohio
Christine Witt, Massachusetts

Dewayne & Audrey Imsand, Alabama

Chiquita & Dewey Prestwood, North Carolina

Joanne & Glenn Lindberg, New Jersey

Polly & John Sweetman, Delaware

Frank Heller, Virginia

Carol Seman, Ohio

Dan Eggert, Ohio

Brian Donaldson, Ohio

Frank Poolas, New Jersey

Doug Dreher, Texas

Colleen & John Vorisek, New York

Shelley & David Perry, Pennsylvania

Judie & Jeff Snyder, Ohio

Debra Thorson, Minnesota

Mark & Marilyn Cooley, Wisconsin

In our first two volumes, we presented the history of the Nelson McCoy Pottery Company from its beginning in 1910 through the decades from the 1920s to the 1980s. For more detail please read our history in the early pages of Volume I and Volume II. What we want to share here is the earlier family history that led to the establishment of the Nelson McCoy Pottery Company in 1910.

In the early 1800s, plentiful natural resources of Zanesville and the surrounding area attracted many settlers. Rich clay, coal, natural gas, and petroleum were some of the resources found. Pottery made from local clay and the ready natural source of fuel for use in the kilns allowed this region to eventually become a major pottery-producing area in the nation.

In the late 1840s two brothers, W.M. and W.N. (Nelson) McCoy, immigrated to the United States. W.M. settled in Harper's Ferry, West Virginia. W.N. traveled to Putnam, Ohio, near Zanesville.

W.N. acquired land and set out to provide for his family. With the region well suited for production of stoneware, W.N. built a small pottery factory in 1848. With primitive equipment, the ware produced was rough and unfinished. However, crude pottery was needed to withstand the rough pioneer life. Therefore, concentration was on making the pottery serviceable and not necessarily ornamental.

Pottery containers were needed by settlers, and since not found in nature, they had to be produced by man. Many farmers made their own crocks, jars, jugs, and churns vital to the daily life of a pioneer. The farmer-potters soon realized utilitarian vessels they produced were universally needed and a marketable commodity. This was the climate emerging when W.N. built his pottery factory in 1848. That same year W.N. had a son, J.W., who later became the founder of the first major McCoy pottery company.

In 1856, W.N. became associated with Benjamin & Company, a Putnam grocery and dry goods business. Before mid-1860, W.N. acquired his own dry goods business in Putnam. In 1862 or 1863, W.N.'s brother in Harper's Ferry, who was also in the merchandising business, decided to move his family, which included his son Wilbur F., to Putnam, Ohio.

W.M took a partner and established a dry goods store, McCoy & Adamson, in Putnam. Wilber, following his father's example, went to work in another dry goods store in town. After a few years, Wilber became a partner in the Zanesville Hardware Co. During the 1880s, Wilber became one of the largest wholesalers of stoneware in the region. He remained with this company until a year before his death in 1896.

While his cousin W.F. was in the dry goods business in Putnam, J.W. McCoy moved about 10 miles south of Zanesville to Roseville, Ohio around 1871. He opened a general store in 1876. At that time, there were many established potteries in the region, but the high demand for pottery induced him to form a new pottery company in Roseville.

In 1886, J.W. McCoy added his name to the 13 established Roseville potteries with the formation of the Williams and (J.W.) McCoy Pottery Co. About 1890, they merged with another pottery and were renamed the Kildow, Williams and McCoy Pottery Co. In addition to his interest in pottery production, J.W. also became a pottery jobber that supplied pottery to wholesalers and undoubtedly also retailed pottery through his general store.

Billie and Nelson McCoy Jr.
A special thank you for once again providing us their valued support and contributions. Photos of their many one-of-a-kind pieces in the Rare and Non-Production section are wonderful to share with all collectors, and their numerous Floraline catalogs helped present the complete story on the profitable Floraline Line.

Nelson McCoy Pottery Company Employee Photo from 1928

About two years later, the Kildow, Williams and McCoy Pottery Co. was renamed the Midland Pottery Co. In 1898, the company was sold to the Roseville Pottery Co. The next year, J.W. McCoy formed a pottery company solely under his own name. He began his pottery business by producing the same type items as before, those related to foodstuff preparation and storage. Most likely during the later part of the 1800s, J.W. and his cousin Wilber had an arrangement where pottery was produced with the stenciled inscription, "W.F. McCoy Wholesale, dealer of Stoneware Zanesville, Ohio." It seems the arrangement to supply Wilber with pottery could not have been between J.W.'s father and Wilber back in 1848. Wilber would have been only six years old at that time and living in Harper's Ferry.

As early as 1904, the J.W. Pottery Company branched out into the new field of art pottery. This art pottery consisted of decorative vases, jardinieres and pedestals, umbrella stands, and flowerpots. These pieces proved to be desirable to consumers, and the new undertaking was successful. The J.W. McCoy Pottery Co. continued in business under that name until 1911. The directors decided to purchase the Globe Stoneware Co. and the old Owens Pottery building in Zanesville which included molds and equipment. George Brush, owner of the old Owens Pottery building and its equipment, acquired a controlling interest in the J.W. McCoy Pottery Co. when he suggested they purchase his assets in the building. Subsequently, the business became the Brush-McCoy Pottery Company. In 1918, the McCoy family sold their interest in the Brush-McCoy Pottery Company. However, it was not until 1925 that the McCoy name was dropped. The Brush Pottery Co. continued in operation until 1982 when it closed.

The McCoy Pottery story did not end with their sale to the Brush Pottery Co. In 1910, four years before his death, J.W. McCoy assisted his son Nelson in establishing the new Nelson McCoy Sanitary Stoneware Co in Roseville, Ohio. It is the pottery produced by this company about which our three Volumes have been written! Although the new pottery specialized in utilitarian stoneware, while Brush Pottery concentrated more on decorative pieces, there was some direct competition between the two companies.

Around 1933, with demand for stoneware decreasing and the demand for decorative pieces on the rise, the company simplified their name to the Nelson McCoy Pottery Co. This company operated for 57 years until sold in 1967 to the Mount Clemens Pottery Co. that retained the Nelson McCoy Pottery name and continued to run under Nelson McCoy Jr.'s leadership. Interesting to note that for a short period after purchase, they did not include the "McCoy" name on the pottery. The company was again sold in 1974 to Lancaster Colony, but they also chose to retain the company name with Nelson McCoy Jr. at the helm. Nelson retired in 1981. In 1985, with declining sales, the company was sold to Designer Accents that merged the company into theirs and renamed it Nelson McCoy Ceramics. Five years later the company shut down.

The values listed throughout Volume III are again based on pieces without any damage. Damage is defined as any hairlines, cracks, crazing, chips or flakes. Defects or flaws in original manufacture are not considered to reduce the value of a given piece. The true answer to that question is really up to the individual collector. Depending on the original flaw, these pieces can actually be more valuable.

The range of the listed value attempts to account for variation in prices throughout the country. It also considers that one particular piece may have a sharper look than another sample of the same piece. This could be a result of the color quality of the same glaze or the crispness of the piece out of the mold. As a mold is used over and over, the sharpness of its pattern, especially if it is very detailed in its design, starts to fade or dull in appearance. This is how you can tell if a particular piece was "early" out of the mold, (very crisp) or made near the end of the mold's life (detail rather dulled). The range in value also considers the difference in values when a piece was made in several glaze colors, and the value varies from color to color in rareness and desirability. In some cases, we have actually listed the different colors with separate values.

The number of years of manufacture of a piece will also have an effect on the value. As the number of years of production increases, so obviously does the probability of being able to find and add that piece to your collection.

There are a number of pieces that were made for several years but with a variety of glazes used over that time. In some of these examples, the marking of the piece may also have changed. This is especially true of several pieces initially made in the late 1920s to early 1930s. They were available in one or more of the glazes of that era and then continued to be manufactured in the pastel glazes of the late 1930s and 1940s. A few actually were still being made into the 1950s. A good example we have cited before in earlier volumes is that of the lower butterfly porch jar. The early manufactured examples of this piece were not marked and had matte glazes. The ones produced into the 1950s had gloss finishes and were marked McCoy. The manufacture of this piece covered the better part of the 20 years! Other later examples of pieces with a long production life are a couple of the turtle and frog pieces that were all made originally in the 1950s in the same green color and then were made in other glaze colors many years later in the 1970s. The values of these types of pieces can vary greatly. We have again tried to take all of these issues into consideration in the development of the values of these pieces in the book. However, some of these issues can be subtle, and thought should be given to this area, when applicable, before making a purchase.

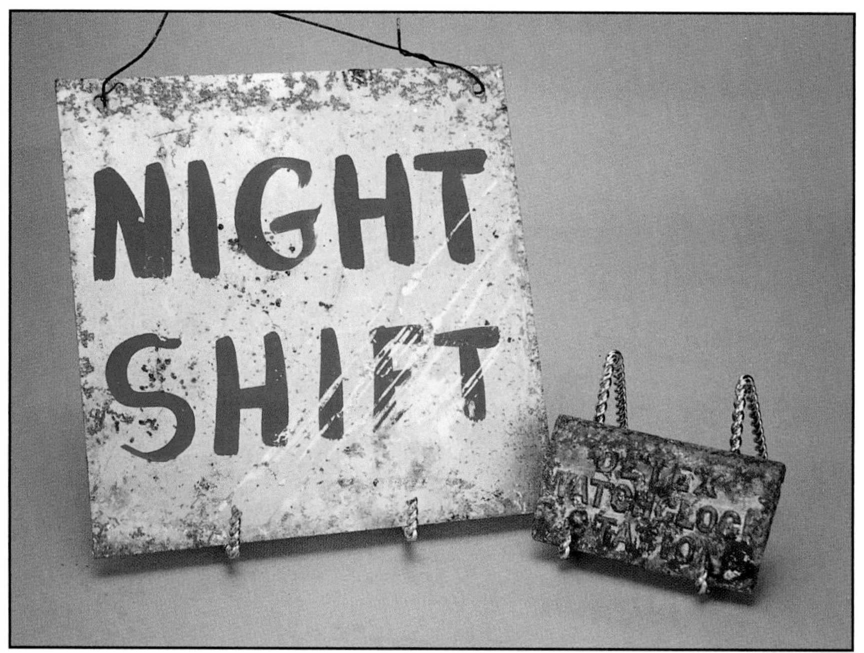

"Night Shift" sign and "Watchclock Station" plate from Nelson McCoy Pottery Plant.

Hand decoration over the glaze in a method commonly described as "cold paint" was done on many pieces, especially in the 1940s and 1950s. This paint was not very durable, and pieces are commonly found with much or all of the paint missing. A piece complete with all the original cold paint will command a premium price over one with no paint at all. The value ranges in the book again have taken this variation into consideration. However, this is another topic that relates to the personal preference of the individual collector in terms of the amount of additional value the cold paint should add to a piece.

Several paper labels were used on a number of lines. They were usually attached to the side of the piece. If a piece in the book has a label, this again has NOT been considered in the value. If the label is in good condition, you should add about $5.00 – $15.00 to the value of the piece. This range covers slight variation in acceptable label condition as well as the rarity of the label. (See the Marks and Labels pages for photo examples of some of these labels.)

Throughout the book we have included additional information on all pieces. Size of a pictured piece is included as well as other sizes of that same style when they existed. Generally, jardinieres are sized by the width of the opening at the top, planters by their width, and vases by their height. We have also included information on other glazes offered on pieces not pictured when available. The difference between cataloged glazes and other unusual or rare glazes found by collectors is noted. An estimate of the original year or era of manufacture of a piece is also included although we remind you of the earlier point made that some pieces were made for many years after initially produced.

Finally, we have included an indication of whether or not a piece is marked. If usually not marked, we will indicate "no mark." If usually marked, we have listed the type of mark style used by category indicated in the Marks and Labels section. We have noted where we know a piece that had been found both with and without a mark or if it has been found with more than one style of mark, such a "NM" and "McCoy."

Hammer and "initial" tool for marking piece to identify employee for piecework credit.

Silt screen from plant used in production operation for skimming impurities. Gnome (3", USA mark, $250.00 – 300.00), pictured with screen for size comparison.

The following are examples of some of the marks used on the bottom of the pottery throughout the history of the Nelson McCoy Pottery Company. There are many different styles of these marks. Variations exist on letter style, position of the "USA" or "Made in USA" mark in respect to the McCoy name, location of mark, etc., but the content should be similar. The following examples provide a range of those styles so that you can make an identification. As we indicate the presence or absence of a mark, you will see that we do it by general style. In addition to a "no mark" indication, we will use either "old mark" for the first style group shown, "NM" for any variation of that mark, and "McCoy" if any style of "McCoy" is used. For Floraline, we will indicate as such. We have also included photo examples of labels as reviewed in the Pricing Information section.

Old Stoneware Marks (1920s)

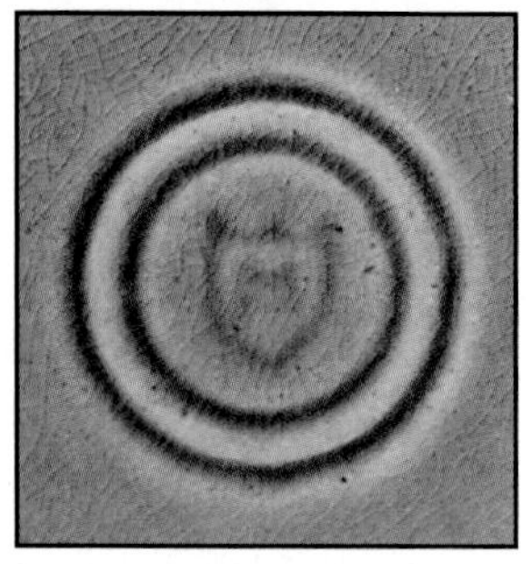

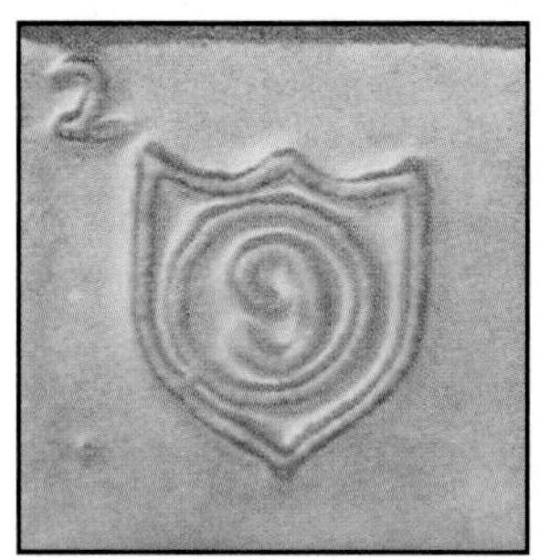

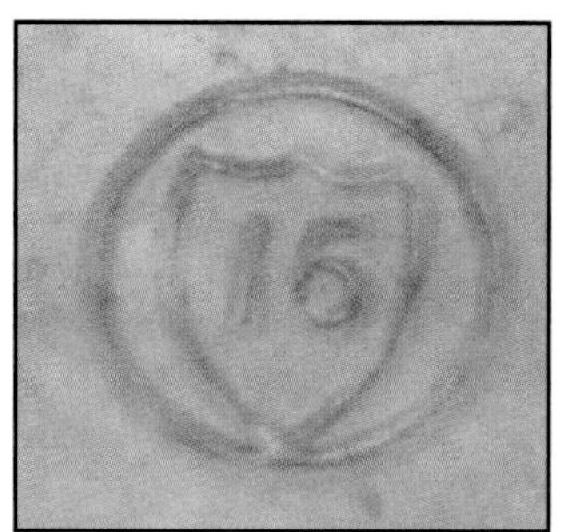

"NM" Marks (Late '30s and '40s) – Small "NM" mark shown on bottom side of piece is typical of the mark used on many of the smaller pieces of this era.

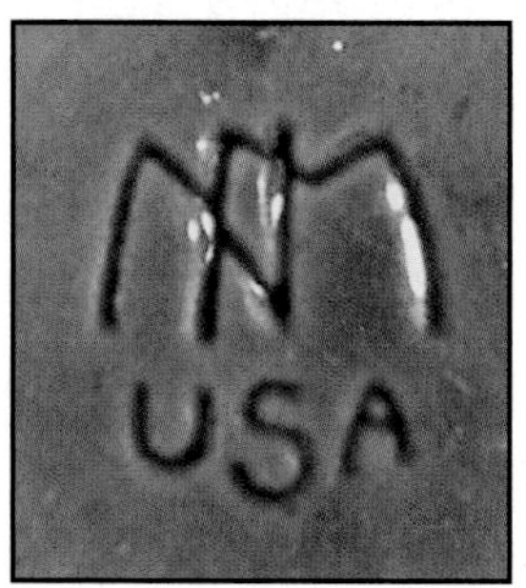

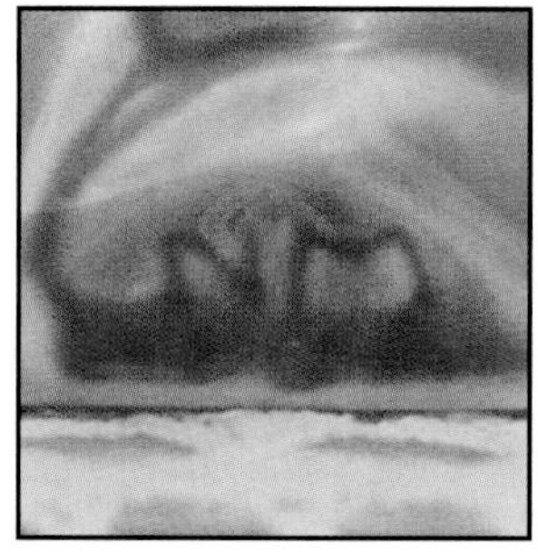

"McCoy" Marks ('40s through the late '60s)

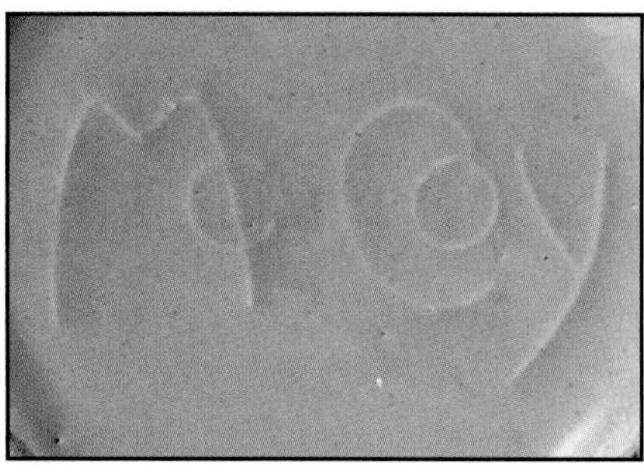

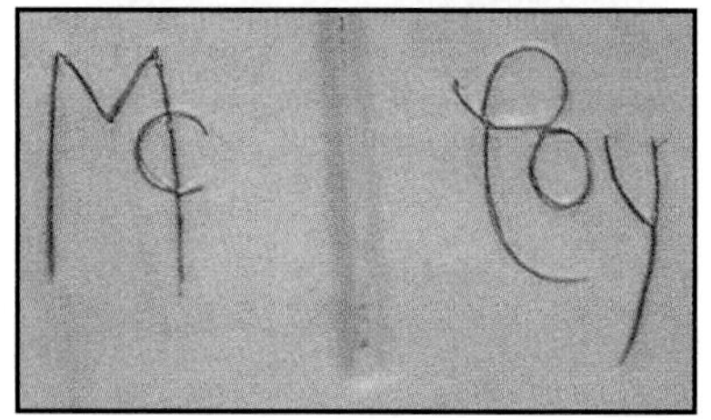

Later Marks ('70s and '80s)

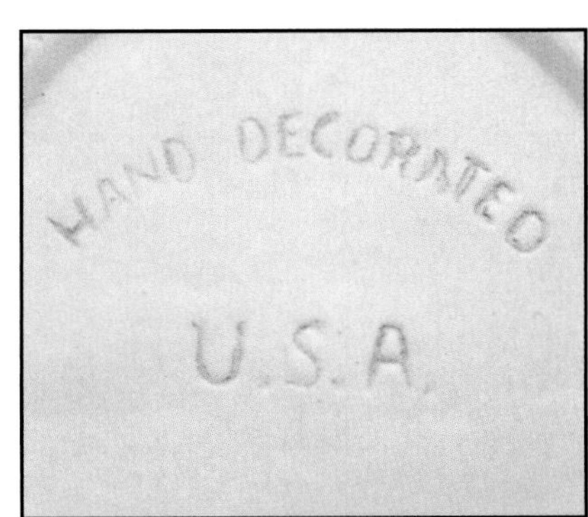

Floraline Marks ('40s through the late '70s)

Labels

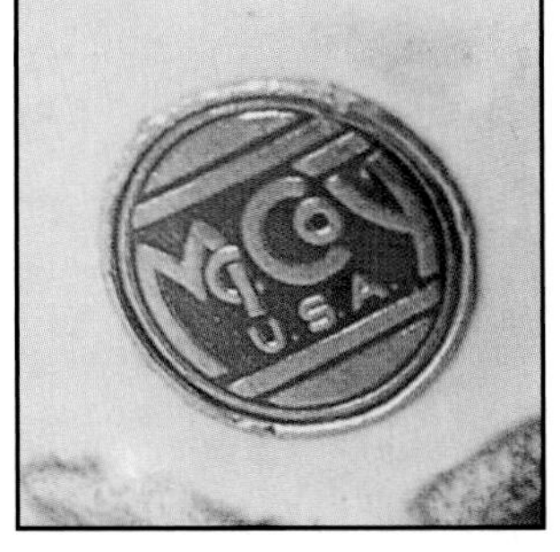

All of the early stoneware pieces on these two pages have no marks on the bottom. Most of them carry the early stencil mark which includes the "M" for McCoy.

Left: Miniature salesman samples from early stoneware. Too rare to price.

#3 Jug with Handle. $80.00 – 100.00.

#4 Jar. $60.00 – 70.00.

#5 & #6 Crocks. $75.00 – 90.00 each.

#3 Crock & #2 Jug. $60.00 – 70.00 and $50.00 – 60.00, respectively.

#2 Crock & #2 Jar. $60.00 – 70.00 and $70.00 – 80.00, respectively.

#10 & #2 Crocks. $90.00 – 110.00 and $50.00 – 60.00, respectively.

Foot Warmer. $75.00 – 100.00.

#4 Water Cooler. $250.00 – 300.00.

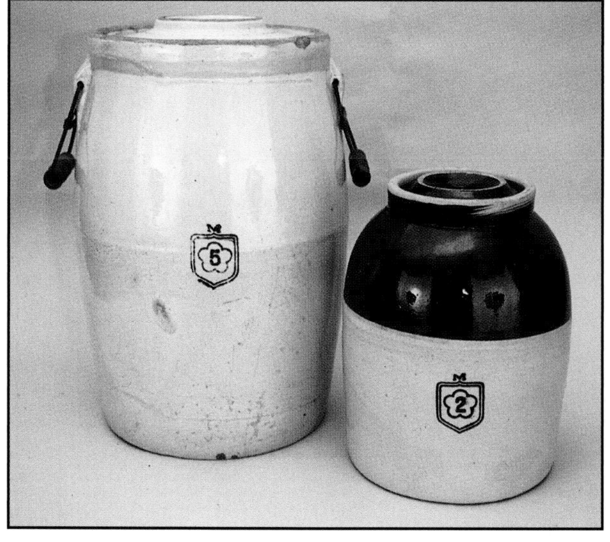

#5 & #2 Jars with Lids. $100.00 – 125.00 and $75.00 – 90.00, respectively.

Mixing Bowls. 10½". $75.00 – 100.00.

The American Clay Products Company

The American Clay Products Company (ACPC) was incorporated in 1919 in Zanesville, Ohio. It was a cooperative venture between a group of stoneware pottery companies. The Nelson McCoy Sanitary Stoneware Co. was a very big partner, and the ACPC affected operations of the NMSSC for seven years. Nelson McCoy was secretary of the ACPC. The member potteries, dates of operation, estimate of production capability, and location are in the table below.

The ACPC plan was to increase stoneware production, broaden product marketing, and improve delivery. With these improvements, the goal was to increase revenue for all the potteries. The ACPC was not formed because of "hard times" or economic conditions specific to the pottery industry. This was over ten years before the stock market crash of 1929, the beginning of the Great Depression.

Member Name	Dates of Operation	Production Quantities (Est.)	Location
AE Hull Pottery Co.	1905 – 1986	9,000 gals/day	Crooksville, OH
Burley (Zane W.) Pottery Co.	1912 – 1922	3,600 gals/day	Crooksville, OH
Burley and Winter Pottery Co.	1885 – 1937	7,500 gals/day	Crooksville/Zanesville, OH
Crooksville Pottery Co.	1903 – 1935	4,000 gals/day	Crooksville, OH
Crooksville Stoneware Pottery Co.	1890 – 1929	4,000 gals/day	Crooksville, OH
Hawthorn Pottery Co.	1893 – 1923	4,000 gals/day	Hawthorn, PA
Logan Pottery Co.	1903 – 1964	7,000 gals/day	Logan, OH
Muskingum Pottery Co.	1910 – 1928+	6,000 gals/day	Crooksville, OH
N. McCoy Sanitary Stoneware Co.	1910 – 1990	3+ cars/day	Roseville, OH
Ransbottom Brothers Pottery Co.	1900 – to present	10 cars/day	Roseville, OH
(In 1920 the pottery merged and was re-named the Robinson-Ransbottom Pottery Co.)			
Star Stoneware Co.	1892 – 1945	9,000 gals/day	Crooksville, OH
Watt Pottery Co.	1922 – 1965	3,600 gals/day	Crooksville, OH
(Watt Pottery began business by purchasing Burley (Zane W.) Pottery in 1922 and thus became an ACPC member.)			

NOTE – Gallons per day is the amount of slip used. One car is equivalent to about 5,000 gallons of slip.

Membership in the ACPC was not open to all area potteries and many potteries were not members. All ACPC members produced stoneware products. Most non-member pottery companies had their own specialties such as Weller, Roseville, and Brush-McCoy which concentrated on producing art pottery and did not choose to participate and produce stoneware items. In addition, an estimated eighteen other non-member potteries existed in the region and produced a variety of wares from porcelain ware to bricks.

Chicken Feeder. $60.00 – 75.00.

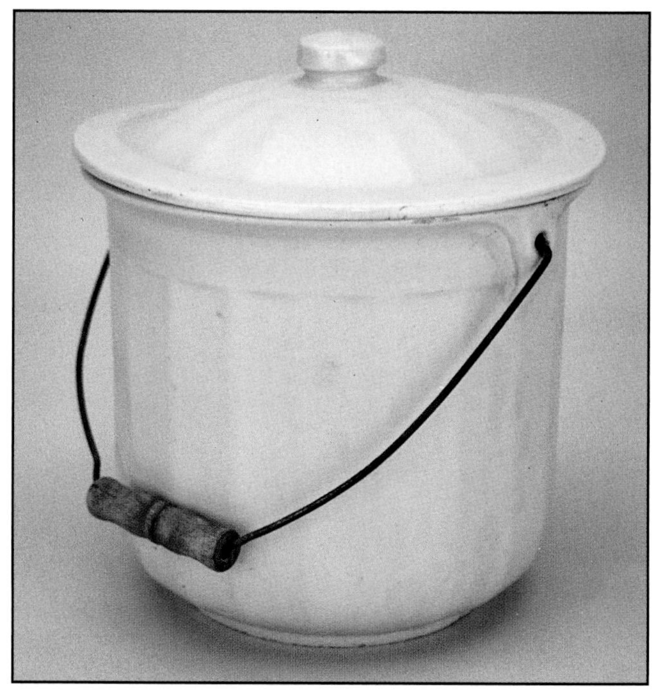

White Combinet. $75.00 – 90.00.

The ACPC organization was led by president, Frank Ransbottom. He and other ACPC organizers, including Nelson McCoy, structured the company so it would purchase the wares produced by each member pottery. ACPC salesmen would present the ACPC catalog to buyers and obtain orders. Orders were distributed among member potteries based on their average percentage of the total stoneware produced by all member potteries during the two year period from 1917 – 1918. The ACPC guaranteed to purchase a minimum of 50% of the average sales volume each member pottery had achieved during those two base years. Without specific ACPC approval, member potteries were not generally permitted to market their wares directly. ACPC issued product catalogs containing pictures of items for sale. One known example is Catalog No. 104, which was issued in 1921. It is 3½" by 9" and shows 65 different items. Another example is Catalog No. 108, which was issued in about 1925. It is 11" wide, 17" long, and is made up of 11 pages showing 94 different items. As intended, a buyer could not generally identify the pottery maker of a specific item. An exception to the no-maker mark rule was found in the 1925 catalog where a symbol used by the Ransbottom Brothers Pottery Co. is depicted next to some of the ware. It is not known exactly how long the anonymous production lasted, but later the ACPC decided that a change was appropriate. A new catalog type began that prominently displayed the name of the pottery maker, in addition to the ACPC name. These new catalogs allowed member potteries to advertise ware that they designed and produced.

The American Clay Products Co.

Illustrated Catalog
No. 104

Zanesville, Ohio, U. S. A.

THE AMERICAN CLAY PRODUCTS COMPANY

ZANESVILLE, OHIO, U. S. A.

Successors to

THE RANSBOTTOM BROS. POTTERY CO.
Roseville, Ohio

THE BURLEY & WINTER POTTERY CO.
Crooksville, Ohio

THE NELSON McCOY SANITARY STONE-WARE CO.
Roseville, Ohio

THE A. E. HULL POTTERY CO.
Crooksville, Ohio

THE STAR STONEWARE CO.
Crooksville, Ohio

THE BURLEY POTTERY CO.
Crooksville, Ohio

THE CROOKSVILLE POTTERY CO.
Crooksville, Ohio

THE LOGAN POTTERY CO.
Logan, Ohio

THE MUSKINGUM POTTERY CO.
White Cottage, Ohio
and
Crooksville, Ohio

THE HAWTHORN POTTERY CO.
Hawthorn, Pa.

Catalogue Number 104
1921

Front cover of 1921 American Clay Products catalog and listing of all member pottery companies.

These procedural changes of the ACPC seemed to be the beginning of a sudden end to the organization. The switch to the use of individually named pottery catalogs by the ACPC salesmen was very significant. Some opinions are that these changes caused several of the member potteries to become disgruntled and created hard feelings among some of the members which resulted in the break-up of the ACPC. Other opinions are that the federal government had intervened and the ACPC actions had been in response to that. Then, with the changes being unsuccessful, the government declared the ACPC a merchandising monopoly which led to the break-up. Regardless of which is opinion may actually be fact, after seven years of successful operation, the result was the liquidation of the ACPC in January 1926, three years before the onset of the Great Depression.

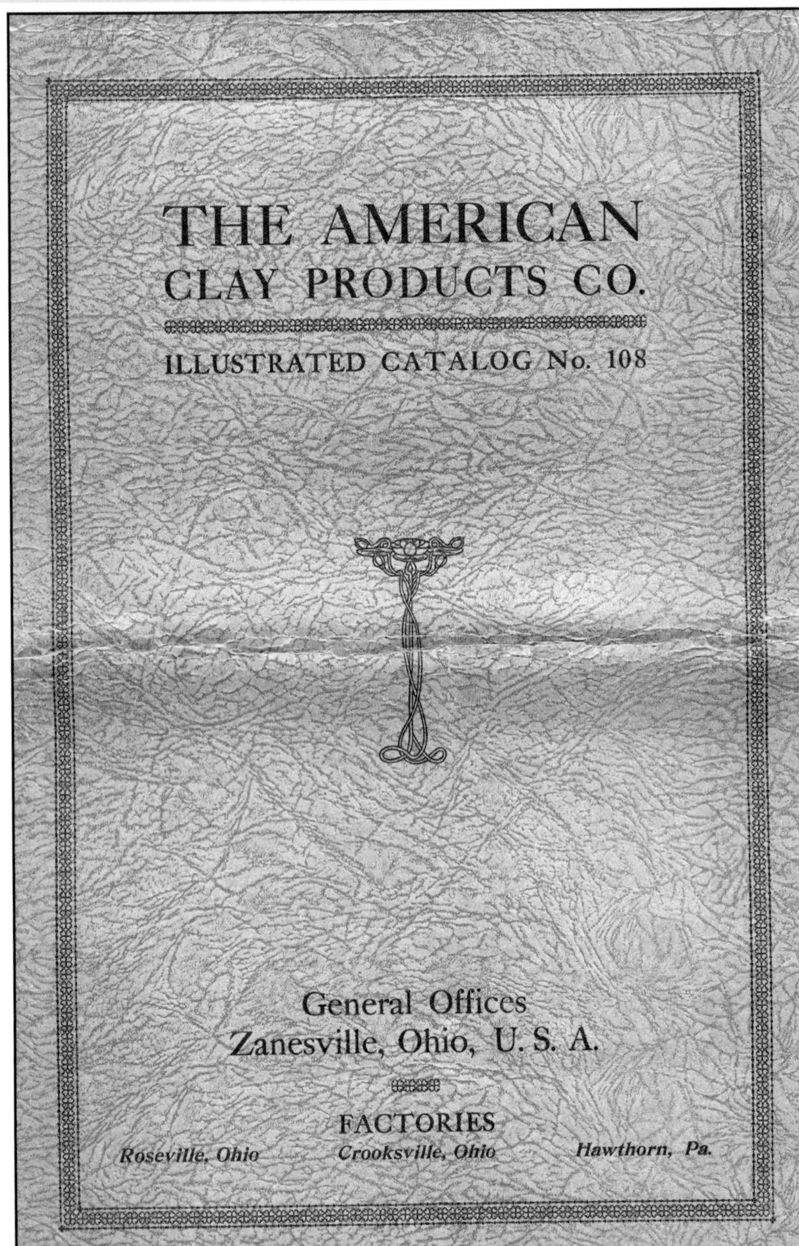

Front cover of 1925 American Clay Products catalog, 11" x 17". On pages 19 – 21 you will find content from this catalog of wares made by the Nelson Sanitary Stoneware Company.

Tulip Pedestal & Jardiniere Set in "Mahogany" glaze. Rare. Late 1920s. No marks. Pedestal 7", Jardiniere 7½". Set, $200.00 – 250.00.

MILK PANS

⅛, ¼, ½, ¾, 1, 1½ and 2 gal size., per gal. White or brown glaze.

STANDARD JARS

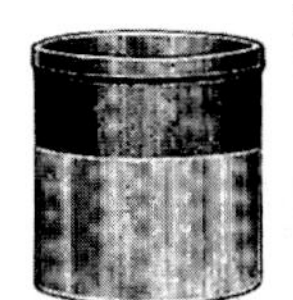

¼, ½, 1, 2, 3, 4, 5 and 6 gallon., per gal. In two colors.

STANDARD JARS OR MEAT TUBS

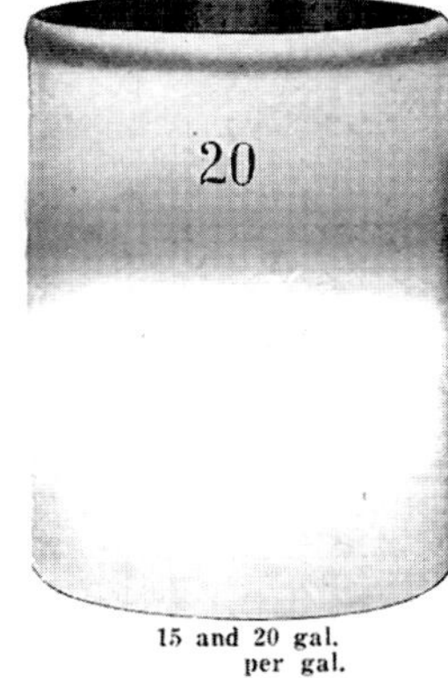

8, 10 and 12 gal. per gal. 15 and 20 gal. per gal. 25 and 30 gal., per gal. 35, 40 and 50 gallon sizes, per gal.

We furnish all size Jars and Meat Tubs with or without Covers. Also any size Jar or Meat Tub with faucet holes any dimension.

SHOULDER JUGS

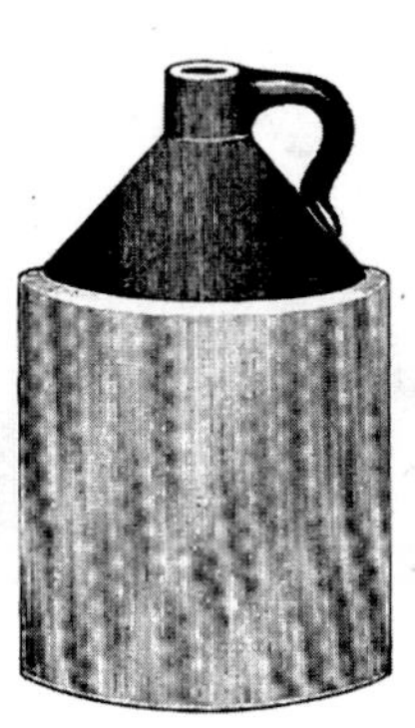

¼, ½, 1, 2, 3, 4, 5 and 6 gallon. per gal. Black glazed top, white body. Uniform corkage.

LOW BUTTERS

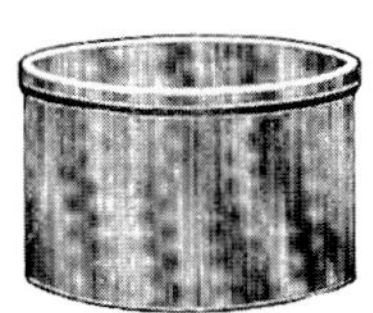

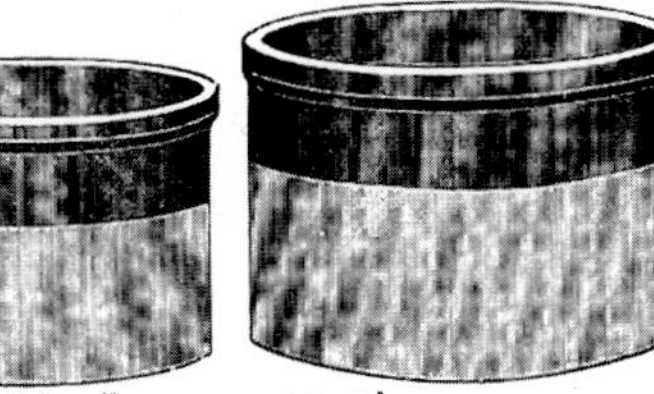

⅛, ¼, ½, 1, 1½, 2 and 3 gallon. per gal.

Catalog page from 1925 American Clay Products catalog.

COVERED BUTTER

Blue Tinted Finish—With or Without Bails.
2, 3, 4 and 5 pound sizes.

BAILED AND COVERED BUTTER JARS

Blue Tinted Finish With or Without Bail.
2, 3, 5 and 10 pound sizes.

STONE COVERED SALT BOXES

Blue Tinted Finish
Stone Covered.

BAILED AND COVERED PRESERVE JARS

2, 3, 5, 10 and 20 lb.

TEA POTS

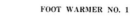

48, 42, 36, 30 and 24 sizes.
Brown—White Lined.

CEMETERY VASE

Glazed or Matt Finish
5x10 in. size.

TULIP JARS

Fine Mahogany Finish.
Made in four sizes, 7, 8, 9 and 10 in.

BOSTON BEAN POTS

1, 2, 3, 4, 6 and 8 quart sizes.

FOOT WARMER NO. 1

No. 1 TANKARD

Blue Tint or Mahogany Glaze.
Full 5 Pints.

No. 6 TANKARD

Blue Tint or Mahogany Glaze
Capacity 5 pints.

No. 5 TANKARD

Blue Tint or Mahogany Glaze
Capacity 5½ pints.

DEER PITCHER

Blue Tint—Full 5 Pints

WORTHMORE FLOWER POTS AND SAUCERS

Sizes—3 in., 4 in., 5 in., 6 in., 7 in., 8 in., 9 in., 10 in., 12 in., 14 in., 16 in.
Flower Pots With or Without Saucers

PLAIN RED BURNED FLOWER POTS AND SAUCERS

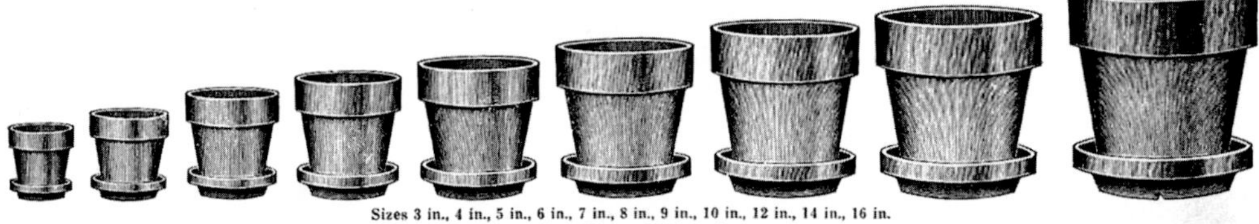

Sizes 3 in., 4 in., 5 in., 6 in., 7 in., 8 in., 9 in., 10 in., 12 in., 14 in., 16 in.
Flower Pots With or Without Saucers.

AZALEA OR LOW FLOWER POTS AND SAUCERS

Sizes—4 in., 5 in., 6 in., 7 in., 8 in., 9 in., 10 in., 12 in.
Azalea Pots With or Without Saucers.

Catalog content from 1925 American Clay Products catalog.

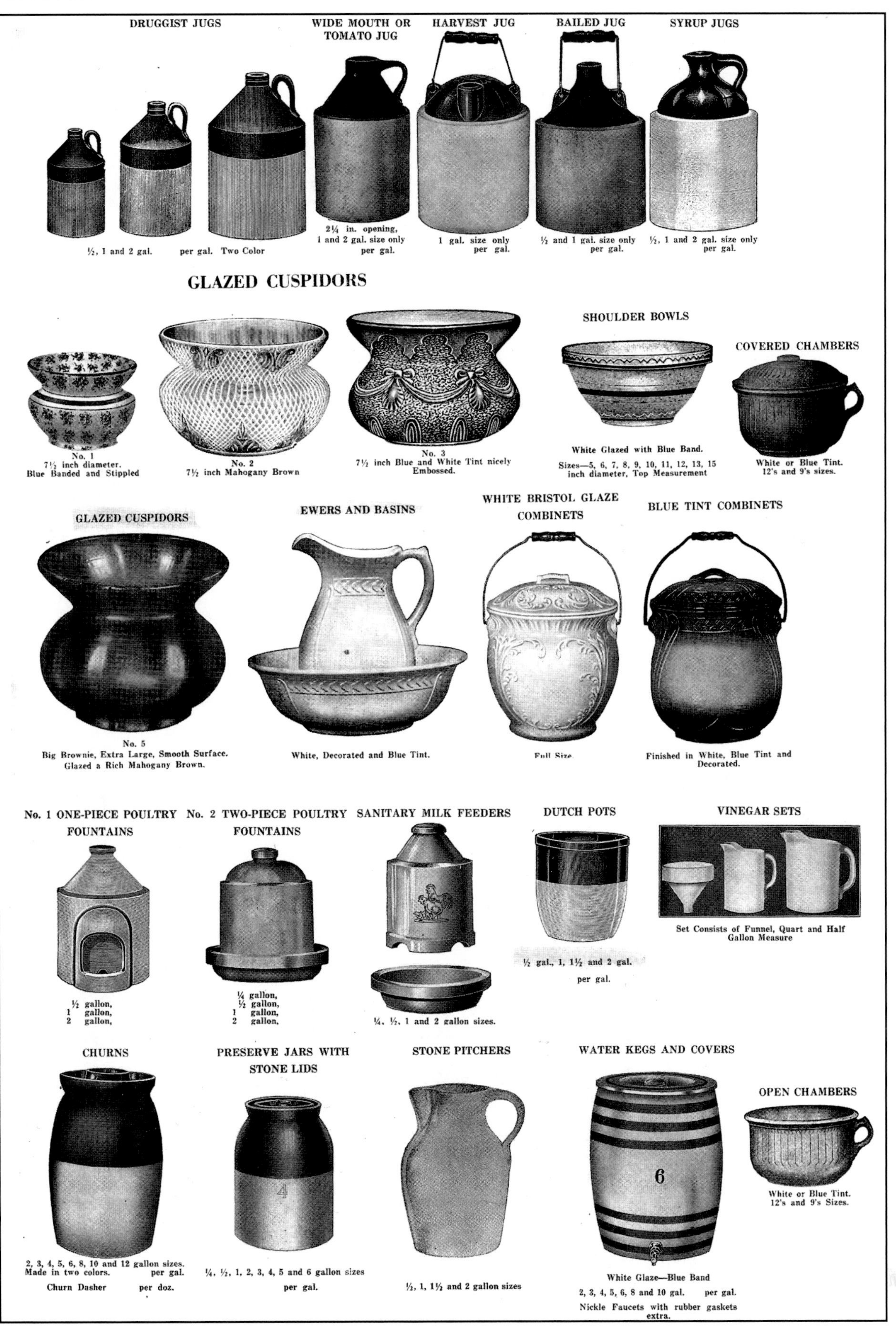

DRUGGIST JUGS
½, 1 and 2 gal.
per gal. Two Color
WIDE MOUTH OR TOMATO JUG
2¼ in. opening, 1 and 2 gal. size only per gal.
HARVEST JUG
1 gal. size only per gal.
BAILED JUG
½ and 1 gal. size only per gal.
SYRUP JUGS
½, 1 and 2 gal. size only per gal.
GLAZED CUSPIDORS
No. 1
7½ inch diameter. Blue Banded and Stippled
No. 2
7½ inch Mahogany Brown
No. 3
7½ inch Blue and White Tint nicely Embossed.
SHOULDER BOWLS
White Glazed with Blue Band.
Sizes—5, 6, 7, 8, 9, 10, 11, 12, 13, 15 inch diameter, Top Measurement
COVERED CHAMBERS
White or Blue Tint. 12's and 9's sizes.
GLAZED CUSPIDORS
No. 5
Big Brownie, Extra Large, Smooth Surface. Glazed a Rich Mahogany Brown.
EWERS AND BASINS
White, Decorated and Blue Tint.
WHITE BRISTOL GLAZE COMBINETS
Full Size.
BLUE TINT COMBINETS
Finished in White, Blue Tint and Decorated.
No. 1 ONE-PIECE POULTRY FOUNTAINS
½ gallon, 1 gallon, 2 gallon,
No. 2 TWO-PIECE POULTRY FOUNTAINS
¼ gallon, ½ gallon, 1 gallon, 2 gallon,
SANITARY MILK FEEDERS
¼, ½, 1 and 2 gallon sizes.
DUTCH POTS
½ gal., 1, 1½ and 2 gal.
per gal.
VINEGAR SETS
Set Consists of Funnel, Quart and Half Gallon Measure
CHURNS
2, 3, 4, 5, 6, 8, 10 and 12 gallon sizes. Made in two colors. per gal.
Churn Dasher per doz.
PRESERVE JARS WITH STONE LIDS
¼, ½, 1, 2, 3, 4, 5 and 6 gallon sizes
per gal.
STONE PITCHERS
½, 1, 1½ and 2 gallon sizes
WATER KEGS AND COVERS
White Glaze—Blue Band
2, 3, 4, 5, 6, 8 and 10 gal. per gal.
Nickle Faucets with rubber gaskets extra.
OPEN CHAMBERS
White or Blue Tint. 12's and 9's Sizes.

Catalog content from 1925 American Clay Products catalog.

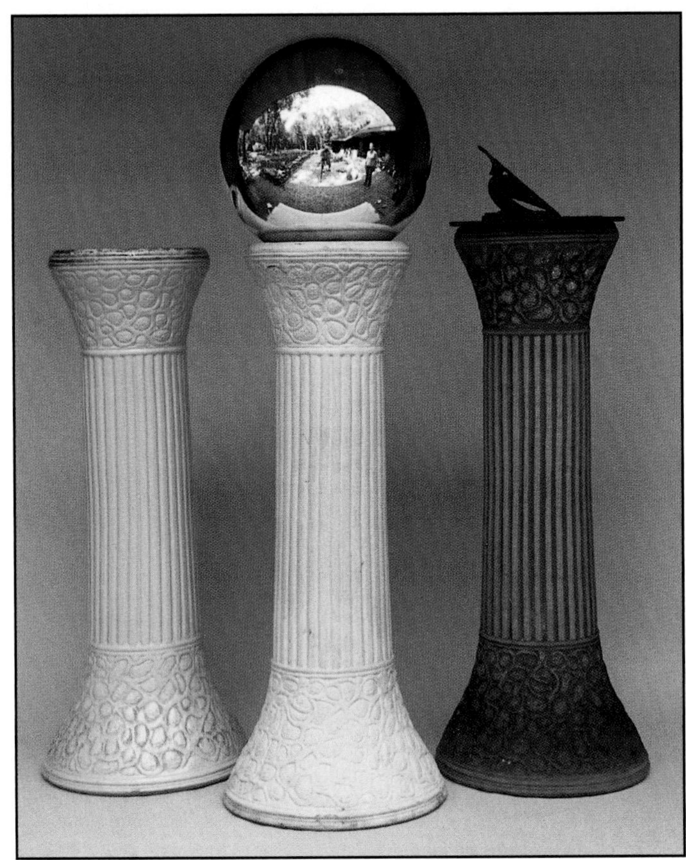

Left: Pedestals for "Glazing Globe" sets and with Sun Dial. No marks. Pedestals 28" tall. 1920s. Glazing Globe Pedestal $150.00 – 200.00, Sun Dial Pedestal Set $300.00 – 400.00.

Lower left: Mugs with Grape Motif. Shield mark. 4½" & 5". $20.00 – 30.00. Matching Pitchers: 8½" $60.00 – 75.00. 9½" $75.00 – 90.00.

Below: Tumblers 5". $40.00 – 50.00.

Right: Jardiniere and Pedestal Set. Jardiniere 10½"-11" and Pedestal 18½". $450.00 – 550.00.

Below: Mugs 5". $25.00 – 35.00. Matching Pitcher 8½". $60.00 – 80.00.

Below right: Tumblers 5". $40.00 – 50.00.

Top: Mixing Bowls. Shield mark. $50.00 – 150.00.

Center: Elephant Dish 8". No marks. Different heights. $40.00 – 55.00.

Below: Covered Butter Dishes, 6" & 5½". No marks. $75.00 – 100.00.

Tankard with floral decoration. No mark. 8½". $70.00 – 90.00. Ring design Pitcher. Shield mark. 7½". $75.00 – 90.00.

Mug 4½". Old mark. $15.00 – 20.00. Tankard 8½". Old mark. $50.00 – 60.00.

Jardiniere with Handles and Pedestal Set. No marks. Jardiniere 10½" and Pedestal 18½". $450.00 – 550.00.

Jardiniere and Pedestal Set. No marks. Jardiniere 10½" and Pedestal 18½". Very rare set. $800.00 – 1,000.00.

Mixing Bowls. Old mark. $60.00 – 225.00.

The catalog information on the following pages is from a 1938 catalog sheet. This was the typical format frequently used for product information during this era. The letter below accompanied the two-sided 1938 catalog sheet pictured on the opposite page. Enlarged portions from these pages can be seen on the following pages through page 35.

The Nelson McCoy Pottery Company

Roseville, Ohio

February 28, 1938

Mr. Kenneth A. Sprague
Roscoe, N.Y.

Gentlemen:

ALL AGREEMENTS ARE CONTINGENT UPON STRIKES, ACCIDENTS AND OTHER DELAYS BEYOND OUR CONTROL. QUOTATIONS SUBJECT TO CHANGE WITHOUT NOTICE.

Enclosed you will find illustrated folder showing many new items which we are making for 1938. You will notice that our line is quite varied, offering you an assortment of pottery that is not only attractive, but in every case made for practical uses.

In addition to illustrations you will find our net price list as of January 1st. All prices are net, f.o.b. factory, Roseville, Ohio, with no extra charge for packing. Our terms are net cash 30 days.

You will note on our price list that we have regular packing units arranged in small quantities, and we believe you will find that these will be very practical for your use. We are operating our plant daily and are prepared to handle your orders promptly. We stand ready to answer any questions you may have and to assist you in any way that we possibly can.

Trusting that we may hear from you, we are,

Sincerely yours,

THE NELSON McCOY POTTERY COMPANY

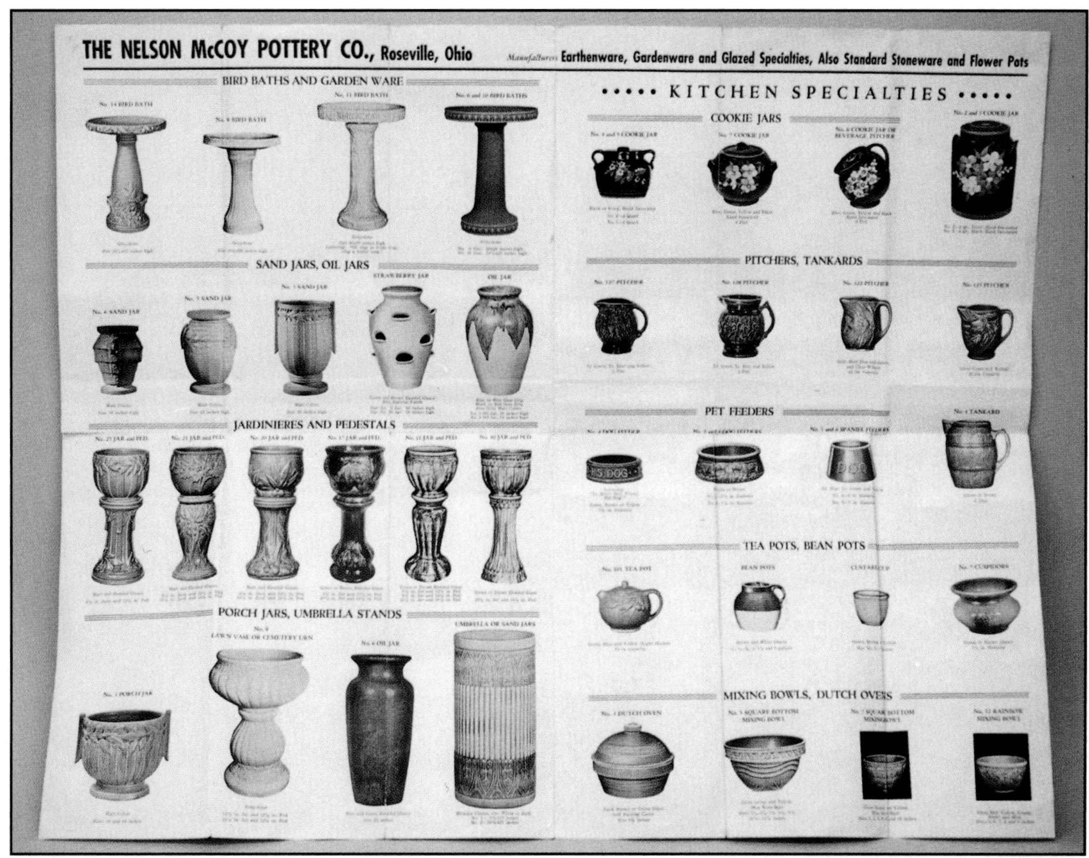

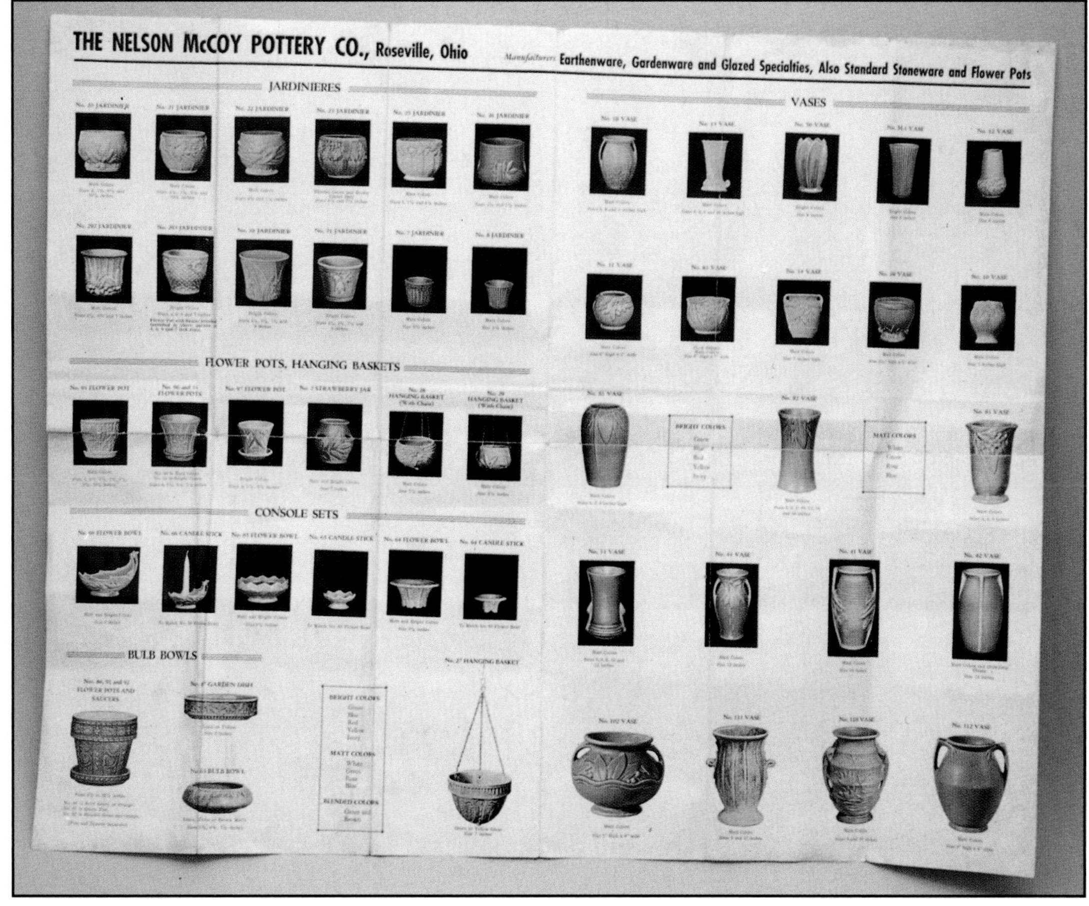

The above photos are of the two sides of the 1938 catalog sheet.

BIRD BATHS AND GARDEN WARE

No. 14 BIRD BATH
Graystone
Size 18¼x25 inches high

No. 9 BIRD BATH
Graystone
Size 18¼x23 inches high

No. 11 BIRD BATH

Graystone
Size 20x26 inches high
Lettering: "Oh sing ye birds sing; sing a joyful song."

No. 6 and 10 BIRD BATHS
Graystone
No. 6 Size: 20x28 inches high.
No. 10 Size: 18¼x25 inches high.

SAND JARS, OIL JARS

No. 6 SAND JAR
Matt Colors
Size 16 inches high

No. 5 SAND JAR
Matt Colors
Size 18 inches high

No. 3 SAND JAR
Matt Colors
Size 20 inches high

STRAWBERRY JAR
Green and Brown Blended Glazes
Also Natural Finish
Size No. 9 Jar: 16 inches high
Size No. 10 Jar: 18 inches high

OIL JAR
Blue on Blue Over-Drip
Black on Red Over-Drip
Also Solid Matt Colors
No. 7 Oil Jar, 16 inches high
No. 8 Oil Jar, 18 inches high

Detail section from the 1938 catalog sheet.

Porch Jar 10". No mark. $150.00 – 300.00. Porch Jar 13". No mark. $300.00 – 500.00.

Oil Jar with drip style glaze. 18" tall. No mark. $350.00 – 400.00. Oil Jar with handles. 15" tall. No mark. $250.00 – 300.00.

No. 25 JAR and PED.
Matt and Blended Glazes
8½ in. Jard. and 12½ in. Ped.

No. 21 JAR and PED.
Matt and Blended Glazes
8½ in. Jard. and 12½ in. Ped.
10½ in. Jard. and 18½ in. Ped.

No. 20 JAR and PED.
Matt and Blended Glazes
8½ in. Jard. and 12½ in. Ped.
10½ in. Jard. and 18½ in. Ped.

No. 17 JAR and PED.
Green or Brown Blended Glaze
8½ in. Jar and 12½ in. Ped.
10½ in. Jar and 18½ in. Ped.

No. 11 JAR and PED.
Green or Brown Blended Glaze
8½ in. Jar and 12½ in. Ped.
9½ in. Jar and 14½ in. Ped.
10½ in. Jar and 18½ in. Ped.

No. 40 JAR and PED.
Green or Brown Blended Glaze
10½ in. Jar and 18½ in. Ped.

PORCH JARS, UMBRELLA STANDS

No. 3 PORCH JAR
Matt Colors
Sizes 10 and 13 inches

No. 9
LAWN VASE OR CEMETERY URN
Graystone
12½ in. Jar and 12½ in. Ped.
15½ in. Jar and 12½ in. Ped.

No. 6 OIL JAR
Blue and Green Derkled Glazes
Size 25 inches

UMBRELLA OR SAND JARS
Blended Glazes, also White or Buff
No. 1— 9½x19 inches
No. 2—10½x21 inches

More detail from the 1938 catalog sheet.

Holly Jardiniere and Pedestal Set. No marks. Jardiniere 10½" and Pedestal 18½". $500.00 – 600.00.

Sand Butterfly Jardiniere and Pedestal Set. No marks. Jardiniere 8½" and Pedestal 12½". $300.00 – 350.00.

Leaves & Berries family of Jardiniere and Pedestal Sets in brown/green glaze. No marks. Jardiniere 10½" and Pedestal 18½" . $600.00 – 700.00.
8½" Jardiniere and 12½" Pedestal. $250.00 – 350.00.
7" Jardiniere and 6½" Pedestal. $200.00 – 250.00.

Oil Jar. 25" tall. No mark. Very rare. $1,000.00 – 1,200.00. Pictured with Zebra Planter for size comparison. 1956. 8½" x 6½". McCoy mark. $650.00 – 800.00.

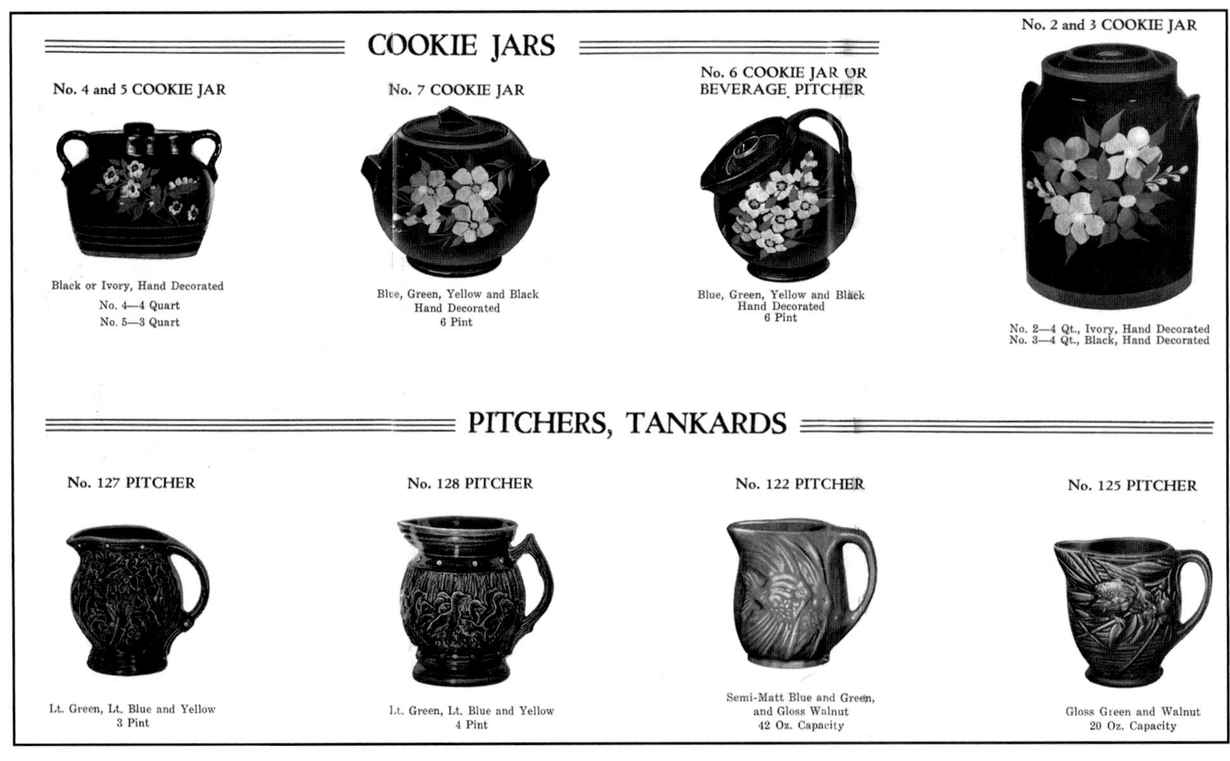

COOKIE JARS

No. 4 and 5 COOKIE JAR
Black or Ivory, Hand Decorated
No. 4—4 Quart
No. 5—3 Quart

No. 7 COOKIE JAR
Blue, Green, Yellow and Black
Hand Decorated
6 Pint

No. 6 COOKIE JAR OR BEVERAGE PITCHER
Blue, Green, Yellow and Black
Hand Decorated
6 Pint

No. 2 and 3 COOKIE JAR
No. 2—4 Qt., Ivory, Hand Decorated
No. 3—4 Qt., Black, Hand Decorated

PITCHERS, TANKARDS

No. 127 PITCHER
Lt. Green, Lt. Blue and Yellow
3 Pint

No. 128 PITCHER
Lt. Green, Lt. Blue and Yellow
4 Pint

No. 122 PITCHER
Semi-Matt Blue and Green, and Gloss Walnut
42 Oz. Capacity

No. 125 PITCHER
Gloss Green and Walnut
20 Oz. Capacity

Another detail from the 1938 catalog sheet.

Leaves & Berries Teapot. Shown in wide variety of glaze colors. No mark. $75.00 – 150.00.

Custard Cup 5 ounce. Variety of colors. Shield mark as shown. $20.00 – 25.00.

From the 1938 catalog sheet.

No. 4 DOG FEEDER

Lettering:
"To Man's Best Friend,
His Dog."
Green, Brown or Yellow
7½ in. diameter

No. 1 and 3 DOG FEEDERS

Green or Brown
No. 1—5½ in. diameter
No. 3—7½ in. diameter

No. 5 and 6 SPANIEL FEEDERS

Lt. Blue, Lt. Green and Yellow
No. 5—6 in. diameter
No. 6—7 in. diameter

Green or Brown
5 Pint

TEA POTS, BEAN POTS

No. 101 TEA POT

Green, Blue and Yellow (Light Shades)
24 oz. capacity

BEAN POTS

Brown and White Glazes
¼, ½, ¾, 1, 1½ and 2 gallons

CUSTARD CUP

Green, Brown or Yellow
Size No. 1—5 ounce

No. 7 CUSPIDORS

Green or Brown Glazes
7½ in. diameter

MIXING BOWLS, DUTCH OVENS

No. 3 DUTCH OVEN

Dark Brown or Green Glaze.
Self Basting Cover.
Size 9¾ inches

No. 5 SQUARE BOTTOM MIXING BOWL

Gloss Green and Yellow.
Blue Semi-Matt
Sizes 5½, 6½ 7½, 8½, 9½,
10½, 11½ inches

No. 7 SQUARE BOTTOM MIXING BOWL

Gloss Green and Yellow.
Blue Semi-Matt
Sizes 5, 6, 7, 8, 9 and 10 inches

No. 32 RAINBOW MIXING BOWL

Gloss Red, Yellow, Green,
White and Blue
Sizes 5, 6, 7, 8 and 9 inches

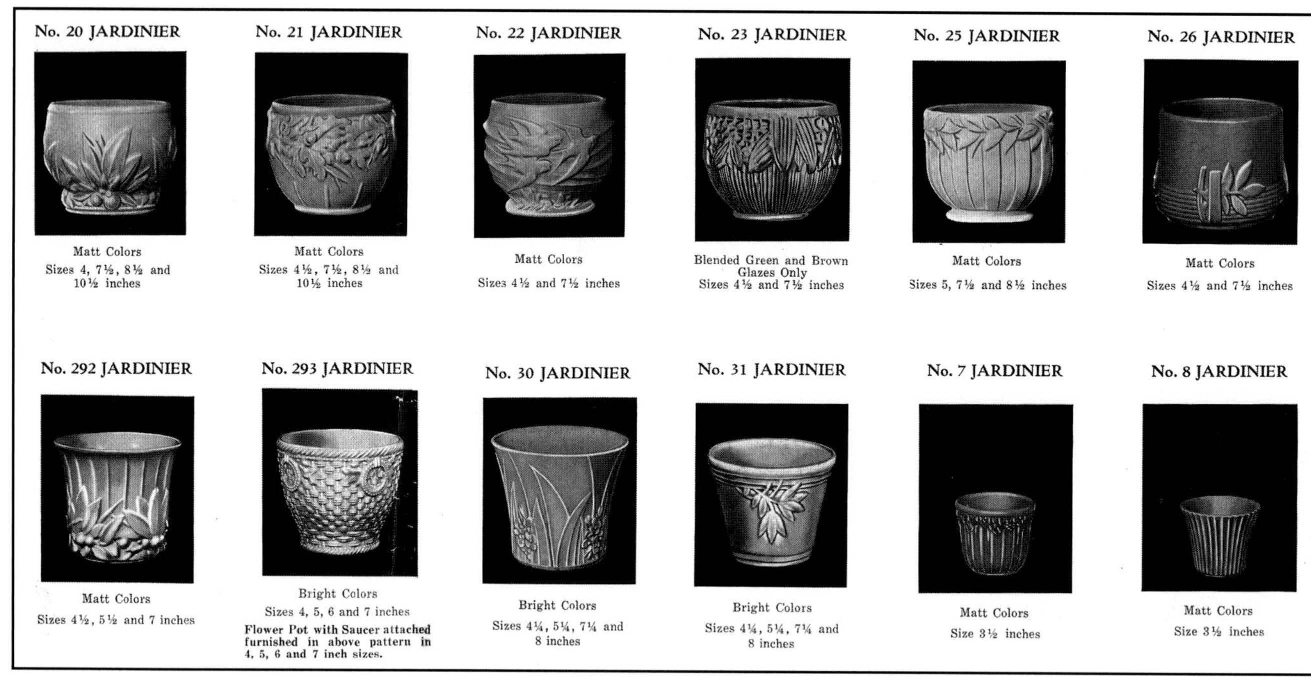

No. 20 JARDINIER
Matt Colors
Sizes 4, 7½, 8½ and 10½ inches

No. 21 JARDINIER
Matt Colors
Sizes 4½, 7½, 8½ and 10½ inches

No. 22 JARDINIER
Matt Colors
Sizes 4½ and 7½ inches

No. 23 JARDINIER
Blended Green and Brown Glazes Only
Sizes 4½ and 7½ inches

No. 25 JARDINIER
Matt Colors
Sizes 5, 7½ and 8½ inches

No. 26 JARDINIER
Matt Colors
Sizes 4½ and 7½ inches

No. 292 JARDINIER
Matt Colors
Sizes 4½, 5½ and 7 inches

No. 293 JARDINIER
Bright Colors
Sizes 4, 5, 6 and 7 inches
Flower Pot with Saucer attached furnished in above pattern in 4, 5, 6 and 7 inch sizes.

No. 30 JARDINIER
Bright Colors
Sizes 4¼, 5¼, 7¼ and 8 inches

No. 31 JARDINIER
Bright Colors
Sizes 4¼, 5¼, 7¼ and 8 inches

No. 7 JARDINIER
Matt Colors
Size 3½ inches

No. 8 JARDINIER
Matt Colors
Size 3½ inches

From the 1938 catalog sheet.

#31 Jardiniere. Variety of colors. No mark. Pictured is 4½" size. Also came in 5½", 7½", and 8" sizes. $30.00 – 60.00.

Three pieces with similar ribbed design. Variety of colors. Left: Vase 6". $30.00 – 40.00. Center: Large Jardiniere, 7" with shield mark. $40.00 – 50.00. Right: No. 8 Jardiniere 3½". $20.00 – 30.00.

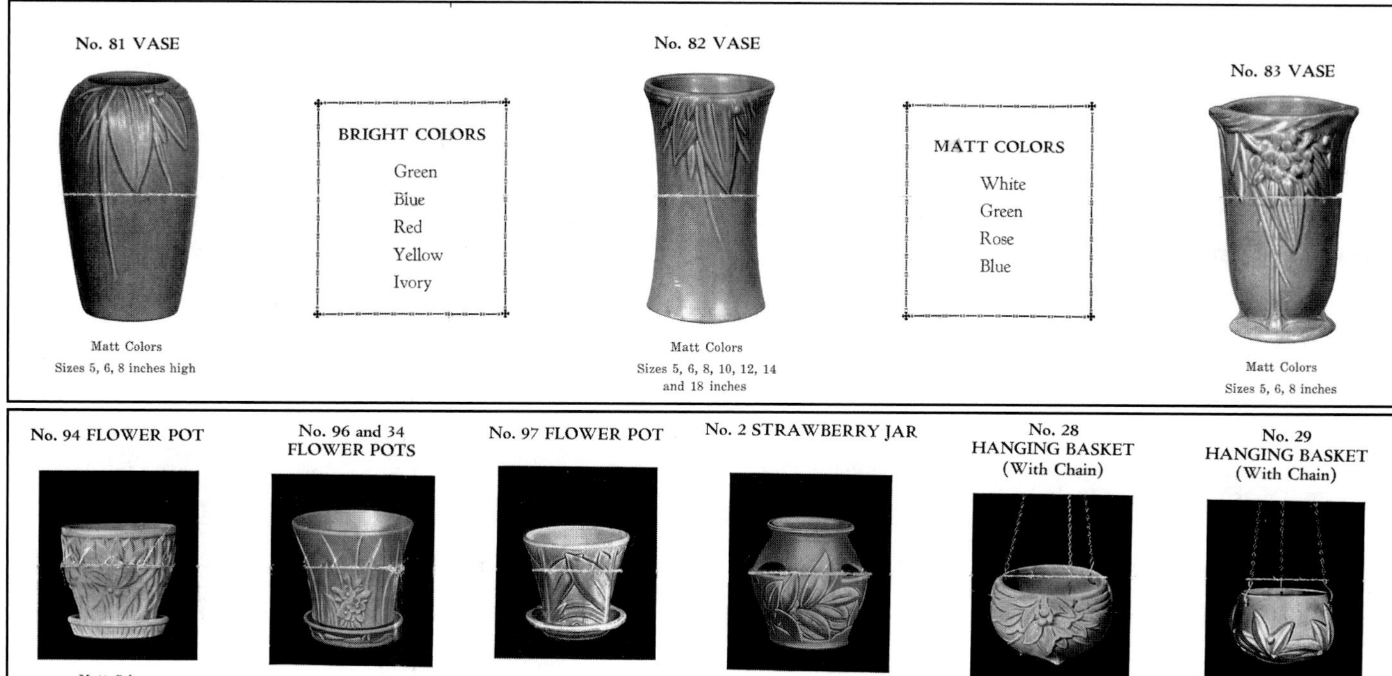

No. 81 VASE

Matt Colors
Sizes 5, 6, 8 inches high

BRIGHT COLORS
Green
Blue
Red
Yellow
Ivory

No. 82 VASE

Matt Colors
Sizes 5, 6, 8, 10, 12, 14 and 18 inches

MATT COLORS
White
Green
Rose
Blue

No. 83 VASE

Matt Colors
Sizes 5, 6, 8 inches

No. 94 FLOWER POT

Matt Colors
Sizes 4, 5½, 6½, 7½, 8½, 9½, 10½ inches

No. 96 and 34 FLOWER POTS

No. 96 in Matt Colors.
No. 34 in Bright Colors.
Sizes 4, 5½, 6½, 7½ inches

No. 97 FLOWER POT

Bright Colors
Sizes 4, 5½, 6½ inches

No. 2 STRAWBERRY JAR

Matt and Bright Colors
Size 7 inches

No. 28 HANGING BASKET (With Chain)

Matt Colors
Size 7½ inches

No. 29 HANGING BASKET (With Chain)

Matt Colors
Size 6½ inches

From the 1938 catalog sheet.

No. 5 Square Bottom Mixing Bowl. Gloss green, yellow, or blue-matt. Sizes 5½" – 11½". $60.00 – 200.00; Smallest and largest sizes demand highest values.

No. 3 Dutch Oven. Gloss green or dark brown. 9¾". Complete, $75.00 – 125.00.

No. 32 Rainbow Mixing Bowl. Gloss green, yellow, red, white or blue. Sizes 5" – 9" (9" size pictured). $100.00 – 200.00.

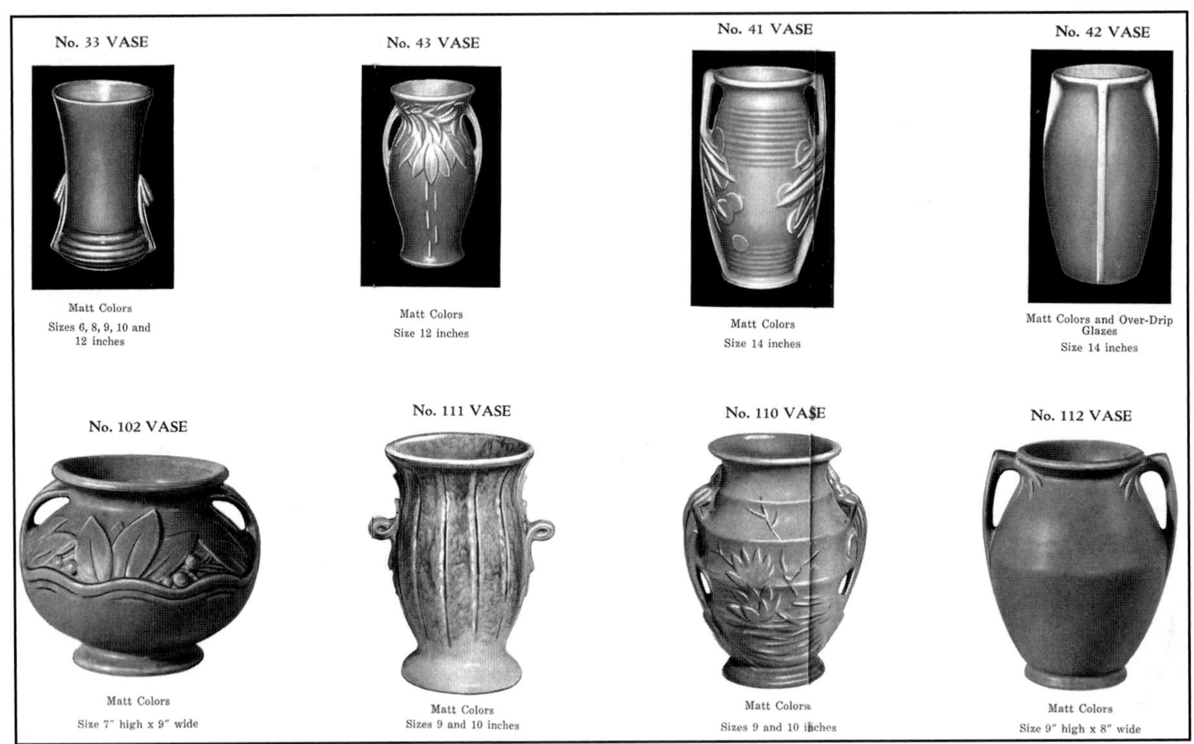

From the 1938 catalog sheet.

Vase No. 18. Matt colors; shown in non-production glaze combination. No mark. 6" pictured. Also made in 8" and 9". 6", $60.00 – 80.00, 8", $80.00 – 100.00, 9", $125.00 – 175.00.

Vase No. 43. Variety of matt colors; shown in rare burgundy. No mark. 12" tall. $225.00 – 325.00.

Vase No. 11. Matt colors; shown in non-production glazes. No mark. 6" tall. $60.00 – 90.00.

VASES

No. 18 VASE

Matt Colors
Sizes 6, 8 and 9 inches high

No. 15 VASE

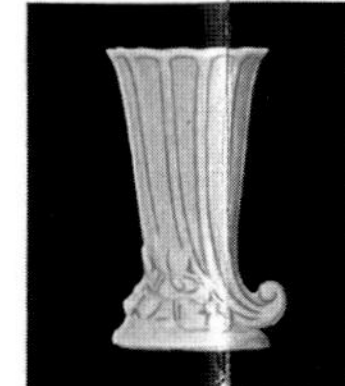

Matt Colors
Sizes 6, 8, 9 and 10 inches high

No. 50 VASE

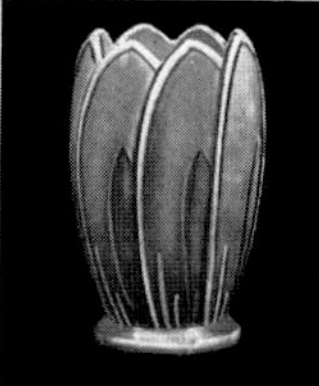

Bright Colors
Size 8 inches

No. M-1 VASE

Bright Colors
Size 8 inches

No. 12 VASE

Matt Colors
Size 8 inches

No. 11 VASE

Matt Colors
Size 6" high x 7" wide

No. 83 VASE

(Low Shape)
Matt Colors
Size 6" high x 7" wide

No. 14 VASE

Matt Colors
Size 7 inches high

No. 19 VASE

Matt Colors
Size 6¼" high x 7" wide

No. 10 VASE

Matt Colors
Size 7 inches high

CONSOLE SETS

No. 66 FLOWER BOWL

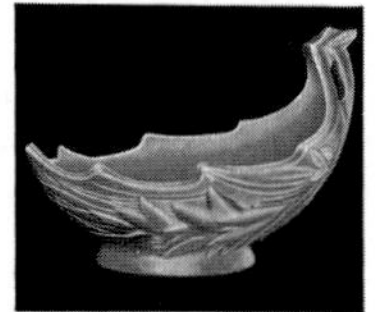

Matt and Bright Colors
Size 9 inches

No. 66 CANDLE STICK

To Match No. 66 Flower Bowl

No. 65 FLOWER BOWL

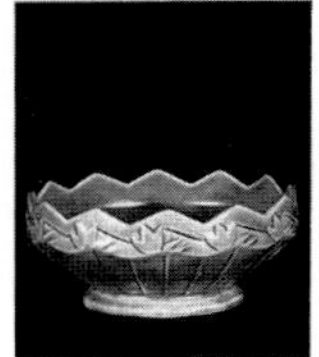

Matt and Bright Colors
Size 8¼ inches

No. 65 CANDLE STICK

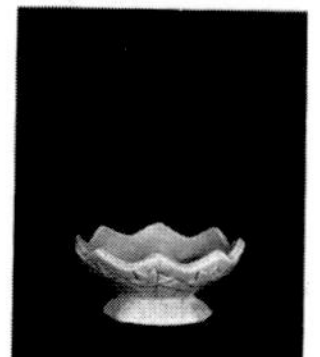

To Match No. 65 Flower Bowl

No. 64 FLOWER BOWL

Matt and Bright Colors
Size 8¼ inches

No. 64 CANDLE STICK

To Match No. 64 Flower Bowl

BULB BOWLS

Nos. 86, 91 and 92 FLOWER POTS AND SAUCERS

Sizes 4½ to 10½ inches

No. 86 is Solid Green or Orange.
No. 91 is Green Tint.
No. 92 is Blended Green and Orange.

(Pots and Saucers Separate)

No. 87 GARDEN DISH

Green or Yellow
Size 8 inches

No. 63 BULB BOWL

Green, White or Brown Matts
Sizes 5½, 6½, 7½ inches

BRIGHT COLORS
Green
Blue
Red
Yellow
Ivory

MATT COLORS
White
Green
Rose
Blue

BLENDED COLORS
Green and
Brown

No. 27 HANGING BASKET

Green or Yellow Glaze
Size 7 inches

From the 1938 catalog sheet.

Oil Jar. Variety of colors. No mark. 25" tall & 15" tall. 25", $400.00 – 500.00. 15", $250.00 – 300.00.

Oil Jar. Variety of colors. No mark. 18" tall. $350.00 – 400.00.

Jardiniere with "fence" pattern. Variety of colors and sizes. 4½" and 7½" shown. $40.00 – 80.00.

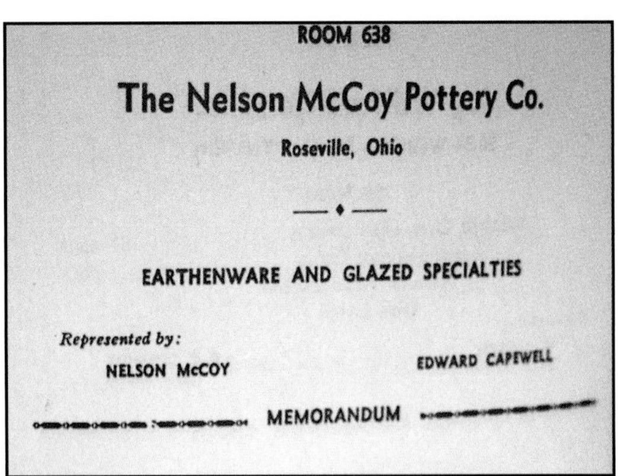

ROOM 638

The Nelson McCoy Pottery Co.

Roseville, Ohio

EARTHENWARE AND GLAZED SPECIALTIES

Represented by:

NELSON McCOY

EDWARD CAPEWELL

MEMORANDUM

New York Housewares Show Book from 1936. Given to all attendees with a page for each company with names of company representatives. Note close-up right of McCoy page with Nelson McCoy listed as an attending representative.

Porch Jar with fancy Handles. 14". Very rare piece. $1,200.00 – 1,500.00. Also made a 17" size which has not been found to date.

Large Jardiniere with Saucer. Unusual glaze finish. No mark. 10". $200.00 – 250.00. Pictured with small Flower Pot, 3", for size comparison. $35.00 – 45.00.

Dog Dish. No mark. 6". $40.00 – 50.00.

Flower Pot with Saucer. Variety of colors. Sizes 3" – 16". $30.00 – 150.00.

Jardiniere. No mark. 7". $60.00 – 80.00.

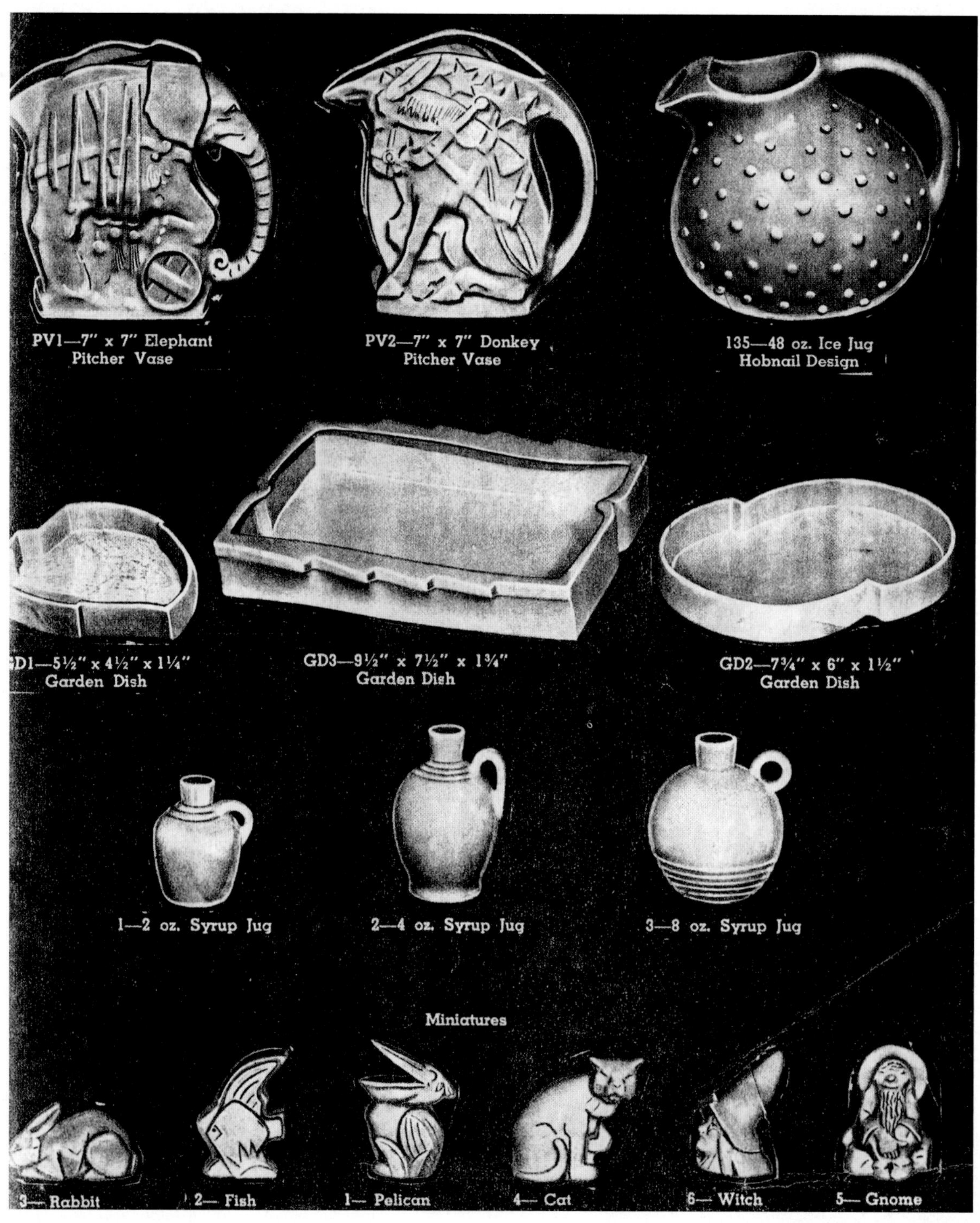

Catalog page from 1939 – 1940 years.

Vases

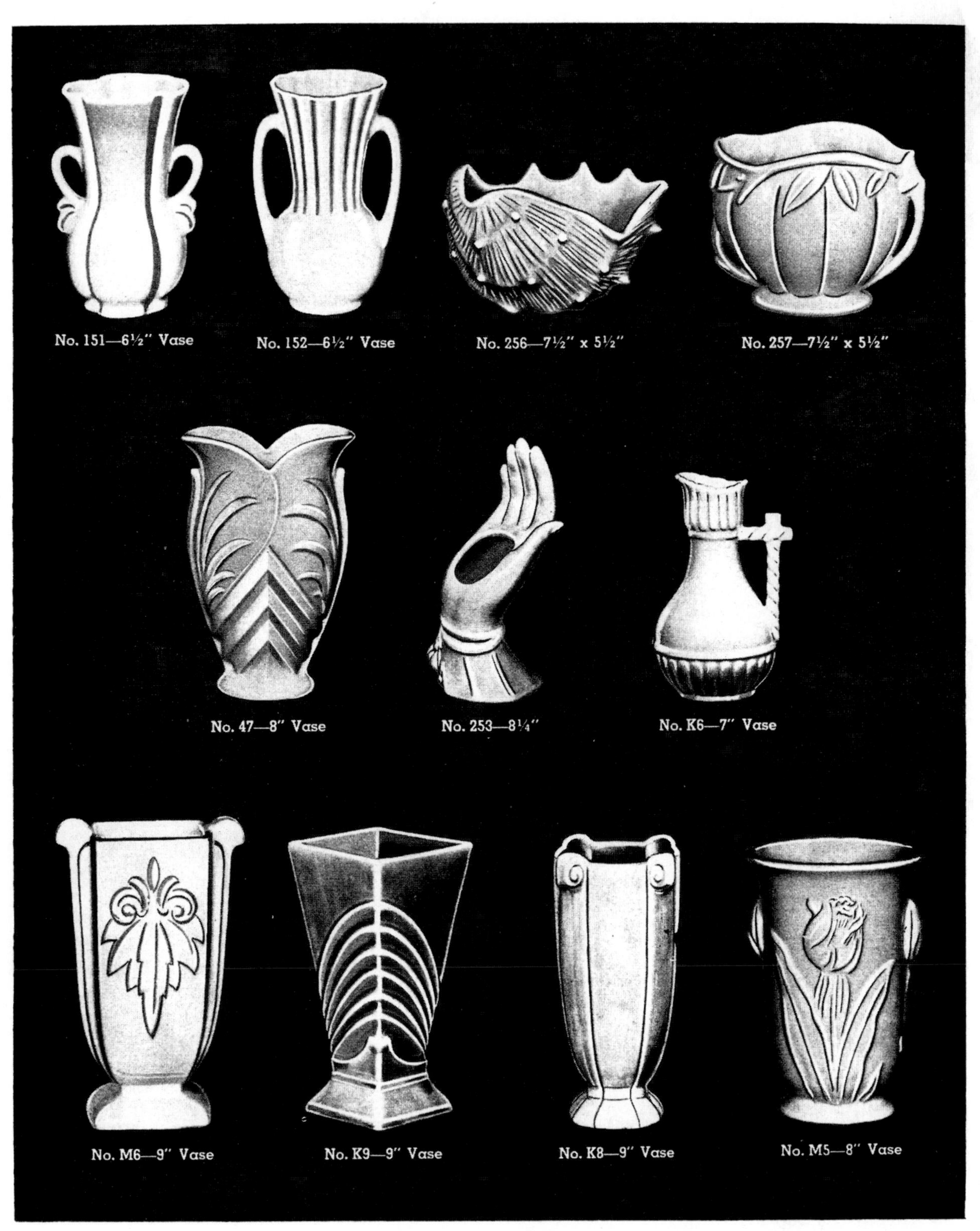

Catalog page from 1941.

Jardiniere 6" and Vase 8". 1930s. No marks. Jardiniere $30.00 – 40.00.
Vase $50.00 – 60.00.

Frog with Lotus Planter. 1940s. Shown in rare oxblood color glaze. Note glaze coding on bottom in smaller photo. Standard glaze colors $15.00 – 20.00. Rare glaze $50.00 – 60.00.

Low Bowl. Variety of colors. No mark. Early 1940s. 6". $30.00 – 35.00.

Little Bowls. No mark. 3½" and 4½". $25.00 – 35.00 each.

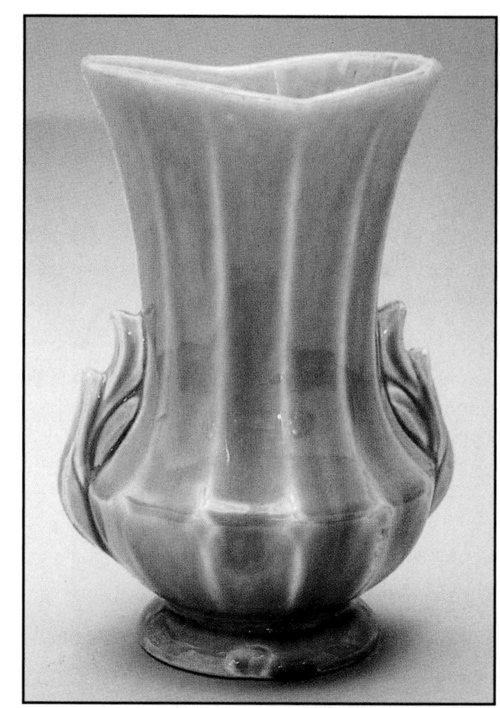

Top left: Flower Pot with Saucer. 3½" and 5". No mark. 3½" $25.00 – 30.00, 5" $35.00 – 40.00.

Top right: Vase. Gloss colors. 7". No mark. Rare find. 1940. $100.00 – 125.00.

Right: Uncle Sam Vase. 7½". McCoy mark. Uncommon light green glaze. 1940s. $50.00 – 60.00. Flower Pot with saucer. 6½". NM mark. Hard to find. Early 1940s. $50.00 – 60.00.

Bottom left: Flower Pot with Saucer. 3½". No mark. $30.00 – 40.00.

Bottom right: Ba-ba Black Sheep Planter. NM mark. Gloss colors. Matte blue glaze unusual. Standard glazes $45.00 – 60.00. Matte glaze $60.00 – 80.00.

Left: Basketweave Jardiniere and Pedestal Set. Jardiniere 8½" and Pedestal 12½". 1940s. Yellow glaze is non-production color. Standard glazes (See Index for examples in Vols. I & II) $250.00 – 350.00. Yellow $350.00 – 450.00.

Right: Horse Bookends. 8". 1942. Shown in uncommon glaze with nice decoration. $125.00 – 175.00.

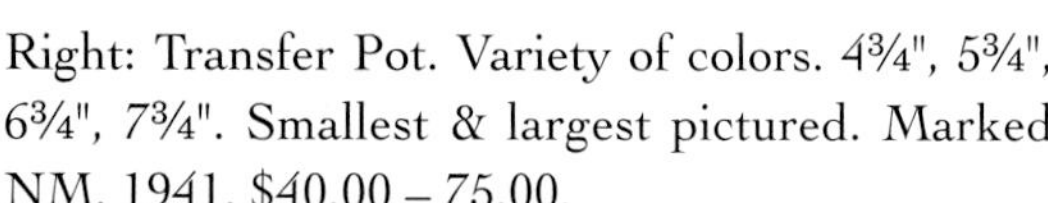

Right: Transfer Pot. Variety of colors. 4¾", 5¾", 6¾", 7¾". Smallest & largest pictured. Marked NM. 1941. $40.00 – 75.00.

Flower Pot with Saucer. Early 1940s. No mark. 5". A tough one to find. $50.00 – 60.00.

Right: Hands Novelty Tray. 1940s. 5¾". NM mark. White glaze example with non-production decoration under glaze. $50.00 – 60.00.

Flower Pot with unusual bottom design. Early 1940s. NM mark. 5". Rare. $50.00 – 60.00.

Butterfly Vase. Early 1940s. USA mark. 7½" x 5½". Pictured in coral glaze in front (only example known as of this writing!) and lavender standard glaze behind for color comparison. These two glazes are frequently confused. Five common glaze colors $75.00 – 100.00. Coral $300.00 – 400.00.

Vase with Handles. Two very similar but slightly different styles shown. 9". Late 1940s. Pastel colors. Marked McCoy. $50.00 – 60.00 each.

Castle Gate Vase, 7" x 6", left, and Fernery, 5½" x 3¼". Early 1940s. Marked USA and NM respectively. Pictured in rose color non-production glaze. Castle Gate: standard glazes, $150.00 – 200.00. Rose color $200.00 – 300.00. Fernery: standard glazes; $30.00 – 40.00. Rose color $60.00 – 80.00.

Butterfly Console Bowl. Early 1940s. 11" x 7½". Non-production glaze. Standard pastel glaze colors $80.00 – 100.00. Non-production glaze pictured $250.00 – 350.00.

From top:
Dog Dishes. 1940s. 6" and 7". Hard to find! $80.00 – 100.00 each.

Scottie Dog Dish. 1940s – 1950s. Marked McCoy. 5". $60.00 – 80.00.

Pig Bank. No mark. 6". 1947. White is commonly found. Aqua and black are rare. White $20.00 – 25.00. Black or aqua $50.00 – 60.00.

Dog with Cart Planter. 8½". Early 1950s. Marked McCoy. Pictured in non-production black glaze. Standard glazes $30.00 – 40.00. Black $80.00 – 90.00.

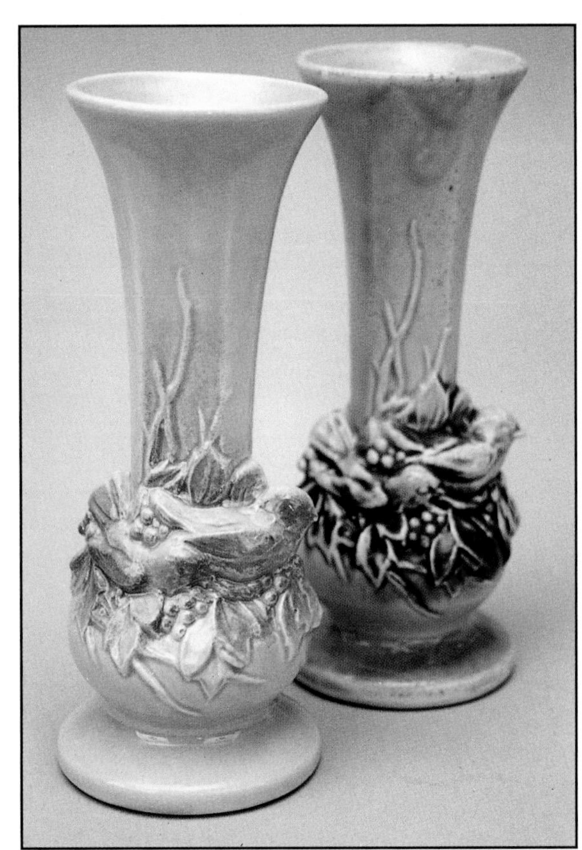

Bud Vase with bird detail. 8" tall. 1950. Marked McCoy. Right is standard blended green and brown glaze; left is non-production color combination. Standard glazes $35.00 – 50.00. Non-production glazes $90.00 – 100.00.

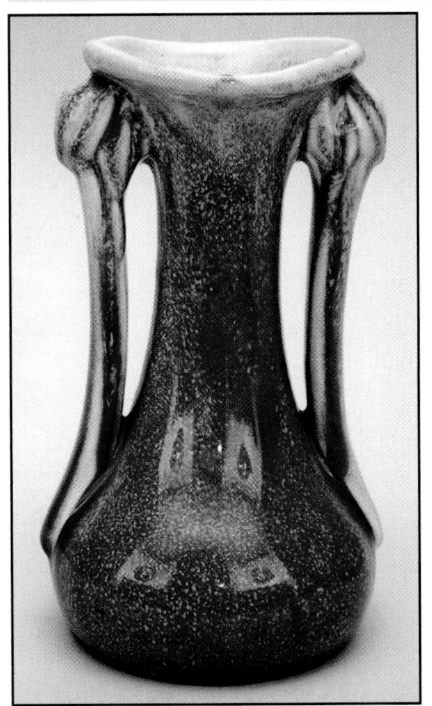

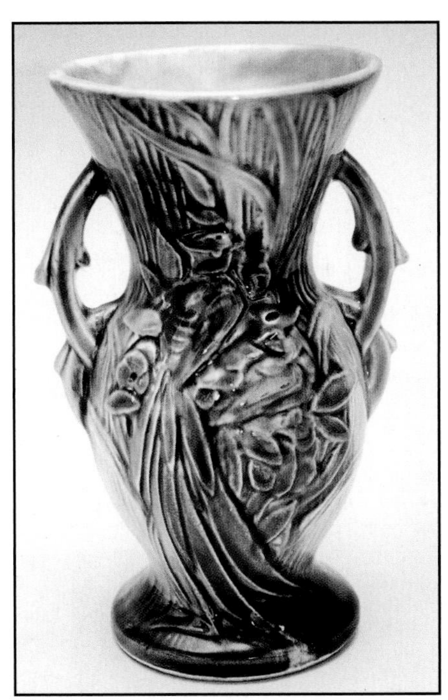

Top left: Vase with Handles. 9" tall. 1940s. Marked McCoy. Pictured in non-production glaze combination. Standard pastel glazes $50.00 – 60.00. Non-production glazes $100.00 – 125.00.

Top center: Vase with Handles. 9" tall. Late 1940s. Marked McCoy. Pictured in unusual glaze detail. Standard pastel glazes $50.00 – 70.00. Unusual glazes $100.00 – 125.00.

Top right: Peacock Vase. 8" tall. 1948. Marked McCoy. Pictured in non-production glaze combination. Standard glazes $50.00 – 60.00. Non-production glazes $125.00 – 150.00.

Above: Shell 6" x 4½" 1948. No mark. Production colors green, coral or yellow. White non-production glaze decoration. Hard to find. Standard glazes $100.00 – 110.00. Matte white with decoration $175.00 – 200.00.

Right: Dripolator. 1943. Marked McCoy. Sold only in white. Requires four components to be complete. $50.00 – 60.00. Second three-piece style shown on page 230 of Volume I.

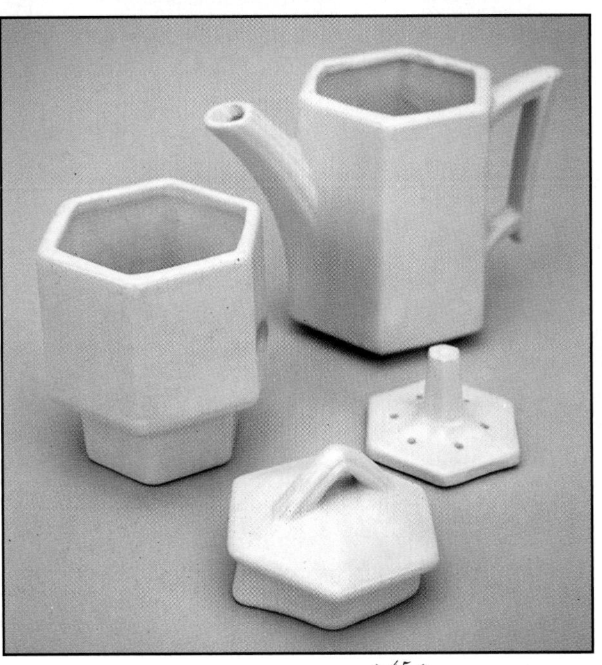

Vases

No. 270—9" Vase
Green, Coral & Yellow
packed 1 doz. Wt. 35 lbs.
$10.40 per dozen

No. 274—9" Vase
Green, Coral & Yellow
packed 1 Doz. Wt. 30 lbs.
$10.40 per dozen

No. 293—9" Vase
Green, Coral & Yellow
packed 1 doz. Wt. 35 lbs.
$10.40 per dozen

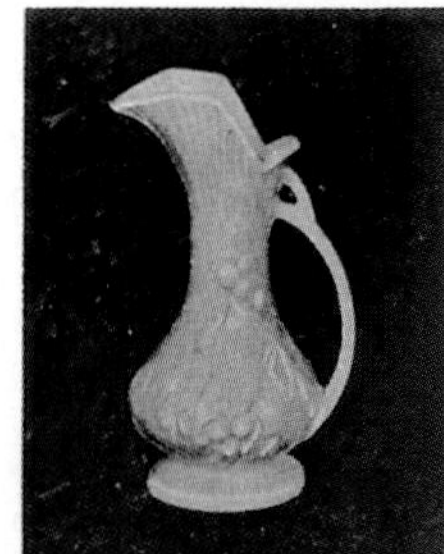
No. 279—9"
Pitcher Vase
Turq., Coral & Yellow
packed 2 doz. Wt. 42 lbs.
$10.40 per dozen

No. 273—8"
Vase
Turq., Coral & Yellow
packed 2 doz. Wt. 35 lbs.
$8.0U per dozen

No. 292—8" Vase
Green, Coral & Yellow
packed 2 doz. Wt. 48 lbs.
$8.80 per dozen

No. 277—8¼" Vase
White, Green & Yellow
packed 2 doz. Wt. 48 lbs.
$8.80 per dozen

No. 5038—8" Vase
White, Green & Yellow
packed 2 doz. Wt. 45 lbs.
$7.20 per dozen

No. 290—7 x 6"
Panel Vase
Green, Coral & Yellow
packed 2 doz. Wt. 52 lbs.
$8.80 per dozen

No. 291—7 x 6"
Embossed Vase
Green, Coral & Yellow
packed 2 doz. Wt. 48 lbs.
$8.80 per dozen

No. WP5—6"
Wall Pocket Vase
Turq., Coral & Yellow
packed 2 doz. Wt. 35 lbs.
$7.20 per dozen

No. 72—7½"
Heart Vase
White, Pink & Maroon gloss
packed 2 doz. Wt. 42 lbs.
$7.20 per dozen

No. K-8—8" x 7½"
Cornicopia Vase
Matt Wht., peach & Yel.
packed 1 doz. Wt. 35 lbs.
$16.00 per dozen

No. 281—8 x 6" Vase
Green, Pink & Yellow
packed 1 doz. Wt. 33 lbs.
$6.40 per dozen

1

No. 282—8 x 6" Vase

No. 283—8 x 6" Vase
Green, Pink & Yellow
packed 1 doz. Wt. 33 lbs.
$6.40 per dozen

1948 catalog page.

Vases & Decorative Items

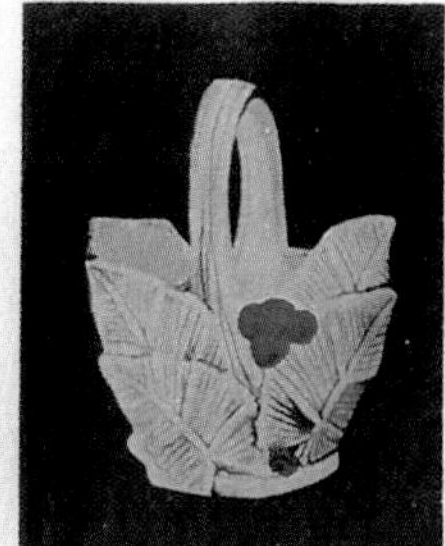

No. 509—9 x 7"
Basket Vase
Sprayed Gr. & Br.
packed 1 doz. Wt. 30 lbs.
$16.00 per dozen

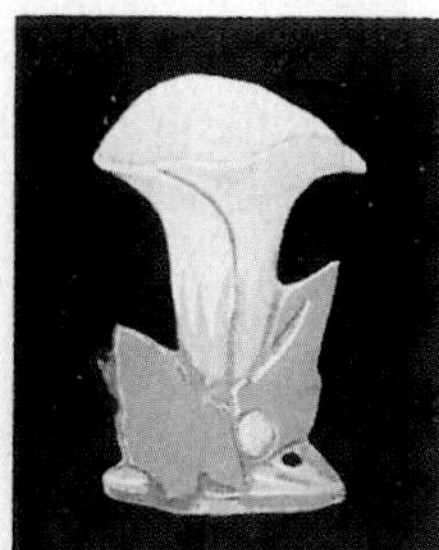

No. 73—8"
Lily Bud Vase
White or Yellow—Dec.
packed 1 doz. Wt. 22 lbs.
$17.60 per dozen

No. 74—8"
Tulip Vase
White or Yellow—Dec.
packed 1 doz. Wt. 25 lbs.
$16.00 per dozen

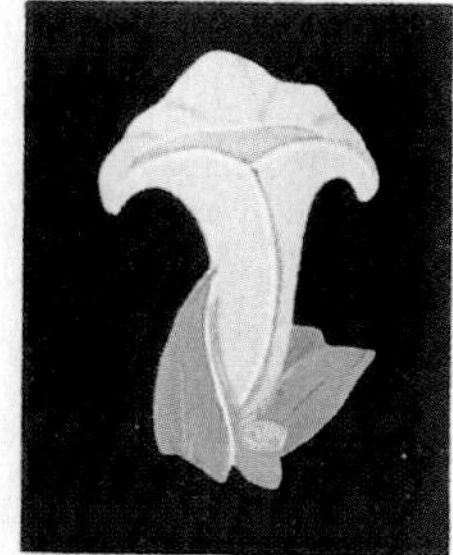

No. 709—6½"
Wall Pocket
White or Yellow—Dec.
packed 2 doz. Wt. 28 lbs.
$14.40 per dozen

No. 32—6½"
Hanging Basket
Green and Yellow
packed 2 doz. Wt. 42 lbs.
$9.60 per dozen

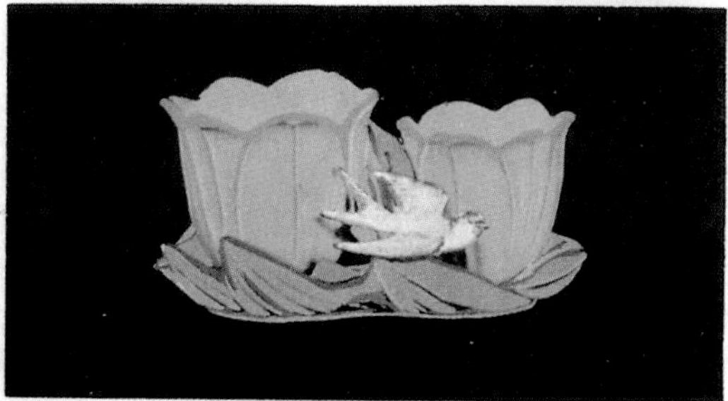

No. 711—10½ x 5½"
Double Cache Pot
Lt. Green or Yellow—Dec.
packed 1 doz. Wt. 35 lbs.
$17.60 per dozen

No. 710—6½ x 5"
Wall Vase W/Bird
Pink, Blue, Yellow—Dec.
packed 3 doz. Wt. 30 lbs.
$13.20 per dozen

No. 45—12" Vase
White & Green Matt
packed ½ doz. Wt. 48 lbs.
$19.20 per dozen

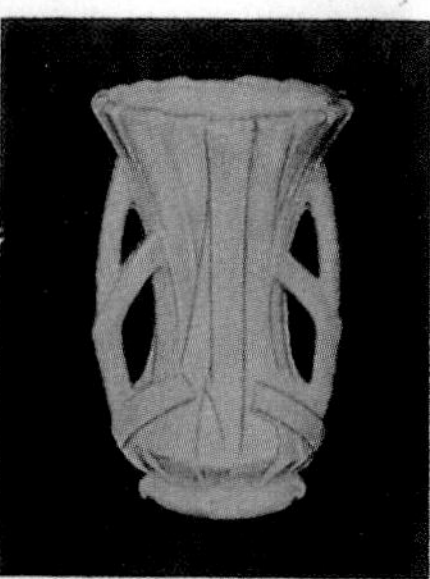

No. 46—12" Vase
White & Green gloss
packed ½ doz. Wt. 35 lbs.
$24.00 per dozen

No. 6—Vase
Size 12"
Gloss Green, Blue, Red
and Matt White
packed 1/3 doz. Wt. 35 lbs.
$19.20 per dozen

No. 16-G—6" x 8"
Vase
Blue, Coral & Green
packed 1 doz. Wt. 35 lbs.
$10.40 per dozen

No. BE1—Horse Book Ends
Gloss White & Yellow
packed 1 doz. pr. Wt. 45 lbs.
$1.80 per pr.

No. BE3—Lily Book End
Green W/Dec. Lily
packed 1 doz. pr. Wt. 30 lbs.
$2.40 per pair

2

No. 104—6 Cup Tea Pot
Gr. & Br. Sprayed
packed 1 doz. Wt. 33 lbs.
$19.20 per dozen

No. 104—Sugar
No. 104—Creamer
Gr. & Br. Sprayed
packed 2 doz. Wt. 16 lbs.
$5.20 per dozen

1948 catalog page.

Planting Dishes & Jardinieres

No. 39—5"
Sq. Jardiniere
Turq., Coral & Yellow
packed 3 doz. Wt. 42 lbs.
$5.80 per dozen

No. 506—7½"
Window Box
Turq., Coral & Yellow
packed 2 doz. Wt. 35 lbs.
$10.40 per dozen

No. 605—8"
Planting Dish
White & Green gloss
packed 2 doz. Wt. 35 lbs.
$7.20 per dozen

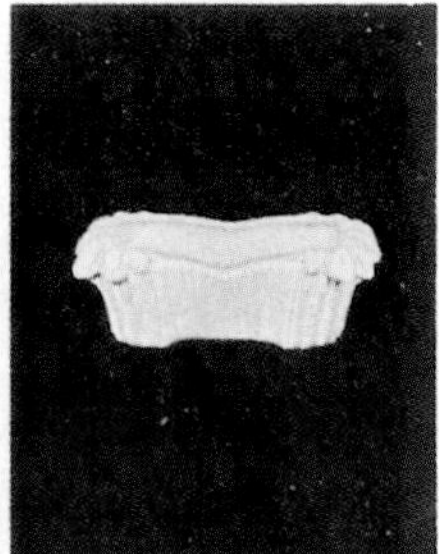

No. 606—9"
Planting Dish
White & Green gloss
packed 2 doz. Wt. 42 lbs.
$10.40 per dozen

No. 71—8¼"
Flower Bowl
Yellow, Green & Coral
packed 2 doz. Wt. 42 lbs.
$7.20 per dozen

No. 75—Bulb Bowl
Sizes 7" & 8¼"
White, Green & Yellow
7"-$7.20 doz. 2 doz. 35 lbs.
8¼" $10.40 doz.
1 doz. 30 lbs.

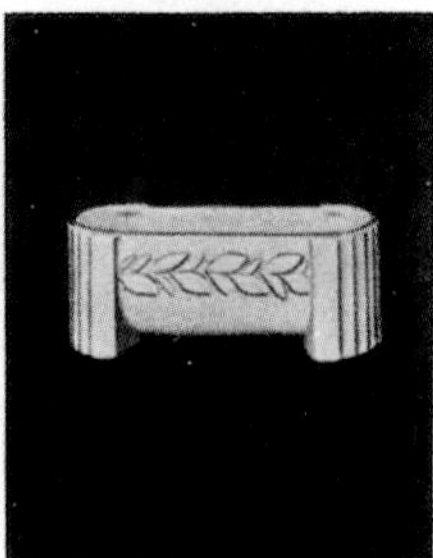

No. 500—Fern Box
Size 4⅜" x 8½"
White, Green & Yellow
packed 2 doz. Wt. 45 lbs.
$9.40 per dozen

No. 278—6" x 8"
Shell Planting Vase
Matt Whit., peach & Yel.
packed 2 doz. Wt. 42 lbs.
$12.00 per dozen

No. M2—8"
Console Bowl
Green, Coral & Yellow
packed 2 doz. Wt. 42 lbs.
$7.20 per dozen

No. M5—11"
Centerpiece
Turq., Green & Yellow
packed 1 doz. Wt. 30 lbs.
$20.40 per dozen

No. 10—3¾"
Jardiniere
White, Green & Yellow
packed 6 doz. Wt. 45 lbs.
$2.20 per dozen

No. 11—No. 12
3¾" Jardinieres
Pink, Yel., & Yel. Gr.
packed 6 doz. Wt. 42 lbs.
$3.00 per dozen

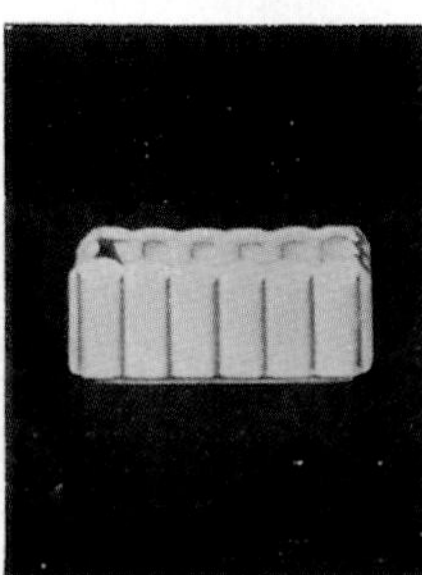

No. 608—6½"
Planting Dish
Green, Coral & Yellow
packed 2 doz. Wt. 30 lbs.
$5.40 per dozen

No. 609—6½"
Planting Dish
Green, Coral & Yellow
packed 2 doz. Wt. 30 lbs.
$5.40 per dozen

3

No. 40—7"
Jardiniere
White, Green & Peach
packed 1 doz. Wt. 42 lbs.
$6.40 per dozen

No. 42—6½"
Jardiniere
Green & Yellow
packed 2 doz. Wt. 55 lbs.
$5.40 per dozen

1948 catalog page.

Jardinieres Flower Pots and Planters

No. 43—7¾"
Jardiniere
White, Green & Coral
packed 1 doz. Wt. 35 lbs.
$6.40 per dozen

No. 600—7¼"
Jardiniere
Sprayed Decoration
packed 1 doz. Wt. 45 lbs.
$9.60 per dozen

No. 38—Jardiniere
Sizes—8½" & 10½"
White, Green & Peach
8½"-$11.60 doz.
2/3 doz. 45 lbs.
10½"-$20.00 doz.
1/3 doz. 35 lbs.

No. 101—Pot & Saucer
Sizes 4"-5"-6"
White, Green & Yellow
4"-$4.00 dz. 3 dz. 35 lbs.
5" 5.20 dz. 3 dz. 35 lbs.
6" 6.40 dz. 1 dz. 30 lbs.

No. 60—6 x 4" Snow Man
Planter
White decorated
packed 3 doz. Wt. 30 lbs.
$5.60 per dozen

No. 63—7 x 3¼"
Duck W/Egg
Planter
White & Yellow—Dec.
packed 3 doz. Wt. 40 lbs.
$7.20 per dozen

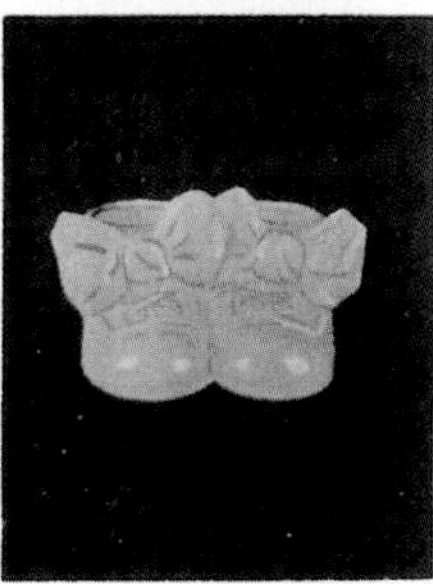

No. 64—4½" x 5½"
Twin Shoes
Pink and Blue
packed 2 doz. Wt. 25 lbs.
$4.90 per dozen

No. 65—6 x 3"
Double Duck W/Egg
Planter
White & Yellow—Dec.
packed 3 doz. Wt. 30 lbs.
$7.20 per dozen

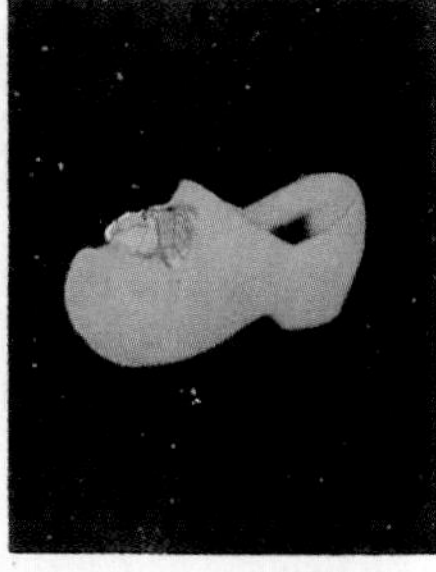

No. 23—7½"
Dutch Shoe
Turq., Blue & Yellow
packed 2 doz. Wt. 30 lbs.
$10.40 per dozen

No. 68—Swan
Underglaze Decoration
packed 1 doz. Wt. 25 lbs.
$16.00 per dozen

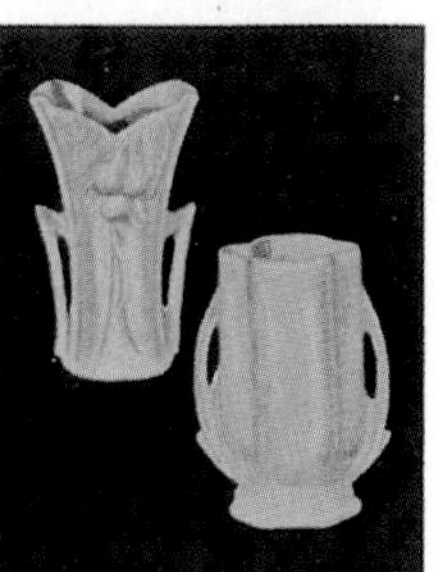

No. 104—No. 105
5¾" Vases
Green, Coral & Yellow
packed 3 doz. Wt. 32 lbs.
$4.40 per dozen

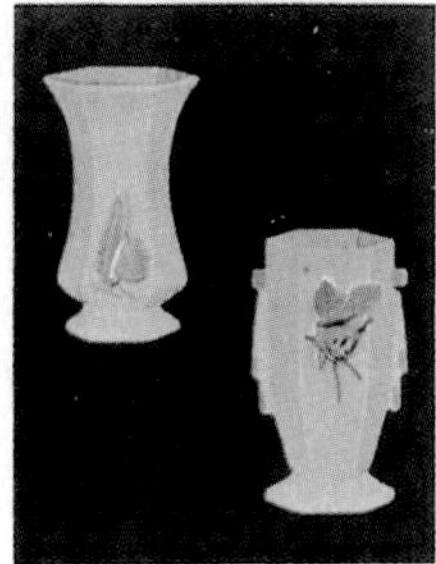

No. 803—No. 802
5¾" Vases
Wht., Pink & Yel. Dec.
packed 3 doz. Wt. 32 lbs.
$8.00 per dozen

No. 49—Swan
Wht., Pink & Yel. Dec.
packed 2 doz. Wt. 35 lbs.
$8.00 per dozen

No. 51—Calf
Pink, Coral & Yel. Dec.
packed 2 doz. Wt. 35 lbs.
$8.00 per dozen

4

No. 55—Pelican
White, Blue, & Yel, Dec.
packed 2 doz. Wt. 35 lbs.
$8.00 per dozen

No. 57—Goose Cart
White, Green & Yel. Dec.
packed 2 doz. Wt. 35 lbs.
$8.00 per dozen

1948 catalog page.

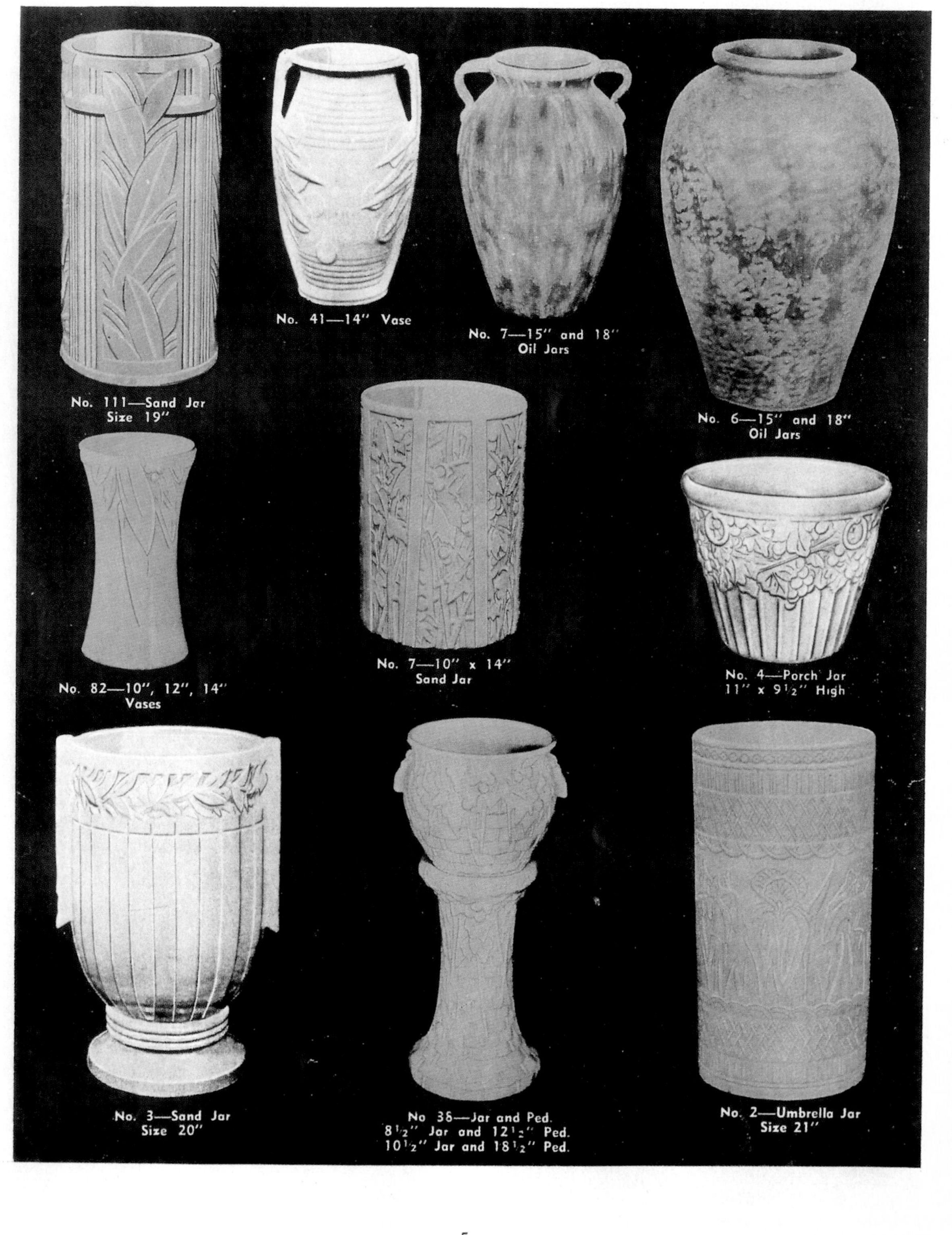

Jardinieres & Pedestals, Vases & Sand Jars
No. 111—Sand Jar Size 19"
No. 41—14" Vase
No. 7—15" and 18" Oil Jars
No. 6—15" and 18" Oil Jars
No. 82—10", 12", 14" Vases
No. 7—10" x 14" Sand Jar
No. 4—Porch Jar 11" x 9½" High
No. 3—Sand Jar Size 20"
No 38—Jar and Ped. 8½" Jar and 12½" Ped. 10½" Jar and 18½" Ped.
No. 2—Umbrella Jar Size 21"
5

1948 catalog page.

Cookie Jars, & Kitchen Items

*No. 105—38 oz. Tea Pot
*No. 106—12 oz. Tea Pot
Brown Gloss
No. 106—2 doz.
30 lbs. $8.00 doz.
No. 105—1 doz.
30 lbs. $12.00 doz.

* No. 5—1 pt. French
Casserole
Brown W/Yellow cover
packed 2 doz. Wt. 30 lbs.
$7.20 per dozen

No. 2—2 qt. Bean Pot
Brown Gloss
packed 1 doz. Wt. 40 lbs.
$7.60 per dozen

No. 138—55 oz.
Pitcher
Green, Yel. & Maroon
packed 1 doz. Wt. 35 lbs.
$10.40 per dozen

No. 9—Mixing Bowls
Green, Yellow & Maroon
6"-3 dz. 40 lbs. $3.30 dz.
8"-1 ½" dz. 45 lbs.
$6.40 dz.

No. 141—48 oz.
Ice Jug
Green, Yellow & Maroon
packed 1 doz. Wt. 35 lbs.
$10.40 per dozen

No. 137—32 oz.
White, Green & Yellow
packed 1 ½ doz. Wt. 33 lbs.
$6.40 per dozen

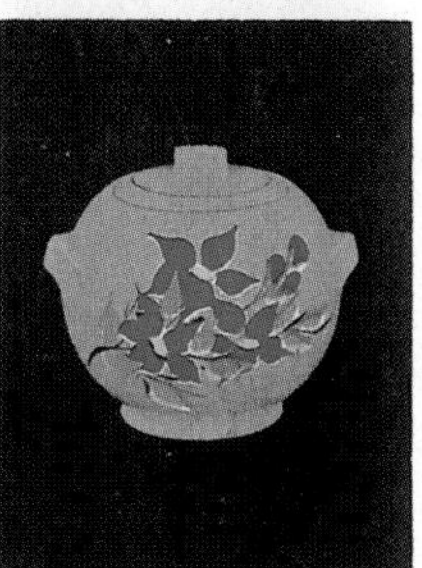

No. 7—6 pt. Cookie Jars
Green, Yellow & Blue Dec.
packed 2/3 doz. Wt. 40 lbs.
$14.40 per dozen

No. 17—Mammy
White W/Decoration
packed ½ doz. Wt. 30 lbs.
$24.00 per dozen

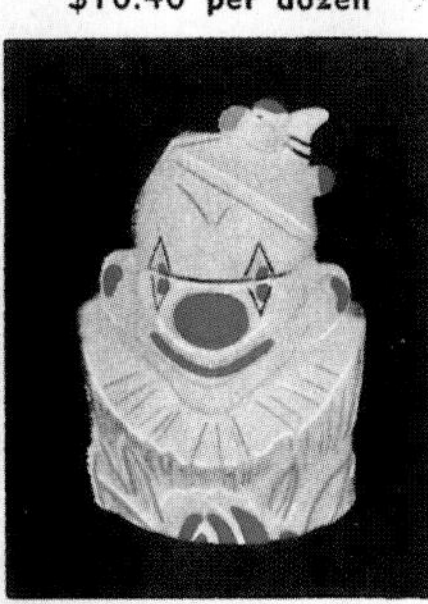

No. 19—Clown
White W/Decoration
packed ½ doz. Wt. 30 lbs.
$24.00 per dozen

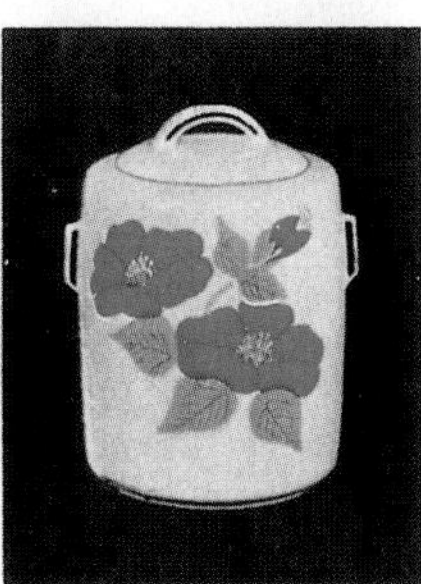

No. 28—Cookie Jar
White W/Red Decoration
packed ½ doz. Wt. 33 lbs.
$24.00 per dozen

No. 32—Cookie Jar
White W/Red Decoration
packed ½ doz. Wt. 30 lbs.
$24.00 per dozen

No. 7—Cuspidors
Green or Brown Glazes
7 ½" Diameter
packed 1 doz. Wt. 35 lbs.
$5.80 per dozen

No. 44—8" Casserole
Brown gloss
packed 1 doz. Wt. 46 lbs.
$10.40 per dozen

6

No. 4—Dog Feeder
Green or Brown
7 ½" Diameter
Lettering:
To Man's Best Friend,
His Dog
packed 2 doz. Wt. 55 lbs.
7.20 per dozen

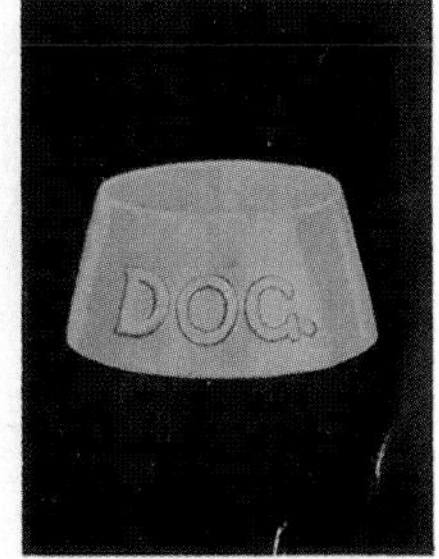

No. 5—6"
Spaniel Feeder
Green & Maroon
packed 2 doz. Wt. 50 lbs.
$7.20 per dozen

1948 catalog page.

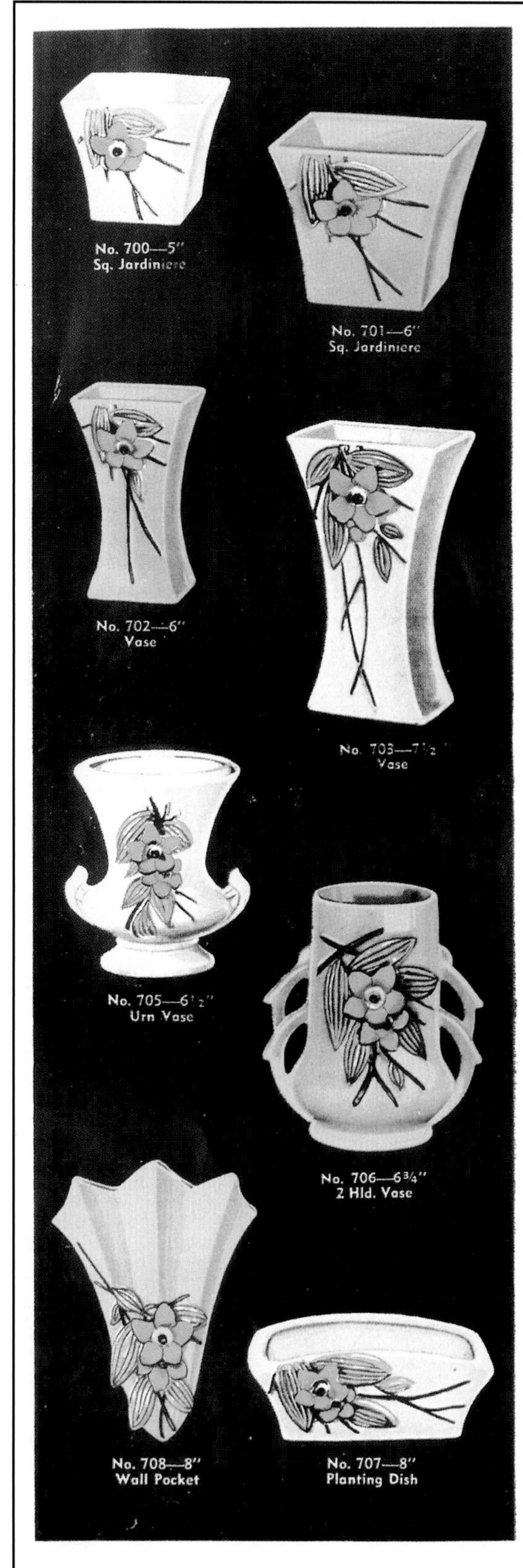

No. 700—5" Square Jardinieres ....$11.60 Doz.
Packed 2 Doz.—Wt. 30 lbs.

No. 701—6" Square Jardinieres .... 17.60 Doz.
Packed 1 Doz.—Wt. 30 lbs.

No. 702—6" Vases .... 14.10 Doz.
Packed 2 Doz.—Wt. 30 lbs.

No. 703—7½" Vases .... 17.60 Doz.
Packed 1 Doz.—Wt. 30 lbs.

No. 705—6½" Urn Vases .... 17.60 Doz.
Packed 1 Doz.—Wt. 25 lbs.

No. 706—6¾" 2 Hld. Vases .... 17.60 Doz.
Packed 1 Doz.—Wt. 25 lbs.

No. 708—8" Wall Pocket .... 16.00 Doz.
Packed 1 Doz.—Wt. 18 lbs.

No. 707—8" Planting Dish .... 16.00 Doz.
Packed 2 Doz.—Wt. 35 lbs.

———o———

This line may also be ordered in the following assortments.

No. G—16-Piece Assortment ....$21.35 Ea.
Consisting of 2 pieces of each item.
1 Carton—Wt. 35 lbs.

No. H—30-Piece Assortment .... 38.70 Ea.
Consisting of:
6 No. 700, 2 No. 701,
6 No. 702, 6 No. 705,
6 No. 706, 4 No. 708,
3 Cartons—Wt. 40 lbs.

No. F—42-Piece Assortment .... 55.50 Ea.
Consisting of:
6 No. 700, 2 No. 701, 6 No. 702,
6 No. 703, 6 No. 705, 6 No. 706,
6 No. 707, 4 No. 708,
4 Cartons—Wt. 60 lbs.

Terms: 30 days net, f. o. b. factory.
No charge for packing.

8

Blossom Time Line from 1948 catalog page.

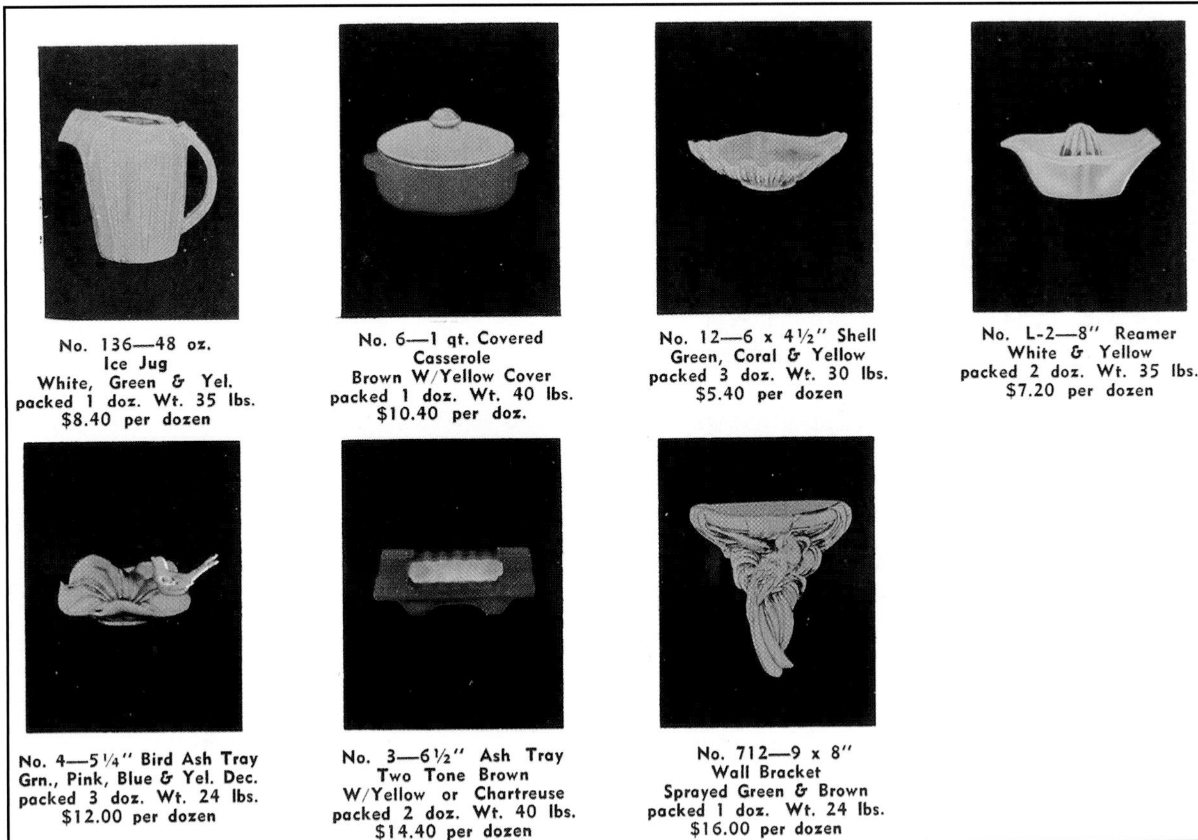

No. 136—48 oz.
Ice Jug
White, Green & Yel.
packed 1 doz. Wt. 35 lbs.
$8.40 per dozen

No. 6—1 qt. Covered
Casserole
Brown W/Yellow Cover
packed 1 doz. Wt. 40 lbs.
$10.40 per doz.

No. 12—6 x 4½" Shell
Green, Coral & Yellow
packed 3 doz. Wt. 30 lbs.
$5.40 per dozen

No. L-2—8" Reamer
White & Yellow
packed 2 doz. Wt. 35 lbs.
$7.20 per dozen

No. 4—5¼" Bird Ash Tray
Grn., Pink, Blue & Yel. Dec.
packed 3 doz. Wt. 24 lbs.
$12.00 per dozen

No. 3—6½" Ash Tray
Two Tone Brown
W/Yellow or Chartreuse
packed 2 doz. Wt. 40 lbs.
$14.40 per dozen

No. 712—9 x 8"
Wall Bracket
Sprayed Green & Brown
packed 1 doz. Wt. 24 lbs.
$16.00 per dozen

Kitchen items and ash trays from the 1948 catalog page.

Mixing Bowl Set. Gloss glaze colors. 1950s. Sizes 5" – 9". $40.00 – 100.00.

Vase with Handles. 8" tall. 1950s. Marked McCoy. $40.00 – 50.00.

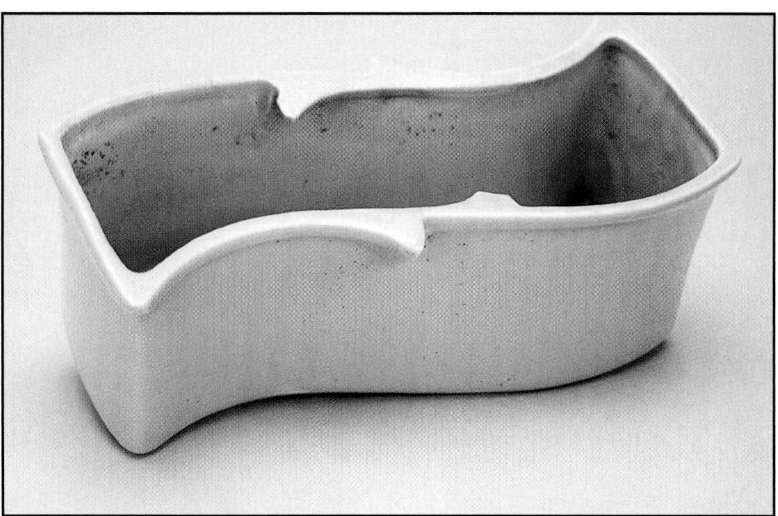

Planter 7½". 1950s. Unusual shape. Marked McCoy. $60.00 – 70.00.

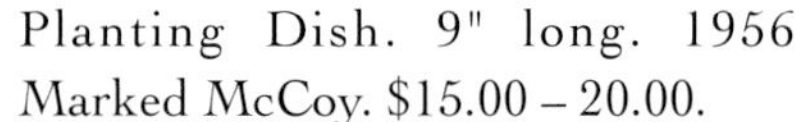

Planting Dish. 9" long. 1956. Marked McCoy. $15.00 – 20.00.

Mixing Bowl Set 5" –10". Variety of colors. 1950s. $30.00 – 80.00.

Vase 9½" tall. 1955. Marked McCoy. Pictured with web decoration. This particular vase has a glaze formula "1/2-800, 1/2-801" on the bottom. Production vase $50.00 – 60.00. Vase with formula $70.00 – 80.00.

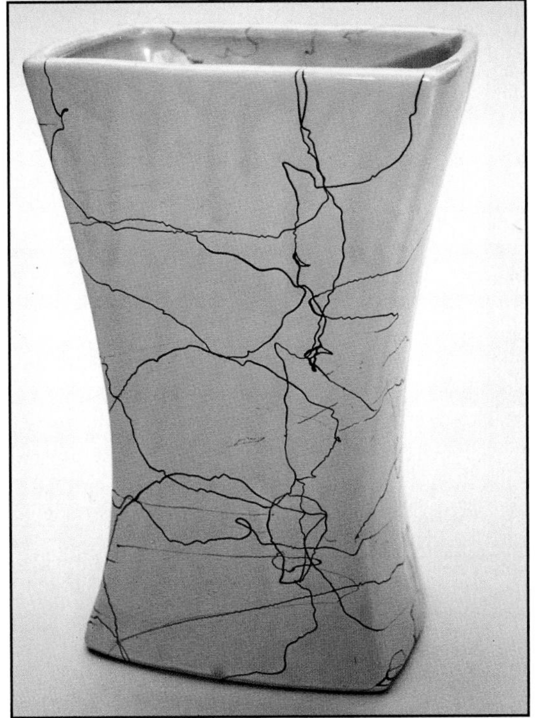

Planter with applied dragonfly. 5½" x 4". 1956. Marked McCoy. $100.00 – 125.00.

Vase 9½" tall. 1955. Marked McCoy. Same vase shape as pink vase above. Multicolored glaze. With special glaze $100.00 – 125.00.

Vase 9½" tall. 1955. Marked McCoy. Same shape as pink and multicolored vases only with production overdrip design. $50.00 – 60.00. Planting Dish 9", also with overdrip design glaze. 1956. $25.00 – 30.00.

Pine Cone Tea Set. Same as green and brown production glaze set from late 1940s – 1950s. (See pg. 228, Vol. I.) Unusual set in blue glaze. Marked McCoy. Standard set $75.00 – 100.00. Blue glaze $100.00 – 125.00.

Capri Line. 1957. All marked McCoy.
Left to right:
Bud Vase 7" tall. $30.00 – 40.00.
Jardiniere 7" x 7½". $30.00 – 40.00.
Planter 5" x 4". $15.00 – 20.00.
Square Planter 5½" x 3½". $20.00 – 25.00.

Capri Line. 1957. All marked McCoy.
Left to right:
Planting Dish 14½". $40.00 – 50.00.
Vase 8¼". $25.00 – 30.00.
Centerpiece 11" x 7½". $35.00 – 45.00.
Planting Dish 11". $20.00 – 25.00.

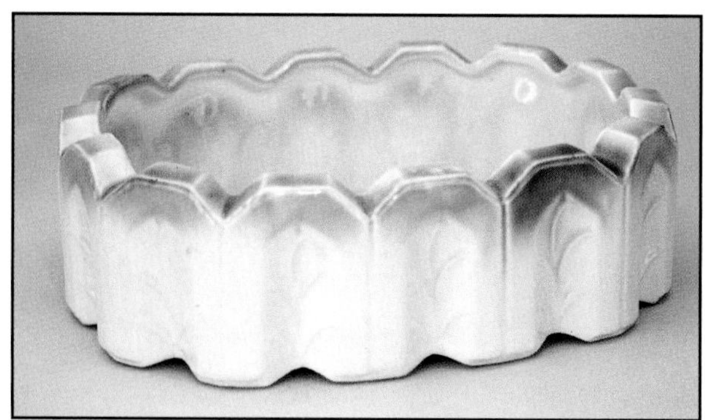

Planting Dish 9½" x 7¼". 1956. Marked McCoy. White with green or yellow with green decoration. $30.00 – 40.00.

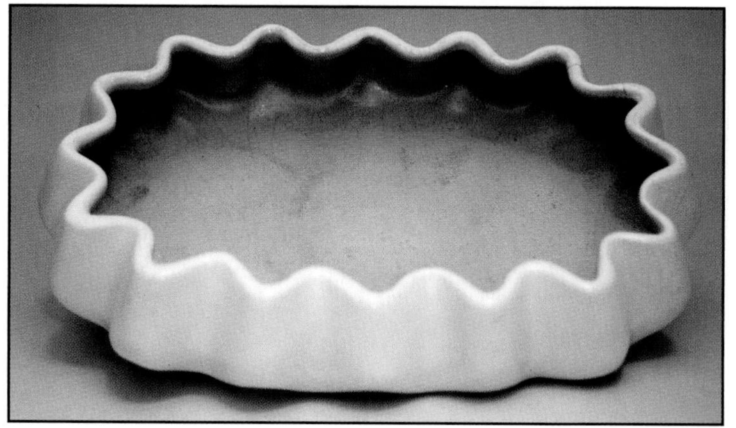

Planting Dish 10½". 1950s. Marked McCoy. $30.00 – 40.00.

Teapot with rare plate in lost glaze decoration. Marked McCoy. \$100.00 – 125.00.

Flower Pot with Saucer. Unique design. 5". Marked. A hard one to find. \$60.00 – 70.00.

Set made up of pair of lost glaze Covered Casseroles with stand. Marked McCoy. \$200.00 – 250.00.

Planting Dish 9" x 7". Yellow with green or pink with turquoise decoration. 1956. Marked McCoy. \$35.00 – 50.00.

Planting Dish 9½" x 7¼". Pictured in both glaze combinations made. 1956. Marked McCoy. \$35.00 – 50.00.

Serving Dish. 11" Marked McCoy on bottom in unusual way. $50.00 – 60.00.

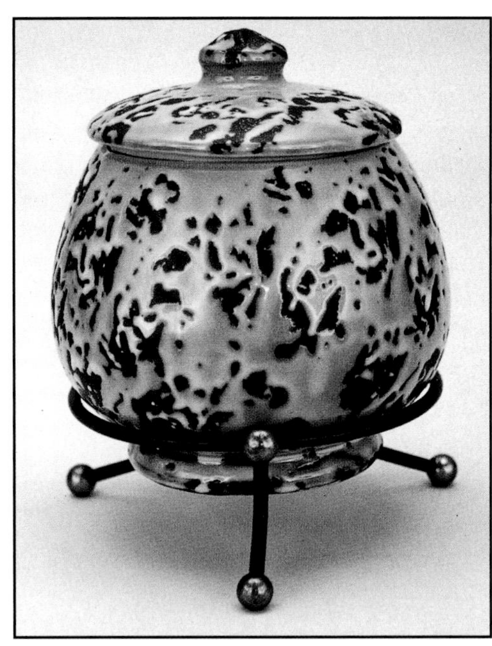

Candy Dish with stand. Brocade Line glaze. 5" x 5". 1950s. Marked McCoy. $50.00 – 60.00.

Left to right:
Pot & Saucer. 1956. Sold in 5" and 6" sizes. Marked McCoy. $25.00 – 35.00.
Artisan Line Vase 10". 1965. Marked McCoy. $50.00 – 60.00.
Vase 5¾". 1952. Pictured with Brocade Line style glaze. $30.00 – 40.00.

Two Artisan Line pieces, both marked McCoy. 1965. Left: Pot with pedestal design 4". $25.00 – 30.00. Right: Jardiniere 5". $30.00 – 35.00.

Artisan Line Planter 7½". 1965. Marked McCoy. $35.00 – 45.00.

Pieces with shapes from earlier Grecian Line. All white with green decoration. Late 1950s. Marked McCoy.
Left to right:
Small Pedestal Dish 5½". $25.00 – 30.00.
Large Centerpiece 12". $40.00 – 50.00.
Jardiniere 5½" x 5½". $30.00 – 35.00.
Small Jardiniere 5½" x 4¼". $25.00 – 30.00.

Bud Vase. 7¼". Gold finish. Marked McCoy. $60.00 – 80.00.

Planting Dish 12". Yellow with brown decoration. Also made in white with maroon or green decoration. 1959. Marked McCoy. $50.00 – 60.00.

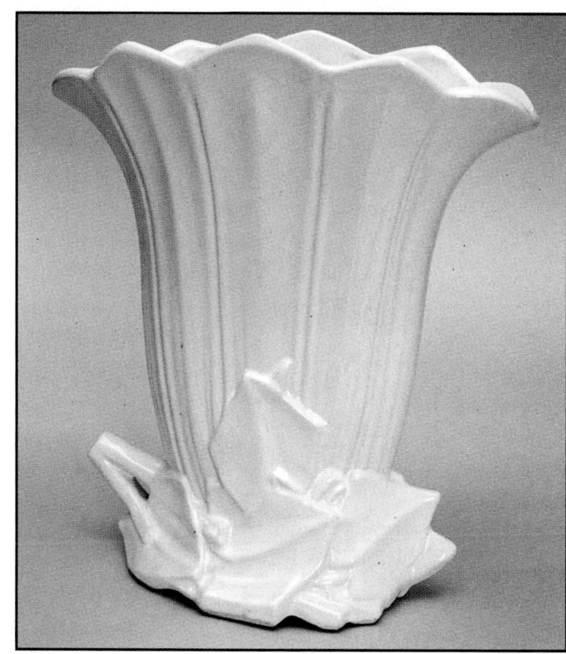

Tall Fan Vase 14½. Marked McCoy. 1954. Pictured non-production white glaze. (See page 173, Volume I, for production glazes.) Production glazes $150.00 – 200.00. White $250.00 – 300.00.

Planting Dish 9½". Marked McCoy. $30.00 – 35.00. Right: Filigree Planting Dish 8¾" x 5". 1953. Sold with a liner. Marked McCoy. $60.00 – 75.00.

Cook-Serve Line Pieces. Late 1940s – 1950s. Marked McCoy
Clockwise from bottom left:
Skillet 10". $25.00 – 30.00.
Oval Dish. $30.00 – 35.00.
Pie Plate 9". $25.00 – 30.00.
Pitcher 24 oz. $25.00 – 30.00.
Skillet with Cover. $40.00 – 50.00.
Stick Handled Creamer 3½".
$20.00 – 25.00.

Additional Cook-Serve Line pieces.
Marked McCoy.
Left to right:
Bean Pot with Cover 2 qt. $35.00 – 45.00.
French Casserole with Cover 1 pt. $25.00 – 30.00.
Pie Plate 9". $25.00 – 30.00.

Planter with leaf design. 1950s. 7". Marked McCoy. $35.00 – 45.00.

Left: Novelty Planter. 1950s. 7". No mark. $20.00 – 25.00. Right: Flower Box. 1956. Marked McCoy. Shown in 12" size. $25.00 – 30.00. Also made in 6½" and 9". $20.00 – 25.00 each.

Left: Vase $9\frac{1}{4}$". Mid-1950s. McCoy mark. Made in green, white or pink. \$30.00 – 40.00. Right: Two-Tone Vase. Mid-1950s. Marked McCoy. \$30.00 – 40.00.

Vase. Mid-1950s. Marked McCoy. \$30.00 – 40.00. Also pictured: Jardiniere in three sizes made in 1" increments in sizes from $4\frac{1}{2}$" through $10\frac{1}{2}$". \$25.00 – 75.00.

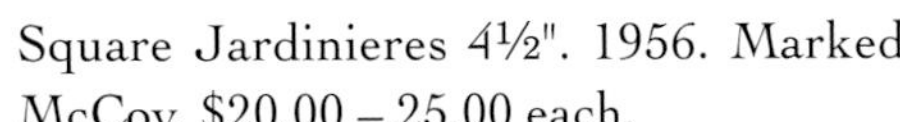

Square Jardinieres $4\frac{1}{2}$". 1956. Marked McCoy. \$20.00 – 25.00 each.

Left: Square Jardiniere $4\frac{1}{2}$". 1956. Marked McCoy. \$20.00 – 25.00. Right: Planting Dish with Handles 10". 1959. Offered in white, green or yellow. \$30.00 – 35.00.

Sunburst Gold pieces, both marked McCoy. Left: Jardiniere. $25.00 – 30.00. Right: Planting Dish 7". $25.00 – 30.00.

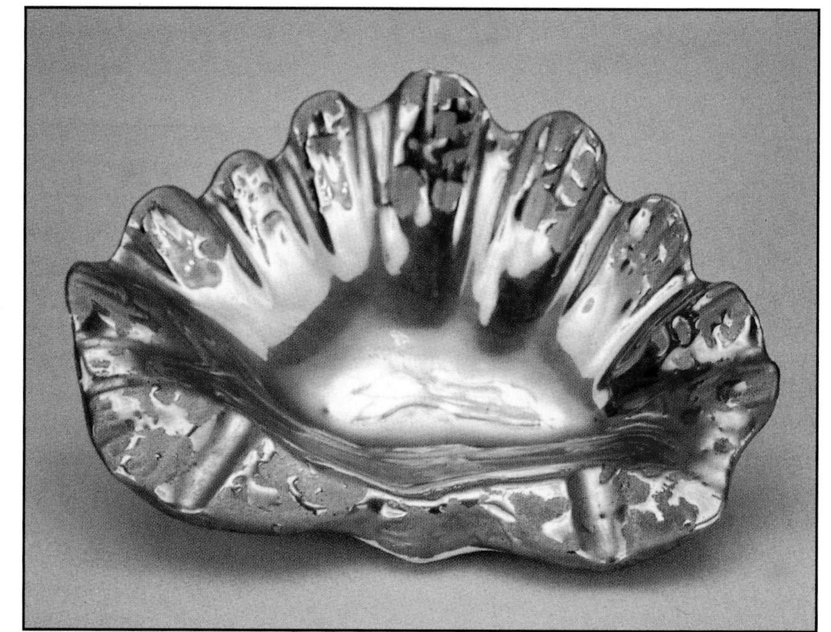

Sunburst Gold Shell Ashtray. 6¼" x 4½". No mark. 1957. HTF. $60.00 – 70.00.

Sunburst Gold pieces, both marked McCoy. Left: Planter 9¼". $30.00 – 35.00. Right: Footed Planter 6". $25.00 – 30.00.

Jardinieres with Saucers. All marked McCoy. Late 1960s. Notice differences in top rim design. Made in sizes 4", 5", 6", and 7". $30.00 – 60.00.

Large Planting Dish 14". Also sold in 10". Marked McCoy. 1959. Made in green, white, and yellow. $35.00 – 40.00. Two Planters. Marked McCoy. 1961. Shown in 6" and 8". Also made in 9". $25.00 – 35.00.

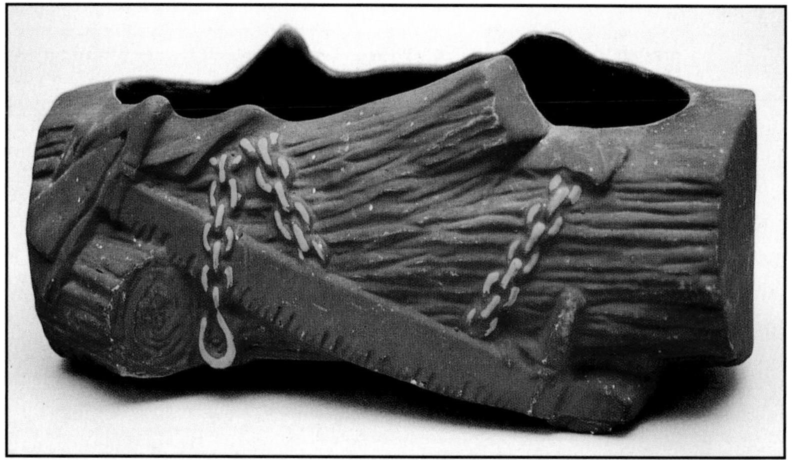

Chocolate Bisque Line pieces from 1958. Both marked McCoy. Left: Jardiniere sold in 6½" and 7½" sizes. $30.00 – 35.00. Right: Log Planter 8¾". $35.00 – 40.00.

Early in the 1960s pottery sales were almost taking care of themselves. The question was, what about the future? The first answer was the release of the Roseville Floraline Line which was extremely successful. A couple of years later, another new idea was proposed. The idea was simple — take standard McCoy designs and modify them slightly to accommodate artificial flowers. The new product consisted of a selection of several pots and saucers and some jardinieres, ready for use with a nice assortment of artificial flowers. Examples can be seen in the photos on this page. A plastic grommet which held the flower stems in place remains in yellow pot and saucer pictured.

The manufacturing was not complex; only a slight modification to the standard mold of each piece was necessary to properly hold the flowers. A ledge in the shape of a ring was created on the inside wall of the pot. The ledge served as a seat for a ceramic disk. The pre-formed disks were about ¼" thick and had a ¾" hole in the center for inserting the flowers.

Following the dipping of the basic piece in its glaze, while the glaze was still wet, the disk was put into position. When the piece was fired, the glaze adhered to the bottom and sides of the disk and kept it in place.

This new idea seemed to be a good one but did not bear the fruits that Roseville Floraline produced. In fact, after initial sales the newcomer seems to fizzle quickly. Production volume of these pieces was likely not too great judging from their relative scarcity. Competition with the plastics industry was becoming fierce at this time, and that may explain the short life of this new product.

Examples of the insert style products. Note the inside step in the green jardiniere for supporting the clay insert. All pieces marked McCoy. Complete with insert $50.00 – 70.00. Without insert but with the inner ring for the insert $30.00 – 40.00.

Standard Style Pot and Saucers. 1960s. Marked McCoy. Sizes 4", 5", and 6". Shown in all four colors made. $25.00 – 40.00.

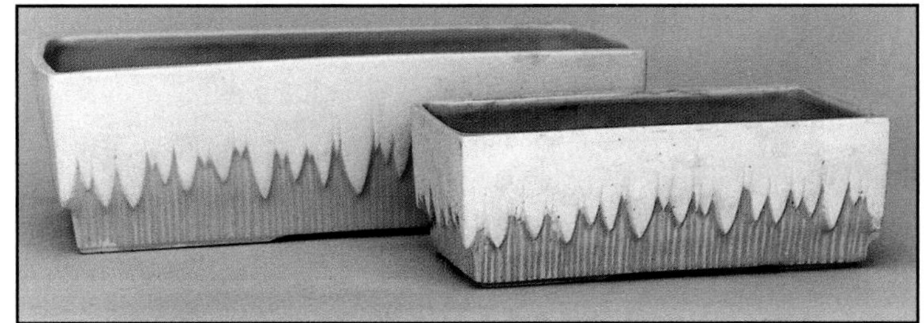

Planting Dish with icing design. Late 1950s. 10" & 14". Marked McCoy. $30.00 – 40.00 and $40.00 – 50.00, respectively.

Planting Dishes, both marked McCoy. Yellow dish same style as dishes pictured above. Late 1950s. 10" $30.00 – 40.00. Orange dish in back. 14". Early 1960s. $40.00 – 50.00.

Pouring Bowl Set. 1962. Marked McCoy. Bowls in three sizes, 6", 7", and 8". Set, $90.00 – 110.00. Individual bowls, $30.00 – 40.00.

Mixing Bowl Set with pouring spout. 1965. Marked McCoy. Bowls in three sizes, 6", 7", and 8". Set, $100.00 – 125.00. Individual bowl, $30.00 – 50.00.

Jardiniere. 1960s. Made in 1" increment sizes, $3\frac{1}{2}$" through $10\frac{1}{2}$". Marked McCoy. $25.00 – 75.00.

January Additions to 1956 Catalog

No. 800—5½x4"
Jewelled Pillow Vase
Pink, White
Packed 1 Doz. Wt. 15 lbs.
$17.60 Per Dozen

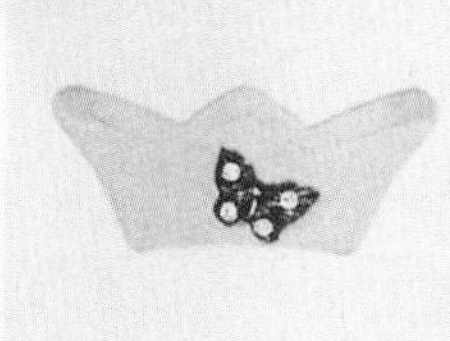

No. 801—8½"
Jeweled Planter
White or Pink
Packed 1 Doz. Wt. 15 lbs.
$17.60 Per Dozen

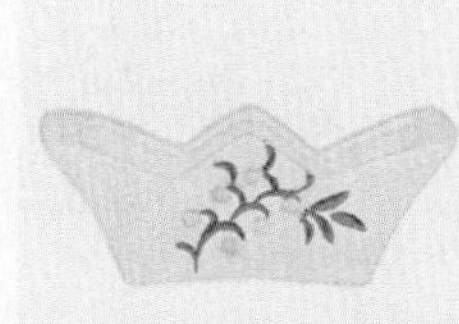

No. 802—8½"
Jeweled Planter
Ivory Decorated
Packed 1 Doz. Wt. 15 lbs.
$17.60 Per Dozen

No. 803—7½"
Jewelled Planter
Pink, White
Packed 1 Doz. Wt. 18 lbs.
$17.60 Per Dozen

No. 422—4½"
Square Jardiniere
Green, White, Maroon
Packed 2 Doz. Wt. 30 lbs.
$8.40 Per Dozen

No. 421—6"
Square Jardiniere
Green, White, Maroon
Packed 1 Doz. Wt. 24 lbs.
$10.40 Per Dozen

No. 420—9½"
Vase
Green, White, Maroon
Packed 1 Doz. Wt. 42 lbs.
$17.60 Per Dozen

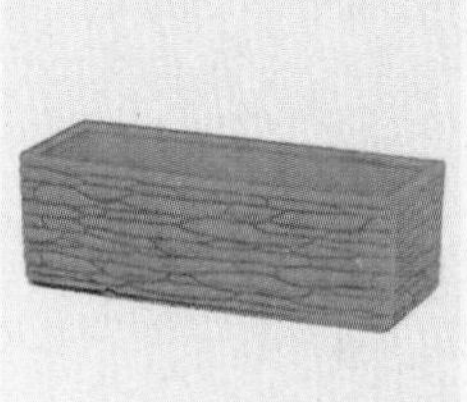

No. 423—9"
Planting Dish
Green, White, Maroon
Packed 1 Doz. Wt. 24 lbs.
$12.00 Per Dozen

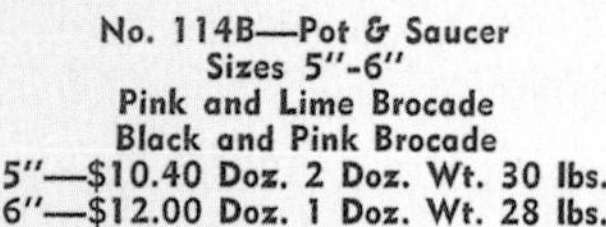

No. 114B—Pot & Saucer
Sizes 5"-6"
Pink and Lime Brocade
Black and Pink Brocade
5"—$10.40 Doz. 2 Doz. Wt. 30 lbs.
6"—$12.00 Doz. 1 Doz. Wt. 28 lbs.

No. BE-8—6x5½"
Swallow Book Ends
Ivory w/Hand Decoration
Packed ½ Doz. Pr. Wt. 24 lbs.
$36.00 Per Dozen Pair

No. WP-17—10¼"
Violin Wall Pocket
Brown or Aqua
w/Contrasting Strings
Packed 1 Doz. Wt. 18 lbs.
$17.60 Per Dozen

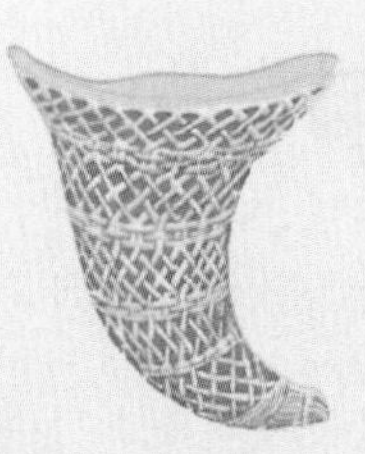

No. WP-18—8x6½"
Basket Weave Wall Pocket
Ivory w/Green Bisque
Yellow w/Brown Bisque
Packed 1 Doz. Wt. 16 lbs.
$17.60 Per Dozen

No. WP-19—6½"
Urn-Shaped Wall Pocket
Pink w/Black Flecks
Chartreuse w/Brown Flecks
Packed 2 Doz. Wt. 30 lbs.
$8.80 Per Dozen

The Nelson-McCoy Pottery Company . . . . . Roseville, Ohio

Sheet No.

Catalog page from 1956.

Jardinieres & Peds
Oil Jars Pet Feeders

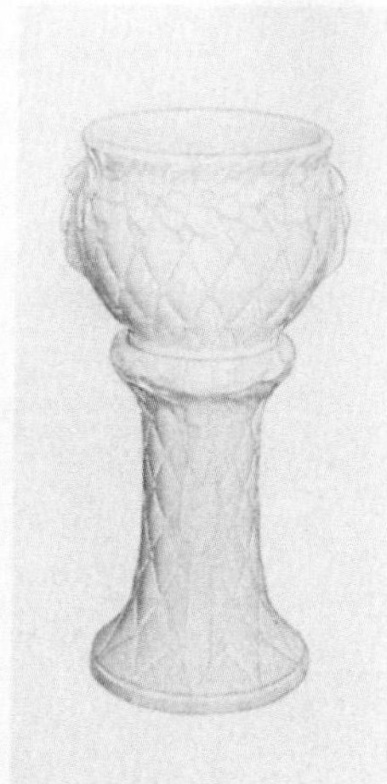

No. 48—Jar and Ped.
Green and White
8½" Jard. and 12½" Pedestal
$1.60 each 1 only—18 lbs.

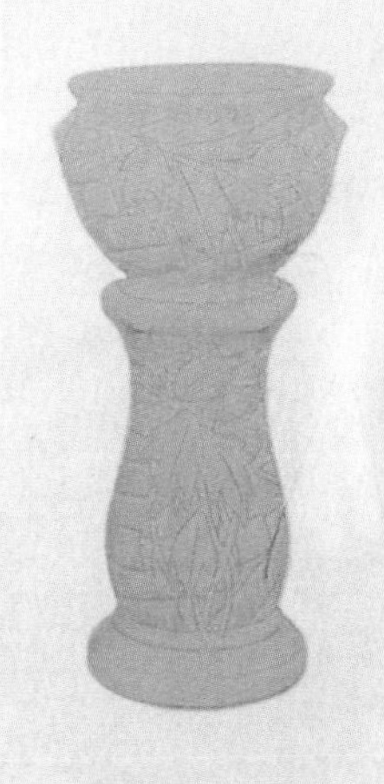

No. 39—Jar and Ped.
Green and White
9½" Jar and 14½" Ped.
$2.20 each 1 only—22 lbs.
Brown and Green Blend
$2.90 each 1 only—22 lbs.

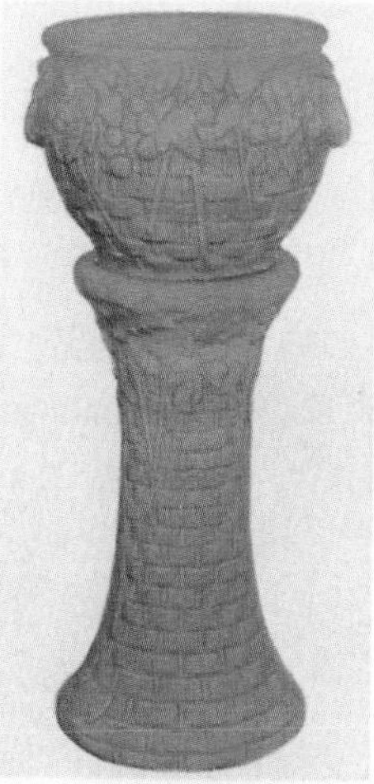

No. 38—Jar and Ped.
Green and White
10½" Jard. and 8½" Pedestal
$3.60 each 1 only—30 lbs.
Brown and Green Blend
$4.20 each 1 only—30 lbs.

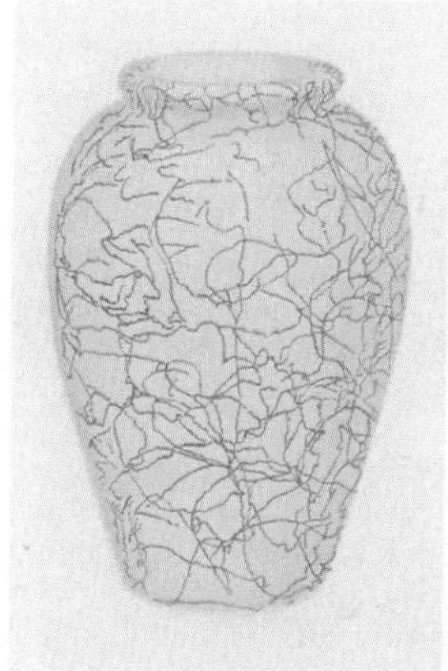

No. 6—Oil Jar
Sizes 15"-18"
Yellow, Maroon, Green
w/Chromoveil Decoration
15"—$ 2.40 each 1 only—Wt. 25 lbs.
18" $ 3.60 each 1 only—Wt. 30 lbs.

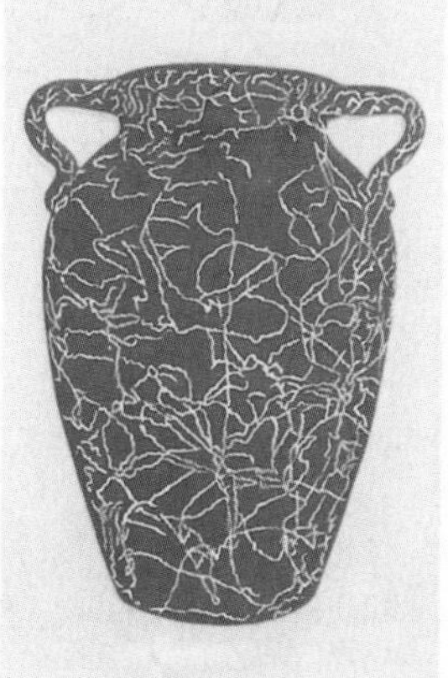

No. 7—Oil Jar
Sizes 15"-18"
Yellow, Maroon, Green
w/Chromoveil Decoration
15"—$2.90 each 1 only—Wt. 25 lbs.
18"—$4.20 each 1 only—Wt. 30 lbs.

No. 7—7½" Cuspidors
Green and Brown Glazes
Packed 1 Doz. Wt. 35 lbs.
$3.60 Per Dozen

No. 9—6" Cat Feeder
Yellow and Green
Packed 3 Doz. Wt. 60 lbs.
$2.88 Per Dozen

No. 4—7½" Dog Feeder
Green and Brown Lettering
To Man's Best Friend, His Dog
Packed 2 Doz. Wt. 55 lbs.
$3.30 Per Dozen

No. 5—6" Spaniel Feeder
Green and Maroon
Packed 2 Doz. Wt. 50 lbs.
$3.30 Per Dozen

7

Catalog page from 1956.

Flower Pots

No. 19—Pots & Saucers
Sizes 3½"-4½"-5½"-6½"
Pink, Green & Yellow
3½"—$1.20 Doz. 4 Doz. 33 lbs.
4½"—$1.84 Doz. 3 Doz. 42 lbs.
5½"—$2.48 Doz. 2 Doz. 50 lbs.
6½"—$3.12 Doz. 1 Doz. 38 lbs.

No. 14 Violet Pot & Saucer
Sizes 4", 5", 6"
Green, Yellow & White
4"—$1.80 Doz. 3 Doz. 28 lbs.
5"—$2.40 Doz. 2 Doz. 30 lbs.
6"—$3.00 Doz. 1 Doz. 28 lbs.

No. 111—Pots & Saucers
Sizes 4", 5", 6"
Yellow, Green, White & Pink
4"—$1.80 Doz. 3 Doz. 28 lbs.
5"—$2.40 Doz. 2 Doz. 30 lbs.
6"—$3.00 Doz. 1 Doz. 28 lbs.

No. 114—Pot & Saucer
Sizes 5", 6"
White, Yellow, Pink & Green
w/Chromoveil Decoration
5"—$3.00 Doz. 2 Doz. 30 lbs.
6"—$3.60 Doz. 1 Doz. 28 lbs.

Decorated Planting Dishes

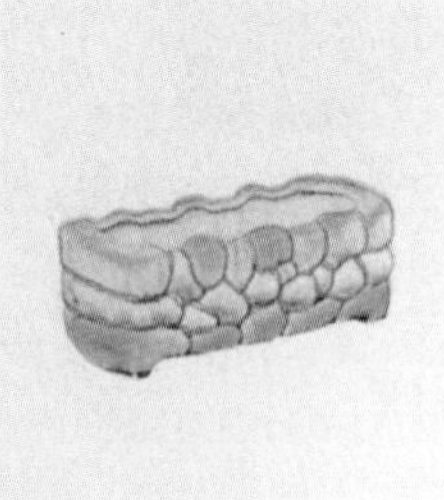

No. 635—6¾"
Stone Window Box
Birchwood, Chartreuse w/Green,
Gray w/Ruby
Packed 2 Doz. Wt. 28 lbs.
$3.00 Per Dozen

No. 648—7½" x 3¾"
Basket Weave Planter
Yellow, Pink, Lime
w/Spray Decoration
Packed 2 Doz. Wt. 36 lbs.
$3.60 Per Dozen

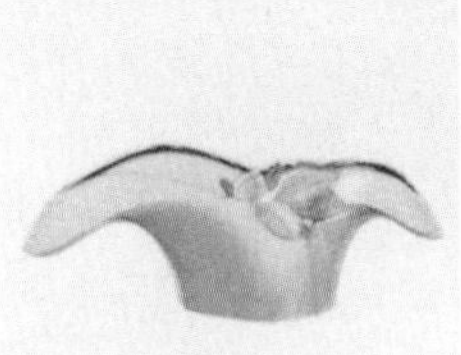

No. 60—11" x 4½"
Planting Dish
w/Applied Bud
Yellow or Chartreuse
Decorated Bud
Packed 1 Doz. Wt. 20 lbs.
$6.00 Per Dozen

No. 711—10½" x 5½"
Double Cache Pot
Lt. Green or Yellow—Dec.
Packed 1 Doz. Wt. 47 lbs.
$7.80 Per Dozen

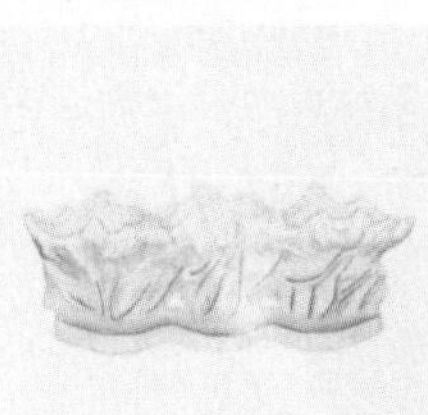

No. 774—12½" x 4½"
Triple Pot
Pink w/Dark Green Spray
Yellow w/Dark Green Spray
Orange Tan w/Dark Brown Spray
Packed 1 Doz. Wt. 30 lbs.
$6.00 Per Dozen

No. 649—12" x 4" x 4"
Log Planter
Ivory w/Brown Spray
Ivory w/Green Spray
Packed 1 Doz. Wt. 36 lbs.
$6.00 Per Dozen

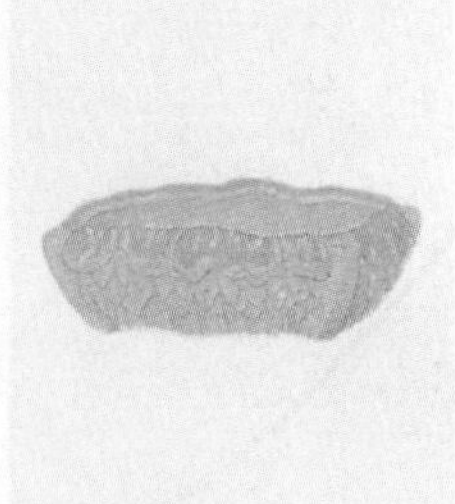

No. 644—9" x 7"
Planting Dish
Yellow w/Green Spray
Pink w/Turquoise Drip
Packed 1 Doz. Wt. 33 lbs.
$6.00 Per Dozen

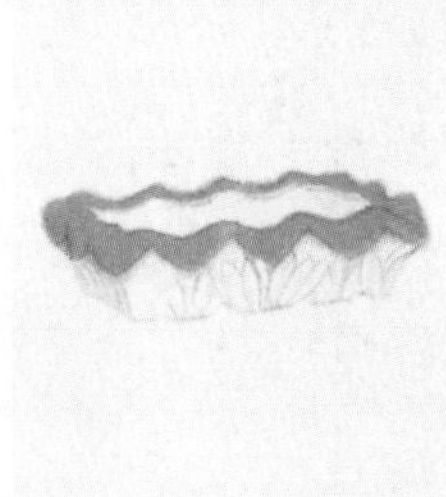

No. 645—9½" x 7¼"
Planting Dish
White w/Green Spray
Pink w/Turquoise Drip
Packed 1 Doz. Wt. 33 lbs.
$6.00 Per Dozen

No. 646—9¼" x 7"
Oval Planting Dish
Yellow w/Green Spray
White w/Green Spray
Packed 1 Doz. Wt. 36 lbs.
$6.00 Per Dozen

4

Catalog page from 1956.

Vases-Decorated

No. 708—5" x 5¾"
Vase
Pink w/Black Base
Chartreuse w/Brown Fleck
Packed 3 Doz. Wt. 50 lbs.
$2.40 Per Dozen

No. 709—4¼" x 5¾"
Basket Weave Vase
Yellow w/Brown Spray
Chartreuse w/Brown Spray
Packed 3 Doz. Wt. 48 lbs.
$2.40 Per Dozen

No. 709-D—6½" x 5¾"
Basket Weave Vase
Lime w/Green Bisque
Pink w/Brown Bisque
Packed 2 Doz. Wt. 44 lbs.
$3.60 Per Dozen

No. 74—8" Tulip Vase
White or Yellow Decorated
Packed 1 Doz. Wt. 25 lbs.
$6.00 Per Dozen

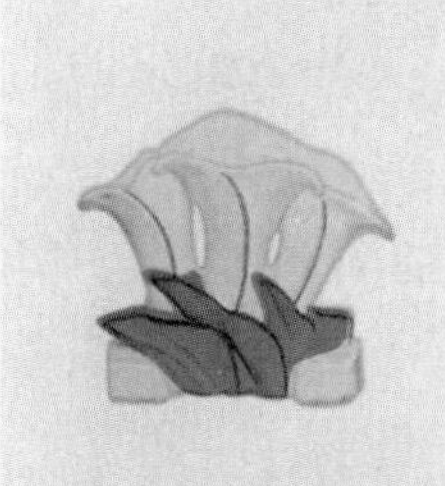

No. 78—8½" x 7"
Triple Lily Vase
White or Yellow Decorated
Packed 1 Doz. Wt. 30 lbs.
$6.00 Per Dozen

No. 80—6½" x 8"
Double Tulip Vase
White w/Hand Decoration
Packed 1 Doz. Wt. 25 lbs.
$6.00 Per Dozen

No. 84—8½"
Lily Vase
White or Yellow Decoration
Packed 1 Doz. Wt. 28 lbs.
$6.00 Per Dozen

No. 289—10" x 8"
Fan Vase
Chartreuse w/Green Dec.
Yellow w/Brown Dec.
Packed 1 Doz. Wt. 35 lbs.
$6.24 Per Dozen

No. 305—9" Fawn Vase
Birchwood, Chartreuse w/Green
White w/Pink
Packed 1 Doz. Wt. 28 lbs.
$6.24 Per Dozen

No. 89—14½" Tall Fan Vase
Green and Yellow w/Dec. Foot
Packed 1/3 Doz. Wt. 42 lbs.
$18.00 Per Dozen

Catalog page from 1956.

Nelson McCoy's

Contemporary Ceramic Group CAPRI

Modernistic shapes with permanent fired-on colors. Semi-gloss textured pastel glazes of BLUE, PINK, WHITE, YELLOW, and LIME outside with interiors glazed in contrasting complementary hues.

No. 201—5½ x 3½" Sq. Planter
Yel. w/Lime, White w/Blue, Pink w/Blue
Packed 2 Doz. Wt. 20 lbs.
$3.60 per Dozen

No. 202—5 x 4" Planter
Lime w/Yel., White w/Blue, Pink w/Blue
Packed 2 Doz. Wt. 20 lbs.
$3.60 per Dozen

No. 203—6½" Rd. Planter
Yel. w/Lime, White w/Blue, Pink w/Blue
Packed 1 Doz. Wt. 18 lbs.
$4.80 per Dozen

No. 204—7" Planting Dish
Blue w/Pink, White w/Blue, Pink w/Blue
Packed 1 Doz. Wt. 10 lbs.
$4.80 per Dozen

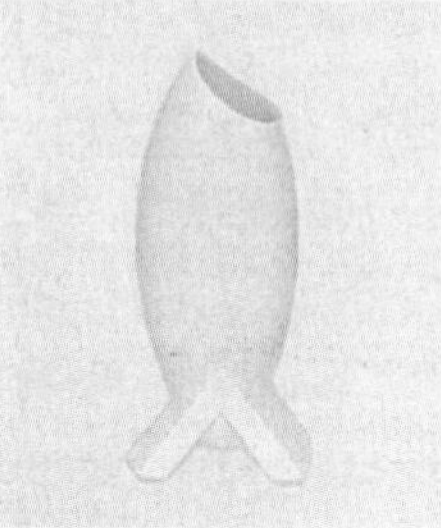

No. 205—7" Bud Vase
Blue w/Pink, White w/Blue, Pink w/Blue
Packed 1 Doz. Wt. 10 lbs.
$4.80 per Dozen

No. 206—8¼" Vase
Blue w/Pink, Lime w/Yel., Pink w/Blue
Packed 1 Doz. Wt. 20 lbs.
$6.00 per Dozen

No. 207—9 x 3½" Planting Dish
Blue w/Pink, Yel. w/Lime, Pink w/Blue
Packed 1 Doz. Wt. 15 lbs.
$6.00 per Dozen

No. 208—11" Planting Dish
Blue w/Pink, Lime w/Yel., Pink w/Blue
Packed ½ Doz. Wt. 9 lbs.
$7.20 per Dozen

No. 212—11 x 7½" Centerpiece
Blue w/Pink, White w/Blue, Lime w/Yel.
Packed ½ Doz. Wt. 14 lbs.
$7.20 per Dozen

No. 209—7 x 7½" Jardiniere
Blue w/Pink, Yel. w/Lime, Pink w/Blue
Packed ½ Doz. Wt. 17 lbs.
$7.20 per Dozen

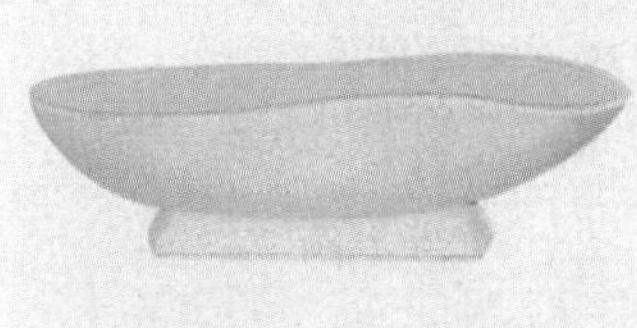

No. 210—14½" Planting Dish
Blue w/Pink, Yel. w/Lime, Pink w/Blue
Packed ½ Doz. Wt. 18 lbs.
$12.00 per Dozen

No. 200NM—24 pc. Capri Assortment
(All 11 items—Asst. Colors)
3—Nos. 201, 202
2—Ea. All other Nos.
1 Ctn. Wt. 34 lbs.—$11.80 each

No. 211NM—24 pc. Capri Assortment
(Asst. Colors)
4—ea. items 201, 202, 203, 204, 205, 207
1 Ctn. Wt. 28 lbs.—$ 9.20 each

No. 222NM—80 pc. Capri Assortment
(All 11 items—Asst. Colors)
12—ea. Nos. 201, 202; 8—ea. Nos. 203, 204, 207; 6—ea. Nos. 205, 206, 208, 212; 4—ea. Nos. 209, 210.
3 Ctns. Wt. 111 lbs.—$ 36.60 each

Catalog page, Capri Line, 1957.

Vases

No. 310—8 x 5"
Vase
White, Green, Yellow
Packed 2 Doz. Wt. 57 lbs.
$4.20 per Dozen

No. 278—8 x 5" Vase
White, Yellow and Green
Packed 2 Doz. Wt. 56 lbs.
$4.20 per Dozen

No. 282—8 x 6" Vase
Green, Yellow and White
Packed 1½ Doz. Wt. 47 lbs.
$4.20 per Dozen

No. 304—9" Swan Vase
White, Yellow and Black
Packed 1 Doz. Wt. 28 lbs.
$4.80 per Dozen

No. 312—9¼"
Vase
White, Green, Pink
Packed 1 Doz. Wt. 35 lbs.
$4.80 per Dozen

No. 320—9"
Vase w/Handles
White, Green, Yellow
Packed 1 Doz. Wt. 40 lbs.
$4.80 per Dozen

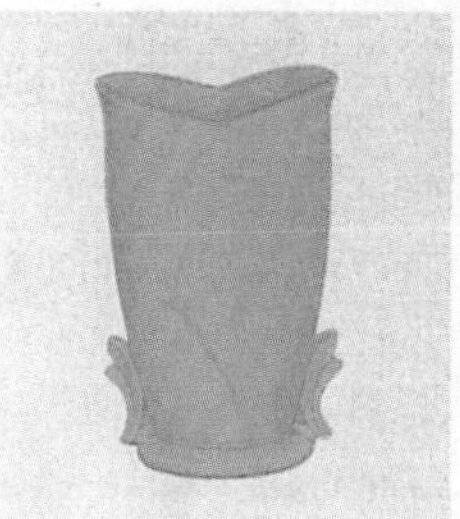

No. 321—9"
Vase
White, Green, Pink
Packed 1 Doz. Wt. 38 lbs.
$4.80 per Dozen

No. 316—10½ x 8½"
Fan Vase
White, Yellow, Green
Packed 1 Doz. Wt. 38 lbs.
$6.00 per Dozen

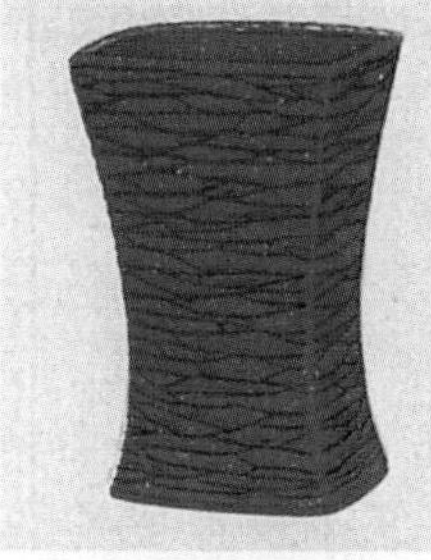

No. 420—9½"
Vase
Green, White, Maroon
Packed 1 Doz. Wt. 47 lbs.
$6.00 per Dozen

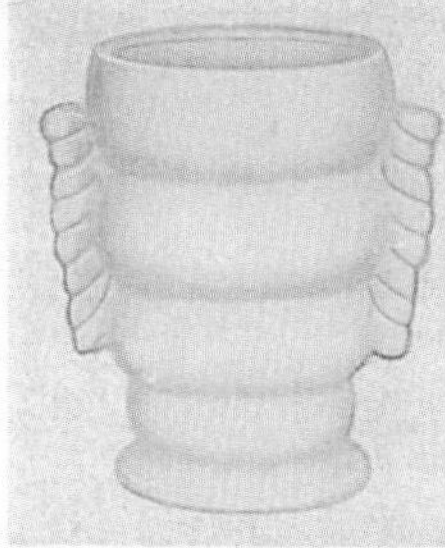

No. 313—9 x 8½"
Vase
White, Green, Yellow
Packed 1 Doz. Wt. 49 lbs.
$6.00 per Dozen

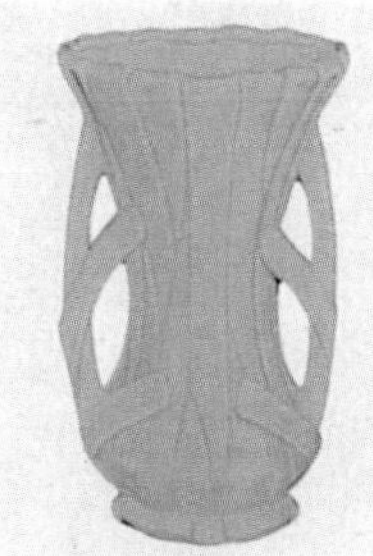

No. 46—12" Vase
White and Green Gloss
Packed ½ Doz. Wt. 40 lbs.
$9.60 per Dozen

No. 85—Vase
Sizes 10"-12"-14"
Green, White
10"—$ 6.00 per Doz. 1 Doz. 38 lbs.
12"—$ 9.00 per Doz. ½ Doz. 42 lbs.
14"—$13.50 per Doz. ½ Doz. 47 lbs.

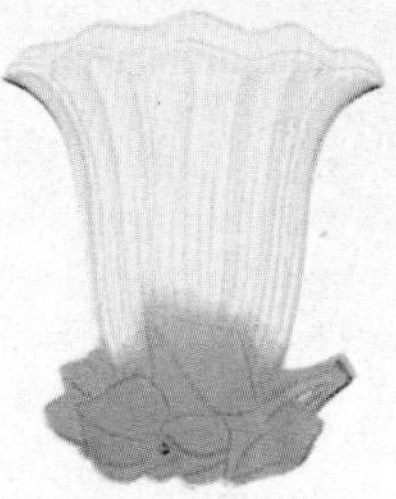

No. 89—14½" Tall Fan Vase
Green or Yellow w/Dec. Front
Packed 1/3 Doz. Wt. 40 lbs.
$18.00 per Dozen

Catalog page from 1957.

Grecian Line

Ivory with Green Spray Decorated in 24 K Gold Marbleizing

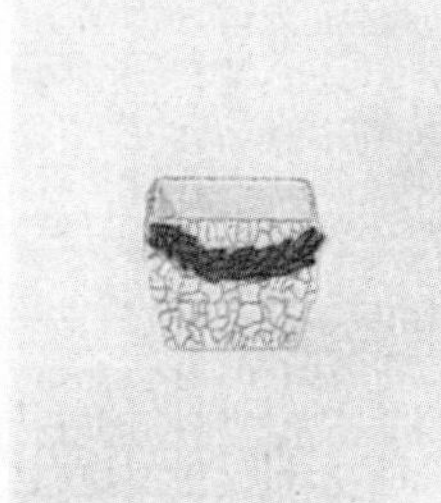

No. 439—3½" Sq. Planter
Packed 1 Doz. Wt. 9 lbs.
$4.80 per Dozen

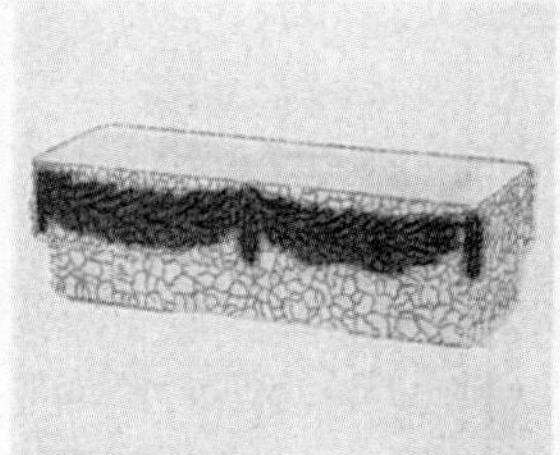

No. 435—12" Planting Dish
Packed ½ Doz. Wt. 18 lbs.
$14.40 per Dozen

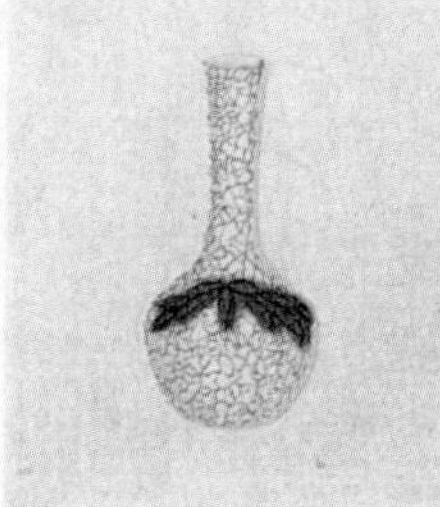

No. 433—7¼" Bud Vase
Packed 1 Doz. Wt. 9 lbs.
$6.60 per Dozen

No. 431—9x7" Vase
Packed ½ Doz. Wt. 28 lbs.
$12.00 per Dozen

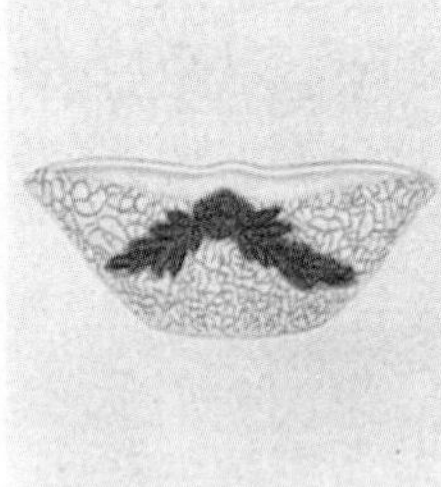

No. 441—8½" Planting Dish
Packed 1 Doz. Wt. 14 lbs.
$7.20 per Dozen

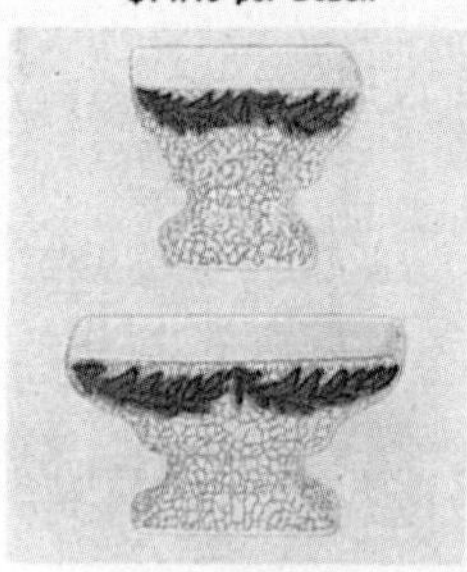

No. 442—5½"-8" Pedestal Bowl
5½"—$7.20 Doz. 1 Doz. 16 lbs.
8"—$9.00 Doz. 1 Doz. 24 lbs.

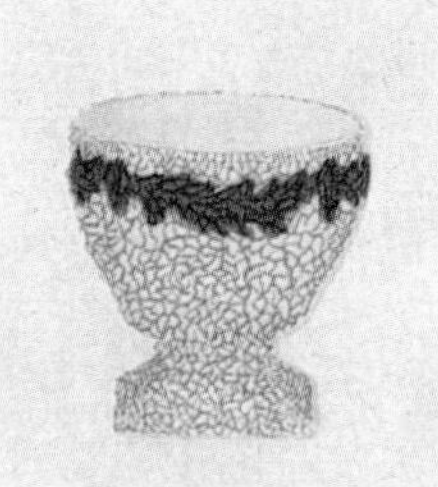

No. 449—6½" x 5½"
Pedestal Bowl
Packed 1 Doz. Wt. 20 lbs.
$9.00 per Dozen

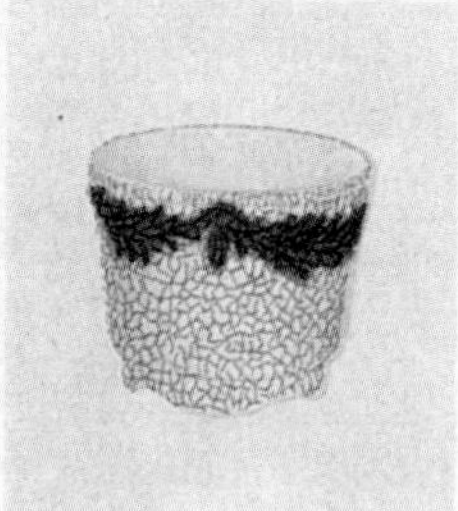

No. 448—5½"x4½" Jardiniere
Packed 1 Doz. Wt. 16 lbs.
$7.20 per Dozen

No. 445—5½x5½" Rd. Jardiniere
Packed 1 Doz. Wt. 22 lbs.
$7.20 per Dozen

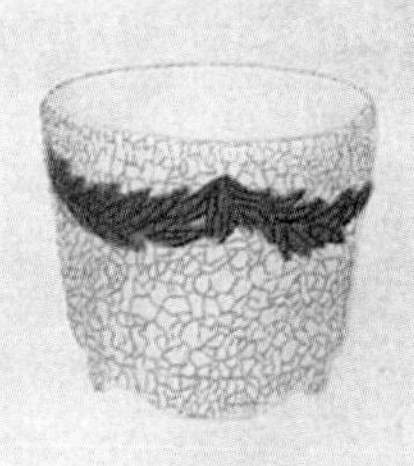

No. 447—6½x5½" Jardiniere
Packed 1 Doz. Wt. 24 lbs.
$9.00 per Dozen

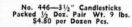

No. 444—8"-12" Centerpiece
8"—$ 8.40 Doz. 1 Doz. 26 lbs.
12"—$18.00 Doz. ½ Doz. 28 lbs.

No. 446—3½" Candlesticks
Packed ½ Doz. Pair Wt. 9 lbs.
$4.80 per Dozen Pcs.

No. 444—3 Pc. Console Set
(1-12" Bowl, 2-Candlesticks)
Packed 6 Sets Wt. 24 lbs.
$2.40 per Set

No. 444-S 3-Pc. Console Set
(1-8" Bowl, 2-Candlesticks)
Packed 6 Sets Wt. 22 lbs.
$1.60 per Set

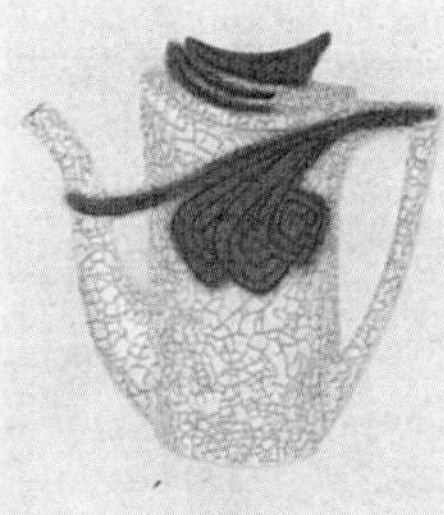

No. 453—10½x9½"
60 oz. Beverage Jug
Packed ½ Doz. Wt. 22 lbs.
$18.00 per Dozen

No. 453—5 pc. Beverage Set
(1-60 oz. Bev. Jug w/cover,
1-Sugar w/cover, 1-Creamer)
Packed 6 Sets Wt. 34 lbs.
$2.80 per Set

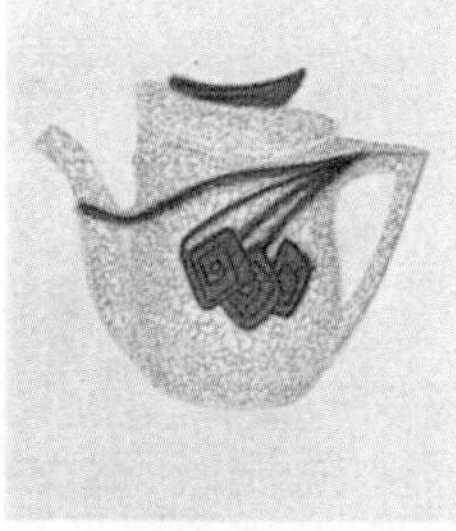

No. 453—9½x6½" 48 oz. Tea Pot
Packed 1 Doz. Wt. 30 lbs.
$13.20 per Dozen

No. 453-T—5 pc. Tea Set
(1-48 oz. Tea Pot w/Cover,
1-Sugar w/Cover, 1-Creamer)
Packed 6 Sets Wt. 20 lbs.
$2.40 per Set

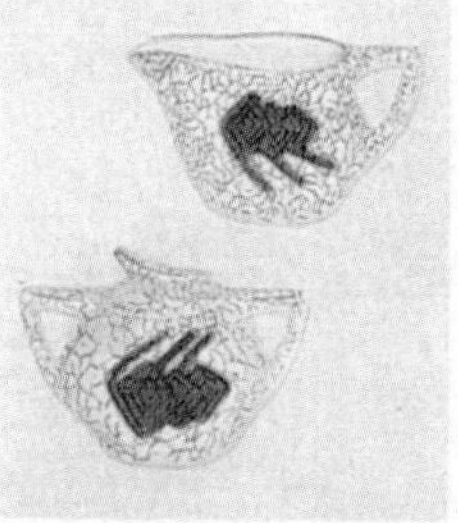

No. 453—12 oz. Sugar w/ Cover
No. 453—12 oz. Creamer
Packed 1 Doz. Wt. 12 lbs.
$7.20 per Dozen

No. 30GL — 30 pc. Grecian Line
Assortment Consisting of:
2—each Nos. 439, 435, 433, 431, 441, 442—5½", 442—8", 449, 445, 448, 447, 444—8", 444—12".
4—each No. 446.
1 Carton Wt. 45 lbs.
$22.35 per Asortment

No. 42GL—42 pc. Grecian Line
Assortment Consisting of:
2—each Nos. 439, 435, 433, 441, 442—5½", 442—8", 449, 445, 448, 447, 444—8", 444—12", 453 Bev. Jug, 453 Tea Pot.
4—each Nos. 446, 453, Sugar, 453 Creamer.
2 Cartons Total Weight 66 lbs.
$32.75 per Assortment

No. 72GL—72 pc. Grecian Line
Assortment Consisting of:
2—each Nos. 439, 441, 444—8", 444—12", 453—Bev. Jug.
4—each Nos. 435, 433, 431, 445, 448, 447, 446, 453 Tea Pot.
6—each Nos. 442—5½", 442—8", 449, 453 Sugar, 453 Creamer.
3 Cartons Total Weight 100 lbs.
$56.00 per Assortment

The Nelson-McCoy Pottery Company . . . Roseville, Ohio

Catalog page, Grecian Line, 1957.

Flower Pots Wall Pockets Bulb Bowls Hanging Baskets

No. 19—Pots & Saucers
Sizes 3½"-4½"-5½"-6½"
Turq., Pink, Green & Yellow
3½"—$1.20 per Doz. 4 Doz. 30 lbs.
4½"—$1.84 per Doz. 3 Doz. 45 lbs.
5½"—$2.48 per Doz. 2 Doz. 50 lbs.
6½"—$3.12 per Doz. 1 Doz. 38 lbs.

No. 115—Pots & Saucers
Sizes 4¼"-5¼"-6¼"
Dark Green, Yellow, Turquoise, Decorated
4¼"—$2.40 Doz. 3 Doz. 40 lbs.
5¼"—$3.00 Doz. 2 Doz. 45 lbs.
6¼"—$3.60 Doz. 1 Doz. 38 lbs.

No. 14—Violet Pot & Sauce
Sizes 4", 5", 6"
Green, Yellow & White
4"—$1.80 per Doz. 3 Doz. 25 lbs.
5"—$2.40 per Doz. 2 Doz. 32 lbs.
6"—$3.00 per Doz. 1 Doz. 23 lbs.

No. WP-14—8¾ x 6"
Umbrella Wall Pocket
Black, Yellow, Green
Packed 2 Doz. Wt. 18 lbs.
$3.60 per Dozen

No. WP-6—7 x 6"
Apple Wall Pocket
Natural Color
Packed 2 Doz. Wt. 30 lbs.
$4.80 per Dozen

No. WP-7—7 x 6"
Pear Wall Pocket
Natural Color
Packed 2 Doz. Wt. 30 lbs.
$4.80 per Dozen

No. WP-10—7 x 6"
Orange Wall Pocket
Packed 2 Doz. Wt. 30 lbs.
$4.80 per Dozen

No. WP-17—10¼"
Violin Wall Pocket
White or Tan
w/Contrasting Strings
Packed 1 Doz. Wt. 18 lbs.
$6.00 per Dozen

No. WP-19—6½"
Urn-Shaped Wall Pocket
Pink w/Black Flecks
Chartreuse w/Brown Flecks
Packed 2 Doz. Wt. 30 lbs.
$3.00 per Dozen

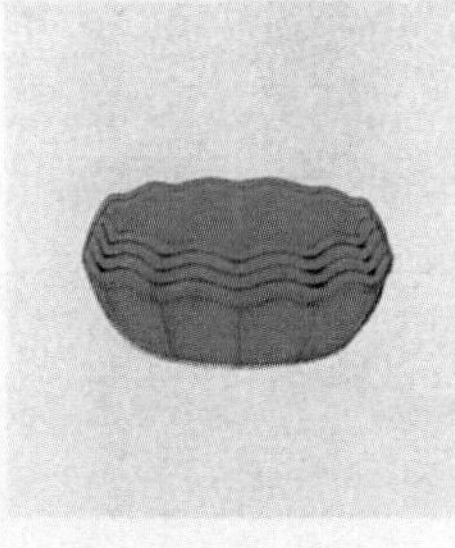

No. 72—Bulb Bowl
Sizes 6½"-8"
White, Green, Yellow
6½"—$2.88 per Doz. 2 Doz. 37 lbs.
8"....—$3.60 per Doz. 1 Doz. 30 lbs.

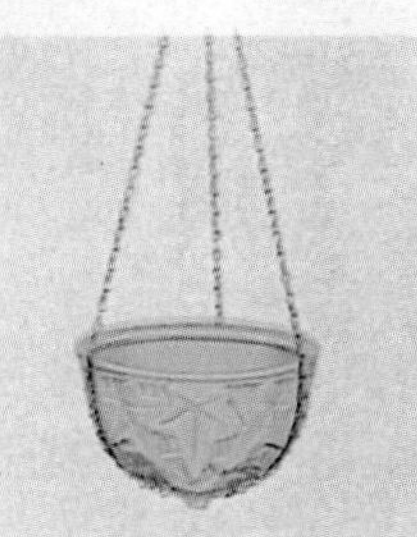

No. 32—6½"
Hanging Basket w/Chain
Green and Yellow
Packed 2 Doz. Wt. 45 lbs.
$4.20 per Dozen

Catalog page from 1957.

SUNBURST GOLD

SPARKLING 24K FIRED ON GOLD IN A COMBINATION MATT AND GLOSS DECORATION

No. 160—4½ x 3½"
Swan
Packed 3 Doz. Wt. 15 lbs.
$4.92 per Dozen

No. 163—3½ x 3¾"
Pitcher
Packed 3 Doz. Wt. 15 lbs.
$4.92 per Dozen

No. 164—3½ x 3½"
Cornucopia
Packed 3 Doz. Wt. 15 lbs.
$4.92 per Dozen

No. 169—5 x 5"
Rd. Candy Dish w/Cover
Packed 1 Doz. Wt. 20 lbs.
$9.60 per Dozen

NOS. 160-163-164 MAY BE ASSORTED TO CARTON.

No. 182—6¼"
Sq. Vase
Packed 1 Doz. Wt. 11 lbs.
$6.00 per Dozen

No. 183—6¼"
Bud Vase
Packed 1 Doz. Wt. 12 lbs.
$6.00 per Dozen

No. 185—5¾"
Vase
Packed 1 Doz. Wt. 11 lbs.
$6.00 per Dozen

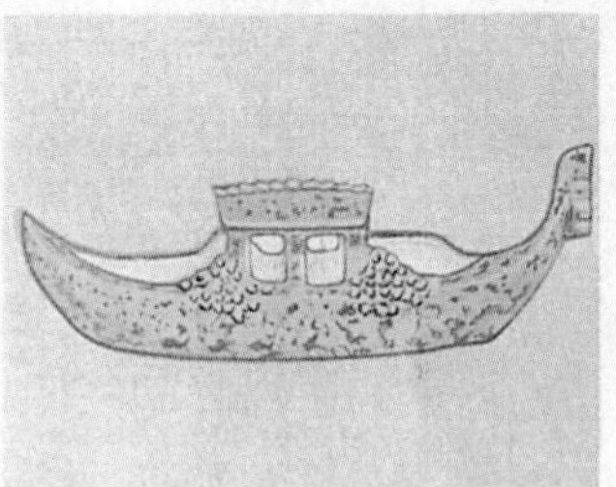

No. 191—11½ x 3½"
Gondola Candy Boat
Packed 1 Doz. Wt. 18 lbs.
$9.60 per Dozen

NOS. 182-183-185 MAY BE ASSORTED TO CARTON.

No. 166—6¼ x 4½"
Shell Ash Tray
Packed 1 Doz. Wt. 9 lbs.
$6.60 per Dozen

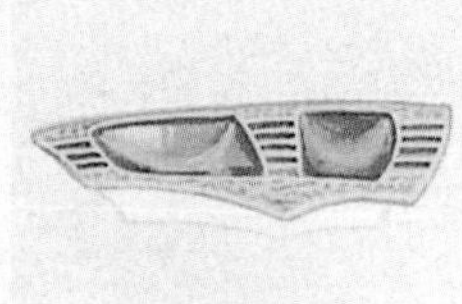

No. 167—8 x 5"
Ash Tray
Packed 1 Doz. Wt. 12 lbs.
$7.20 per Dozen

NOS. 166-167 MAY BE ASSORTED TO CARTON.

No. 197—8¾ x 6"
Umbrella Wall Pocket
Packed 1 Doz. Wt. 12 lbs.
$7.20 per Dozen

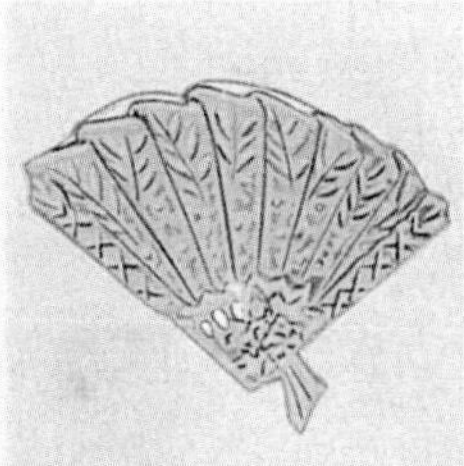

No. 198—8½ x 8"
Fan Wall Pocket
Packed 1 Doz. Wt. 16 lbs.
$7.20 per Dozen

NOS. 197-198 MAY BE ASSORTED TO CARTON.

No. 263—5 pc.
Beverage Set
Packed 6 sets. Wt. 36 lbs.
$2.40 per Set

No. 262—12 oz.
Sugar w/Cover

No. 262—12 oz.
Creamer
Packed 1 Doz. Wt. 25 lbs.
$7.20 per Dozen

No. 263—6 cup
Beverage Jug w/Cover
Packed 1 Doz. Wt. 33 lbs.
$13.20 per Dozen

No. 264—36 oz.
Tea Pot
Packed 1 Doz. Wt. 27 lbs.
$10.80 per Dozen

ASSORTMENTS AVAILABLE IN SUNBURST GOLD

No. 24SG—24 Pc. Sunburst Gold Assortment
(2 ea. Nos. 160, 163, 164, 182, 183, 185, 166, 167, 197, 198, 169, 191)
1 Carton—Wt. 28 lbs.—Price $13.50

No. 32SG—32 Pc. Sunburst Gold Assortment
(2 ea. every item in the line)
1 Carton—Wt. 37 lbs.—Price $20.00

No. 100SG—102 Pc. Sunburst Gold Assortment
(12 ea. Nos. 160, 163, 164; 6 ea. Nos. 166, 167, 197, 198; 4 ea. Nos. 182, 183, 185, 169, 191, 264; 6 Sets No. 263)
6 Cartons—Total Wt. 100 lbs.—Price $60.00

Catalog page, Sunburst Gold Line, 1957.

Cookie Jars

No. 20R—Apple Cookie Jar
Decorated with Bright Red Overglaze and 24K Gold Leaf
Packed ½ Doz. Wt. 27 lbs.
$13.10 per Dozen

No. 136—Cabin Cookie Jar
Ivory w/Brown Spray
Decorated
Packed ½ Doz. Wt. 29 lbs.
$10.80 per Dozen

No. 137—Tepee Cookie Jar
White w/Black Spray
Decorated
Packed ½ Doz. Wt. 27 lbs.
$11.40 per Dozen

No. 138—Floral Cookie Jar
Yellow w/Blue Flower
White w/Red Flower
Packed ½ Doz. Wt. 28 lbs.
$8.40 per Dozen

No. 20—Apple Cookie Jar
Yellow or Aqua
w/Sprayed Decoration
Packed ½ Doz. Wt. 27 lbs.
$9.60 per Dozen

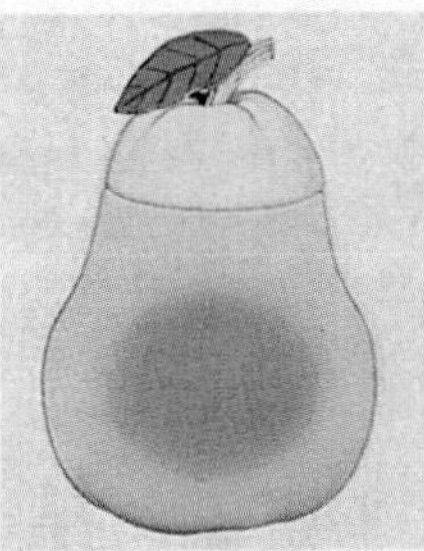

No. 18—Pear Cookie Jar
Yellow w/Pink Spray
Packed ½ Doz. Wt. 24 lbs.
$9.60 per Dozen

No. 52—Pineapple Cookie Jar
Sprayed Natural Color
Packed ½ Doz. Wt. 25 lbs.
$9.60 per Dozen

No. 54—Strawberry Cookie Jar
Red w/Green Cover
Packed ½ Doz. Wt. 27 lbs.
$10.80 per Dozen

Note: Two each of any three styles of above jars may be assorted to ½ doz. carton.

No. 126—Kitten Cookie Jar
White Cover—Pink Base
Decorated
Packed ½ Doz. Wt. 27 lbs.
$9.60 per Dozen

No. 127—Lamb Cookie Jar
Brown Cover — Brown Base
Decorated
Packed ½ Doz. Wt. 27 lbs.
$9.60 per Dozen

No. 128—Dog Cookie Jar
Black Cover—Black Base
Decorated
Packed ½ Doz. Wt. 27 lbs.
$9.60 per Dozen

No. 55—Rooster Cookie Jar
White w/Black Spray
Brown Blend
Packed ½ Doz. Wt. 28 lbs.
$10.80 per Dozen

Note: Two each of any three styles of above jars may be assorted to ½ doz. carton.

No. 133—Pine Cone Cookie Jar
Brown Decorated
Packed ½ Doz. Wt. 27 lbs.
$9.60 per Dozen

No. 134—Apple Cookie Jar
Natural Color—Decorated
Packed ½ Doz. Wt. 27 lbs.
$9.60 per Dozen

No. 135—Pear Cookie Jar
Natural Color—Decorated
Packed ½ Doz. Wt. 27 lbs.
$9.60 per Dozen

No. 17—Mammy
White w/Decoration
Packed ½ Doz. Wt. 32 lbs.
$9.60 per Dozen

Above 3 Numbers May Be Assorted to Carton.
Specify No. 133/4/5 Cookie Jar Assortment.

Catalog page, Cookie jars, 1957.

Kitchen Items

No. 12—6 Cup
Beverage Jug w/Cover
Black w/Pink Cover
Packed 1 Doz. Wt. 36 lbs.
$6.00 per Dozen

No. 12—Sugar w/Cover
No. 12—Creamer
Black and Pink
Packed 2 Doz. Wt. 25 lbs.
$3.60 per Dozen

No. 12—5 pc. Beverage Set
Black and Pink
Packed 6 Sets Wt. 33 lbs.
$1.20 per set

No. 106—12 oz. Tea Pot
Brown, Green, or Yellow
Packed 2 Doz. Wt. 25 lbs.
$3.00 per Dozen

No. 105—36 oz. Tea Pot
Brown, Green, or Yellow
Packed 1 Doz. Wt. 25 lbs.
$4.80 per Dozen

No. 15—Mixing Bowls
Maroon 5" Bowl in 4 pc. sets
Sizes 5", 6", 7", 8"
Pink, Yellow, Aqua
5"—$1.20 per Doz. 3 Doz. 28 lbs.
6"—$1.80 per Doz. 3 Doz. 43 lbs.
7"—$2.40 per Doz. 2 Doz. 40 lbs.
8"—$3.00 per Doz. 1½ Doz. 42 lbs.
3 Pc. Set 6-7-8"
2/3 Doz. Wt. 50 lbs.
4 Pc. Set 5-6-7-8"
2/3 Doz. Wt. 55 lbs.
3 pc. 6-7-8"—$7.20 per Doz. sets
4 pc. 5-6-7-8"—$8.40 per Doz. sets

Oven Proof
McCoy
Cook Serve

Cook-Serve Line

YELLOW OVENPROOF WARE

With Hand Decorated Bright Red Cherries, Green Leaves, and Brown Stems

(All Colors Fired Into Ware)

No. C1—10 oz. French Casserole w/Cover
Packed 2 Doz. Wt. 28 lbs.
$4.20 per Dozen

No. C9—3 Pt. Covered Casserole
Packed 1 Doz. Wt. 38 lbs.
$9.60 per Dozen

No. C18—4 Pt. Covered Casserole
Packed 1 Doz. Wt. 58 lbs.
$12.00 per Dozen

No. C3—2 Qt. Bean Pot w/Cover
Packed 1 Doz. Wt. 36 lbs.
$8.40 per Dozen

No. C7—6" Salad Bowl
Packed 3 Doz. Wt. 36 lbs.
$1.50 per Dozen

No. C10—10" Salad Bowl
Packed 1 Doz. Wt. 30 lbs.
$4.80 per Dozen

No. C150—22 oz. Pitcher
Packed 2 Doz. Wt. 30 lbs.
$2.40 per Dozen

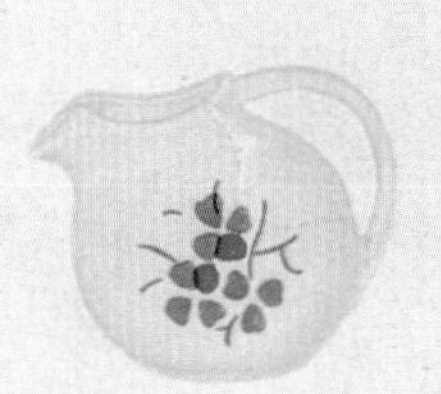

No. C141—48 oz. Ice Jug
Packed 1 Doz. Wt. 32 lbs.
$4.80 per Dozen

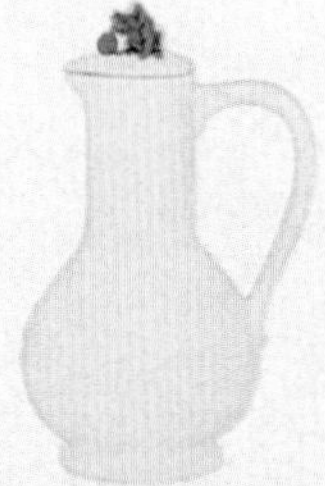

No. C12—6 Cup
Beverage Jug w/Cover
Packed 1 Doz. Wt. 36 lbs.
$7.20 per Dozen

No. C12—5 pc. Beverage Set
Packed 6 Sets Wt. 27 lbs.
$1.40 per Set

No. C12—Creamer
Packed 2 Doz. Wt. 25 lbs.
$3.60 per Dozen

No. C12—Sugar w/Cover
Packed 2 Doz. Wt. 23 lbs.
$4.80 per Dozen

No. C105—36 oz. Tea Pot
Packed 1 Doz. Wt. 25 lbs.
$6.00 per Dozen

No. C32—32 pc. COOK-SERVE Assortment
Consisting of: 8 ea. No. C7; 4 ea. No. C1;
2 Sets No. C12; 2 ea. Nos. C9, C18, C3, C10,
C150, C141, C105.
2 Cartons—Total Wt. 62 lb.
Price $13.40 per Assortment

Catalog page, Kitchen Items, 1957.

GARDEN CLUB LINE

Flower Bowls—Centerpieces

No. 341—Planting Dish
Sizes 8"—10"—15½"
White, Yellow, Peach
8 "—$ 9.70 per Doz. 2 Doz. 30 lbs.
10 "—$14.40 per Doz. 1 Doz. 25 lbs.
15½"—$32.00 per Doz. 1 Doz. 38 lbs.

No. 601—10 x 8" Centerpiece
Yellow, Peach, Gray
Packed 1 Doz. Wt. 30 lbs.
$21.30 per Dozen

No. 520P—Planter Bowl
Sizes 5½"-6½"-7½"
White, Green, Peach, Black
5½"—$ 9.70 per Doz. 2 Doz. 32 lbs.
6½"—$14.40 per Doz. 2 Doz. 60 lbs.
7½"—$17.60 per Doz. 1 Doz. 40 lbs.

No. 333—9½ x 7½" Pedestal Bowl
White, Peach, Black
Packed ½ Doz. Wt. 30 lbs.
$36.00 per Dozen

No. 340—8 x 8 x 2"
Sq. Centerpiece
White, Green, Gray
Packed 1 Doz. Wt. 30 lbs.
$17.60 per Dozen

No. 325M—Pedestal Bowl
Sizes 5½"-8"
White, Green, Black, Yellow
5½"—$ 9.70 per Doz. 2 Doz. 34 lbs.
8 "—$14.40 per Doz. 1 Doz. 27 lbs.

Vases • Jardinieres

No. 710M—5½ x 4" Pillow Vase
White, Peach, Black, Yel., Gray, Green
Packed 3 Doz. Wt. 50 lbs.
$7.20 per Dozen

No. 331—6½" Bud Vase
Peach, Yellow, White
Packed 2 Doz. Wt. 14 lbs.
$8.80 per Dozen

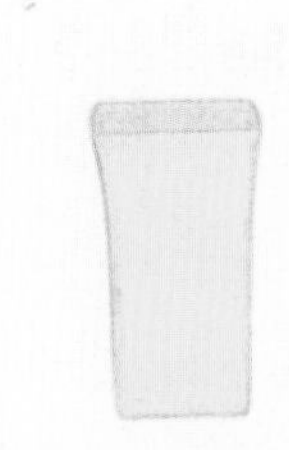

No. 338—7¼" Sq. Vase
White, Yellow, Peach
Packed 2 Doz. Wt. 47 lbs.
$14.40 per Dozen

No. 335—8" Pitcher Vase
Yellow, Peach, Gray
Packed 2 Doz. Wt. 43 lbs.
$14.40 per Dozen

No. 334—9½ x 11" Vase
White, Green, Yellow
Packed ½ Doz. Wt. 40 lbs.
$42.60 per Dozen

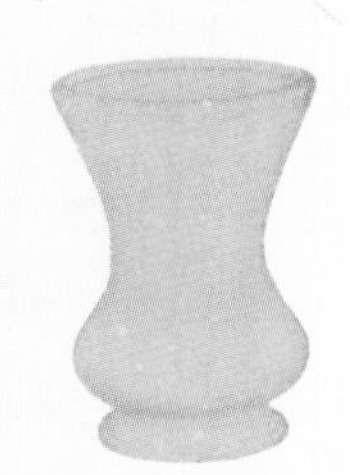

No. 336—9" Vase
White, Green, Peach
Packed 1 Doz. Wt. 43 lbs.
$17.60 per Dozen

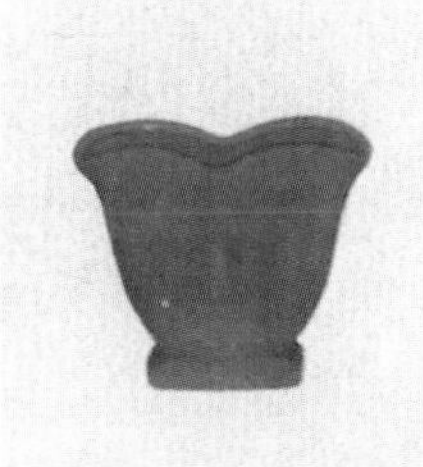

No. 309M—7 x 6" Vase
White, Green, Yellow
Packed 2 Doz. Wt. 50 lbs.
$14.40 per Dozen

No. 337—7½" Jardiniere
White, Green, Peach
Packed 1 Doz. Wt. 43 lbs.
$17.60 per Dozen

No. 339—6½" Jardiniere
White, Green, Yellow
Packed 1½ Doz. Wt. 45 lbs.
$14.40 per Dozen

No. 332—12" Vase
White, Peach, Gray
Packed ½ Doz. Wt. 29 lbs.
$32.00 per Dozen

No. 42GC—42 pc. Garden Club Assortment
Consisting of: 2 pcs. each of every item in the line
(Assorted Colors)
3 cartons Total Weight 106 lbs. $63.40 per Assortment.

No. 84GC—84 pc. Garden Club Assortment
Consisting of: 8—ea. nos. 520P—5½", 710M
6—ea. nos. 325M—5½", 331, 341-8"
4—ea. nos. 520P-6½", 325M-8", 341-10", 338, 335, 309M, 336, 339, 337
2—ea. nos. 520P-7½", 341-15½", 601, 333, 340, 332, 334
(Assorted Colors)
5 Cartons Total Wt. 173 lbs. $104.00 per Assortment.

Catalog page, Garden Club, 1958.

Novelty Planters

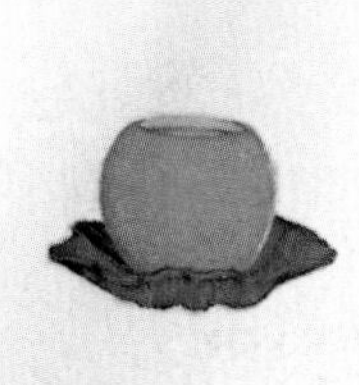

No. 403—6½ x 5½"
Orange Planter
Natural Color w/Brown or Lime Leaf
Packed 1 Doz. Wt. 16 lbs.
$14.40 per Dozen

No. 402—7½ x 5"
Barrel Planter
Brown Spray w/Decorated Features
Packed 1 Doz. Wt. 22 lbs.
$17.60 per Dozen

No. 401—11" Banana Boat Planter
Brown Spray w/Decorated Features
Packed 1 Doz. Wt. 31 lbs.
$24.60 per Dozen

No. 760—10¾ x 8½"
Flying Ducks Planter
Chartreuse w/Pink Ducks
Ivory w/Brown Ducks
Packed ½ Doz. Wt. 26 lbs.
$36.00 per Dozen

No. 637—11½ x 3½"
Gondola Planter
Black, Green, Yellow
Packed 1 Doz. Wt. 18 lbs.
$17.60 per Dozen

No. 765—9 x 7"
Quail Planter
Ivory or Tan Blend
Packed 1 Doz. Wt. 33 lbs.
$20.00 per Dozen

No. 725—6¾ x 6"
Wishing Well
Brown Blend
Packed 1 Doz. Wt. 25 lbs.
$20.00 per Dozen

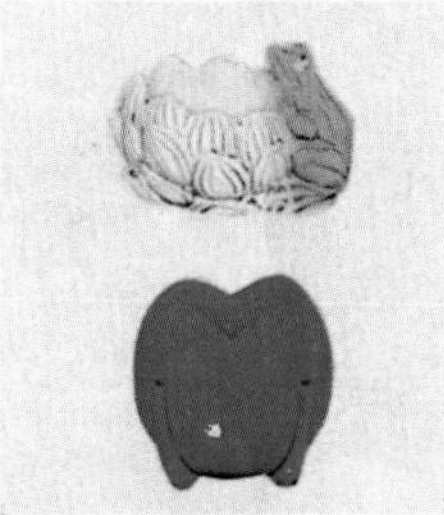

No. 21—5 x 4"
Frog & Lotus Planter
Green & Yellow w/Green Frog
Packed 3 Doz. Wt. 26 lbs.
$7.20 per Dozen

No. 27—4½" Ball Planter
Green, Yellow & Maroon
Packed 3 Doz. Wt. 32 lbs.
$7.20 per Dozen

No. 31—5 x 4"
Frog Planter
Yellow or Green
Packed 3 Doz. Wt. 27 lbs.
$7.20 per Dozen

No. 32—5 x 4"
Stump Planter
Green or Yellow
Packed 3 Doz. Wt. 36 lbs.
$7.20 per Dozen

No. 33—5 x 4"
Shell Planter
Yellow or Green
Packed 3 Doz. Wt. 24 lbs.
$7.20 per Dozen

No. 34—5 x 4½"
Squirrel Planter
Brown or Grey Decorated
Packed 3 Doz. Wt. 30 lbs.
$7.20 per Dozen

No. 35—5 x 3½"
Fawn Planter
Brown w/Green or Tan
Decorated
Packed 3 Doz. Wt. 25 lbs.
$7.20 per Dozen

No. 36—5 x 4"
Bird Planter
Yellow or Green Decorated
Packed 3 Doz. Wt. 26 lbs.
$7.20 per Dozen

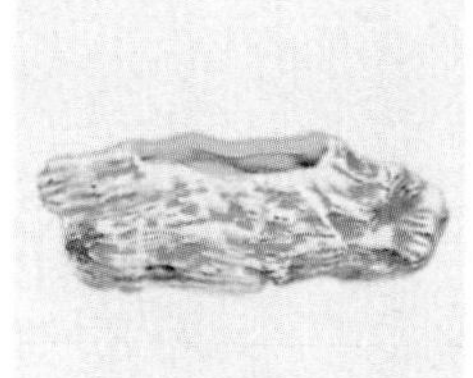

No. 787—8½ x 3½"
Driftwood Planter
White w/Gray Bisque
Chartreuse w/Green Bisque
Birchwood
Packed 2 Doz. Wt. 29 lbs.
$12.00 per Dozen

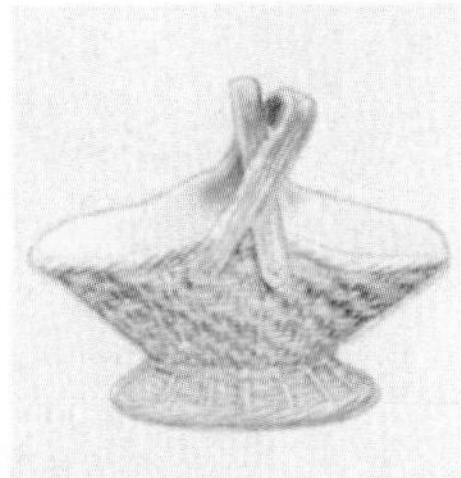

No. 786—9 x 5¼"
Basket Planter
Ivory w/Green Spray
Yellow w/Brown
Packed 1 Doz. Wt. 25 lbs.
$20.00 per Dozen

Catalog page, Novelty Planters, 1958.

Novelty Planters

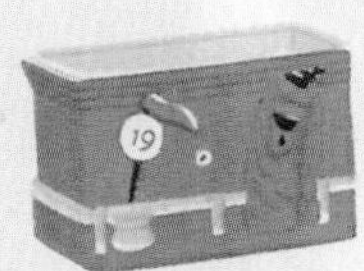

No. 551—6 x 4" Golf Planter
Brown Spray w/Yellow or Green Interior Dec.
Pkd. 1 Doz. Wt. 20 lbs.
$4.80 per Dozen

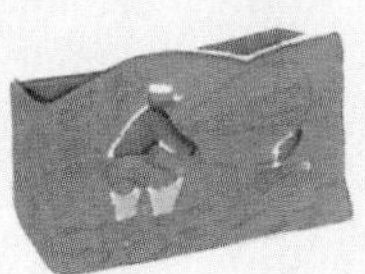

No. 552—6 x 4½"
Fisherman Planter
Brown Spray w/Yellow or Green Interior Dec.
Pkd. 1 Doz. Wt. 20 lbs.
$4.80 per Dozen

No. 553—6½ x 4"
Bowling Planter
Brown Spray w/Yellow or Green Interior Dec.
Pkd. 1 Doz. Wt. 20 lbs.
$4.80 per Dozen

No. 748—9 x 4½"
Automobile Planter
Brown Spray w/Yellow or Green Interior Dec.
Pkd. 1 Doz. Wt. 36 lbs.
$7.20 per Dozen

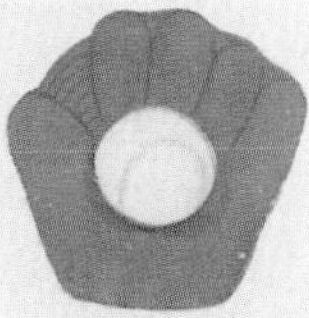

No. 554—6 x 6"
Baseball Planter
Brown Spray w/Yellow or Green Interior Dec.
Pkd. 1 Doz. Wt. 22 lbs.
$4.80 per Dozen

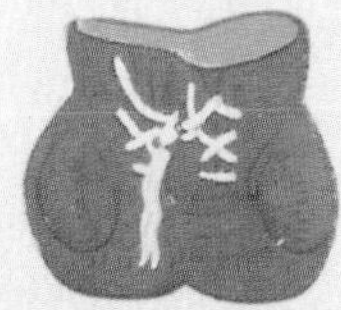

No. 555—6½ x 5½"
Boxing Glove Planter
Brown Spray w/Blue or Pink Interior Dec.
Pkd. 1 Doz. Wt. 17 lbs.
$4.80 per Dozen

No. 559—7" Football Planter
Brown Spray w/Yellow or Green Interior Dec.
Pkd. 1 Doz. Wt. 17 lbs.
$4.80 per Dozen

No. 750—9½ x 4½"
Convertible Auto Planter
Brown Spray w/Yellow or Green Interior Dec.
Pkd. 1 Doz. Wt. 36 lbs.
$7.20 per Dozen

No. 793—7¾"
Bird Dog Planter
Brown or White w/Spray Dec.
Packed 1 Doz. Wt. 21 lbs.
$6.00 per Dozen

No. 794—7½" x 6"
Pheasant Planter
Brown & Green Spray Dec.
Packed 1 Doz. Wt. 22 lbs.
$6.00 per Dozen

No. 795—6¼" x 6"
Puppy Planter
White w/Black & Brown Dec.
Packed 1 Doz. Wt. 20 lbs.
$6.00 per Dozen

No. 725—6¾ x 6"
Wishing Well
Brown Blend
Packed 1 Doz. Wt. 25 lbs.
$6.60 per Dozen

No. 402—7½ x 5"
Barrel Planter
Brown Spray w/Decorated Features
Packed 1 Doz. Wt. 22 lbs.
$6.00 per Dozen

No. 401—11" Banana Boat Planter
Brown Spray w/Decorated Features
Packed 1 Doz. Wt. 31 lbs.
$8.40 per Dozen

No. 637—11½ x 3½"
Gondola Planter
Black, Green, Yellow
Packed 1 Doz. Wt. 18 lbs.
$6.00 per Dozen

No. 765—9 x 7"
Quail Planter
Ivory or Tan Blend
Packed 1 Doz. Wt. 33 lbs.
$6.60 per Dozen

Catalog page, Novelty Planters, 1959.

NELSON McCOY'S NEW BASKET LINE

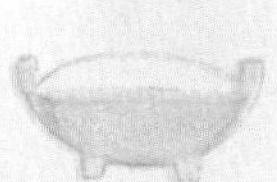

No. 240—6½" Planter
Brown Bisque w/Dark Green Interior
Yellow Bisque w/White Interior
Green Bisque w/Yellow Interior
Packed 2 Doz. Wt. 20 lbs.
$3.60 per Dozen

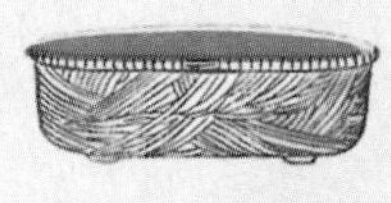

No. 241—9½" Planting Dish
Brown Bisque w/Dark Green Interior
Yellow Bisque w/White Interior
Green Bisque w/Yellow Interior
Packed 1 Doz. Wt. 18 lbs.
$4.80 per Dozen

No. 242—11½" Planting Dish w/Handle
Brown Bisque w/Dark Green Interior
Yellow Bisque w/White Interior
Green Bisque w/Yellow Interior
Packed 1 Doz. Wt. 16 lbs.
$7.20 per Dozen

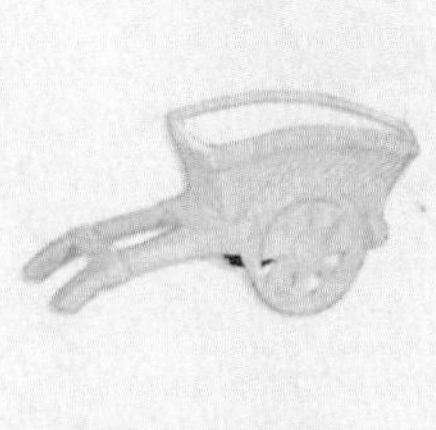

No. 243—10" Cart Planter
Brown Bisque w/Dark Green Interior
Yellow Bisque w/White Interior
Green Bisque w/Yellow Interior
Packed ½ Doz. Wt. 14 lbs.
$8.40 per Dozen

No. 244—9x6" Cornucopia Centerpiece
Brown Bisque w/Dark Green Interior
Yellow Bisque w/White Interior
Green Bisque w/Yellow Interior
Packed ½ Doz. Wt. 14 lbs.
$8.40 per Dozen

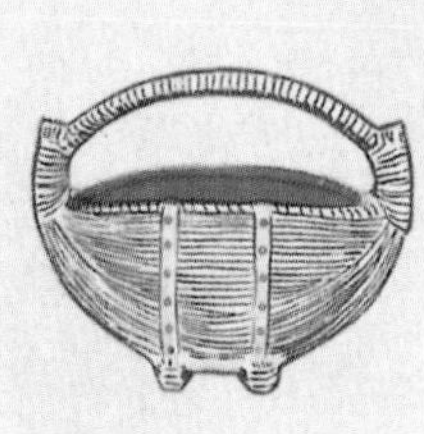

No. 245—10½" Basket Centerpiece
Brown Bisque w/Dark Green Interior
Yellow Bisque w/White Interior
Green Bisque w/Yellow Interior
Packed ½ Doz. Wt. 18 lbs.
$10.80 per Dozen

No. 246—9" Jardiniere
Brown Bisque w/Dark Green Interior
Yellow Bisque w/White Interior
Green Bisque w/Yellow Interior
Packed 1/3 Doz. Wt. 22 lbs.
$12.00 per Dozen

No. 247—8" Vase
Brown Bisque w/Dark Green Interior
Yellow Bisque w/White Interior
Green Bisque w/Yellow Interior
Packed 1 Doz. Wt. 24 lbs.
$6.00 per Dozen

AVAILABLE IN OPEN STOCK OR THE FOLLOWING 24-PIECE ASSORTMENT.

No. 1459—24 Piece BASKET LINE ASSORTMENT
Consisting of:
4 each Nos. 240, 241, 242, 243
2 each Nos. 244, 245, 246, 247
PACKING: 1 Carton
WEIGHT: 44 Pounds
COST: $14.20 Per Assortment

The Nelson-McCoy Pottery Company . . . Roseville, Ohio

Catalog page, Basket Line, 1959.

JANUARY ADDITIONS TO 1959 CATALOG

No. 798—6x5" Piano Planter
White, Black, Matt,
Yellow Fleck
Packed 1 Doz. Wt. 20 lbs.
$6.00 per Dozen

No. 799—10"
Violin Planter Bookends (Felted)
White, Turq. Fleck, Black Matt
Packed 1/4 Doz. Pr. Wt. 14 lbs.
$14.40 per Dozen

No. 73B—8 3/4"
Jardiniere w/Brass Stand
White, Green, Yellow
Packed 2/3 Doz. Units Wt. 57 lbs.
$1.35 per Unit

No. 672—Planting Dish
Sizes 10"—14"
White, Green, Yellow
10"—$4.20 per Doz. 2 Doz. 47 lbs.
14"—$8.40 per Doz. 1 Doz. 35 lbs.

No. 670—Planting Dish
Sizes 8"-10"
Green, Fawn, White
8"—$4.80 per Doz. 1 Doz. 38 lbs.
10"—$6.00 per Doz. 1/2 Doz. 23 lbs.

No. 671—10"
Planting Dish w/Handles
White, Green, Yellow
Packed 1 Doz. Wt. 29 lbs.
$6.00 per Dozen

No. 323—7 1/2x5 1/2" Flower Bowl
Ivory or Green
Packed 1 1/2 Doz. Wt. 50 lbs.
$3.60 per Dozen

No. 324—13 1/2x10" Vase
White, Green Agate, Black
Packed 1/3 Doz. Wt. 28 lbs.
$14.40 per Dozen

No. 322—Vase
Sizes 5"-8"-10"
White, Green, Yellow
5"—$3.00 per Doz. 2 Doz. 29 lbs.
8"—$4.80 per Doz. 1 1/2 Doz. 52 lbs.
10"—$7.80 per Doz. 1 Doz. 53 lbs.

The Nelson-McCoy Pottery Company . . . Roseville, Ohio

Catalog page from 1959.

ANTIQUE ROSE LINE

Flower Bowls, Planters, Vases Designed For An Antique Look

Available in two colors—Pure white or two-tone brown and flecked blue—Decorated in an old fashioned moss rose pattern and trimmed in bright gold.

No. 370—7 x 6"
Sprinkling Can Planter
White or Two-tone Brown and Flecked Blue. Red Rose Decoration. GOLD Trim
Pkd. 1 doz. Wt. 16 lbs.
$7.20 per Dozen

No. 371—7½ x 5½" Swan Planter
White or Two-tone Brown and Flecked Blue. Red Rose Decoration. GOLD Trim.
Pkd. ½ Doz. Wt. 12 lbs.
$9.60 per Dozen

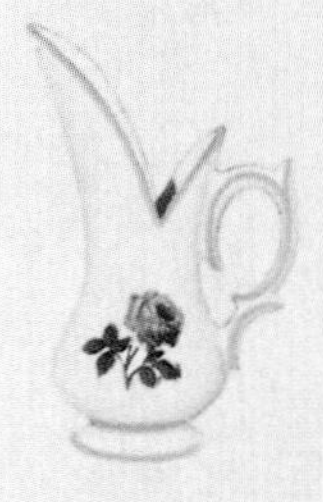

No. 372—9" Pitcher Vase
White or Two-tone Brown and Flecked Blue. Red Rose Decoration. GOLD Trim
Pkd. ½ Doz. Wt. 10 lbs.
$9.60 per Dozen

No. 373—9½ x 6½" Flower Bowl
White or Two-tone Brown and Flecked Blue. Red Rose Decoration. GOLD Trim
Pkd. ½ Doz. Wt. 15 lbs.
$11.40 per Dozen

No. 374—12 x 7½" Low Flower Bowl
White or Two-tone Brown and Flecked Blue. Red Rose Decoration. GOLD Trim
Pkd. 1/3 Doz. Wt. 14 lbs.
$14.40 per Dozen

Order Open Stock or in the Following 12 Pc. Trial Assortment
No. 95068—12 Pc. "ANTIQUE ROSE" Planter-Vase Assortment
Consisting of:
4 Only No. 370 — 2 Each Nos. 372; 373
3 Only No. 371 — 1 Only No. 374
Pkd. 1 Carton—Wt. 25 lbs.
$9.50 per Assortment

Pedestal Line

Contemporary styling on a group of planter bowls, planting dishes, jardinieres and vases in green, white, yellow and pink gloss glazes with a decorated bisque foot.

No. 802—Pedestal Jardiniere
Sizes 7" - 9"
Green, Yellow or White
w/Decorated Foot
7"—$4.80 per Doz. 1 Doz. 26 lbs.
9"—$8.40 per Doz. ½ Doz. 26 lbs.

No. 803—Pedestal Planter Bowl
Sizes 5" - 6"
Green, Yellow or Pink
w/Decorated Foot
5"—$3.00 per Doz. 2 Doz. 22 lbs.
6"—$3.60 per Doz. 1 Doz. 19 lbs.

No. 804—6½"
Hanging Basket w/Cord
Green, Yellow or Pink
w/Decorated Foot
Pkd. 1 Doz. Wt. 14 lbs.
$4.80 per Dozen

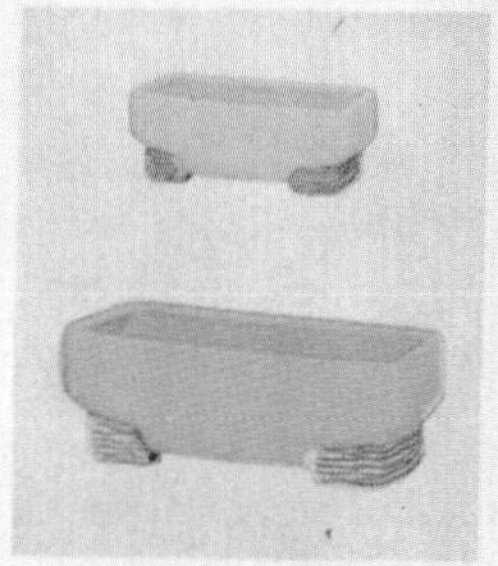

No. 805—Pedestal Planting Dish
Sizes 7" - 11"
Green, Yellow or Pink
w/Decorated Foot
7"—$3.30 per Doz. 2 Doz. 28 lbs.
11"—$6.00 per Doz. 1 Doz. 28 lbs.

No. 806—8"
Low Centerpiece
Green, Yellow or White
w/Decorated Foot
Pkd. 1 Doz. Wt. 22 lbs.
$4.80 per Dozen

No. 807—Vase
Sizes 8" - 10"
Green, Yellow or White
w/Decorated Foot
8"—$4.80 per Doz. 1 Doz. 23 lbs.
10"—$8.40 per Doz. ½ Doz. 25 lbs.

Order Open Stock or from the Following 72 Pc. Assortment
No. 2968—72 Pc. "PEDESTAL LINE" Assortment
Consisting of:
8 Only No. 802—7"
4 Only No. 802—9"
8 Each Nos. 803—5"; 803—6"; 804; 805—7"; 805—11"; 806; 807—8"
4 Only No. 807—10"
Pkd. 4 Cartons—Wt. 145 lbs.
$29.00 per Assortment

1

Catalog page from 1959.

Cookie Jars

New!

No. 151—9 x 8" House Cookie Jar
Green and Brown Spray Decorated
Packed ½ Doz. Wt. 35 lbs.
$11.40 per Dozen

New!

No. 153—9½ x 8"
Wren House Cookie Jar
Pink w/Black Trim
Brown w/Green Trim
Packed ½ Doz. Wt. 30 lbs.
$11.40 per Dozen

New!

No. 155—11 x 8½"
Tulip Cookie Jar
White w/Red Tulip
White w/Yellow Tulip
Packed ½ Doz. Wt. 32 lbs.
$11.40 per Dozen

New!

No. 156—12 x 7"
Corn Cookie Jar
NATURAL COLOR
Packed ½ Doz. Wt. 26 lbs.
$11.40 per Dozen

NEW - PROMOTIONALLY PRICED

No. 28F—10 x 7½"
Fruit Cookie Jar
NATURAL COLOR
Packed ½ Doz. Wt. 29 lbs.
$10.20 per Dozen

No. 28V—10 x 7½"
Vegetable Cookie Jar
NATURAL COLOR
Packed ½ Doz. Wt. 29 lbs.
$10.20 per Dozen

No. 28C—10 x 7½"
Chef Cookie Jar
Black Outline w/Brown,
Red and Yellow Decoration
Packed ½ Doz. Wt. 29 lbs.
$10.20 per Dozen

No. 20—7¾ x 7½"
Apple Cookie Jar
Yellow or Aqua
w/Sprayed Decoration
Packed ½ Doz. Wt. 26 lbs.
$11.40 per Dozen
Also available in solid Red w/Green
Leaves specified as No. 20R—
Same Price.

No. 144—9½ x 7"
Jug Cookie Jar
White w/Brown Cover
Packed ½ Doz. Wt. 31 lbs.
$11.40 per Dozen

No. 147—10 x 7½"
Barrel Cookie Jar
Brown Decorated
Packed ½ Doz. Wt. 31 lbs.
$11.40 per Dozen

No. 136—8½ x 6¾"
Cabin Cookie Jar
Ivory w/Brown Spray
Decorated
Packed ½ Doz. Wt. 29 lbs.
$11.40 per Dozen

No. 126—10 x 6"
Kitten Cookie Jar
White Cover—Pink Base
Decorated
Packed ½ Doz. Wt. 26 lbs.
$11.40 per Dozen

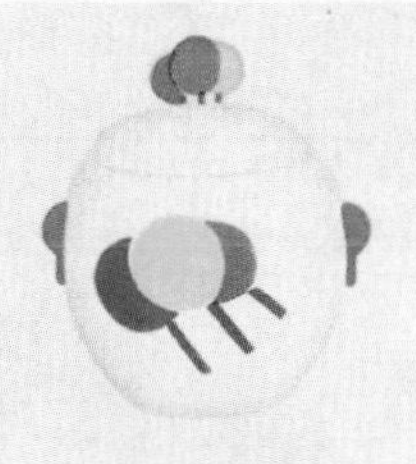

No. 143—9 x 8½"
Lollipop Cookie Jar
White w/Hand Painted
Lollipops
Packed ½ Doz. Wt. 26 lbs.
$11.40 per Dozen

No. 139—10 x 8"
Hen on Nest Cookie Jar
Brown Hen w/Yellow Nest
Packed ½ Doz. Wt. 28 lbs.
$11.40 per Dozen

No. 137—11 x 8"
Tepee Cookie Jar
White w/Black Spray
Decorated
Packed ½ Doz. Wt. 27 lbs.
$11.40 per Dozen

Note: All Cookie Jars Individually Boxed. In addition, you may make up your own Assortment of any THREE Jars Illustrated above which will be packed 2 each in a ½ Dozen Master Carton.

10

Catalog page from 1959.

Garden Club Line. 1958. All marked McCoy. Square Vase. 5" tall. $25.00 – 30.00. Square Centerpiece. 8" square x 2" deep. $40.00 – 50.00.

Garden Club Line. 1958. All marked McCoy. Jardiniere 7½". Two colors shown. $40.00 – 50.00. Pedestal Bowl 9½" x 7½". $40.00 – 50.00.

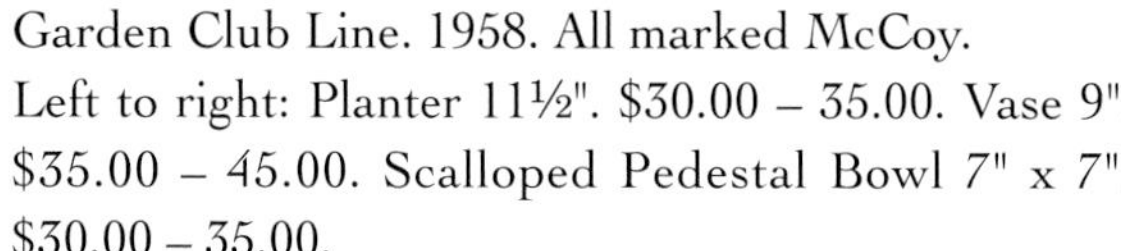

Garden Club Line. 1958. All marked McCoy.
Left to right: Planter 11½". $30.00 – 35.00. Vase 9". $35.00 – 45.00. Scalloped Pedestal Bowl 7" x 7". $30.00 – 35.00.

Jardiniere 10", Silhouette Line. 1961. $50.00 – 60.00. Pot with Saucer. 8½" tall. 1960. Both marked McCoy. $30.00 – 40.00.

Pillow Vase. Garden Club Line. 1958. Marked McCoy. Shown in a rainbow of colors! 5½" x 4". $20.00 – 40.00.

Garden Club Line. 1958. Both marked McCoy. Vase 5" tall. $50.00 – 60.00. Oval Pedestal Bowl 10" x 6". $30.00 – 40.00.

All marked McCoy. Left to right: Low Dish 6". Silhouette Line. 1961. $15.00 – 20.00. Pedestal Bowl 5½" x 4". Garden Club Line. 1958. $20.00 – 25.00. Low Centerpiece 10¼" x 7". Silhouette Line. 1961. $20.00 – 25.00.

All marked McCoy. Left: Goblet Vase 7". Silhouette Line. 1961. $30.00 – 35.00. The following are all Garden Club. Planting Dish 8" x 4". 1958. $30.00 – 35.00. Planter Bowl. Made in three sizes: 5½", 6½ , 7½". $30.00 – 45.00 each. Fan Vase 7½" x 7". Garden Club Line. 1958. $60.00 – 70.00.

Brown Antique Rose. 1959. All marked McCoy. Left to right: Vase 9" tall. $40.00 – 50.00. Planting Dish 8". $25.00 – 30.00. Also made in 10". $30.00 – 35.00. Planting Dish 15½". $40.00 – 50.00. Ice Jug 48 oz. $40.00 – 50.00. Vase 9" tall. $40.00 – 50.00.

Brown Antique Rose. 1959. Cup and Saucer. $25.00 – 35.00. Small Plate. $20.00 – 30.00.

Uncommon decal design. Late 1950s. Left to right: Swan Planter 7½". $50.00 – 60.00. Console Bowl 9". $40.00 – 50.00. Ice Jug 48 oz. $40.00 – 50.00.

Brown Antique Rose. 1959. All marked McCoy. Left to right: Pedestal Bowl 5½" x 4". $25.00 – 30.00. Vase 8" tall. $40.00 – 50.00. Vase 5" tall. $40.00 – 50.00. Vase 8" tall. $40.00 – 50.00. Pillow Vase 5½" x 4". $25.00 – 30.00.

Brown Antique Rose. 1959. Vase 7". $30.00 – 40.00. Individual Covered Casserole. $20.00 – 25.00. Vase 8". $35.00 – 45.00.

Coffee Pot. Late 1950s. Marked McCoy. Unusual decoration. $30.00 – 40.00.

Both pieces marked McCoy with unusual decal designs. Planting Dish 8". $25.00 – 30.00. Coffee Pot. $30.00 – 40.00.

Vesta Line. 1963. Bowl 6¾". Marked McCoy. Two glazes shown. $25.00 – 30.00. Bud Vase 8" tall. No mark. $20.00 – 25.00.

Vesta Line. 1963. Bud Vase 8" tall. No mark. $20.00 – 25.00. Planting Dish 8¼". Marked McCoy. $20.00 – 25.00.

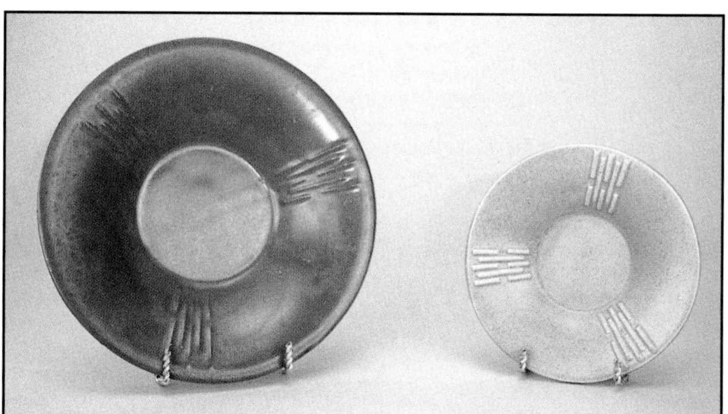

Vesta Line. 1963. Bowl 9". $20.00 – 25.00. Bowl 7". $20.00 – 25.00.

Individual Casserole 4½". 1960s. $25.00 – 30.00.

Oil & Vinegar Set with stoppers. No mark. $15.00 – 20.00 each.

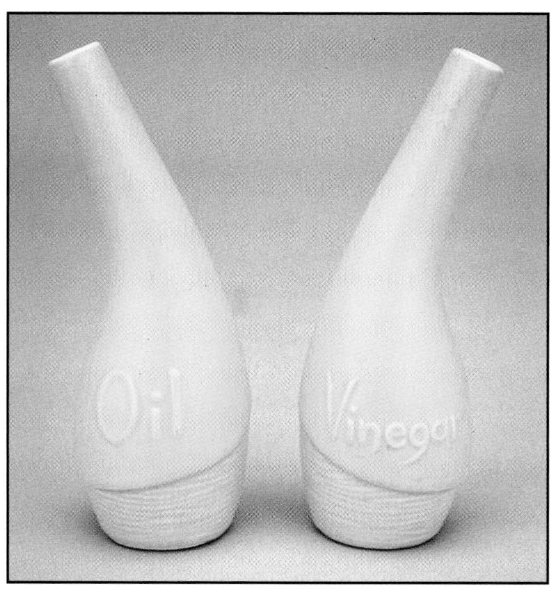

Oil & Vinegar Set. 1962. $20.00 – 25.00 each.

Sugar with Cover 12 oz. 1962. $20.00 – 25.00.
Bean Baker with Cover 2 qt. 1962. $35.00 – 40.00.

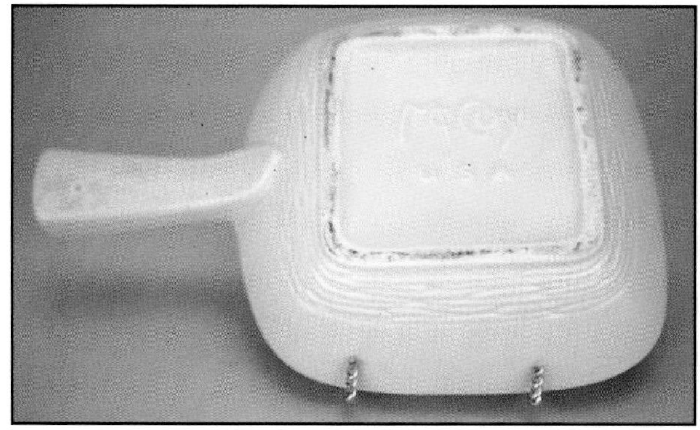

Individual Serving Dish 7". 1958. Marked McCoy. $25.00 – 30.00.

Teapots with same unusual decals but different handles. 36 oz. Early 1960s. Marked McCoy. $40.00 – 50.00.

Bowl 6" and Salad Bowl 10". Early 1960s. Marked McCoy. 6", $10.00 – 15.00; 10", $25.00 – 30.00.

Coffee Pot 40 oz. Sugar and Creamer. Marked McCoy. Cook-Serve Line. Late 1950s. Coffee Pot. $30.00 – 40.00; Sugar or Creamer. $20.00 – 25.00 each.

Vase with original sticker, 14½". Crestwood Line. 1964. Marked McCoy. $60.00 – 70.00.

Planter 13". Crestwood Line. 1964. Marked McCoy. $40.00 – 50.00.

Pedestal Vase 8½" and Pedestal Planter 7". Early American Line. 1967. Marked McCoy. Vase $50.00 – 60.00. Planter $35.00 – 45.00.

Vases with ball footed design 9½" and 6½", respectively. 1953. Marked McCoy. 9½", $35.00 – 40.00; 6½", $25.00 – 30.00.

All pieces with rose decal decoration and marked McCoy. Late 1950s. Left to right: Vase 8" tall. $35.00 – 45.00. Pot & Saucer 6". $20.00 – 25.00. Vase 9" tall. $40.00 – 50.00. Jardiniere 6". $30.00 – 35.00. Vase 9" tall. $40.00 – 50.00.

Rose decal decoration and marked McCoy. Late 1950s. Vase 7½". $35.00 – 40.00. Bowl 10". $30.00 – 35.00.

Rose decal decoration, all marked McCoy. Late 1950s. Left to right: Vase 6" tall. $30.00 – 40.00. Vase 8" tall. $35.00 – 45.00. Flower Bowl 5". $25.00 – 30.00. Vase 8" tall. $35.00 – 45.00. Vase 6½" tall. $30.00 – 40.00.

All pieces from Blue Country Line. 1982. Left to right: Covered Bowl with handle. $35.00 – 45.00. Pitcher & Bowl Set. $40.00 – 50.00. Candlesticks. $15.00 – 18.00 each. Chamber tray. $20.00 – 25.00.

Vase 8". 1954. Marked McCoy. Made in green, black, and white. Not an easy one to find! $50.00 – 60.00.

Corinthian Line. 1960s. Marked McCoy. Planter 9" x 4". $20.00 – 25.00. Tall Pedestal Bowl 8" x 6½". $25.00 – 35.00.

Three pieces with unusual finish. Marked McCoy. Likely from mid-1950s. Some may be from the Golden Fantasy Line, especially the middle planter. The other two might also be a style similar to the Sunburst Gold glaze. Covered Box. $25.00 – 30.00. Pedestal Planter. $25.00 – 30.00. Planter. $25.00 – 30.00.

Covered Casserole with original stand. 1960s. Esmond by McCoy. $60.00 – 75.00.

Pieces from Floral Country Line. 1982. Left to right: Pitcher & Bowl Set. $40.00 – 50.00. Pitcher. $25.00 – 30.00. Utensil Holder. $25.00 – 30.00. Candle Holder with Chimney. $40.00 – 50.00.

Classic Line. 1962. Marked McCoy. Low Dish 6". $ 12.00 – 15.00. Bud Vase 6". $15.00 – 20.00.

Classic Line. 1962. Marked McCoy. Springwood style Jardiniere with Classic Line finish 7". $40.00 – 50.00. Jardiniere 10". $50.00 – 60.00.

Classic Line. 1962. Marked McCoy. Goblet Vase 6½". $25.00 – 30.00. Low Dish 8" x 6". $15.00 – 20.00.

Low Centerpiece 8". Pedestal Line. 1959 – 1960. Marked McCoy. $25.00 – 30.00.

Vase 10". Pedestal Line. 1959 – 1960. Marked McCoy. $30.00 – 40.00. Jardiniere 9". Basket Line. 1959 – 1960. Marked McCoy. $40.00 – 50.00.

Both marked McCoy. Long Planter 14". $25.00 – 30.00. Low Dish 8". $15.00 – 20.00.

Happytime Line Mugs. 1974. Marked USA. $15.00 – 18.00 each.

Happytime Line Pieces. 1974. Jug. $20.00 – 25.00. Mug. $15.00 – 18.00. Pitcher. $20.00 – 25.00.

Wonderful jagged edge-shaped planter. 9½" long. Likely late 1950s. Marked McCoy. $60.00 – 75.00.

All pieces from Tonecraft Line. 1967. All marked McCoy. Left to right: Low Pedestal Dish 7". $15.00 – 18.00. Square Pedestal Planter 4¼". $15.00 – 18.00. Rectangle Planter 10½". $20.00 – 25.00. Round Flower Bowl 6". $18.00 – 20.00.

Classic Line. 1962. Marked McCoy. Planter with stand 6". $20.00 – 25.00. Pedestal Bowl. 5" x 3½". $15.00 – 20.00.

Jardiniere 6½". Tonecraft Line. 1967. Marked McCoy. $30.00 – 40.00.

Classic Line. 1962. Marked McCoy. Left to right: Round Pedestal Planter 5½". $18.00 – 20.00. Vase 12". $30.00 – 35.00. Vase 8". $20.00 – 25.00.

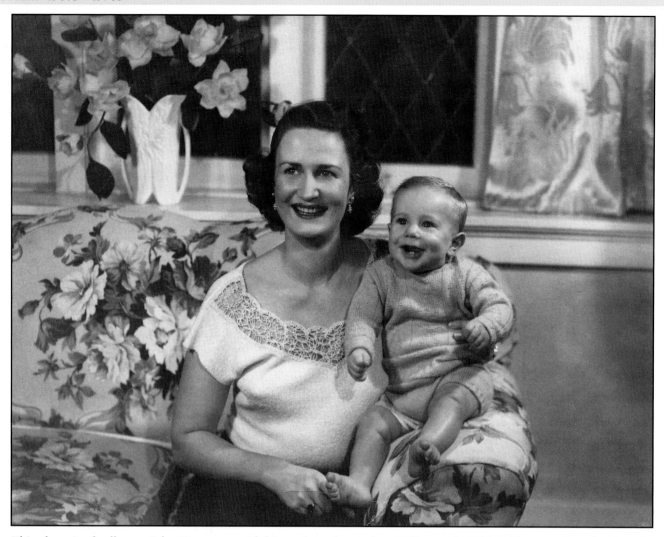

This photo is of collector John Hauseman with his mother taken in late 1950 or early 1951 in Toronto, Canada. Note the wonderful double handle Butterfly Vase in the background made in early 1940s, 10" tall, and valued at $150.00 – 225.00. What a great photo!

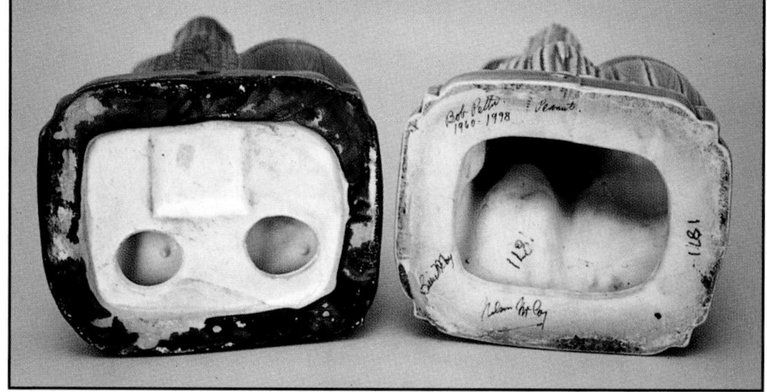

Whaling Man Lamp on right made by Nelson McCoy Pottery in 1950s. About 16¾" tall. No mark. Not very many of these produced. $350.00 – 400.00. Similar Whaling Man figure pictured on left is not a McCoy product. The best way of determining this is by checking the construction from the bottom; see smaller photo. The glaze type and coloring may tell the collector if a lamp is the McCoy product, but the foolproof method is definitely by checking out the piece from the bottom!

Catalog page, Antique Curio Line, 1962.

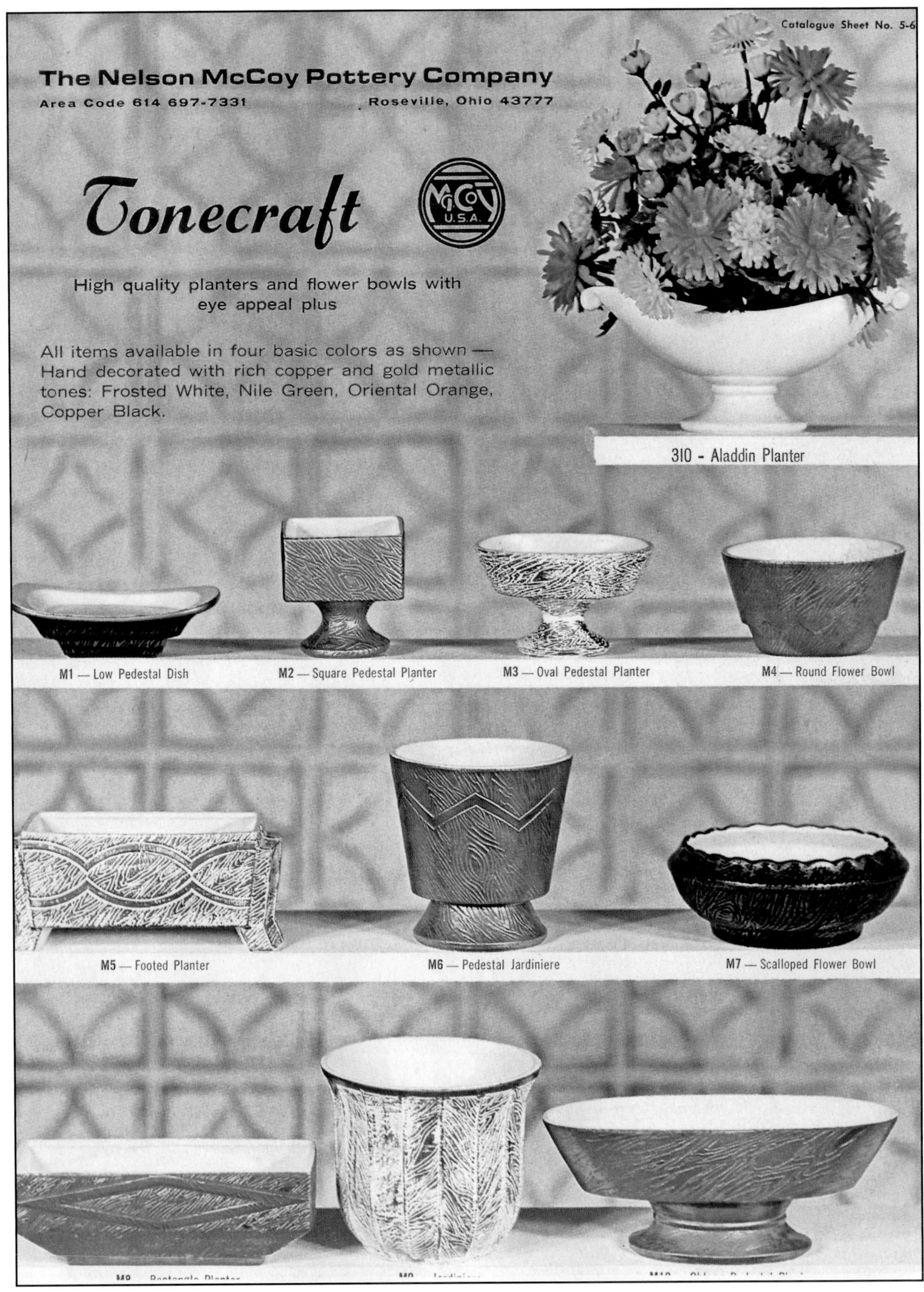

Catalog page, Tonecraft Line, 1965.

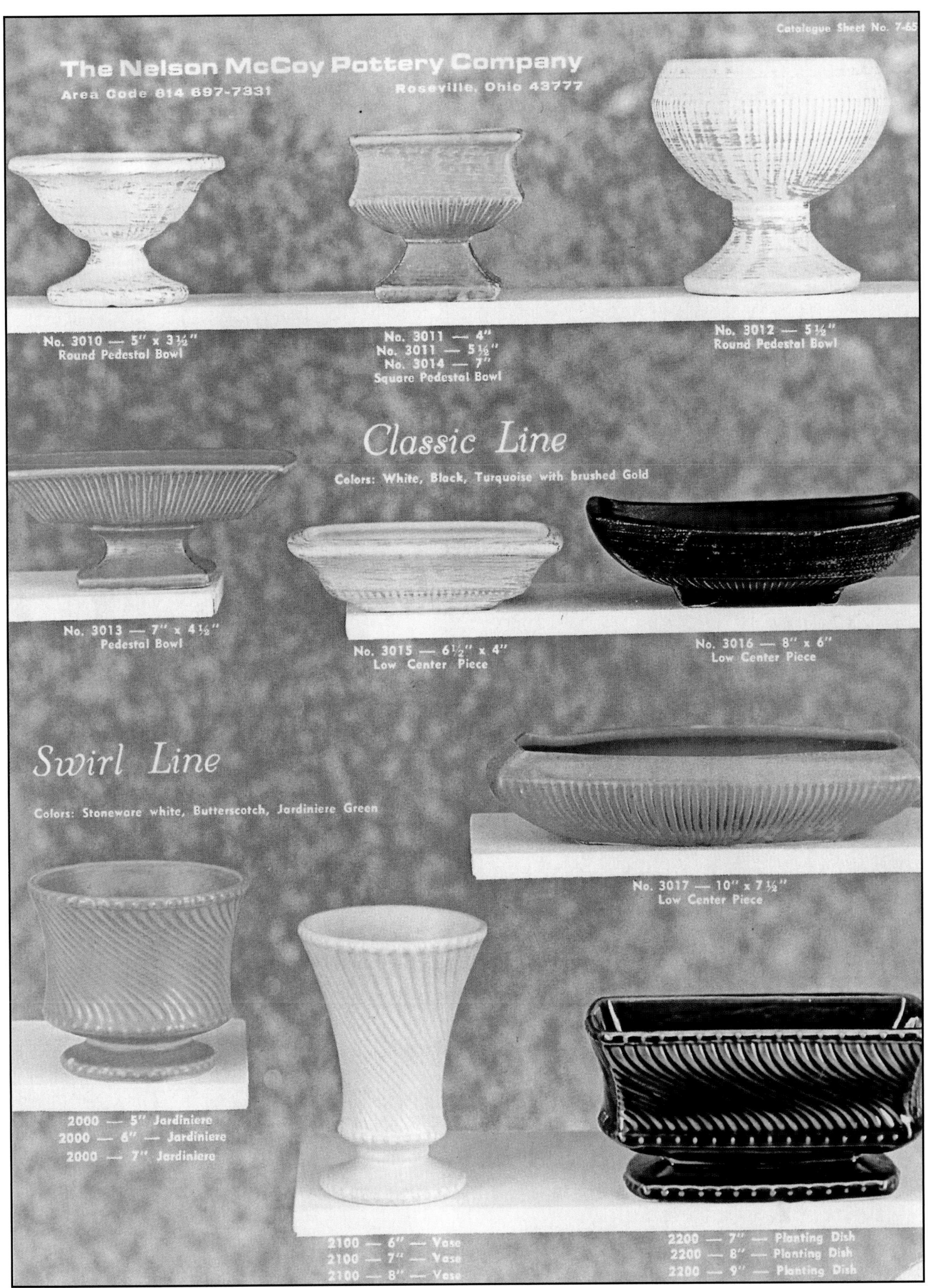

Catalog page, Classic & Swirl Lines, 1965.

Catalog page, Modern Cope Originals, 1965.

Catalog page, Mixing Bowls, 1965.

KOOKIE KETTLE
No. 171—Kookie Kettle
9½ x 8"
COOKIE Kettle
No. 243—Cookie Kettle
8 x 8"
No. 178—Oaken Bucket
9 x 8½"
Ceramic Cookie Jars
HAND DECORATED
3 styles to 6 pack
COOKIES
No. 207—"Coalby" Cat
No. 208—"Mac" Dog
No. 188—Black Kettle
8½ x 8"
No. 213—Early American
7 x 8½"
Wish I Had a Cookie
Cookies
No. 180—Wishing Well
9 x 7¼"
No. 190—Stove
9 x 9"
No. 179—Coffee Grinder
10 x 7"
No. 236—Country Stove
6½ x 6½ x 10½"
The Nelson McCoy Pottery Company
Subsidiary of Mount Clemens Pottery Company
Area Code 614 697-7331
Roseville, Ohio 43777
10

Catalog page, Cookie Jars, 1967.

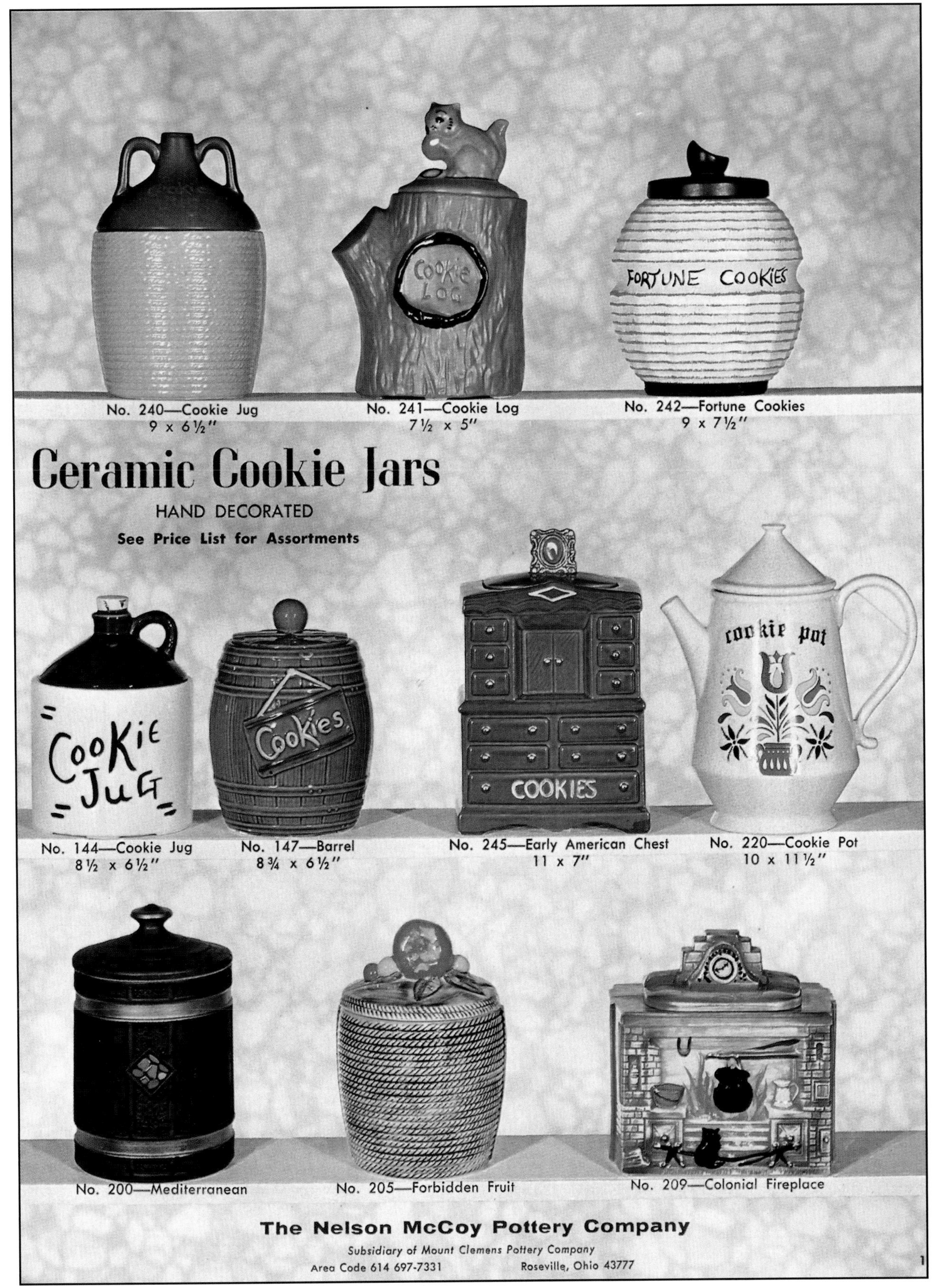

Cookie Log
Fortune Cookies
No. 240—Cookie Jug
9 x 6½"
No. 241—Cookie Log
7½ x 5"
No. 242—Fortune Cookies
9 x 7½"
Ceramic Cookie Jars
HAND DECORATED
See Price List for Assortments
Cookie Jug
Cookies
COOKIES
cookie pot
No. 144—Cookie Jug
8½ x 6½"
No. 147—Barrel
8¾ x 6½"
No. 245—Early American Chest
11 x 7"
No. 220—Cookie Pot
10 x 11½"
No. 200—Mediterranean
No. 205—Forbidden Fruit
No. 209—Colonial Fireplace
The Nelson McCoy Pottery Company
Subsidiary of Mount Clemens Pottery Company
Area Code 614 697-7331
Roseville, Ohio 43777
1

Catalog page, Cookie Jars, 1967.

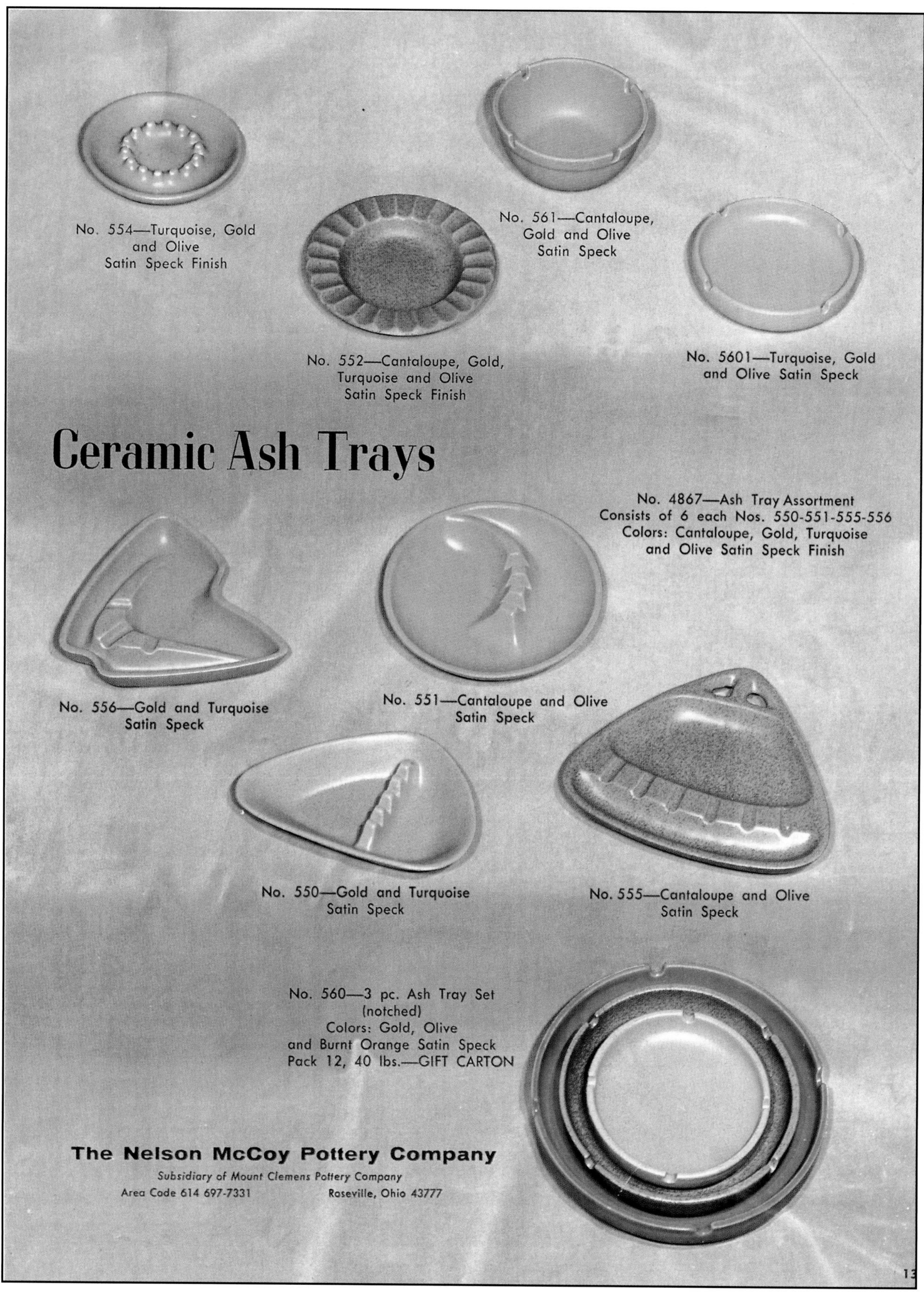

No. 554—Turquoise, Gold
and Olive
Satin Speck Finish
No. 561—Cantaloupe,
Gold and Olive
Satin Speck
No. 552—Cantaloupe, Gold,
Turquoise and Olive
Satin Speck Finish
No. 5601—Turquoise, Gold
and Olive Satin Speck
Ceramic Ash Trays
No. 4867—Ash Tray Assortment
Consists of 6 each Nos. 550-551-555-556
Colors: Cantaloupe, Gold, Turquoise
and Olive Satin Speck Finish
No. 556—Gold and Turquoise
Satin Speck
No. 551—Cantaloupe and Olive
Satin Speck
No. 550—Gold and Turquoise
Satin Speck
No. 555—Cantaloupe and Olive
Satin Speck
No. 560—3 pc. Ash Tray Set
(notched)
Colors: Gold, Olive
and Burnt Orange Satin Speck
Pack 12, 40 lbs.—GIFT CARTON
The Nelson McCoy Pottery Company
Subsidiary of Mount Clemens Pottery Company
Area Code 614 697-7331
Roseville, Ohio 43777
13

Catalog page, Ashtrays, 1967

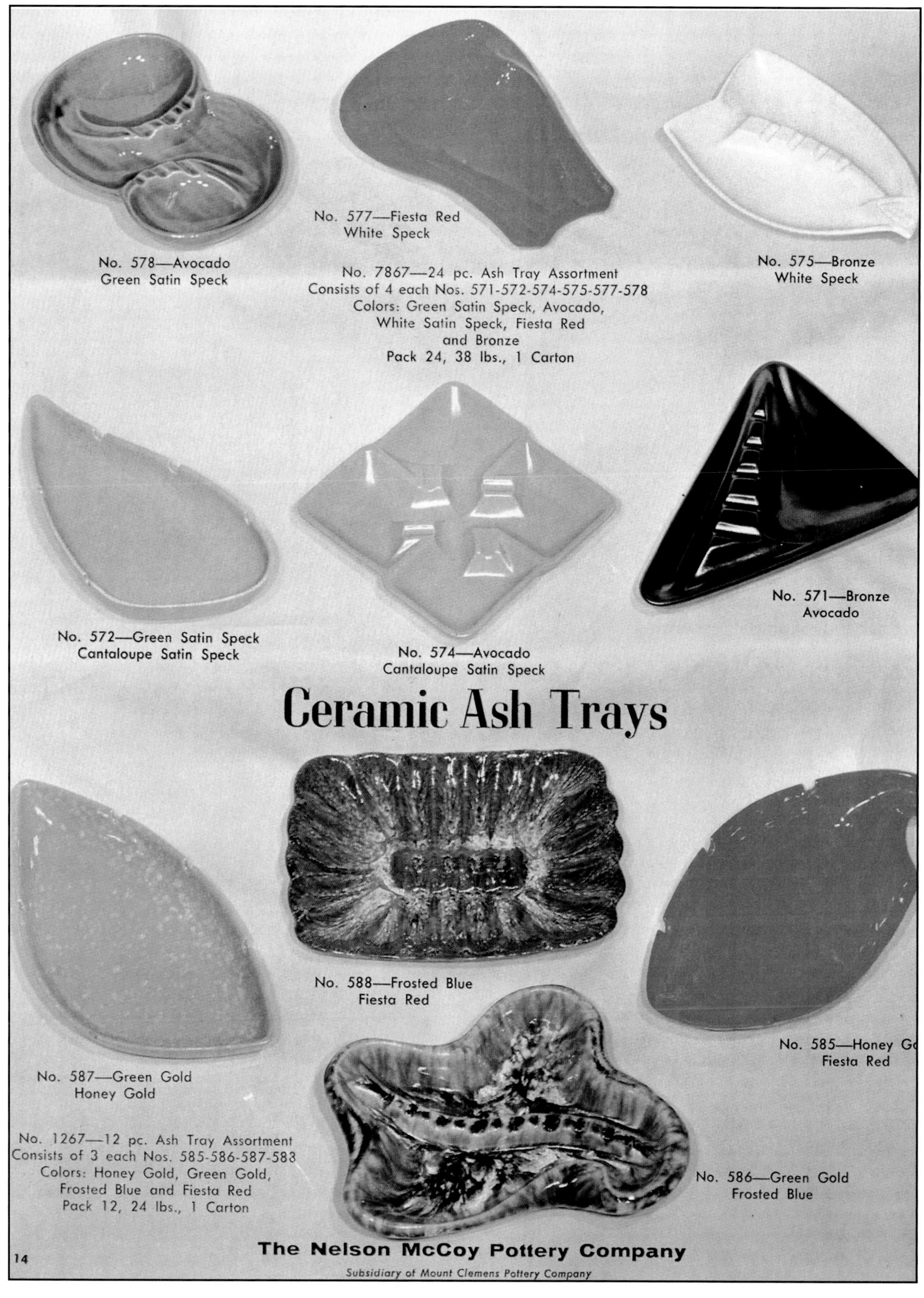

No. 578—Avocado
Green Satin Speck
No. 577—Fiesta Red
White Speck
No. 575—Bronze
White Speck
No. 7867—24 pc. Ash Tray Assortment
Consists of 4 each Nos. 571-572-574-575-577-578
Colors: Green Satin Speck, Avocado,
White Satin Speck, Fiesta Red
and Bronze
Pack 24, 38 lbs., 1 Carton
No. 571—Bronze
Avocado
No. 572—Green Satin Speck
Cantaloupe Satin Speck
No. 574—Avocado
Cantaloupe Satin Speck
Ceramic Ash Trays
No. 588—Frosted Blue
Fiesta Red
No. 585—Honey G
Fiesta Red
No. 587—Green Gold
Honey Gold
No. 1267—12 pc. Ash Tray Assortment
Consists of 3 each Nos. 585-586-587-583
Colors: Honey Gold, Green Gold,
Frosted Blue and Fiesta Red
Pack 12, 24 lbs., 1 Carton
No. 586—Green Gold
Frosted Blue
14
The Nelson McCoy Pottery Company
Subsidiary of Mount Clemens Pottery Company

Catalog page, Ashtrays, 1967.

Early American

Featuring Antique Crackle and Blue-Green Colors *for* Artificial Flower Arrangements and the Horticultural Department.

No. 757
Vase
Blue-Green

No. 753

No. 756

No. 757

No. 754

No. 751

No. 752

No. 755

No. 751	No. 752	No. 753	No. 754	No. 755	No. 756	No. 757
Pitcher & Bowl	Footed Bowl	Pedestal Bowl	Tall Pedestal Vase	Planter	Vase	Vase
8″ x 8″	7″ x 3½″	5½″ x 7″	8½″ x 6½″	7½″ x 4″	9″ x 6″	8″ x 5″

(See Price List for Assortment.)

The Nelson McCoy Pottery Company

Subsidiary of Mount Clemens Pottery Company

Area Code 614 697-7331 Roseville, Ohio 43777

Catalog page, Early American Line, 1967.

Dish Gardens
PROMOTIONALLY PRICED FOR VOLUME USERS
Colors: Green
White
No. 682
No. 610
No. 685
No. 606
No. 611
No. 607
No. 609
No. 608
6" PLANTERS
No. 701
No. 700
No. 690
7" PLANTERS
9" PLANTER
No. 683
No. 668
No. 697
8" PLANTERS
No. 662—4¼ x 2½"
No. 655—5 x 2½"
No. 654—3½ x 2½"
No. 656—3½ x 3"
The Nelson McCoy Pottery Company
Subsidiary of Mount Clemens Pottery Company
Area Code 614 697-7331
Roseville, Ohio 43777

Catalog page, Garden Dishes, 1967.

Mugs

IN GAY COLORS

No. 3667—8 oz. Mug Assortment
Packed 72 pcs. 44 lbs.
1 Carton
(5 Styles—Assorted Colors)
Olive, Cantaloupe, Gold and Turquoise
Satin Speck Finish

No. 43—Roman   No. 42—Ionic   No. 41—Utility

No. 45—Delmont   No. 44—Trigger

No. 29—16 oz.   No. 25—14 oz.   No. 26—15 oz.   No. 27—10 oz.

No. 6067 Mug Assortment—Consists of 6 each of the following
Nos. 25-26-27-29
Packed 24, 27 lbs., 1 Carton
Olive, Cantaloupe, Gold and Turquoise Satin Speck

No. 21—12 oz.   No. 23—12 oz.   No. 22—10 oz.   No. 24—12 oz.

No. 9067 Mug Assortment—Consists of 6 each of the following
Nos. 21-22-23-24
Packed 24, 38 lbs., 1 Carton
Green Gold, Honey Gold, Satin Gray and Frosted Blue

The Nelson McCoy Pottery Company

Subsidiary of Mount Clemens Pottery Company

Area Code 614 697-7331   Roseville, Ohio 43777

8

Catalog page, Mugs, 1967.

Kitchen Accessories
MIXING BOWLS AND LAZY SUSANS
Natural Finish with Hand Decorated Apple
OVENPROOF—Shrink Pack
No. 80—3 pc. Bowl Set
6-7-8"
No. 95—7 pc. Salad Set
10½" Salad, 4-5" Salads
Wooden Fork and Spoon
No. 90—6 pc. Bean Pot Set
2 qt. Bean Pot W/Cover and
4-6 oz. Bean Pots
Yellow, Pumpkin and Chartreuse
Satin Speck Finish
No. 75—3 pc. Bowl Set
6-7-8"
No. 32—3 pc. Bowl Set
8-10-12"
Yellow, Pumpkin and Chartreuse
Satin Speck Finish
Available in Open Stock
as per Price List
No. 70—Bean Pot
Brown and Green Drip
12" Avocado
No. 905 with Gift Carton
12" Butterscotch
No. 905 with
Gift Carton
No. 950—12" W/Cover
White and Black
No. 900—12"
Gold and Green
The Nelson McCoy Pottery Company
Subsidiary of Mount Clemens Pottery Company
12

Catalog page, Kitchen Accessories, 1967.

Illustrations by Frank Heller.

In this Finders Keepers section, we selected 50 pieces of Nelson McCoy pottery and assembled them in relative chronological order. The criteria used to qualify for this section is as follows:

• The piece had to be highly desirable to Nelson McCoy collectors!

• The item had to be a hard to find piece, not impossible, but definitely very difficult. This is to the contrary of the HNH Top 100 Findables in Volume II, where the pieces are also high in demand by collectors, but are likely findable within a few years. The Finders Keepers pieces are more rare, so a collector will likely have fewer opportunities to acquire one for their collection.

• The most important criteria to make the list was that there must be known documentation that the piece was an actual production item listed on a catalog page or advertising sheet.

To include all eras of Nelson McCoy pottery, we have selected pieces from all decades of production. Fellow McCoy collector Frank Heller did this outstanding artwork on pages 110 and 111. Have fun and good luck in pursuit of your Finders Keepers piece. Our conclusion: If you "find" it, you'd better "keep" it!

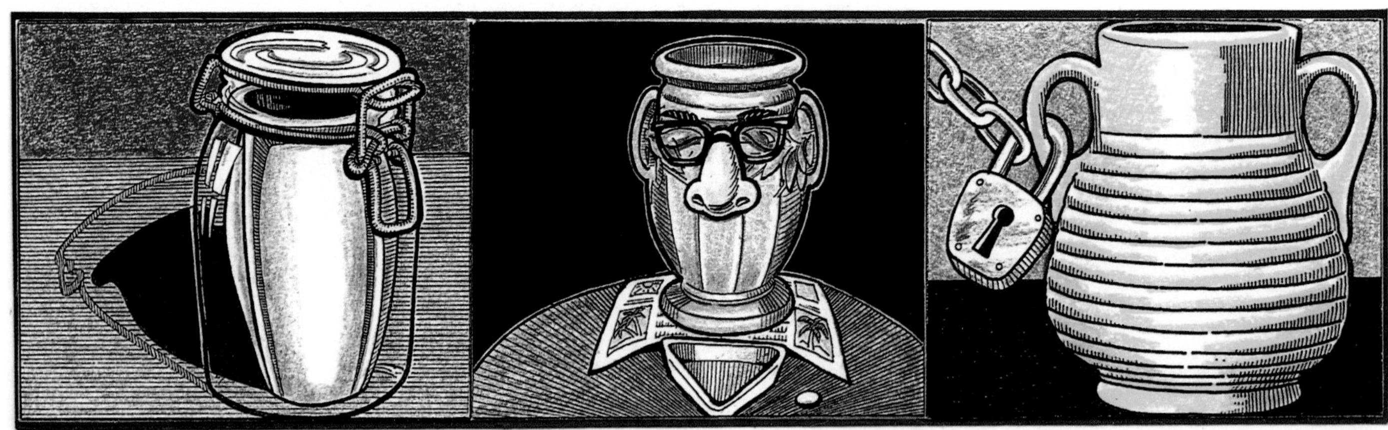

1. Jardiniere and Pedestal Set. Jardiniere, 12½", Pedestal 20½". 1920s – 1930s. No marks. This set is big and heavy. Fewer than six sets known to exist. Muffy seems to enjoy the higher view! $600.00 – 700.00.

2. Umbrella Stand. Shown in both glaze coloring combinations. 18" tall. One of the earliest umbrella stands made and a tough one to find. No marks. $300.00 – 350.00.

3. Ringed Vase with Handles. 7½" tall. Shield mark. Great vase design from this early era. $80.00 – 100.00.

4. Large Holly Jardiniere and Pedestal Set. No marks. Jardiniere 10½" and Pedestal 18½". Came in several matte and onyx glaze colors. No marks. $500.00 – 600.00.

5. Large Cameo Jardiniere and Pedestal Set. Jardiniere 10". Pedestal 18½". No marks. Not many of these larger Cameo sets in existence! $700.00 – 800.00.

6. Vase. Pictured in two glaze color offerings. Also made in white. 7" high x 9" wide. 1930s. No mark. One of the most sought after vases from this era. $200.00 – 250.00.

7. Sphinx Sand Jar (No. 6 Sand Jar designation in catalog). 16" tall. No mark. Made in several matte colors. Highly desirable piece to collectors of this era! $1,500.00 – 2,500.00.

8. Leaves and Berries Jardiniere and Pedestal Set. Jardiniere 10", Pedestal 18½". No marks. Like the Holly Design Set, this was made in several matte and onyx glaze colors. This pedestal is a tough one to acquire! $600.00 – 700.00.

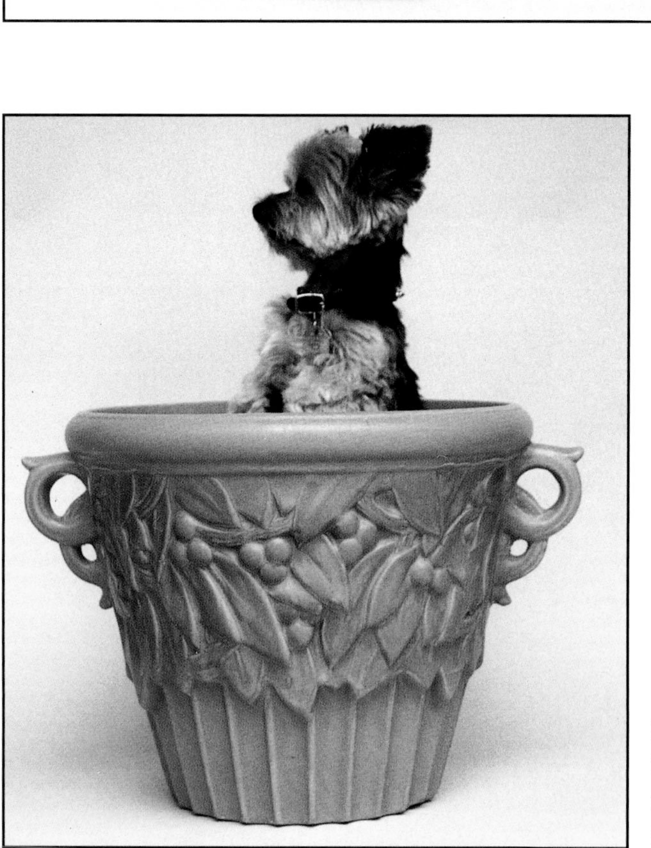

9. Porch Jar with Handles. 14". Came in matte colors. Only a few of these are presently known to exist. Hard to find is no exaggeration here! Plenty of room for Fergie in this one. $1,200.00 – 1,500.00.

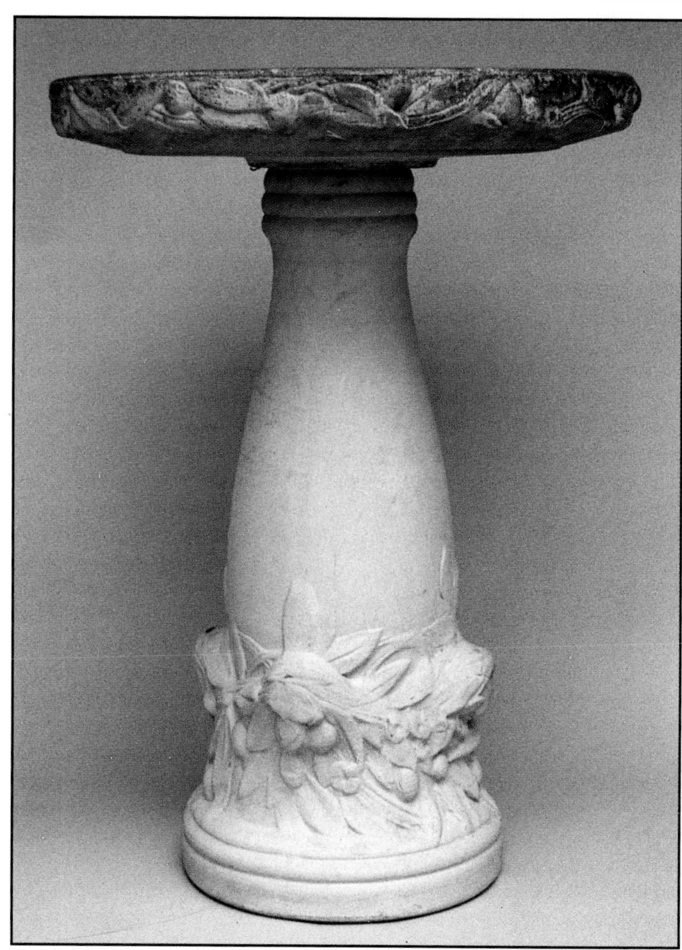

10. Bird Bath Set. 18¼" wide top, 25" total height. No marks. Graystone finish. Beautiful detail in this scarce piece. $400.00 – 500.00.

11. Ribbed Vase 14" tall. Shown in two photos. No mark. Made in matte glazes and overdrip glazes as shown. $300.00 – 450.00.

12. Sand Jar (No. 5 Sand Jar designation in catalog). 18" tall. No mark. Made in several matte colors. Highly desirable piece to collectors of this era! $1,200.00 – 1,500.00.

13. Vase (No. 82 designation in catalog). 18" tall. Made in several other sizes which are much more findable. Pictured with 5" size for comparison. No mark. Matt colors. 18", $300.00 – 400.00; 5". $50.00 – 60.00.

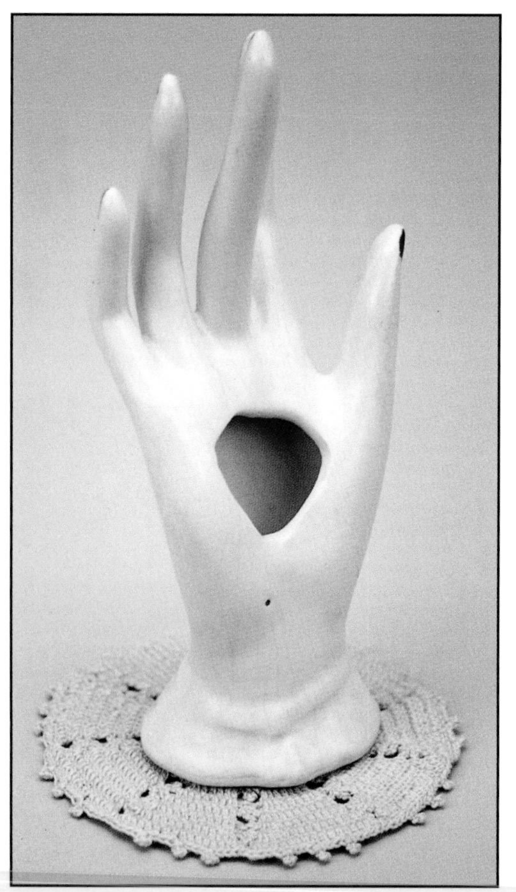

14. Hand Vase 6½" tall. Early 1940s. Usually dry bottom with no mark but has been found with NM mark on bottom also. White glaze color only. Cold paint on fingernails is original. $150.00 – 200.00.

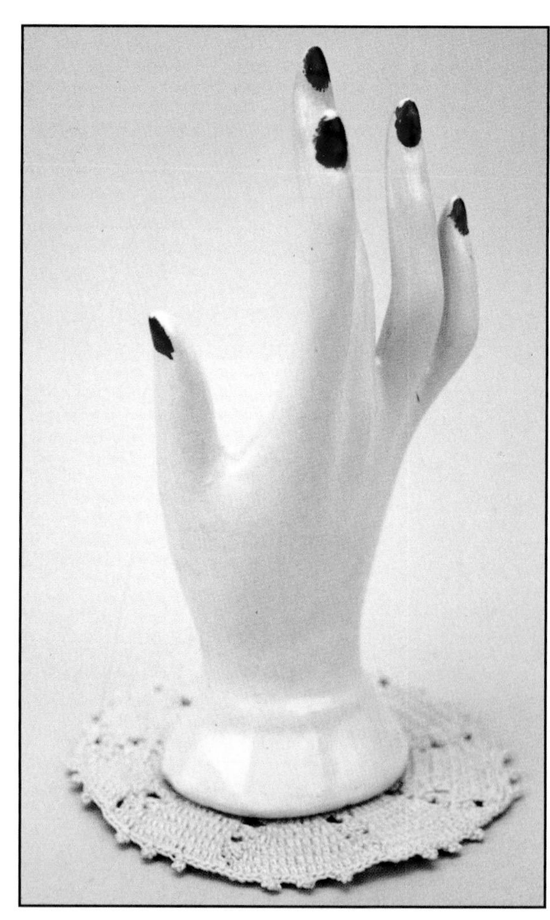

15. Vase with Lily Bud Design. 5" tall. Dry bottom, usually without any mark visible on sides. Pastel matte colors. A tough find to complete a Lily Bud collection! $80.00 – 100.00.

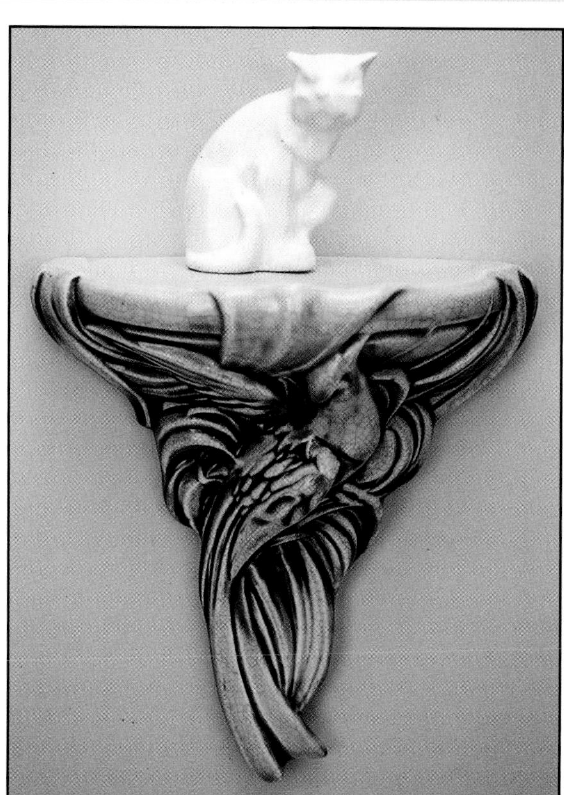

16. Wall Bracket (Bird Shelf) 9" long x 8" wide. 1948. Shown with Cat Miniature for size comparison (see Cat below). No mark. Made in glaze combination pictured and all white glaze. Only 6 – 7 examples known to exist at this time. $800.00 – 1,000.00.

17. Witch 3" tall. Early 1940s. Open cored bottom; marked USA on lower side. Gloss solid colors. $400.00 – 500.00.

18. and 19. Rabbit, 1½" tall; Pelican, 3" tall. Early 1940s. Rabbit marked USA on lower side; Pelican, no mark. Variety of solid colors. Rabbit $300.00 – 400.00; Pelican $250.00 – 350.00.

20. and 21. Cat, 3" tall; Fish, 3" tall. Early 1940s. Cat marked USA on lower side; Fish, no mark. Variety of solid colors. Cat $300.00 – 400.00; Fish $150.00 – 200.00.

22. Gloved Hand Vase. 8¼" tall. Early 1940s. Marked NM. Variety of gloss glazes. $250.00 – 350.00

23. Wall Pocket, Leaves and Berries pattern. 7" long. Early 1940s. No mark. Variety of gloss glazes. $200.00 – 300.00.

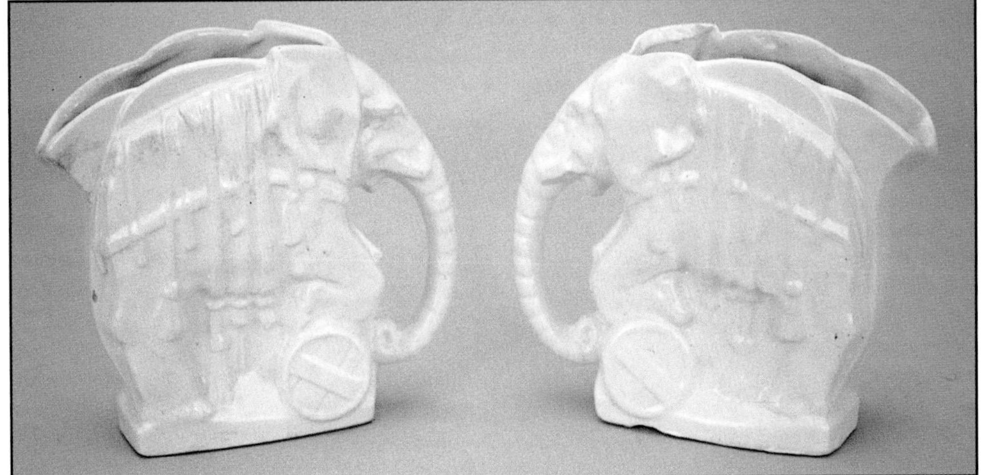

24. Elephant Pitcher 7" tall. Early 1940s. Marked NM. Gloss solid colors. $350.00 – 400.00.

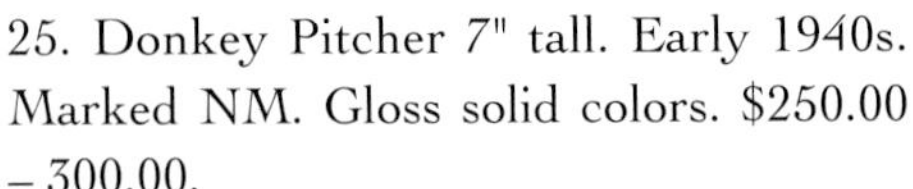

25. Donkey Pitcher 7" tall. Early 1940s. Marked NM. Gloss solid colors. $250.00 – 300.00.

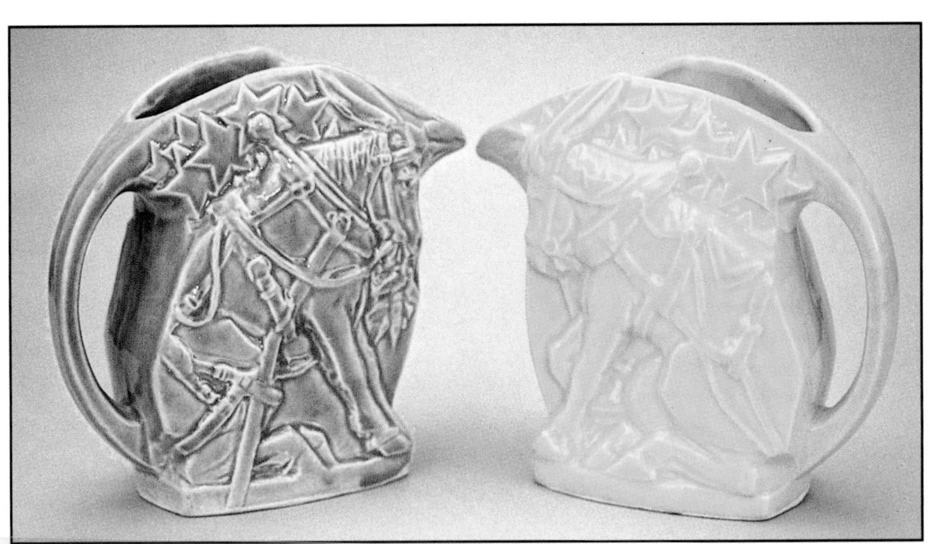

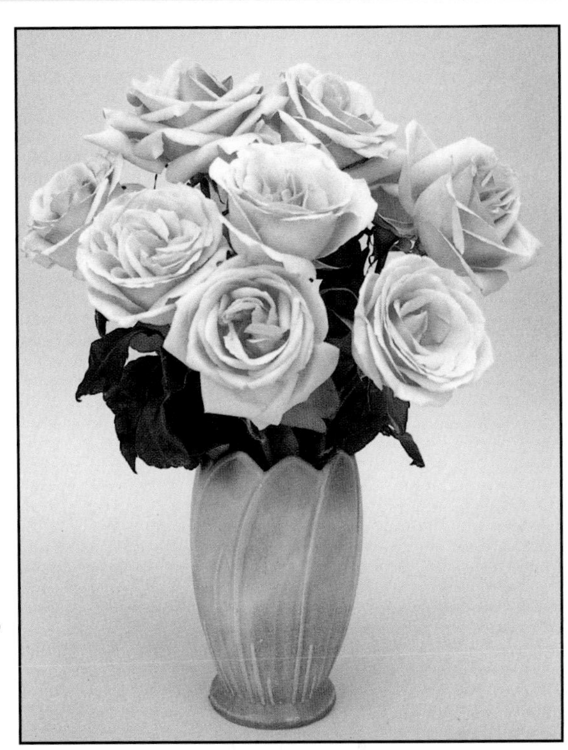

26. Vase (No. 50 designation in catalog). 8" tall. Shown in two photos. No mark. Late 1930s. Variety of glaze colors. $100.00 – 150.00.

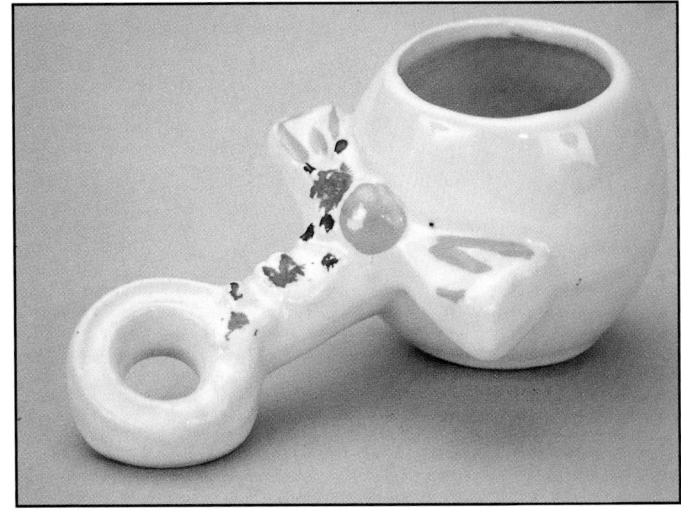

27. Baby Rattle Planter with excellent cold paint decoration. 5½" x 3". 1954. No mark. Made only in white glaze color. $90.00 – 110.00.

28. Vase 6¾" tall. Early 1940s. Shown in two photos. Marked USA. Variety of glazes. $100.00 – 150.00.

29. Vase 5" tall. No mark. Shown in two photos. Early 1940s. Found with and without center area filled. Variety of glaze colors. $80.00 – 100.00.

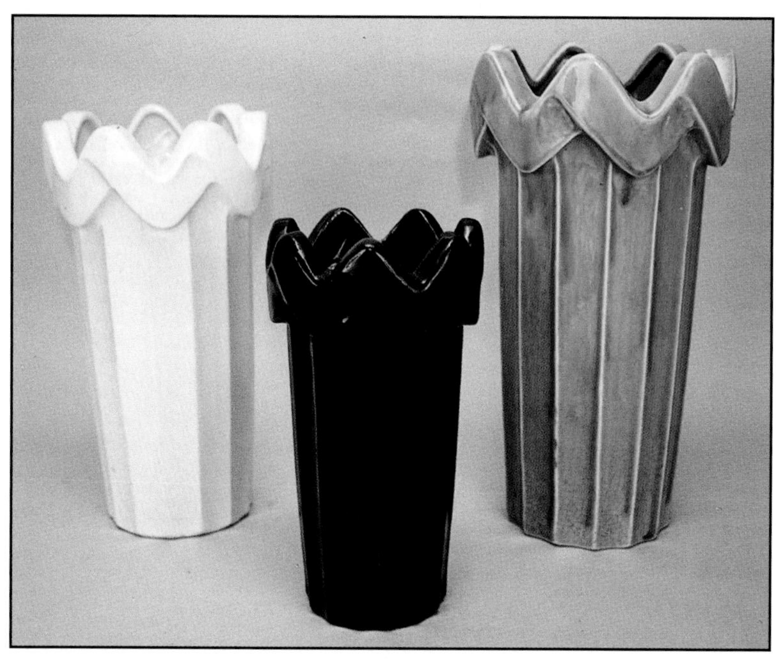

30. Vase, shown in the three sizes made: 12", 10" and 14". 1950s. Marked McCoy. The 14" size is the Finders Keepers piece. None of these sizes is an easy find, but only a few 14" ones have been found! 14", $150.00– 200.00; 12", $100.00 – 125.00; 10", $80.00 – 100.00.

31. Planter 3" x 5". Early 1940s. No mark. Shown in two photos. Variety of colors. $70.00 – 90.00.

32. Vase 5½" tall. No mark. Early 1940s. Shown in two photos. Variety of glaze colors. $100.00 – 150.00.

33. Penguin Spoonrest 7" long. 1953. Marked McCoy. Also made in a two-tone green glaze combination. Hard to find without wing or beak damage. $100.00 – 150.00.

34. Fish Pitcher. 7". 1949. Marked McCoy. Green/brown color combination as shown, also solid green. Blue non-production glaze has also been found. Very few of these are known to exist! $650.00 – 800.00.

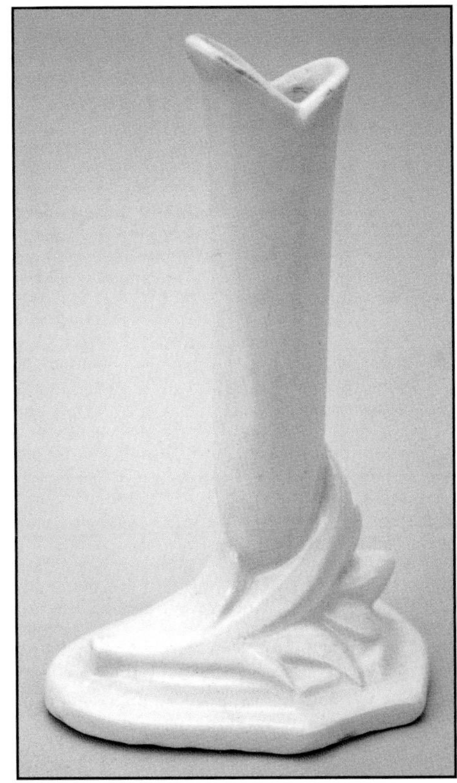

35. Bud Vase 5" tall. Late 1930s – early 1940s. Old McCoy mark. Variety of glaze colors. $100.00 – 150.00.

36. Vase with Contrasting Leaf. 9" tall. 1955. Marked McCoy. Glaze color options as pictured with overdrip design. Not only a tough vase to find but even harder to find without any damage to the leaf! $150.00 – 200.00.

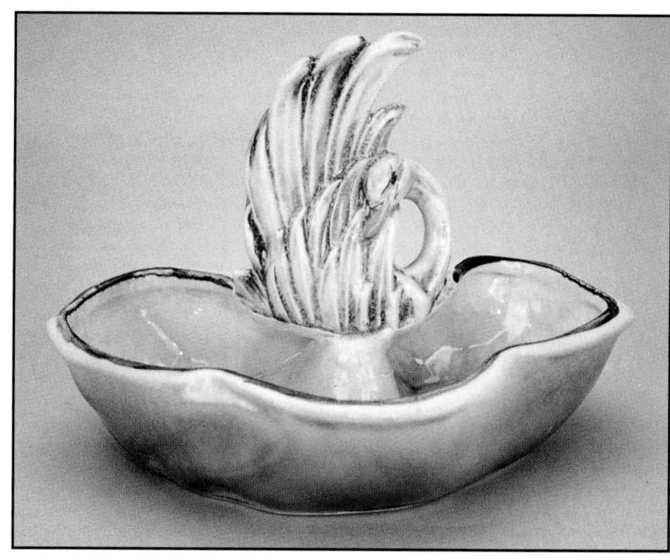

37. Swan Planting Dish 10½". 1955. Marked McCoy. Produced with white base coloring or yellow base. $300.00 – 350.00.

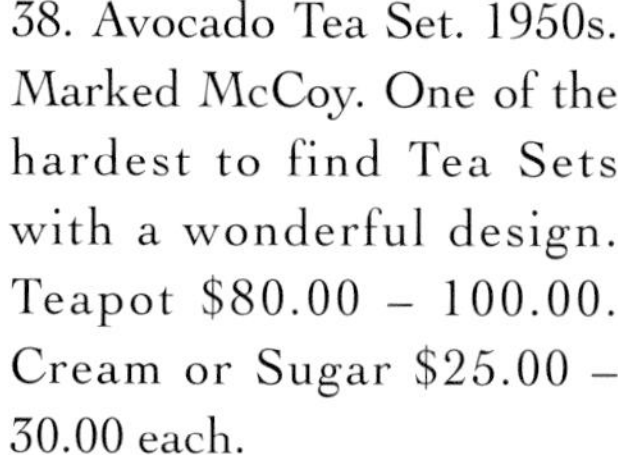

38. Avocado Tea Set. 1950s. Marked McCoy. One of the hardest to find Tea Sets with a wonderful design. Teapot $80.00 – 100.00. Cream or Sugar $25.00 – 30.00 each.

39. Antelope Centerpiece. About 12" wide. 1955. No mark. Sold with black or green base. $350.00 – 450.00.

40. Three-Piece Cabbage Set. Grease Jar 7", Shakers 4". 1954. Marked McCoy. Shaker Set $75.00 – 100.00; Grease Jar $125.00 – 150.00.

41 and 42. Grapes and Pomegranate Planters 6½" x 5". 1953. Marked McCoy. These are scarcest of the fruit planter line. $200.00 – 300.00 each.

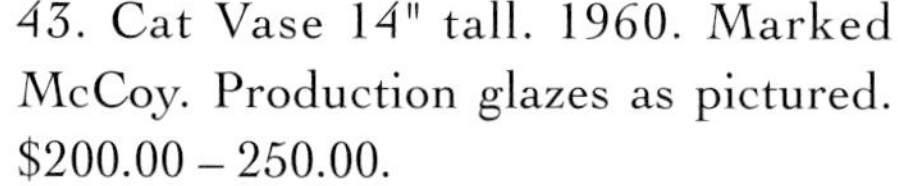

43. Cat Vase 14" tall. 1960. Marked McCoy. Production glazes as pictured. $200.00 – 250.00.

44. Footed Vase 14". 1959. Marked USA. Produced in glaze colors white, green or fawn (light brown). $75.00 – 100.00.

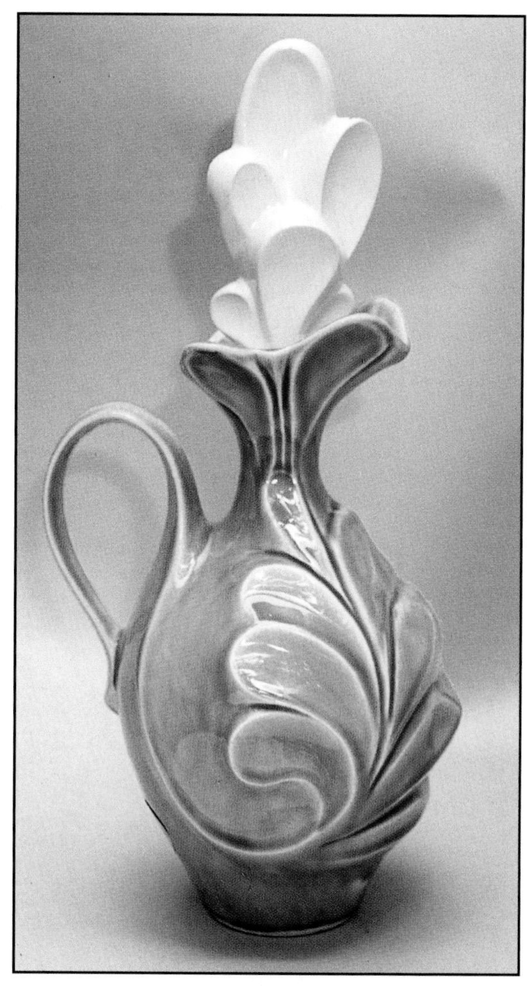

45. Pitcher with Stopper from the Morano Line. 12". 1967. A very rare piece. $100.00 – 125.00.

46. Teddy Bear Planter 5" x 4". Cute planter from the Floraline Line. Marked Floraline. One of the more elusive Floraline pieces! Production colors as pictured and also with a blue bear. $80.00 – 110.00.

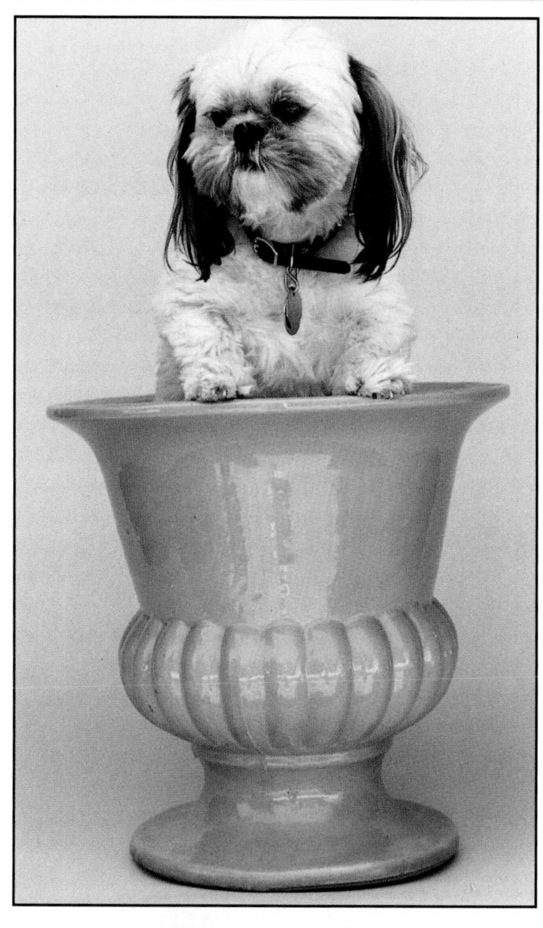

47. Large Urn 15". 1961. Marked McCoy. Produced in green or white. Looks just the right size for Sophie! $150.00 – 200.00.

48. Vase 14". 1959. Marked McCoy. Produced in green gloss or white matt. A tall elusive vase with nice detail. $100.00 – 125.00.

49. Madonna Planter. 7" x 6". Rare planter from the Floraline Line. Marked Floraline. Produced only in white. $200.00 – 250.00.

50. Decanter from the Wine Cellar Line 13¾" tall. 1973. Marked USA. From the 1970s, this is definitely still a scarce bird! The eyes are easily lost, make sure they are the originals. $60.00 – 80.00.

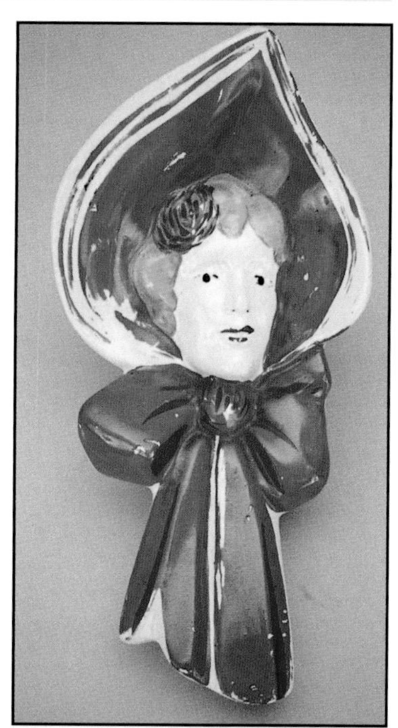

Lady with Bonnet Wall Pocket 8" long. 1940s. Marked McCoy. Pictured in four photos in variety of non-production decorations. $75.00 – 200.00.

Right: Lady with Bonnet, shown signed by an employee. Owner of this wonderful wall pocket is Edna's son. $350.00 – 400.00.

Fan Wall Pocket 8½" x 8". Mid-1950s. Shown in two photos. This wall pocket is decorated with a great non-production glaze combination and has a different top construction. This may have been the first style tried with a later decision to add the support rib as shown on the standard blue example. Standard $75.00 – 90.00; rare two-tone $300.00 – 400.00.

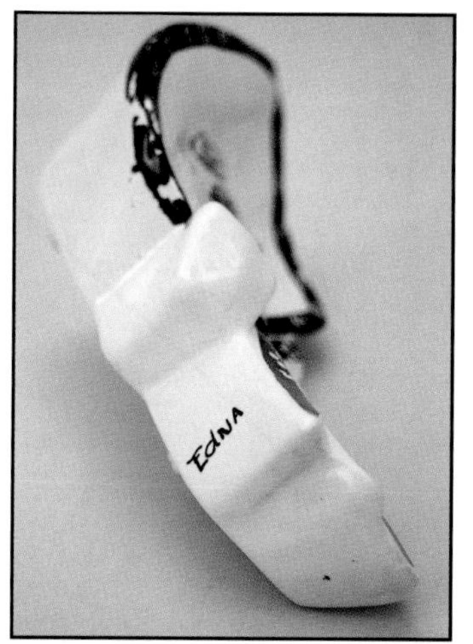

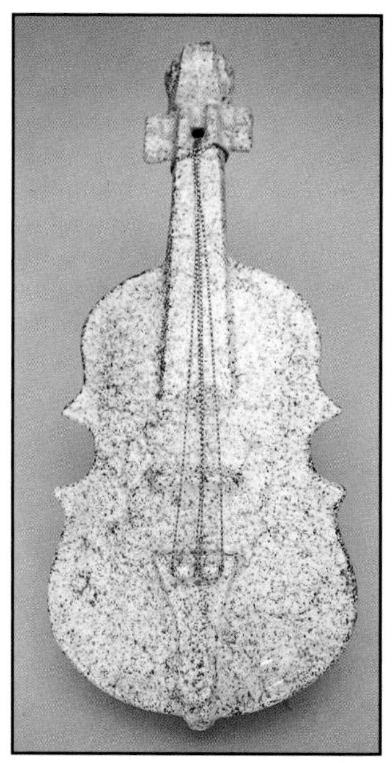

Above left: Violin Wall Pocket 10¼". Mid-1950s. Marked McCoy. Pictured with unusual finish; possibly the first of the Gold Fantasy line which would fit the timing of the era. $150.00 – 200.00.
Above center: Clock Wall Pocket. Body about 8" long. Mid-1950s. Marked McCoy. Pictured with a standard coloring combination, but numerals had the brown glaze wiped away before firing. Standard decoration $100.00 – 150.00; with unglazed numerals $150.00 – 200.00.
Above right: Clock Wall Pocket, same mold. Pictured in non-production glaze coloring combination. $250.00 – 300.00 (without damage).

Leaves and Berries Wall Pocket 7" long. Early 1940s. No mark. Shown in two different aqua/green glaze colors. $200.00 – 300.00.

Flower Wall Pocket 6" square. Late 1940s. No mark. Shown with wonderful underglaze decoration. Standard glazes $35.00 – 50.00. Special decoration $200.00 – 250.00.

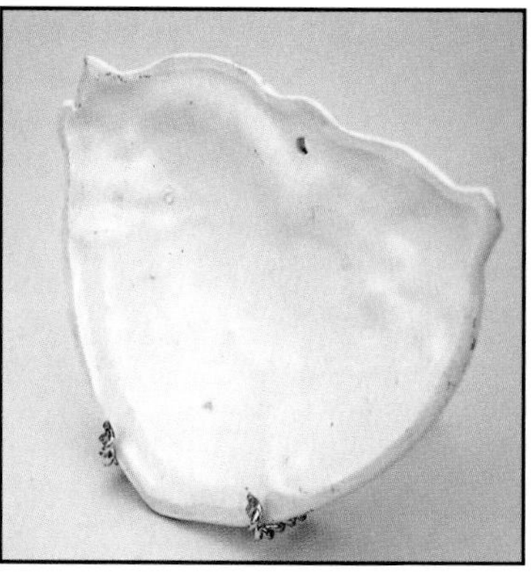

This is a wall piece made from the Heart Vase of the 1940s. This took time and great care to make. Decorated with cold paint. About 6" from top to bottom. $250.00 – 300.00.

Right and below: Umbrella Wall Pocket 8¾" long. Mid-1950s. Marked McCoy. Pictured right in standard green glaze and yellow handle instead of usual white handle. Below example with non-production glaze. Green with yellow handle.$90.00 – 100.00. Green marbleized glaze $150.00 – 200.00.

Leaves with Berries Wall Pocket. About 9" long. Late 1940s. Marked McCoy. Non-production piece; extremely rare. $1,000.00+.

Above and right: Standard Pear Wall Pocket 7" x 6". Early 1950s. No mark. Pictured with pear-shaped portion in oxblood type glaze with formula reference on back. Standard wall pocket $70.00 – 85.00. With glaze formula $100.00 – 125.00.

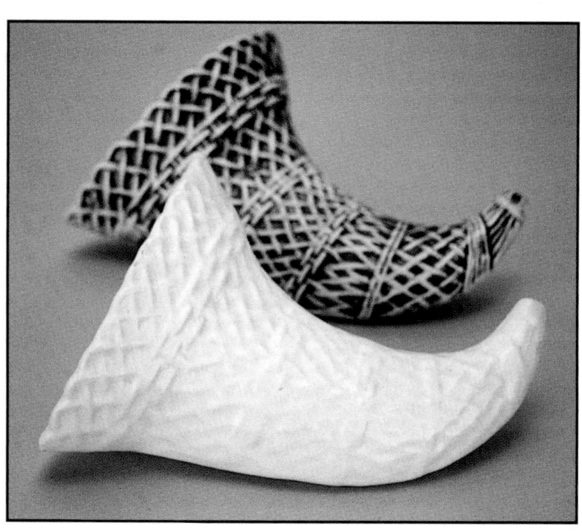

Cornucopia Wall Pocket 8" long. Mid-1950s. Marked McCoy. Ivory with green decoration standard; front all-white coloring not catalogued. Standard $75.00 – 90.00. White $100.00 – 150.00.

Magnolia Vase with non-catalogued factory hole for hanging. 8¼" long. 1953. Marked McCoy. $200.00 – 250.00.

Mailbox Wall Pocket 7" long. Mid-1950s. Marked McCoy. Shown with fabulous cold paint decoration non-standard. Standard (no cold paint) $90.00 – 100.00. Cold paint decoration $150.00 – 200.00.

Tongue Wall Pocket 9½" long. Early 1980s. No mark. Shown with uncommon decoration decal. $75.00 – 90.00.

Trivet Style Backing for Wall Pockets. About 8½" long. Early 1950s. Marked McCoy. This backing was not produced in white. $30.00 – 40.00.

Lovebirds Wall Pocket 8½" long. Early 1950s. Marked McCoy. Shown with unusual cold paint decoration. $100.00 – 125.00.

With only a few exceptions, gold trim pieces were done outside the Nelson McCoy Company after the original glaze firing. Shafer is the most commonly known company that did this 23K decorating. Many of these pieces are quite rare and are high on the Want Lists of many collectors. See Volume I, page 180, and Volume II, page 114, for additional information and pieces.

Beautiful Dragonfly Planter 7½". 1956. Marked McCoy. $150.00 – 200.00.

Scoop with Mammy planter 7½" long. 1953. Marked McCoy. $200.00 – 250.00.

Vase with lower handle design and Vase with Bird, 9" and 8" respectively. 1950s and late 1940s. Marked McCoy. $85.00 – 120.00 each.

Rabbit and Stump Planter 5½". 1951. Marked McCoy. $150.00 – 200.00.

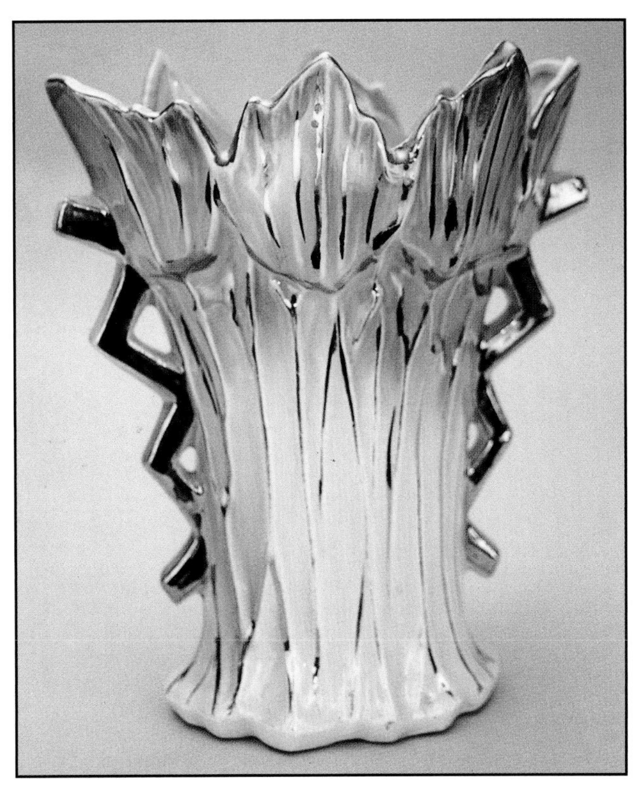

Petal vase 9". 1955. Marked McCoy. $300.00 – 350.00.

Dragonfly Planter (see page 130) with Jeweled Planter 8½". 1956. Marked McCoy. Jeweled Planter: $100.00 – 125.00.

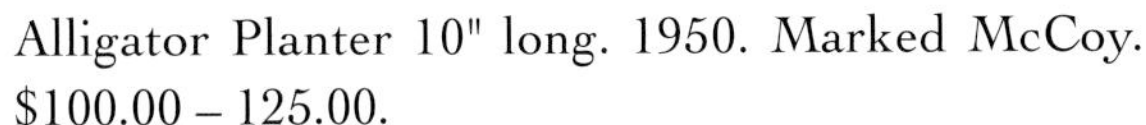

Alligator Planter 10" long. 1950. Marked McCoy. $100.00 – 125.00.

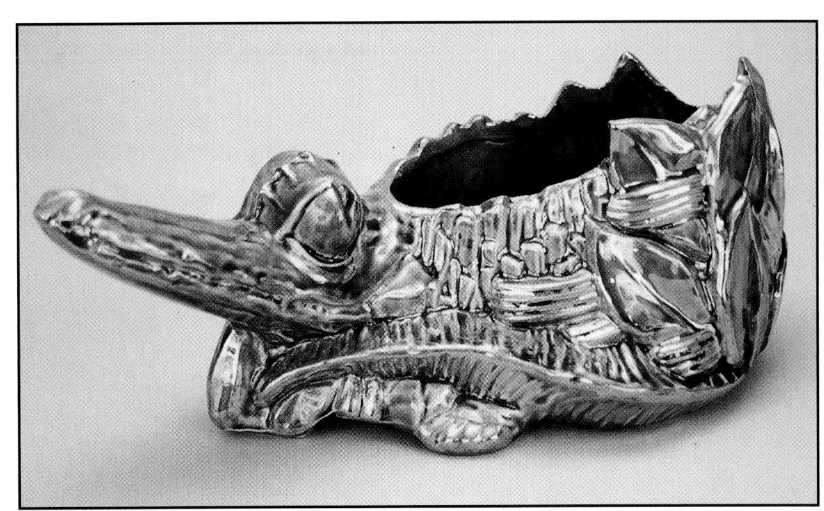

Fawn Planter 12" x 8". 1954. Marked McCoy. $350.00 – 400.00.

Flower Bowl with Grapes 10½". 1954. Cowboy Hat Planter 8". 1956. Both marked McCoy. Flower Bowl $90.00 – 100.00. Hat $65.00 – 90.00.

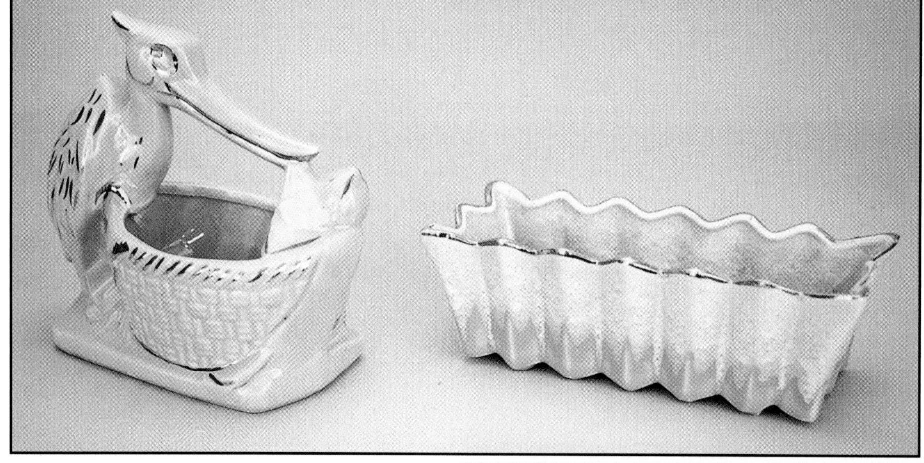

Stork Planter 7½", and Planter 8½". Both 1950s and marked McCoy. Stork Planter $80.00 – 100.00. Planter $40.00 – 50.00.

Lamb Planter 8½", 1954, and Shell Planting Vase 6". 1940s. Both marked McCoy. Lamb $90.00 – 110.00. Vase $100.00 – 125.00.

Hyacinth Vase 8". 1950. Marked McCoy. $200.00 – 250.00.

White Grapes Wall Pocket 7" x 6". Early 1950s. No mark. $300.00 – 400.00.

Clock Wall Pocket. 1952. Marked McCoy. Double rarity here with the yellow glaze clock and the gold trim decoration. $250.00 – 300.00.

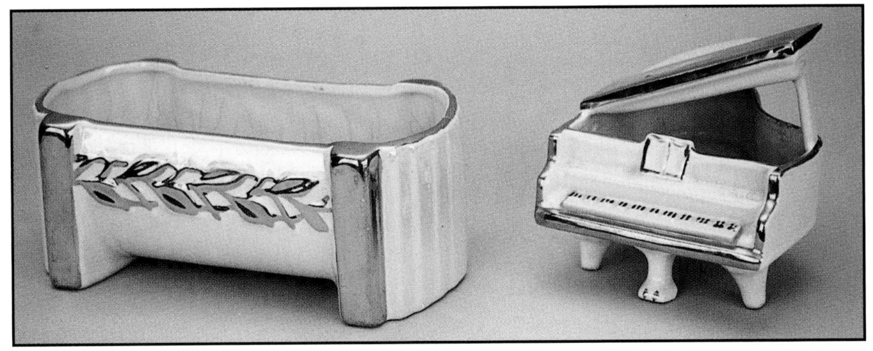

Sand Butterfly Trough 8½". 1940s. No mark. Piano Planter 5" x 6". 1959. Marked McCoy. Trough $60.00 – 75.00, Planter $150.00 – 200.00.

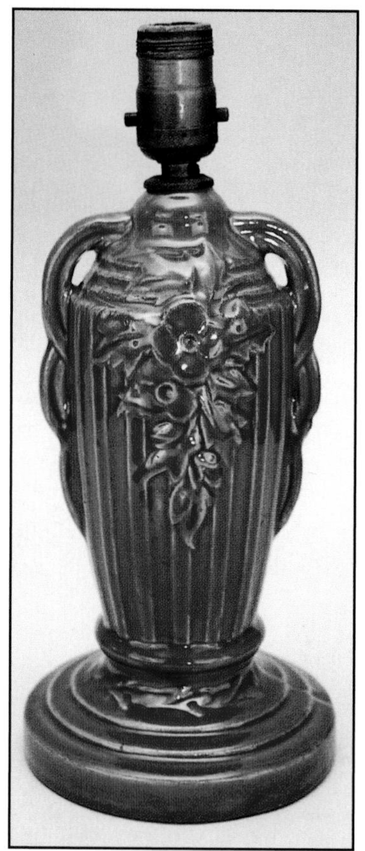

Floral Design Lamp. Pottery base, 10" tall. Late 1930s. $150.00 – 200.00.

Unusual matte glaze Lamp with great handles. 1930s. $150.00 – 200.00.

Leaves and Berries Lamp with socket, 5½". 1930s. Hard to find. $175.00 – 225.00. Similar size lamp without socket even more rare. $200.00 – 250.00.

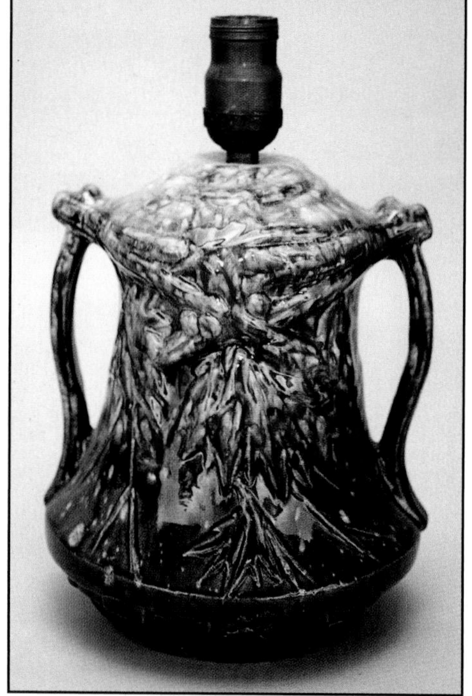

Double Handle Lamp with great handles. 9" tall. 1930s. $150.00 – 200.00.

Floral Design Lamp with handles. 1930s. $150.00 – 200.00.

Lamp with jagged edge handles. 9" tall. 1930s. $150.00 – 200.00.

Fireplace Lamp similar to Cookie Jar design. $75.00 – 100.00.

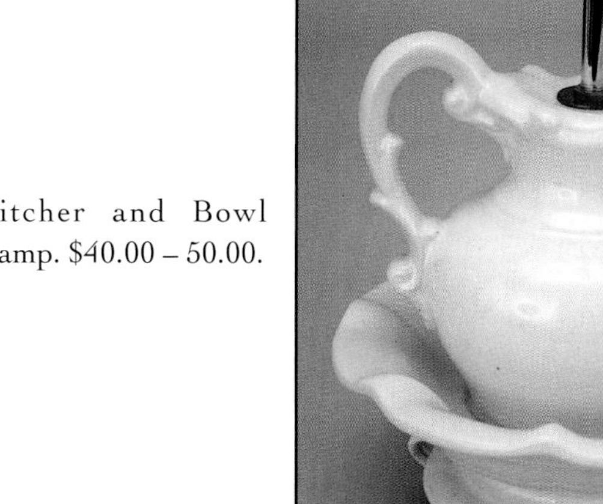

Pitcher and Bowl Lamp. $40.00 – 50.00.

TV Lamp with floral decor. $50.00 – 60.00.

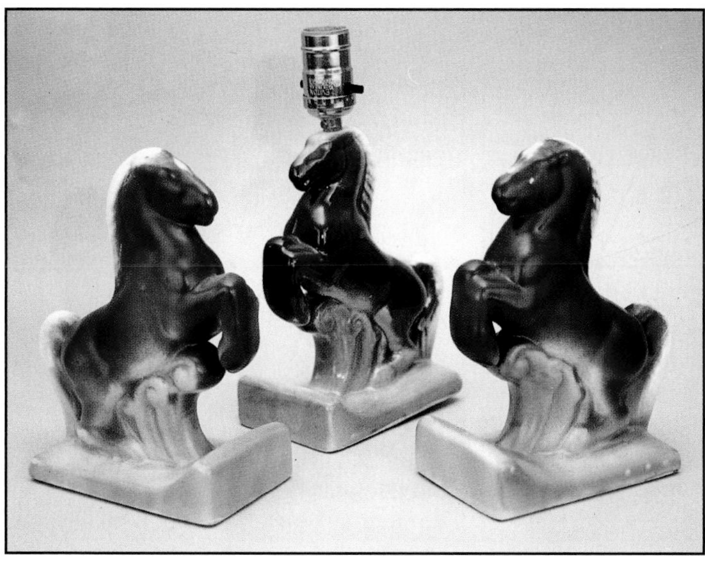

Horse Lamp with unusual glaze decoration. 8" tall. Pictured with Bookends of same design. 1940s. This is not the same lamp base as other horse lamps (see page 207, Vol. I) made in the 1950s. Lamp $125.00 – 175.00. Bookends (Set) $200.00 – 250.00.

Hyacinth Lamp shown in two glaze colors. 8" tall. 1950. $800.00 – 1,000.00.

Squirrel Cookie Jar. 1961. Marked McCoy. Very rare. This photo was taken at Jeff Koehler's auction building in Roseville, Ohio in July of 2000. This was a morning gathering of the small group of lucky collectors who own these jars and brought them to Pottery Week to share and compare details. This is well over half of the Squirrel jars known to exist at this time! Quite a picture of the range of beautiful glaze colorings and decoration. $3,000.00 – 5,000.00+.

Unusual decoration on this Split Trunk Elephant. 1943. Marked McCoy. $350.00 – 400.00.

Oval Plain Jar in burgundy glaze. Marked McCoy. Not an easy find! Early 1960s. $100.00 – 150.00.

Love Birds (Kissing Penguins). 1946. Marked McCoy. Uncommon black glaze color. $200.00 – 250.00.

Clown Bust Jar with wonderful Cope decoration. 1943. Marked McCoy. Standard decoration $50.00 – 75.00; Cope decorated $2,000.00+.

Mammy Jar with "Dem Cookies Sho Got Dat Vitamin A" wording on jar's skirt. 1942. Marked McCoy. One of only two of these jars known to exist. (See pg. 224, Vol. II for the other one in yellow). It may likely be that this jar was never produced. $4,000.00 – 5,000.00.

Cylinder Jars with variety of decoration. 7½" tall. Marked McCoy. $60.00 – 80.00.

Apple Jar with jagged leaf. Marked McCoy. A tough find. $100.00 – 125.00.

Hobnail Heart-Shaped Jar. 1940. No mark. Shown without lid but in non-production glaze color. Complete jar, production colors $400.00 – 550.00. Lime green $600.00 – 700.00.

Jar with wonderful leaf decoration and lid with finial. Hard to find! $250.00 – 350.00.

Pumpkin (Jack-o-Lantern). 1955. Marked McCoy. Rare yellow glaze coloring. $600.00 – 700.00.

Indian. 1954. Marked McCoy. Unusual example with feathers pointed to right and no "cookies" by neck area! Standard configuration $325.00 – 425.00. Rare example pictured $500.00 – 600.00.

Apple with non-production glaze. $150.00 – 200.00.

Rooster with beautiful color decoration. Standard color is white. 1970. Marked McCoy. Standard white $50.00 – 60.00. Special coloring $100.00 – 125.00.

Pear. 1952. Shown in non-production basic green glaze. Marked McCoy. Standard yellow $75.00 – 95.00. Green $100.00 – 150.00.

Kitten on matching pink Basketweave bottom. 1956. Marked McCoy. $75.00 – 90.00.

Leprechaun. No mark. Usually found in red or green but estimated that only 100 made. Examples shown are extremely rare! Green or red $1,800.00 – 2,500.00. Special coloring as pictured $3,000.00+.

Happy Face Jar without the standard "Have a Happy Day" written on pedestal. 1972. Marked McCoy. Standard jar $60.00 – 80.00. Sample as pictured $100.00 – 125.00.

Old-Fashioned Auto (Touring Car). 1962. Marked McCoy. Unusual completely dark glaze coloring. Standard decoration $85.00 – 100.00; Special decoration as pictured $125.00 – 150.00.

Barrel Cookie Jar. 1958. No mark. Shown in gray base color glaze. Usually found in brown. Brown $35.00 – 40.00. Gray $50.00 – 60.00.

Cylinder jar with "lost glaze" decoration. $80.00 – 100.00.

Oaken Bucket. 1961. No mark. Shown in less common green base coloring. $50.00 – 60.00.

Freddy the Gleep. 1974. Marked McCoy. Rare chartreuse green color. Usually found in yellow with red decoration. Yellow $450.00 – 500.00. Green $800.00+.

Asparagus. 1977. No mark. Shown in less common glaze color; normally found in green. Green $40.00 – 50.00. Unusual color pictured $60.00 – 70.00.

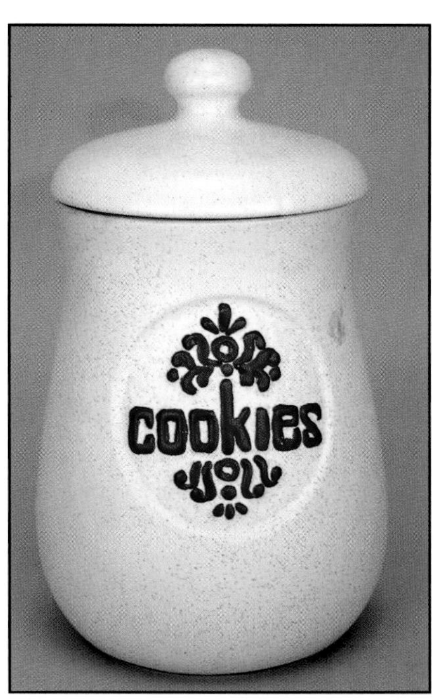

Peanut. 1976. Marked McCoy. Unusual white color with brown detail. Usually found in yellow. Yellow $40.00 – 50.00. White $60.00 – 70.00.

Rag Doll (Raggedy Ann). Marked USA. Pictured in standard decoration on left and slightly different, hard to find decoration on right. Standard $100.00 – 125.00. Uncommon decoration $150.00 – 200.00.

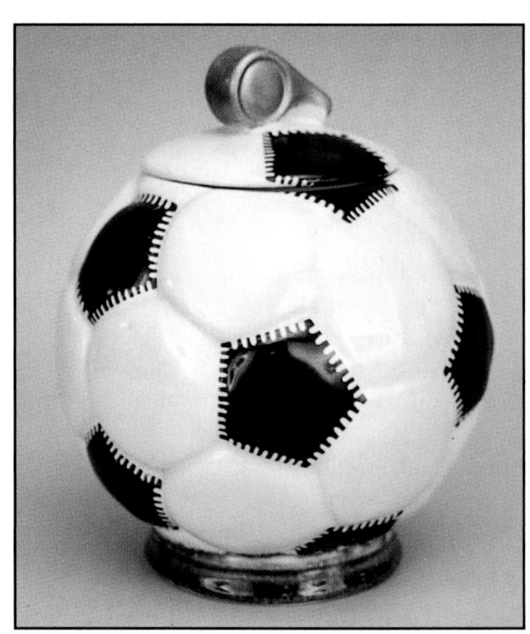

Soccer Ball. 1978. No mark. $1,800.00 – 2,000.00.

Below: Milk Can. Mid-1970s. Some have McCoy mark. Shown with some less common decoration examples. (See pgs. 277 and 280, Vol. II, for others.) $50.00 – 75.00.

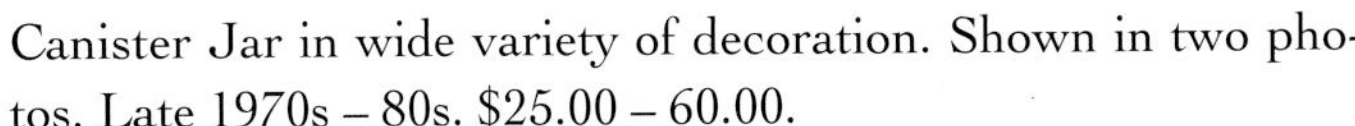

Canister Jar in wide variety of decoration. Shown in two photos. Late 1970s – 80s. $25.00 – 60.00.

Pagoda. 1974. Marked McCoy. Pictured in non-production Christmas decoration. Production decoration was floral decal. Standard $40.00 – 50.00. Christmas $100.00 – 150.00.

Cylinder Jar in two different decorations. 1974. Marked McCoy. $45.00 – 60.00 each.

Cylinder Jar with Christmas decoration. Jar was not produced with this decoration See pg. 300, Vol. II, for another Christmas decoration that has been found on this jar. Not valued due to non-production.

Koala Bear. 1983. Marked McCoy. Pictured in uncommon darker brown glaze; commonly found in a lighter brown (See pg. 289, Vol. II.) Light brown $85.00 – 100.00. Darker brown $300.00+.

Jug with floral decal. 1980s. Marked USA. This jar usually found with Coca-Cola decal. Coca-Cola $80.00 – 100.00. Floral $100.00 – 110.00.

Old-Fashioned Milk Can. Late 1970s. No mark. Found with a variety of decals. $50.00 – 60.00.

Dog House. 1983. Marked McCoy. Pictured in yet another color combination. (See pg. 289, Vol. II, for two others.) $200.00 – 250.00.

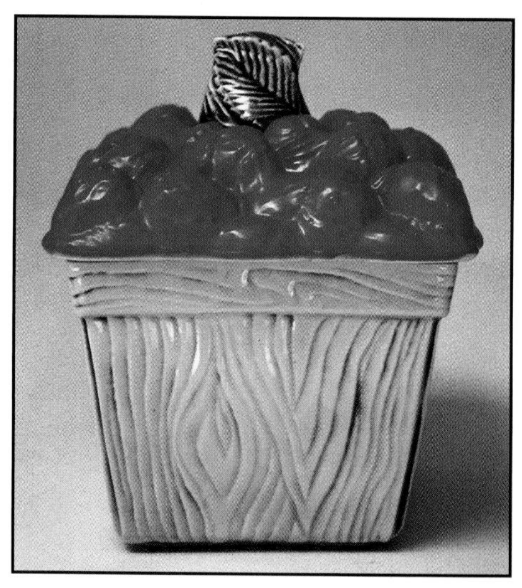

Strawberry Basket. 1978. Marked McCoy. Shown with lighter colored bottom glaze. (See pg. 289, Vol. II, for light brown coloring) Green $40.00 – 50.00. Unusual color pictured $60.00 – 70.00.

Hand Vase from 1940s, 8¼" tall in standard gloss green glaze. Pictured with reproduction piece in white with blue bottom decoration and gold trim accent. Both pieces have the NM mark.

Reproductions of McCoy pottery can be frustrating for the collector and disappointing if discovered after a purchase. McCoy cookie jars have had serious attempts at volume reproductions with the goal to make the reproduction jar look just like the original jar in style and glaze color. For McCoy collectors outside the area of cookie jar collecting, the news is better. No attempts at volume reproduction of non-cookie jar pieces have yet been made. However, on an infrequent basis, a reproduction of a piece of McCoy may be found. The fact that collectors are regularly discovering original production pieces with non-production glazes makes these infrequent reproduction discoveries sometimes even more difficult to identify. The following may be of some help in making that decision of whether or not to buy:

Size: Generally, reproductions found have not been made from a mold copying the size of a piece. Instead, the maker has taken an original piece and used that as a pattern to make a mold. As a result, the final product from that mold is a piece that is smaller than the original. A check this, put an original piece next to the piece in question; the result will be obvious. Of course, that form of test will not always be available at decision time.

McCoy mark: If you check for a McCoy mark, this is no verification of the fact that it's an original piece. If the original piece used as the pattern has a McCoy mark, the reproduced product will have that same mark.

Weight: The weight of the piece is also a clue to assist you in your evaluation. Of the pieces pictured in this article, only one (the frog planter) does not follow this rule. Almost always, the reproduction piece will be lighter than the original. If your instincts tell you that the piece seems too light, it's likely a reproduction!

Glaze color and type: A tough issue, but the more one collects, the more knowledge you obtain on glaze types for a given era. If the glaze color seems off, ask yourself if the type of glaze seems right. Is it too thick? Is it too thin or watery? Is it consistent with glazes from the era of the piece you have found?

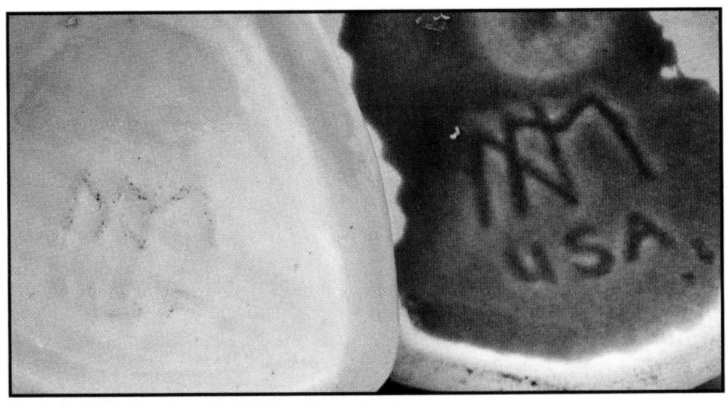

Bottom marks on the hand vases shown above.

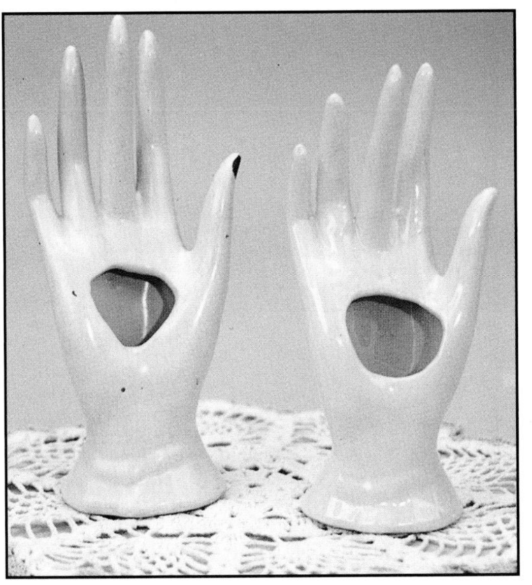

Hand Vase from 1940s, 6½". Usually found dry bottom with no mark but has been found on occasion with NM mark. Pictured with reproduction piece in gloss off-white glaze.

Vase. Late 1940s. 9". Marked McCoy. Pictured with reproduction piece in unusual glaze coloring.

Double Tulip Vase 8". First released in 1948. Pictured with reproduction Vase with a bright lavender glaze and yellow base decoration. Both pieces have McCoy mark.

Leaf Wall Pocket from the mid-1950s in standard blue/pink glaze color combination. 7" x 5½". Reproduction Wall Pocket in white with subtle green shadowing and red decoration on berries. Both pieces have the McCoy mark.

Color of the clay: Look at the bottom of the piece and specifically at the non-glazed surfaces: What is the color of the clay? Study your collection and develop a mental picture of clay color ranges. This may not confirm if the clay color is a definite "yes" for McCoy, but it certainly can help you eliminate some reproductions.

Bottom glaze: Again, look at the bottom of the piece: Is it glazed completely? This condition is frequently found on reproductions. McCoy made many pieces, especially in the late 1930s and early 1940s, that were dry bottom (no glaze on bottom), but rarely will you find a McCoy piece that is completely glazed over the entire bottom.

Detail: Is the mold detail of the piece there? Production pieces made in the latter part of a mold's life do not have clear details. If the detail is poor and the mark on the bottom faint, you may have a questionable candidate depending on the answers to some of the other questions.

Instinct: Possibly the most important: Use your instincts! Get to know your pottery. Hold it, examine it, check those glaze colors, clay colors, the weight, the overall feel of the pottery. If you pick up a piece with unusual coloring and during your examination all the alarms are going off, set it back and chalk it up to experience. Your instincts will almost always be right!

Other reproduction pieces include the Peacock Flower Bowl ornament (HNH Vol. I, pg. 95) reproduced in a gloss off-white glaze, the butterfly shape vase from the early 1940s Butterfly line (HNH Vol. I, pg. 102), and the "Man's Best Friend" Dog Dish (HNH Vol. I, pg. 130).

Flower with Bird Wall Pocket. Late 1940s. 6½" x 5". Both pieces have similar pink glaze flower decoration. However, the reproduction is smaller and the birds are different. The head shape and body width vary from the original. With the similarity in glaze coloring and bird design, this is definitely a tough reproduction to identify without an original for comparison.

Frog with Leaf Planter. 1951. 7½" long. Reproduction Planter in dark rust/brown color glaze. Both pieces have McCoy mark.

Most of these rare and non-production pieces of the Nelson McCoy Pottery Company were not shown in our two earlier volumes. As before, we have not assigned values to these pieces (unless a sold or auction value is known) because there are too few to establish an accurate market value. Let it suffice to say that all of the pieces in this section carry a significant value.

Beautiful Cope designed Candleholders. About 6" tall.

Pedestal and Jardiniere Set in miniature. Likely a salesman's sample. 1920s. Total height 11". No marks. Shown with Duck Flower Bowl Ornament (4" tall) for size comparison.

Cope designed Deer Wall Plaque. Approximately 7" across.

Vase with Leaves and Berries detail. Designed by Walter Bauer. 12" tall.

American Eagle Planter. Late 1940s. Approximately 10" wide. Marked McCoy.

Spittoon. Late 1940s. Marked McCoy.

Uncle Sam with Eagle Planter. 1940s. Approximately 9" wide. Marked McCoy.

V-Vases. 1940s. White vases, no mark. Right vase, 7" tall and marked McCoy.

Hand with Bowl Planter. Marked NM.

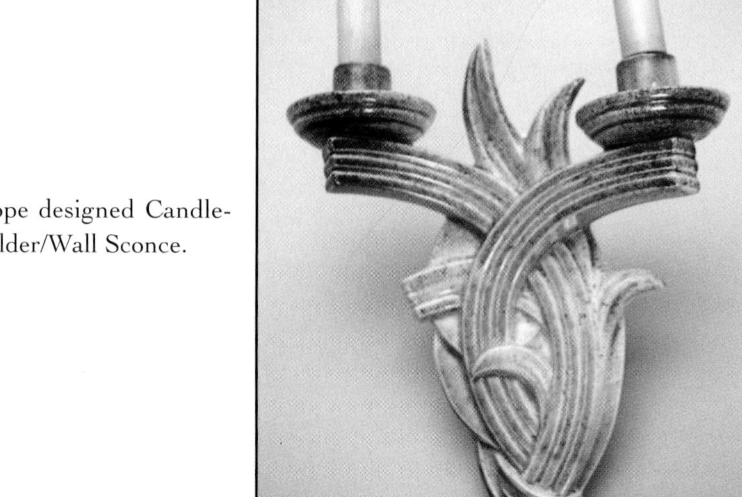

Cope designed Candleholder/Wall Sconce.

Butterfly Flower Holder. Late 1930s. 4" tall. Marked NM. Sold at Koehler Auction in Roseville, Ohio in July, 1999 for $2,100.00.

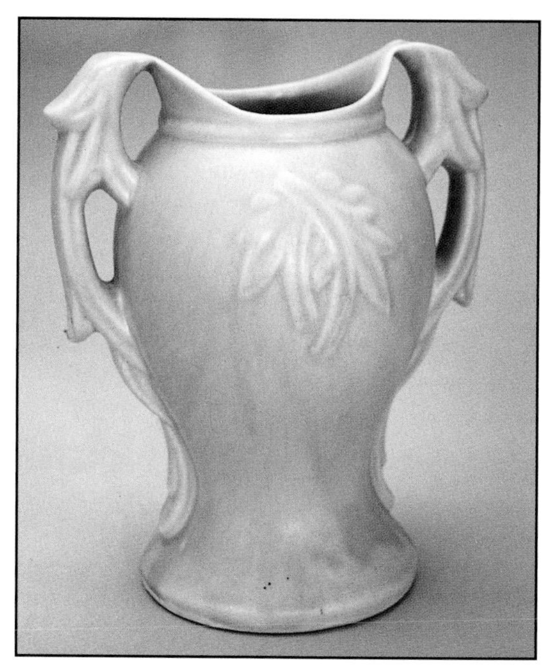

Vase. Late 1940s. About 8". Marked McCoy. Likely a one-of-a-kind as it appears to be a piece where either the mold did not completely fill during the pouring process or a production vase was modified before firing.

Rhinoceros Planter. 1940s. Marked NM.

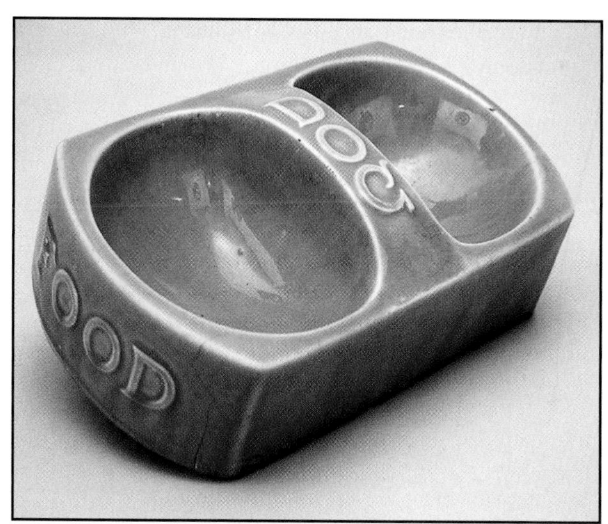

Dog Dish. 1940. About 12" long. Marked NM.

Flower Pot with Saucer. Late 1950s.

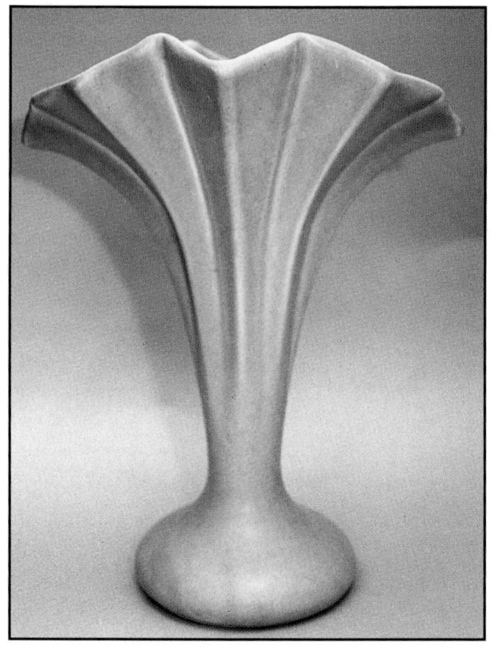
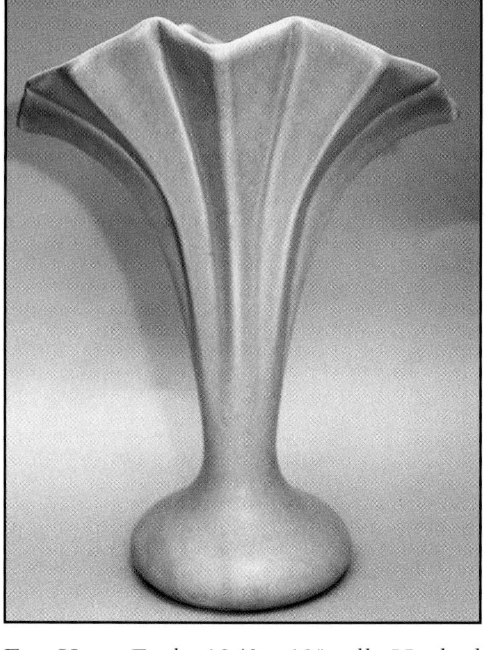

Fan Vase. Early 1940s. 12" tall. Marked USA.

Angelfish in non-production matt coral glaze. 6" tall. 1940. No mark.

Covered Casserole. Cope design. Marked McCoy.

Dog Planter. Early 1940s. Marked NM. Similar to rare Cat Planter, pg. 205, Volume II.

Leaf Design Candy Dish. 6" x 5". Right photo shows the McCoy mark.

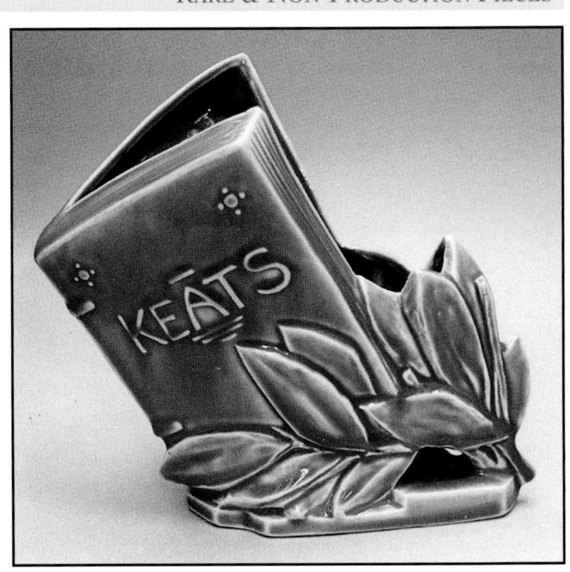

Keats Planter with both sides pictured. Marked McCoy.

Cow Pitcher. 1940s. Marked McCoy.

Pig Archer Pitcher. 1940s. Marked McCoy.

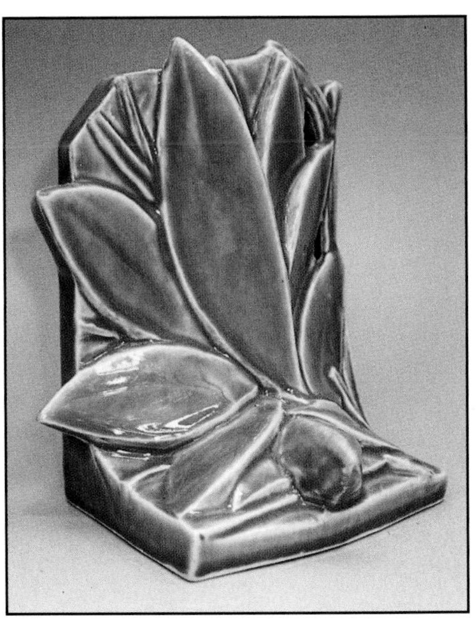

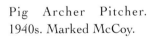

Lily Bud Bookend. Early 1940s. Marked NM.

Dog Creamer. 1950s. Marked McCoy.

General MacArthur Batan Pitcher, shown in two glazes. 1940s. Marked McCoy.

Great Duck Design Pitcher. Marked McCoy.

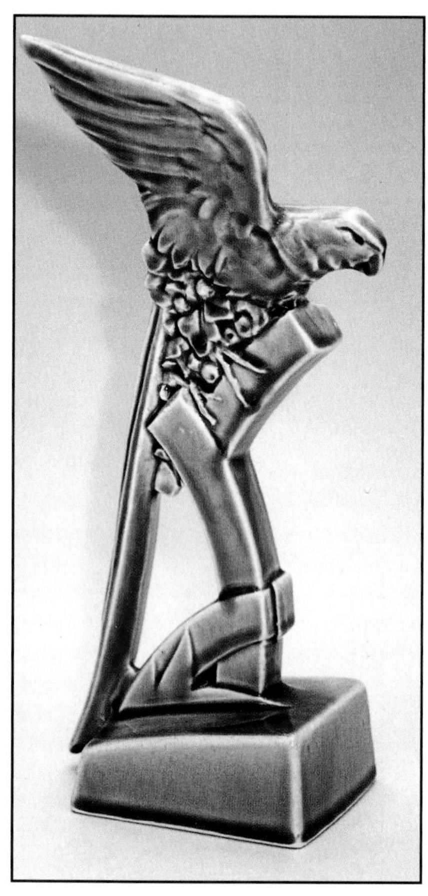

Wonderful perched bird figural piece. About 10" tall.

Pitcher with leaves and vine detail. Marked McCoy.

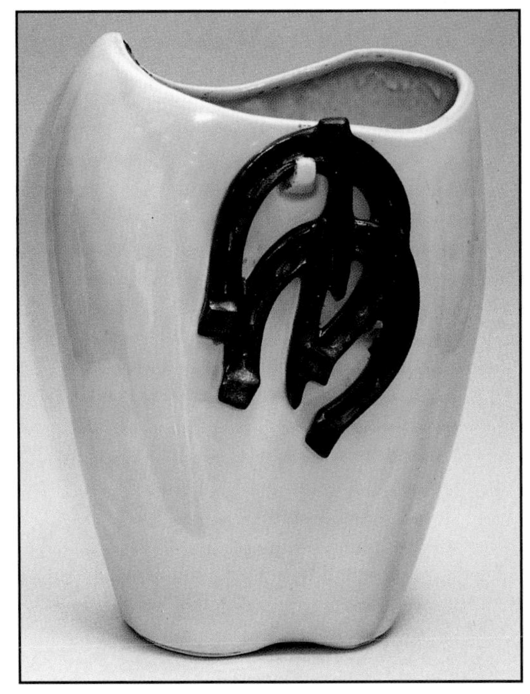

Vase with Horseshoe Decoration. About 11" tall. Marked McCoy. Early 1950s.

Left: Three Bird Plaques, Cope Originals. Approximately 6" x 8".

Bud Vase. 6" tall. Late 1940s. Marked McCoy.

The Cookie Jars pictured on this page were not production jars and are all highly desirable by McCoy Cookie Jar collectors.

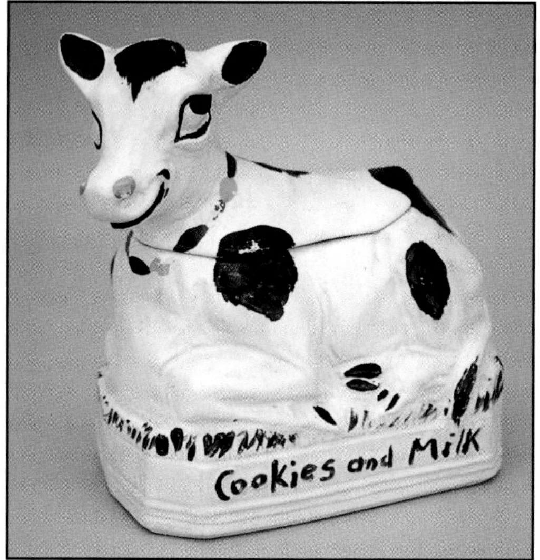

Reclining Cow (Cookies & Milk). Only two are known to exist! The white jar with black detail decoration here and a brown decoration example (see pg. 298, Vol. II) sold for $10,000.00 at auction in 1998.

"Tony Veller." Marked NM. Pictured with Cope decoration. This jar reportedly sold for $10,000.00 in 1998.

Pine Cone Jar. The base of this jar is similar to the Mr. & Mrs. Owl Jar. This is the only known example of this jar with the Pine Cone cover.

Choo Choo with Smoke Jar shown in gray and blue colors. 1974. A red color version sold at auction in 1998 for $4,600.00. (See pg. 299, Vol. II.)

Clown Riding Pig with Cope Decoration. 1940s. Marked McCoy.

Lamb Planter. About 7" wide. Marked McCoy.

Leaves and Berries Vase with beautiful underglaze decoration.

Robin Hood Mug and Robin Hood Planter. Both marked McCoy.

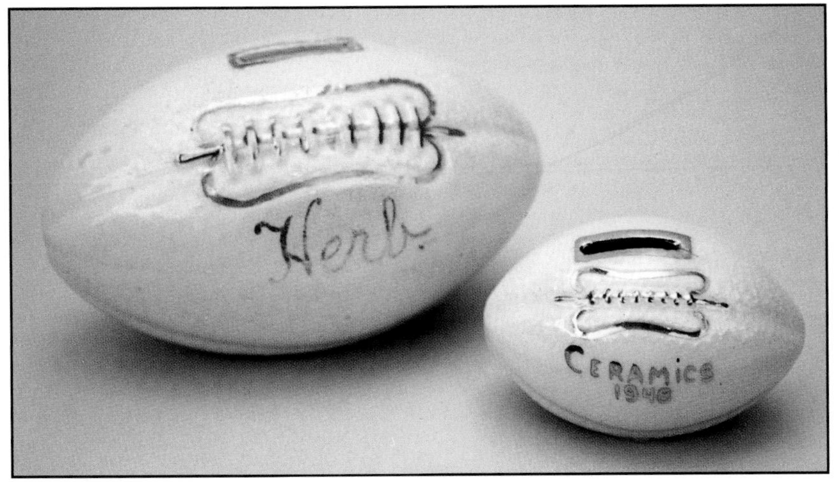

Football Bank from the late 1940s. Approximately 3" in length. Larger one shown for size comparison.

Cope Plate with Leaves and Grapes Design. About 6" in diameter. Sold for almost $2,000.00 at Koehler Auction in Roseville, Ohio in July 2000.

Vase with Pine Cone Decoration. 10" tall. Late 1940s. Marked McCoy.

Planters with Pine Cone Decoration. 1940s. Marked McCoy. Below about 10½" long, Planter above slightly shorter.

Stained Glass Jardiniere. 1950s. About 5" in diameter. Marked McCoy.

Stained Glass Planter. 1950s. About 7" long. Marked McCoy.

Pansy Ring. Approximately 10" in diameter.

Planter with applied birds. About 8" wide. Late 1940s. Shown in three different glaze combinations. Marked McCoy.

Noel Planter. 1940s. Marked McCoy.

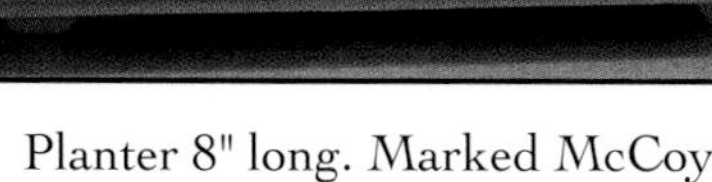

Planter 8" long. Marked McCoy.

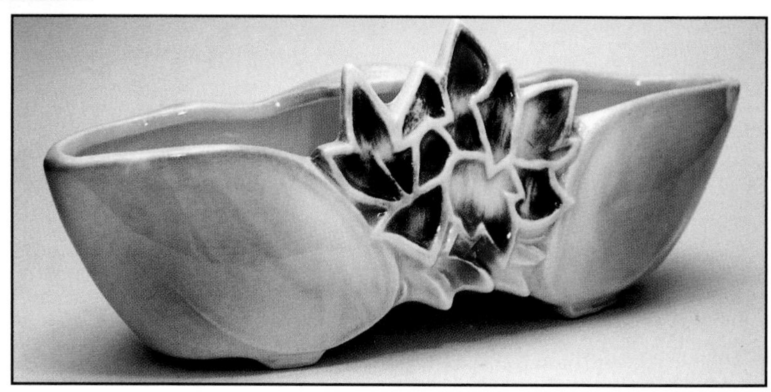

Centerpiece Bowl. 1950s. Marked McCoy.

These three 1950s vases are all about 8" tall and are marked McCoy. The vase on the far left sold for $560.00 at the 2001 McCoy Lovers Reunion in Zanesville, Ohio.

Saddle Planter. 7¼" long. Marked McCoy.

Spinning Wheel Planter. 7" long. Marked McCoy.

Donkey with bananas. 8½" long. No mark.

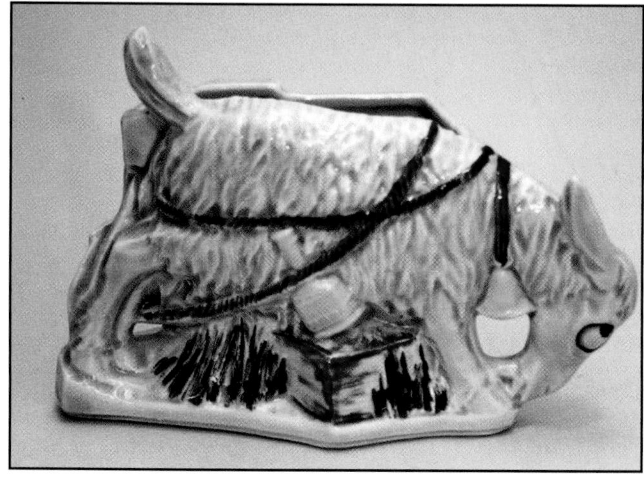

Goat Planter. 6" long. Marked McCoy.

Pail with Birds Planter. About 6" long. Marked McCoy.

Snowman. Cope Original. About 6" tall.

Monkey Head Planter with unusual underglaze decoration and Clown Head, Cope Original. No marks.

Lily Bookend with Cope Decoration.

Buccaneer Mug and Monkey Head Planter in unusual blue color. No marks.

Ashtray/Planter. 7" long. Marked McCoy.

Planter with bow decoration, Cope Original.

Dog in Doghouse Bookends. No mark. Similar to design of production Cookie Jar.

Christmas Tree Bookends.

Bunny Planter. About 8" long. No mark. Rabbit Stump Planter in unusual glaze coloring; marked McCoy. Rabbit Stump Planter shown for size comparison.

Hobby Horse Planter in very rare non-production yellow glaze coloring. Marked McCoy.

Planter. About 7" long. Marked McCoy.

Cleopatra's Boat.
About 12" long

"Y" Bridge Planter. About 3" tall as pictured.

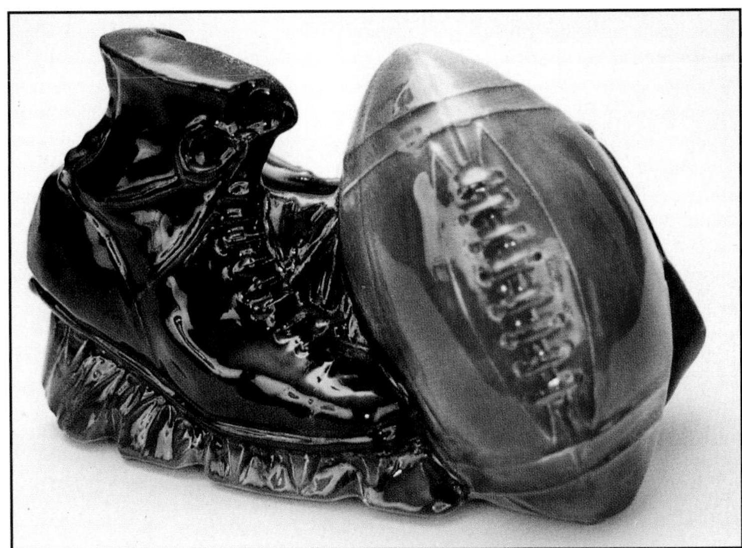

Football and Shoe Planter in rare vivid underglaze colors.

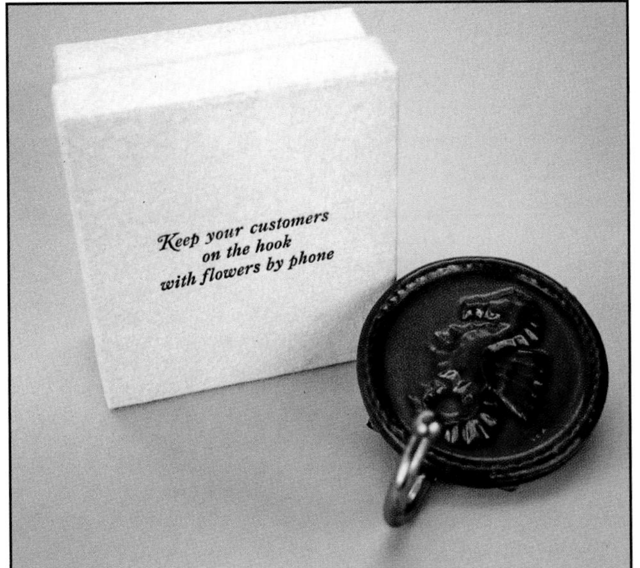

Teleflora Hook Piece with original box. No mark.

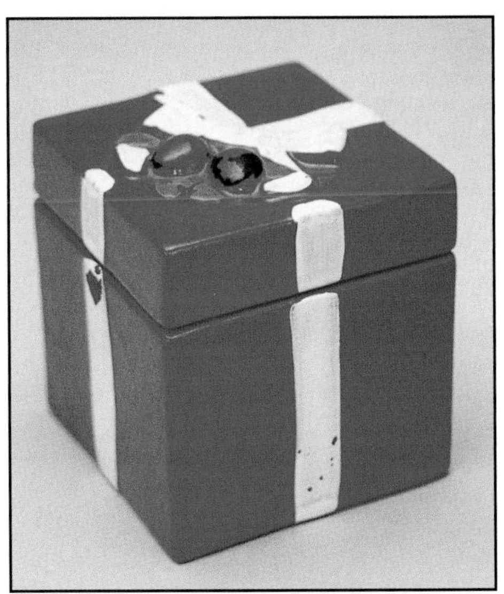

Gift box made for Nieman Marcus. About 4" square.

The Decanter at left was the Landing Module, part of a three-decanter series in 1968 and 1969 commemorating the landing on the moon. This series was made for Thomas W. Sims Distillery of Kentucky. This Decanter is by far the rarest and most difficult to find in the series. The similar Decanter on the right was likely another design alternative and was not produced.

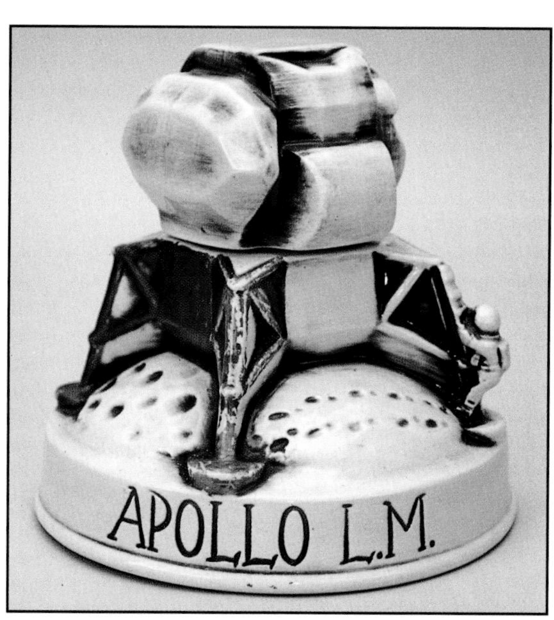

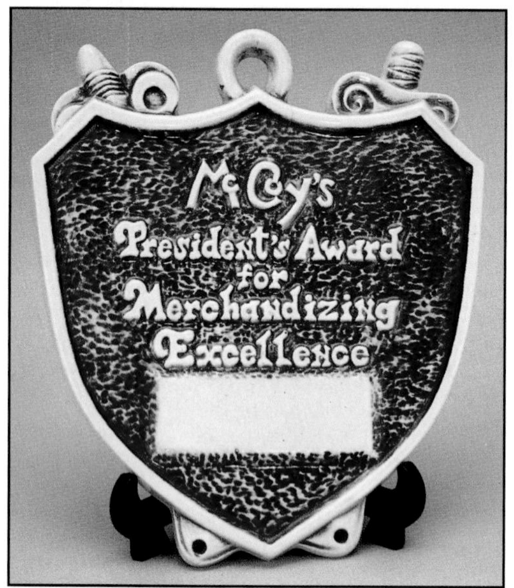

Award Plaque. About 9" tall.

This Pot was made for FTD in 1981 to be their 1982 Mother's Day Pot. It was never produced, and this may be the only example in existence.

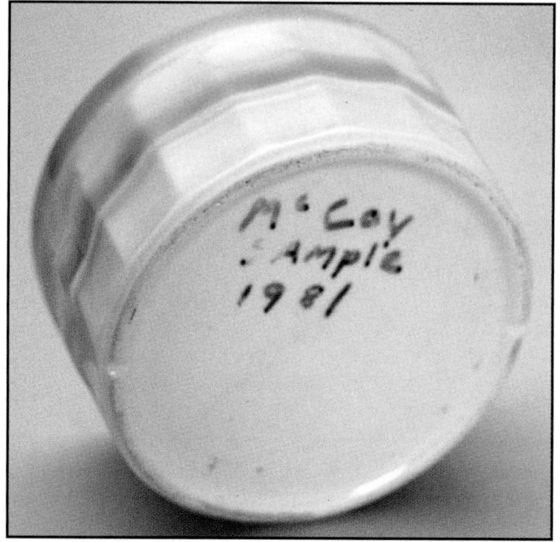

Luminary Piece, all four sides shown in two photos, with special hand decoration of a wide range of marks used throughout the production years of the Nelson McCoy Pottery Company.

Tiger Decanter. Approximately 10" tall.

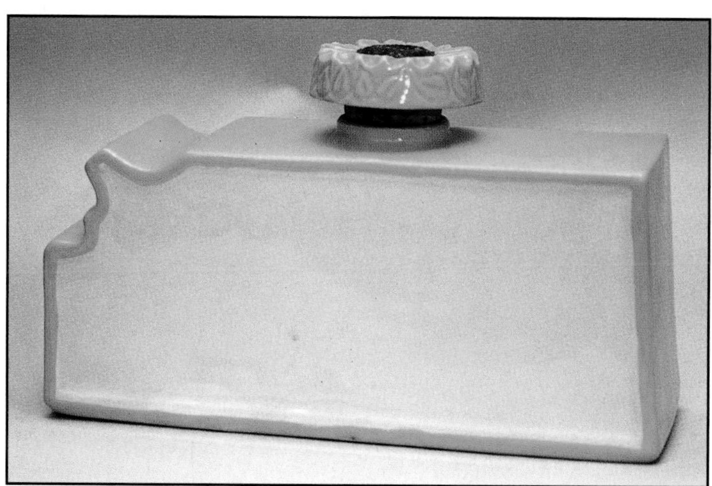

Kansas State Decanter. 1970. About 9" long.

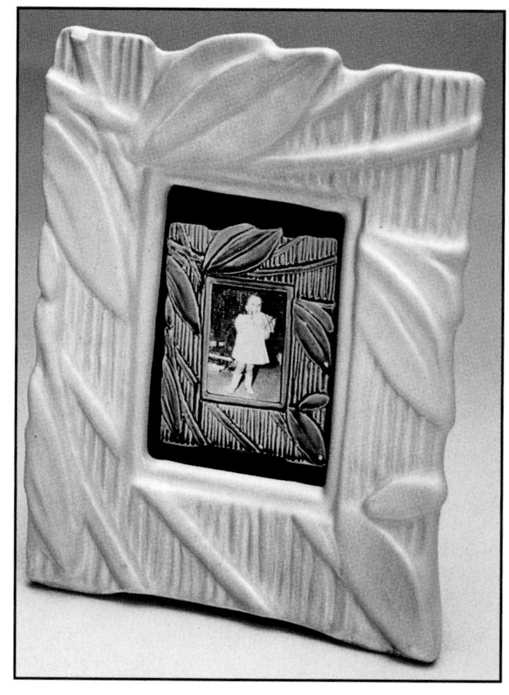

Picture Frame. About 6" x 7". Frame shown with McCoy family photo.

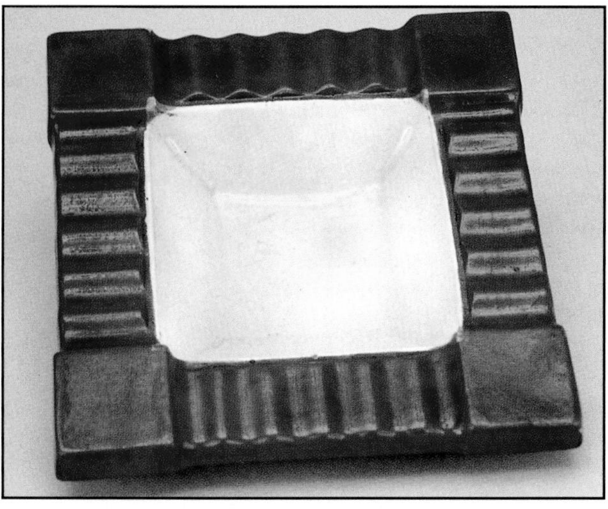

Ashtray 6½" square. 1948. \$25.00 – 30.00.

Ashtray, made from the attached saucer of the pot in photo. Ashtray, \$15.00. – 25.00. 5½" Pot and Saucer, \$20.00 – 25.00.

Bottom of ashtray shown above.

Unmarked 6½" Ashtray. \$25.00 – 30.00.

Square Ashtray. \$25.00 – 30.00.

Ruptured Duck Insignia Ashtray. \$50.00 – 65.00. The original Ruptured Duck was a cloth insignia depicting an eagle inside a wreath. It was worn on uniforms above the right breast pocket of WWII service men and women. It was issued to service personnel who were about to leave the military with an Honorable Discharge. It also allowed them to wear the uniform for 30 days after discharge because of the clothing shortage during the war.

Beautiful Eagle Ashtray. MCP Mark. $100.00 – 125.00.

Yellow Top Hat Ashtray. $20.00 – 25.00.

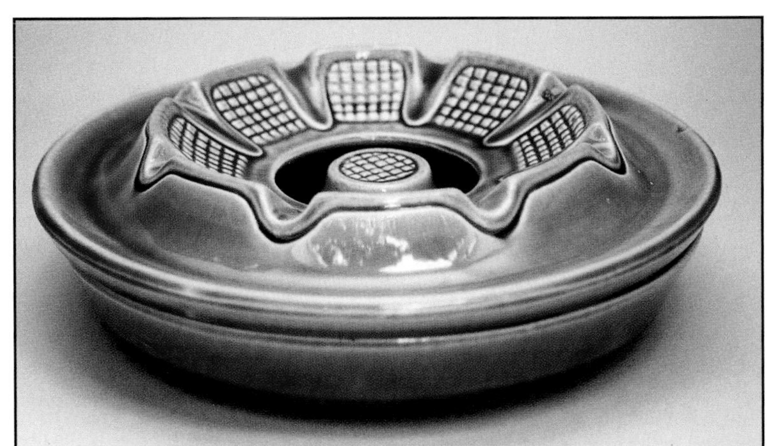

Round Ashtray. $30.00 – 40.00.

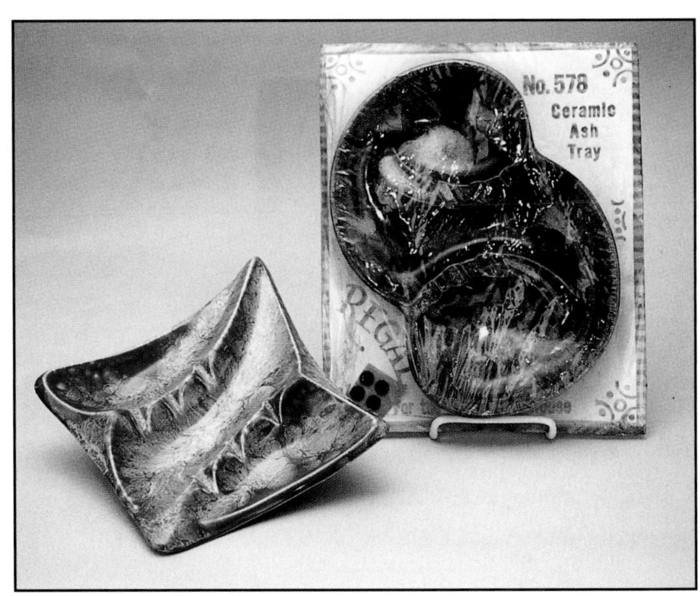

1969 Ashtrays. $20.00 – 30.00.

Spoof Ashtrays. $35.00 – 45.00.

Advertising Ashtray. $25.00 – 35.00.

Spoof Ashtray. $35.00 – 45.00. "Sometimes I wish I'd never been laid!"

Trophy Ashtrays. $30.00 – 40.00.

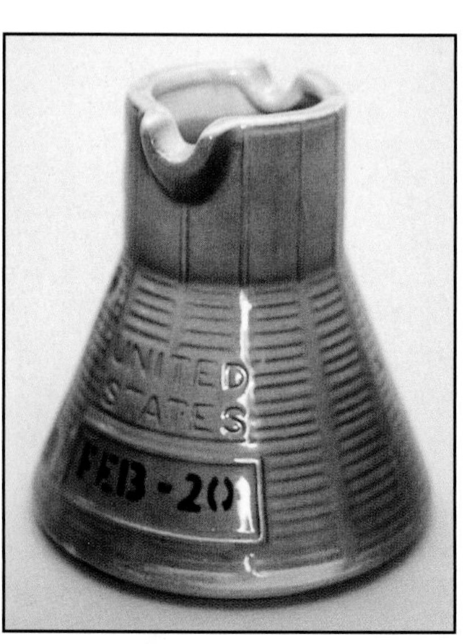

Feb. 20 Space Capsule Ashtray. $40.00 – 50.00.

Hunting Dog Ashtrays. $25.00 – 35.00.

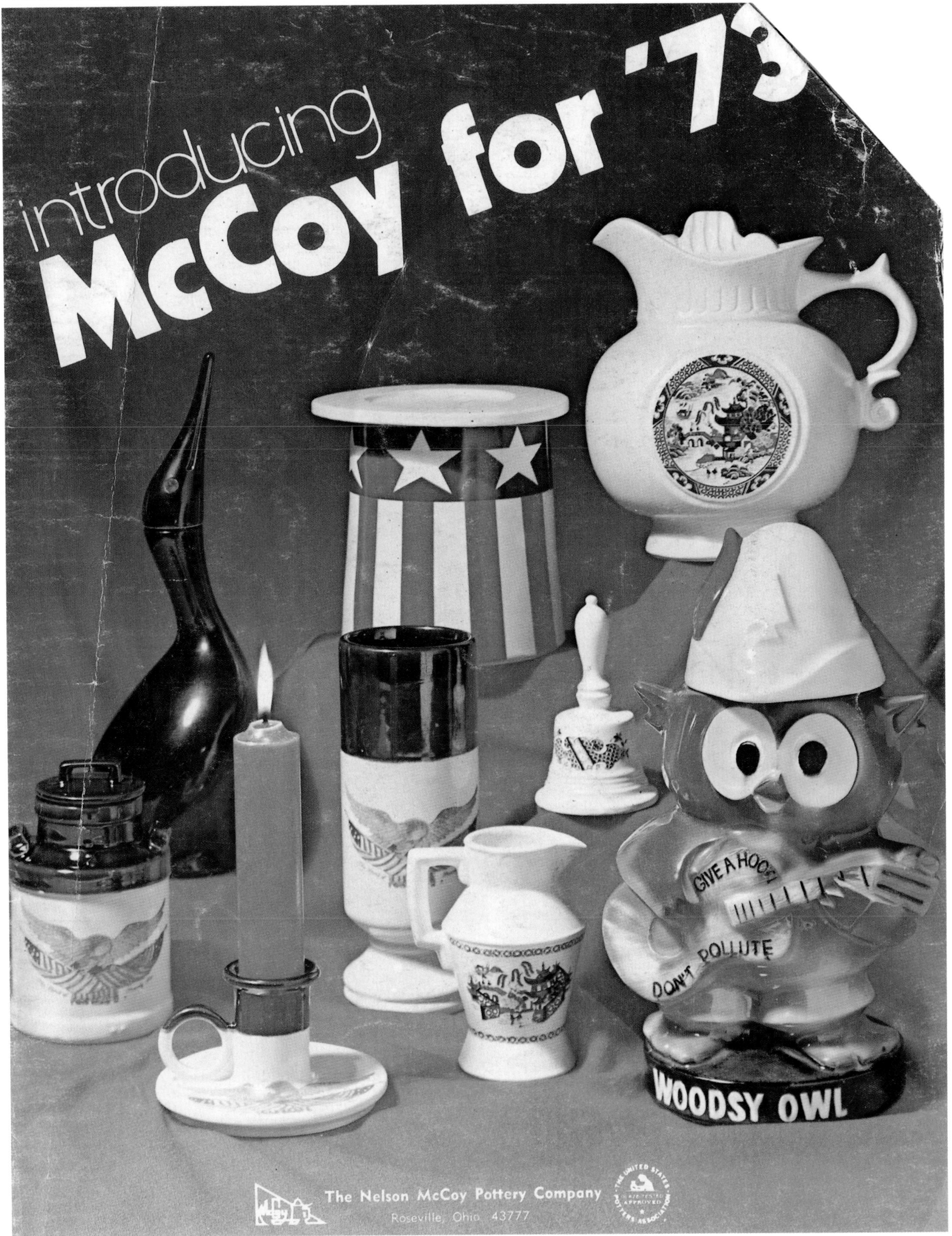
introducing
McCoy for '73
GIVE A HOOT
DON'T POLLUTE
WOODSY OWL
The Nelson McCoy Pottery Company
Roseville, Ohio 43777

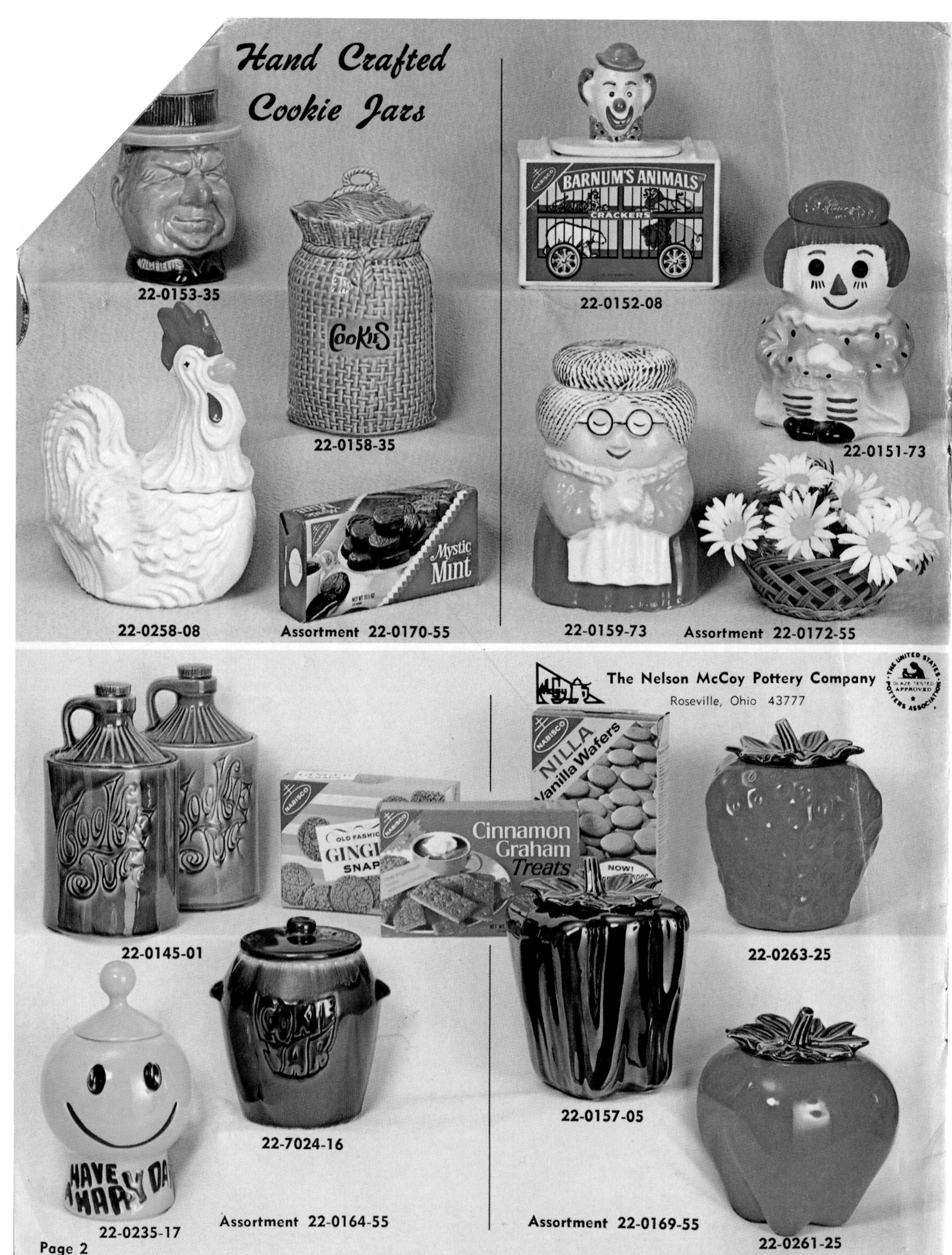
Hand Crafted
Cookie Jars
W.C. FIELDS
22-0153-35
COOKIES
22-0158-35
22-0258-08
Mystic Mint
Assortment 22-0170-55
BARNUM'S ANIMALS
CRACKERS
22-0152-08
22-0151-73
22-0159-73
Assortment 22-0172-55
The Nelson McCoy Pottery Company
Roseville, Ohio 43777
THE UNITED STATES POTTERS ASSOCIATION
GLAZE TESTED APPROVED
22-0145-01
NILLA Vanilla Wafers
Cinnamon Graham Treats
22-0263-25
COOKIE JAR
22-7024-16
22-0157-05
HAVE A HAPPY DAY
22-0235-17
Assortment 22-0164-55
Assortment 22-0169-55
22-0261-25
Page 2

Hand Crafted C
GIVE A HOOT
DON'T POLLUTE
WOODSY OWL

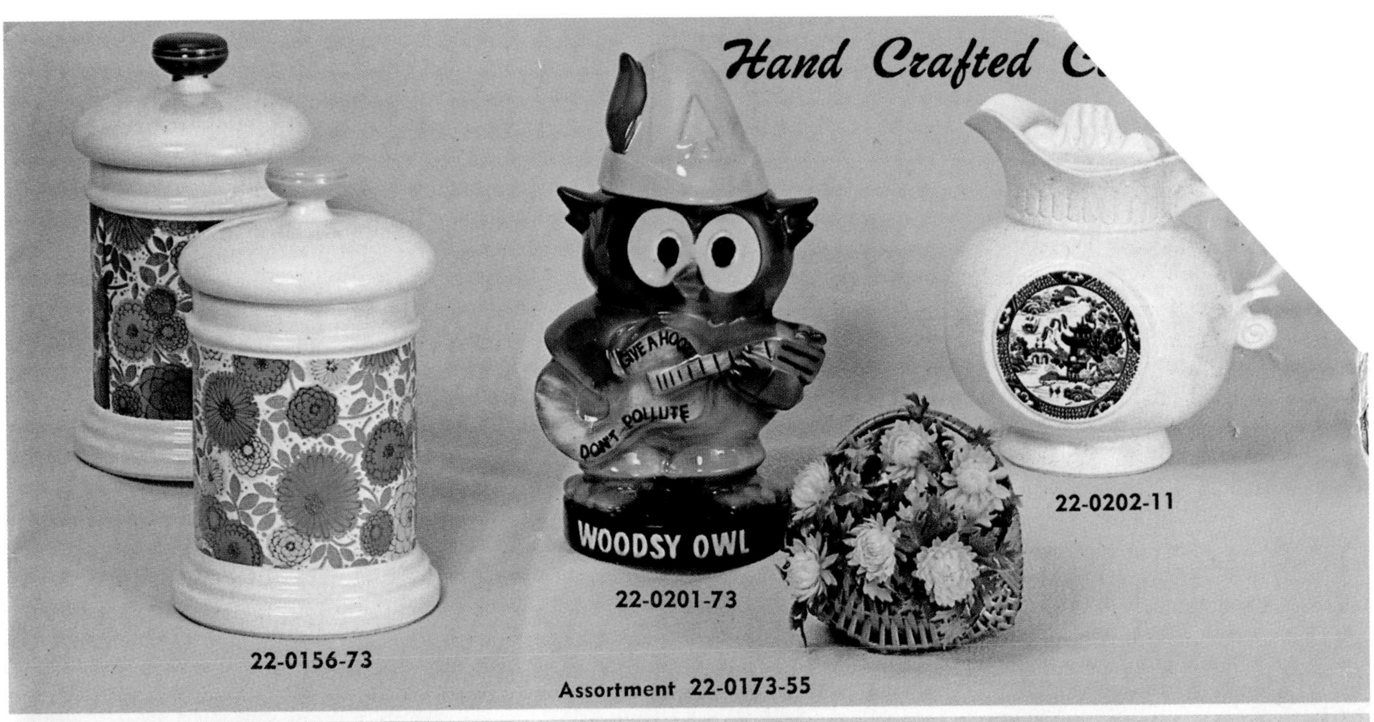

22-0156-73

22-0201-73

22-0202-11

Assortment 22-0173-55

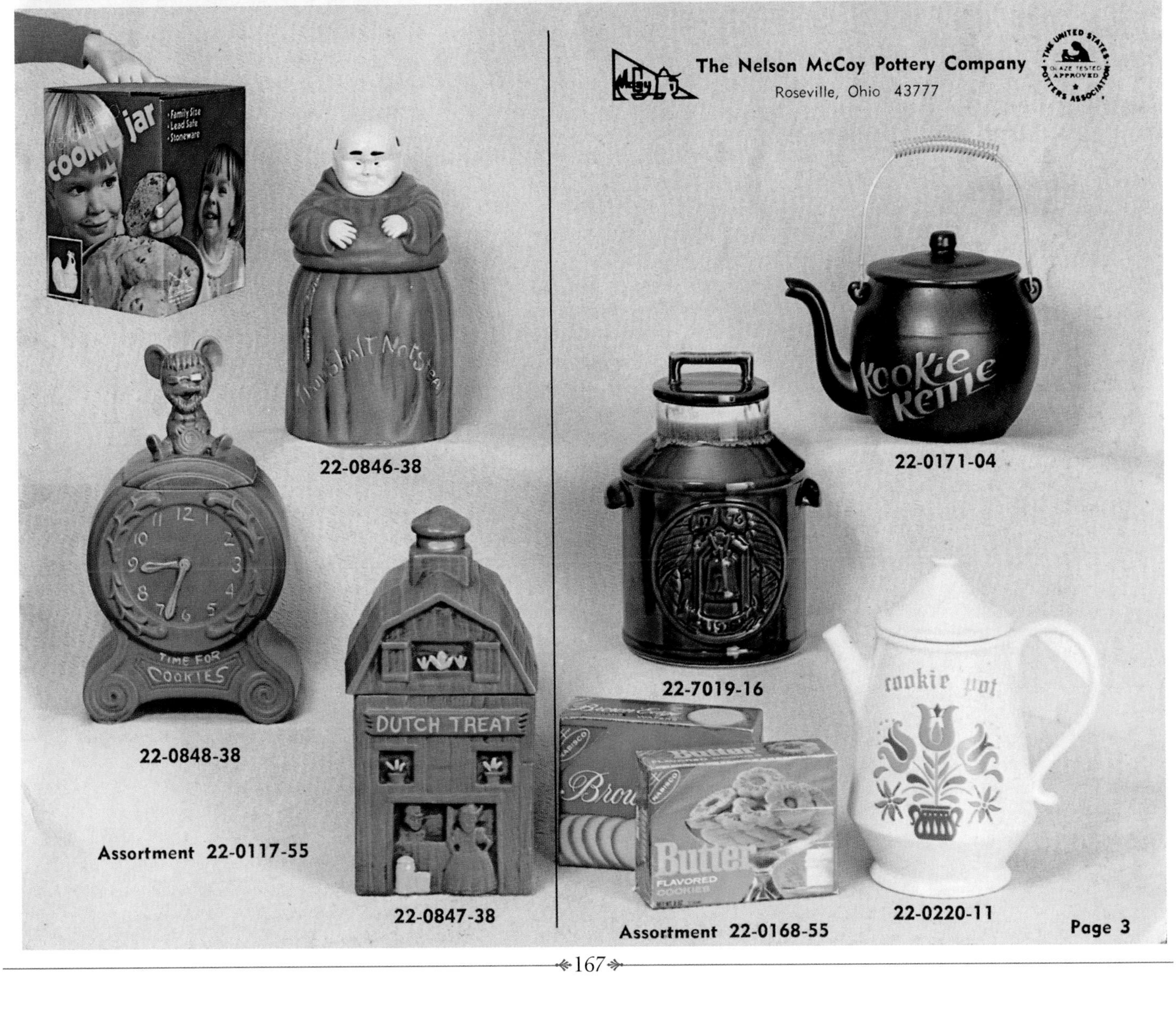

cookie jar
• Family Size
• Lead Safe
• Stoneware
Thou Shalt Not Steal
TIME FOR COOKIES
DUTCH TREAT
Kookie Kettle
cookie pot
Butter
FLAVORED COOKIES
The Nelson McCoy Pottery Company
Roseville, Ohio 43777
THE UNITED STATES POTTERS ASSOCIATION
GLAZE TESTED APPROVED

22-0846-38

22-0848-38

Assortment 22-0117-55

22-0847-38

22-0171-04

22-7019-16

22-0220-11

Assortment 22-0168-55

Page 3

Cookie Jars and Cannister Sets
22-0154-73
22-0345-73
22-0346-73
27-7548-11
28-0333-73
The Nelson McCoy Pottery Company
Roseville, Ohio 43777
28-0352-73
28-0351-73
28-0350-73
22-0200-73
28-0343-73
FLOUR
SUGAR
COFFEE
TEA
22-0207-73
22-0206-17
22-0206-18
Page 4

spirit of '76
28-0335-17
28-0356-73
28-0348-73
28-0347-73
28-0337-73
28-0357-73
Are you keeping up with the growing demand for Early American design? Have what your customers want — stock this new line of Nelson McCoy ceramics. Cookie jars. Candle holders. A full selection of pitchers. Canister sets. Vases. And graduating sizes or individual bean pots. Perfect collectors' items . . . ideal for everyday use. Unique styling will insure fast turnover and high profits!
28-0338-73
28-0336-73
28 0340-73
28-0339-73 (w/o cover)
28-0330-73
28-0331-73
28-0332-73
28-0334-73 8 pc. Cannister Set
28-0333-73
28-0344-73
28-0342-73
28-0341-73
28-0349-73
The Nelson McCoy Pottery Company
Roseville, Ohio 43777
Page 5

blue willow
27-7548-11
27-7547-11
27-7546-11
27-7545-11
27-7542-11
27-7503-55 Bell Assortment
22-0202-11
27-7540-11
27-7543-11
27-7541-11
Colonial design ceramics are the current rage . . . so when your customers ask what you have, you'll want something to fit every need. Like this complete line of Blue Willow. Milk can canister set. Assorted pitchers. Bells. Pitcher-style cookie jar. Milk can cookie jar. And apothecary canister set. Your customers will want to collect them . . . and use them. You will realize high profits from fast turnover.
27-7549-08 6 pc. Canister Set
The Nelson McCoy Pottery Company
Roseville, Ohio 43777
Page 6

Pitchers and Bowls
27-7516-18
27-7516-11
27-7516-06
27-7519-53
27-7512-01
27-7517-11
The Nelson McCoy Pottery Company
Roseville, Ohio 43777
27-7512-01
27-7514-73
27-7512-01
27-7510-11
27-7518-73
27-7510-18
27-7510-06
Assortment 27-7510-01
Page 7

Snack Bowls - Banks - Sprinkling Cans
37-0730-73
28-0295-17
33-0720-73
The Nelson McCoy Pottery Company
Roseville, Ohio
33-0716-01–5½" Rd.
33-0716-01–6" Rd.
33-0717-01–5½" Rd.
33-0717-01–6" Rd.
27-7522-01
27-0055-04
27-0054-01
27-7521-01
SNACKS!
27-7520-11
27-0044-01
Hand Crafted Ceramic Giftware
28-0293-17
28-0290-17
37-0732-59
33-0718-01
33-0719-01
33-0718-01–3¾"
33-0719-01–6¾"
Page 8

Wine Cellar
27-0062-11
27-0060-06
27-0063-13
27-0061-11
27-0050-73
27-0051-73
27-0052-73
27-0058-35
27-0057-35
The Nelson McCoy Pottery Company
Roseville, Ohio 43777
28-7531-15 2 Qt. Copper Kettle W/cover, copper handle. Ind. Box.
28-7532-15 Individual Copper Pot
28-7536-15 Copper Kettle Set—1 large Copper Kettle and 4 Individuals.
Page 9

Brown Drip
29-7009-16
29-7041-16
29-7042-16
29-7043-16
29-7020-16
29-7011-16
29-7007-16
29-7008-16
29-7034-16
29-7052-16
29-7040-16 (w/ cover)
29-7039-16 (w/o cover)
29-7012-16
29-7001-16
29-7016-16
29-7004-16
29-7053-16
29-7005-16
The Nelson McCoy Pottery Company
Roseville, Ohio 43777
29-7002-16
futura
16 Piece Set
29-7003-16
29-7038-16
29-7017-16
Page 10

The Nelson McCoy Pottery Company
Roseville, Ohio 43777
Brown
29-7090-16
29-7084-16
29-7076-16
29-7070-16—9" 29-7071-16—10½"
29-7091-16
29-7054-16
29-7087-16
29-7050-16
29-7072-16—12½"
29-7074-16—14½" 29-7073-16 (Assortment)
Set of 3 includes 9", 10½" and 12"
29-7088-16
29-7023-16
29-7013-16
29-7081-16—9"
29-7082-16—10"
29-7093-16
29-7094-16
29-7067-16
29-7066-16
29-7065-16
Page 11

Accessories
28-0106-37
28-0108-37
28-0110-37
28-0112-37
28-0114-37
28-0317-01
28-0129-37
28-0118-37—12½″
28-0119-37—14″
28-9380-01
28-9381-01
28-0366-01
28-0131-73
28-0132-73
28-0137-01
28-9375-
28-9374-
28-9370-
28-9371-
The Nelson McCoy Pottery Company
Roseville, Ohio 43777
28-0365-08
28-0364-08
28-0363-08
Assortment 28-0368-08
28-0136-01
Page 12

Giftware
36-1039-01
36-1035-01
36-1036-01
36-1035-01
36-1038-01
36-1037 SALAD SET—Contains large salad bowl, four small individual bowls, fork and spoon. (See price page.)
The Nelson McCoy Pottery Company
Roseville, Ohio 43777
36-1034
36-1040
Page 13

38-0032-01
38-0035-01
38-0033-01
Scandia
Line
38-0031-01
38-0034-01
38-0030-01
The Nelson McCoy Pottery Company
Roseville, Ohio 43777
38-0037-01
38-0036-01
38-0677-01
38-0620-01
Page 14

The Nelson McCoy Pottery Co
Roseville, Ohio 43777
38-0615-01
Decorator Vases
38-0616-01
38-0619-01
38-0618-01
38-0036-01
38-0620-01
38-0677-01
Page 15

elson McCoy Pottery Company
Roseville, Ohio 43777
Gold and Silver
24-6034-33
24-2025-
25-6063-44
25-6065-44
24-2030-
50-0557-36
25-6067-44
25-6062-44
24-2032-
25-6066-44
24-2033-
Page 16

Schlitz Steins by McCoy
26-9107-08
26-9106-08
26-9129-08
26-9106-08
26-9112-08
26-9114-08
26-9111-08
26-9109-08
Malt Liquor Stein
Same as Above
No Metal Cover
26-9134-08
26-9132-08
26-9101-08
The Nelson McCoy Pottery Company
Roseville, Ohio 43777
Page 17

English Cavaliers
#6028
40 OZ.
26-6029-01
26-6028-08
Steins
26-6037-01
26-6020-08
26-6035-01
26-6036-01
The Nelson McCoy Pottery Company
Roseville, Ohio 43777
Page 18

The Nelson McCoy Pottery Company
Roseville, Ohio 43777
Beer St
26-6397-08
26-6396-29
26-6042-08
26-6396-29
26-6395-29
26-6039-01
26-6398-98
26-6399-53
26-6398-84
Page 19

The Promotional Line
33-2003
33-1612-55 Ass't
33-1824-55 Ass't
33-0683
33-0611
33-1312-55 Ass't
33-0690
33-2004
33-2002
33-0701
31-0674
33-0697
31-0675
33-2005
31-0676
33-0685
33-1917
31-0673
33-0606
33-0682
Page 20
The Nelson McCoy Pottery Company
Roseville, Ohio 43777

The Tiara Line
The Nelson McCoy Pottery Company
Roseville, Ohio 43777
50-0500-06
50-0546-89
50-0552-06
50-0551-06
31-0636
31-0635
31-0634
31-0672-01
31-0670-01
31-0671-01
31-0628
31-0631
31-0632
31-0633
31-0627
31-0613
31-0667
31-0612
31-1480-01
31-1488-01
31-0637
31-3009-01
31-3014-01
31-3008-01
Page 21

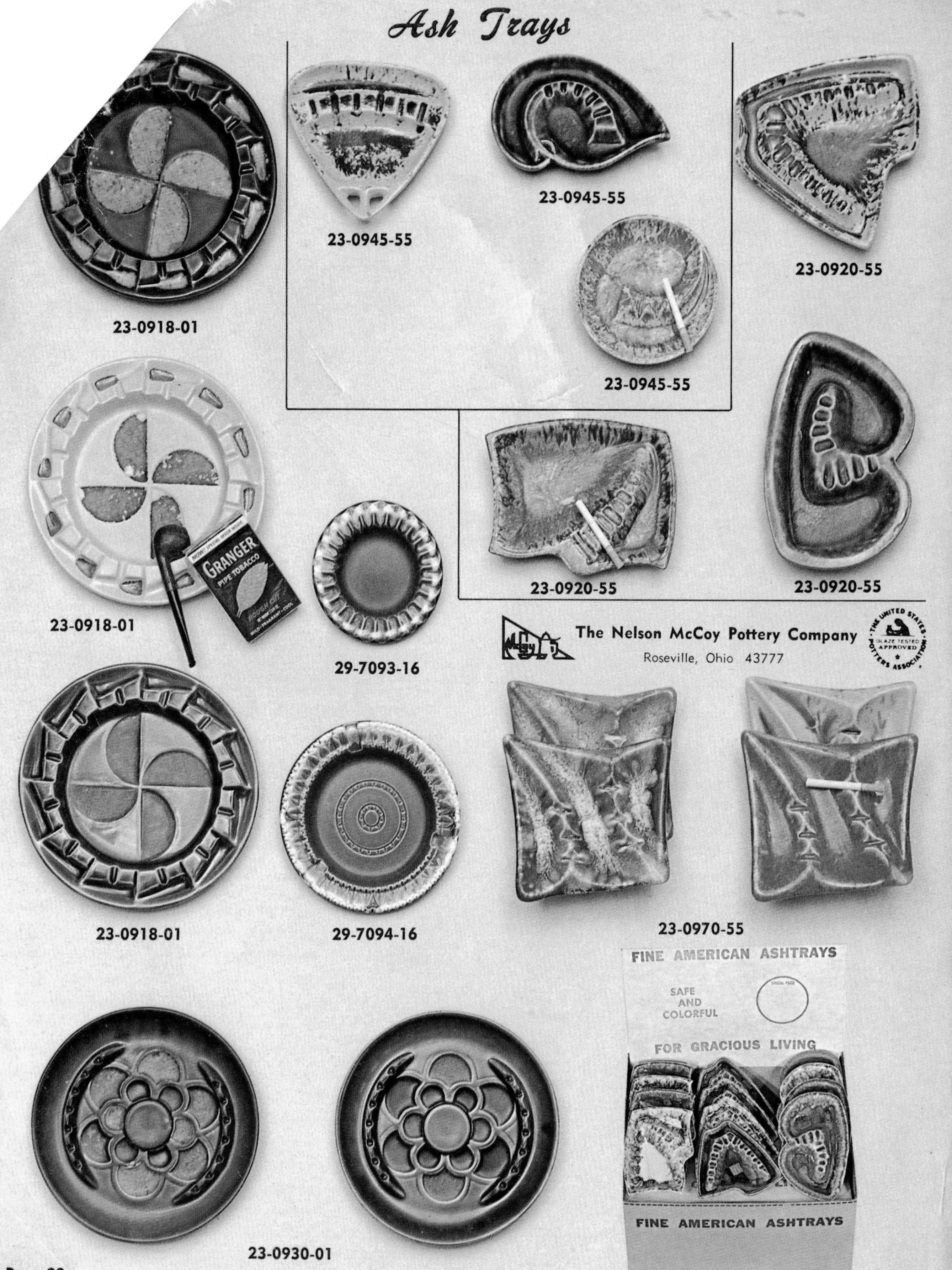
Ash Trays
23-0918-01
23-0945-55
23-0945-55
23-0945-55
23-0920-55
23-0920-55
23-0920-55
23-0918-01
GRANGER
PIPE TOBACCO
29-7093-16
The Nelson McCoy Pottery Company
Roseville, Ohio 43777
23-0918-01
29-7094-16
23-0970-55
FINE AMERICAN ASHTRAYS
SAFE
AND
COLORFUL
FOR GRACIOUS LIVING
FINE AMERICAN ASHTRAYS
23-0930-01
Page 22

Candle Holders
34-0086-01
34-0065-01
34-0078-01
34-0077-01
34-0074-01
34-0020-01
The Nelson McCoy Pottery Company
Roseville, Ohio 43777
34-0087-01
34-0066-01
34-0075-01
34-0067-01
Page 23

Nelson McCoy Pottery Company
Roseville, Ohio 43777
Candle Holders
34-0082-01
34-0082-01
34-0071-01
34-0090-01
34-0071-01
34-0089-01
34-0095-54
34-0097-54
34-0098-54
34-0093-54
34-0096-54
36-0094-54
34-0099-54
34-0101-54
34-0102-54
Page 24
Photography and Lithography by Pappas Brothers, Parkersburg, W. Va.

The Avocado-Capri Drip Line By McCoy
Stone Ware - From Freezer - Oven - Table
8521
8519
915
8514
823
8522
911
913
914
8518
8520
8515
8513
918
8516
916
The Nelson McCoy Pottery Company
Subsidiary of Mount Clemens Pottery Company
Area Code 614 697-7331
Roseville, Ohio 43777

Top left: Early Covered Casserole. $60.00 – 80.00.

Top right: 1979 Western Wear 2½ qt. Pitcher 9" tall. $50.00 – 75.00.

Second left: 1940s – 1960s American Eagle Covered Casserole. Produced for Krug's Grocery & sold with a fruitcake inside. $60.00 – 80.00.

Bottom left: 1979 Western Wear 3⅞" mugs, 10 oz. $20.00 – 25.00.
1979 Western Wear Snack Bowl,10" x 3". $50.00 – 60.00.

Bottom right: 1973 Two gallon Jug with Early American Farmers (Grant Wood's American Gothic) decal. 12½"x 7½". $50.00 – 75.00.

Right: Large Ice Tea Server, 13" high, 1973. $60.00 – $75.00. 1979 Western Wear Mug, 10 oz., 4" high. $30.00 – 35.00.

Left:
Small Server, 9" high. 1973. $50.00 – 60.00. Same mug as in right photo.

1973 Western Theme Snack Bowls.
Left: Double handle snack bowl. $15.00 – 20.00.
Right: Single handle snack bowl. $15.00 – 20.00.

7" Ginger Jar shaped Vase. McCoy mark. $20.00 – 25.00. 4½" Oil Jar similar to the one from the 1940s. Marked McCoy & somewhat hard to find $35.00 – 45.00. 7" Scalloped Container. McCoy mark. $30.00 – 35.00.

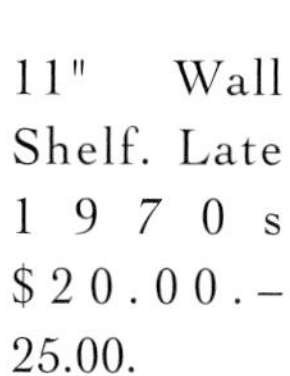

11" Wall Shelf. Late 1970s $20.00.– 25.00.

Happy Face Coffee Mug. $20.00 – 25.00.
Happy Face 14 oz. Beer Mug. $25.00 – 30.00.
McCoy picture puzzle courtesy of John Sweetman.

Happy Face Pitcher 5½"x 4½". $25.00 – 35.00.

Happy Face Planter. $25.00 – 35.00.

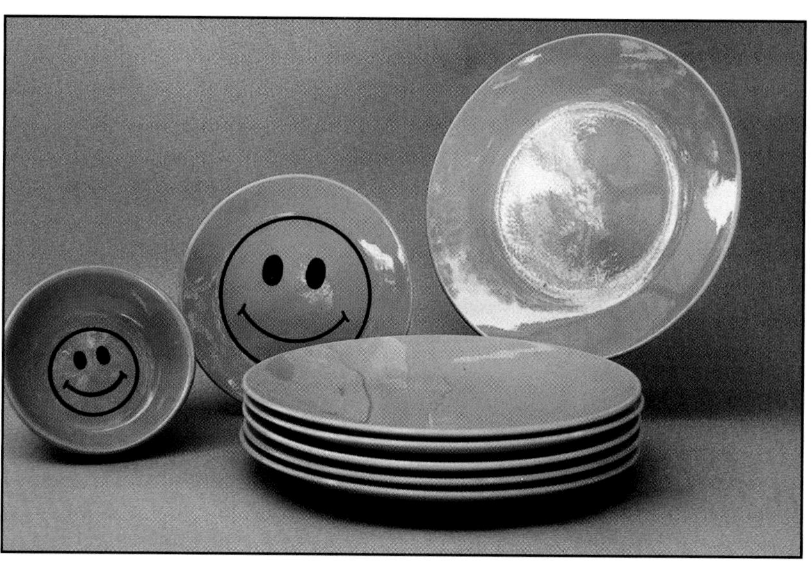

Happy Face 4" Cereal Bowl, $15.00 – 20.00.
Happy Face 7" Sandwich Plate, $15.00 – 20.00.
Happy Face 10" Dinner Plate, $20.00 – 25.00.
(Happy Face cold paint has washed off).

Small Happy Face Bank. $35.00 – 45.00.
New York Savings Bank. $45.00 – 50.00.
Basketball Bank. $45.00 – 50.00.

Assortment of Matchbox Holders. 1970s. $30.00 – 40.00 each.

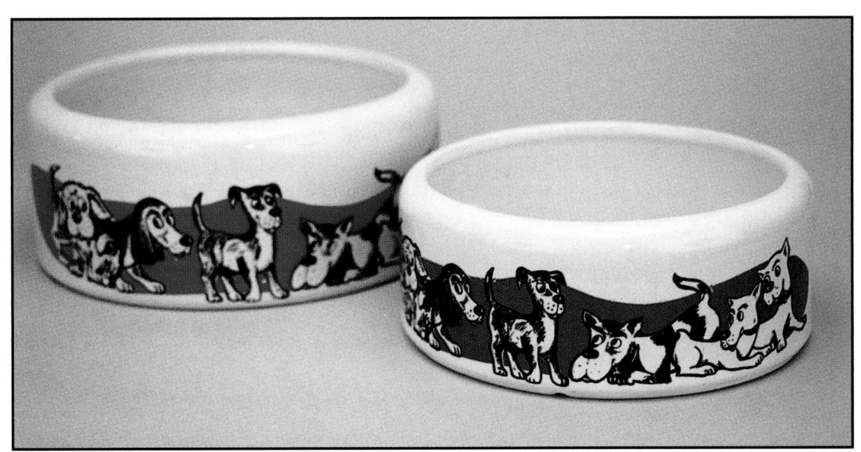

Decal decorated Dog Dishes. Late 1970s. Mt. Clemens mark. $70.00 – 75.00.

1960 Jardiniere in original stand, $8\frac{3}{4}$" $60.00 – 80.00. Also shown without stand on pg. 277, Vol. I.

Covered Casserole. Late 1970s. $40.00 – 50.00.

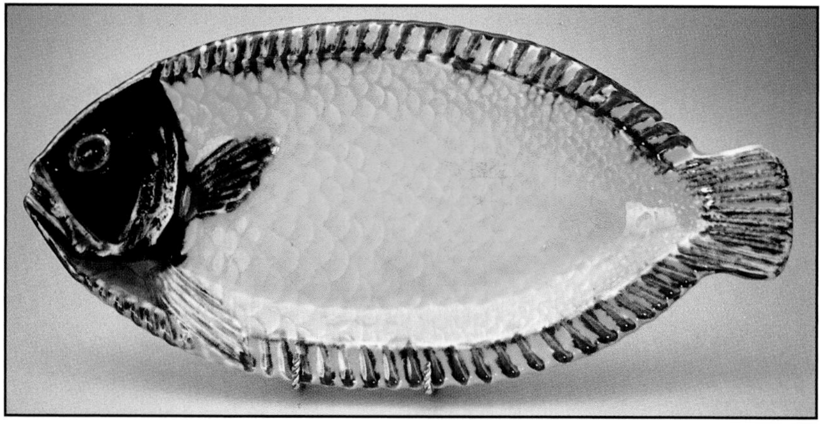

Decorated Fish Platter 18"x 8¼", decorated under glaze. 1973. $150.00 – 200.00. Shown without decoration on pg. 291, Vol. I.

Happy Smile Hanging Basket. Late 1970s. Rare. $75.00 – 80.00.

Decal Decorated Flower Pots. Small $25.00 – 30.00. Produced in 1978. Large $30.00 – 40.00.

Assortment of Trivets, Spoon Holders, Serving Dishes. Late 1970s and early 1980s. Shown in two photos. $10.00 – 25.00 each.

Two-quart Bean Pot with four serving bowls. 1967. Marked Kathy Kale U.S.A. $65.00 – 75.00 set.

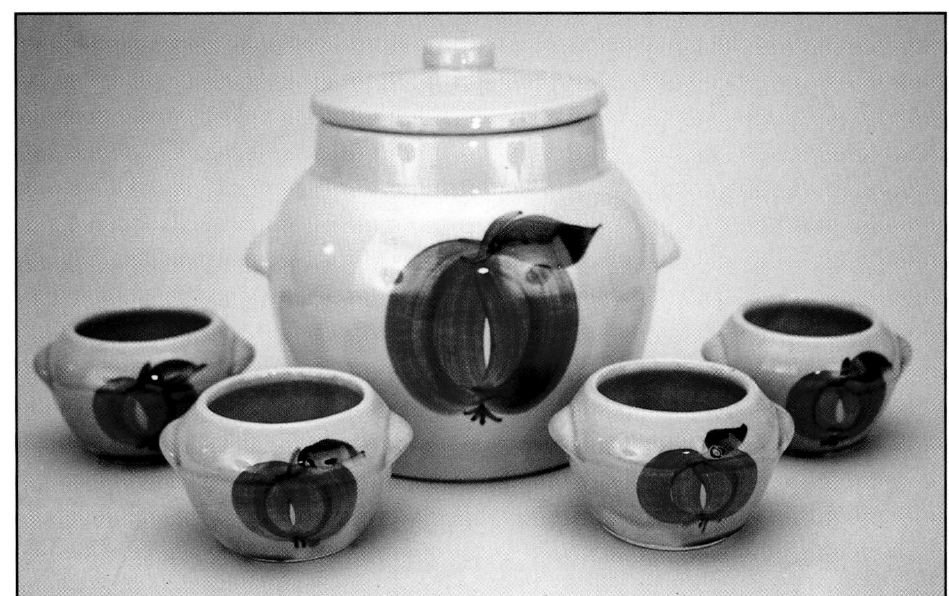

Serving Bowls. 1967. Kathy Kale Design.
6", $20.00 – 30.00.
7", $25.00 – 35.00.
8", $35.00 – 45.00.

Morano Line Serving Dish. #915. 1966. $35.00 – 40.00.

Morano Line Shell Chip and Dip #911. 1966. $35.00 – 40.00.

Plates specifically decorated for McCoy Company Christmas parties and given to plant foremen. A total of about 60 plates were given away. $50.00 – 75.00.

Brown Drip Wine Carafe with Cup. Late 1970s. $20.00 – 30.00. Brown Drip Coffee Mug with Sandwich Plate $20.00 – 30.00.

Blue Windmill Canister Set. $75.00 – 100.00. Four-piece set produced in 1974.

Assortment of Trivets from 1974 – early 1980s. Various shapes and designs. $15.00 – 35.00.

Hostess Line French Casserole. 1973. $10.00 – 15.00 each. Hostess Line Candle Holder. 1973. $7.00 – 10.00.

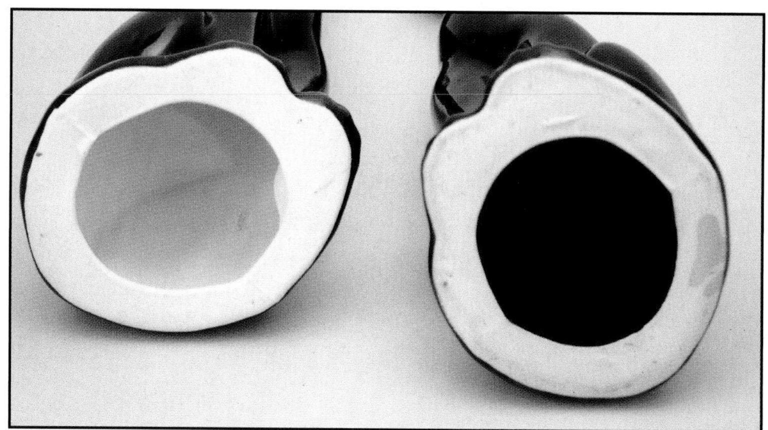

Long-necked Cat Nelson McCoy Figurine pictured on right with identical McCoy Limited Company Cat Figurine on left. The bottoms (above) show the early cat was glazed inside while the newer McCoy Limited version was not. Nelson McCoy $50.00 – 65.00. McCoy Limited $40.00 – 50.00.

Decorated Kitten with ball of yarn planter. $95.00 – 110.00. Decorated Dog Planter. Early 1970s. $95.00 – 110.00. Bottom of Kitten shown (not catalog glaze decoration). See pg. 292, Volume I for production example.

Turtle Serving Dish. 1973. $15.00 – 25.00.

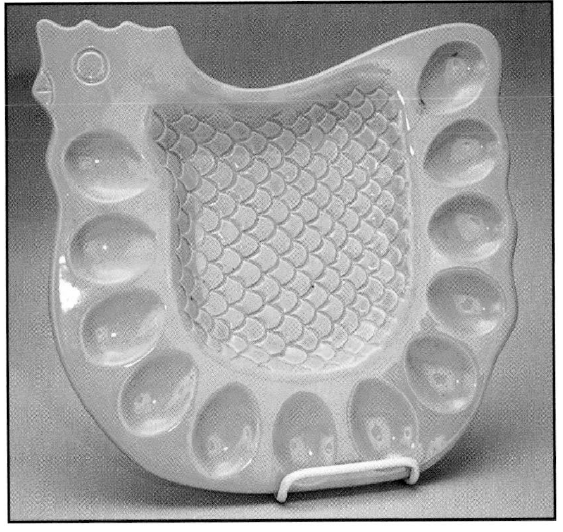

Chicken-Shaped Deviled Egg Plate. 1973. $20.00 – 30.00.

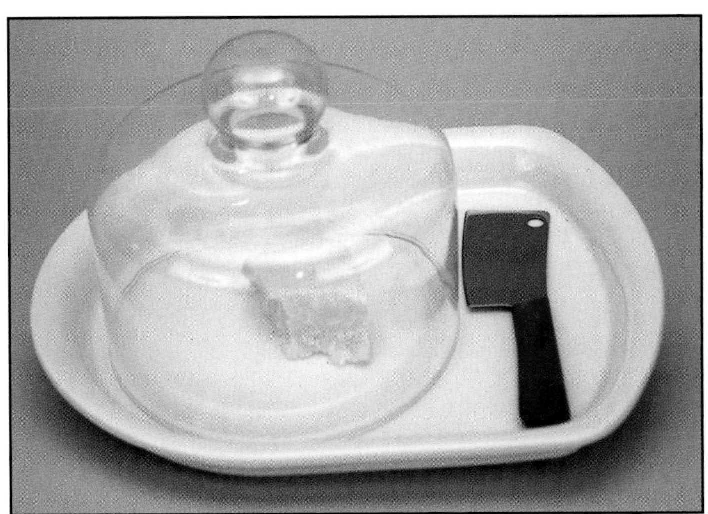

Late 1970s Covered Cheese Dish. $25.00 – 30.00.

Elsie and Elmer Sugar and Creamer Set. $30.00 – 50.00. Made for Borden (double collectible).

Down on the Farm Pitcher and Bowl. Early 1980s. 9" x 10½". $30.00 – 50.00.

Assortment from 1975 Spice Delight Line. 6" Coffee Mug, $ 7.00 – 10.00. Salt and Pepper Shakers. $20.00 – 25.00. Coffee Server with bail, $80.00 – 100.00. Trivet. $15.00 – 20.00.

Blue Fruit Canister. Late 1970s. $30.00 – 40.00.

Wine Cellar Decanter. 1973. $20.00 – 30.00.
Hanging Basket. 1975. $20.00 – 25.00.

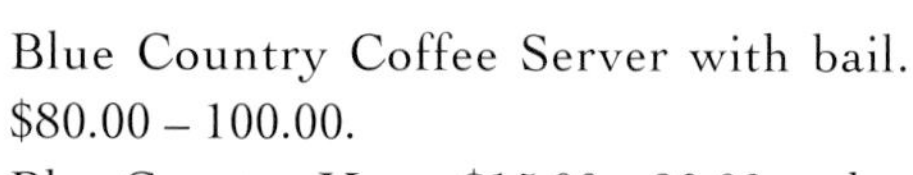

Blue Country Coffee Server with bail. $80.00 – 100.00.
Blue Country Mugs. $15.00 – 20.00 each.

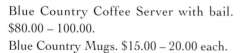

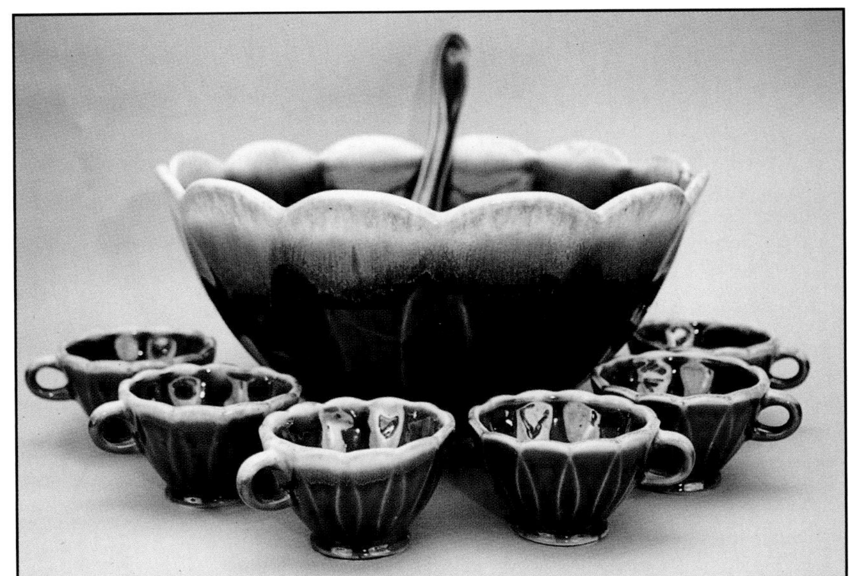

Punch Bowl Set. Late 1960. $80.00 – 100.00.

Flower Pots, Water Guard Planters with reservoirs. Late 1970s. 4". $20.00 – 25.00. 6", $25.00 – 30.00. 8", $30.00 – 35.00.

1970s Lazy Susan Canister Set, $70.00 – 80.00.

Happytime Pitcher and Bowl. 1974. $35.00 – 45.00.
Happytime Spoon Rest. 1974. $10.00 – 15.00.
Happytime Centerpiece Bowl. 1974. $25.00 – 30.00.

Bamboo Canister Set. 1974. $75.00 – 100.00.

Chuck Wagon Food Warmer. 1960s. Unusual non-production mold and glaze. $150.00 – 200.00. (See pg. 309, Vol. I.)

Assorted Advertising Pitchers 6¼" high, 1970s, marked McCoy. $30.00 – 40.00.

Fruit Festival Slow Cooker. 1974. $70.00 – 85.00.
Fruit Festival Individual Casserole. 1974. $30.00 – 35.00.
Pictured with the original owner's manual.

Islander Collection Napkin Holder. 1979. $15.00 – 20.00.
Islander Collection Covered Dish. 1979. $10.00 – 15.00.

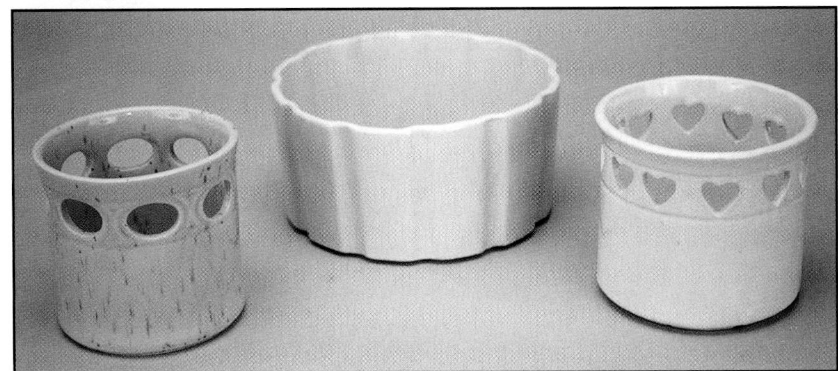

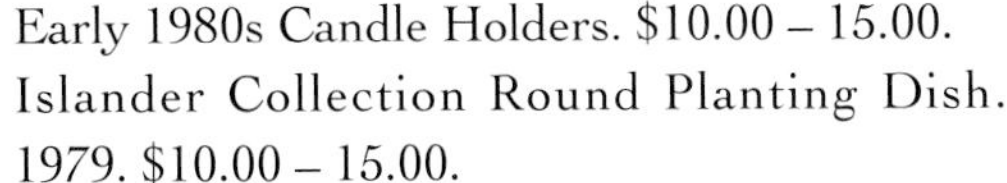

Early 1980s Candle Holders. $10.00 – 15.00.
Islander Collection Round Planting Dish. 1979. $10.00 – 15.00.

Green Thumb Line Yellow Vase 6¼". 1978. $25.00 – 30.00.
Vase 6". 1970s. Marked McCoy $25.00 – 30.00.

Wine Carafe with original box and glasses $25.00 – 35.00.

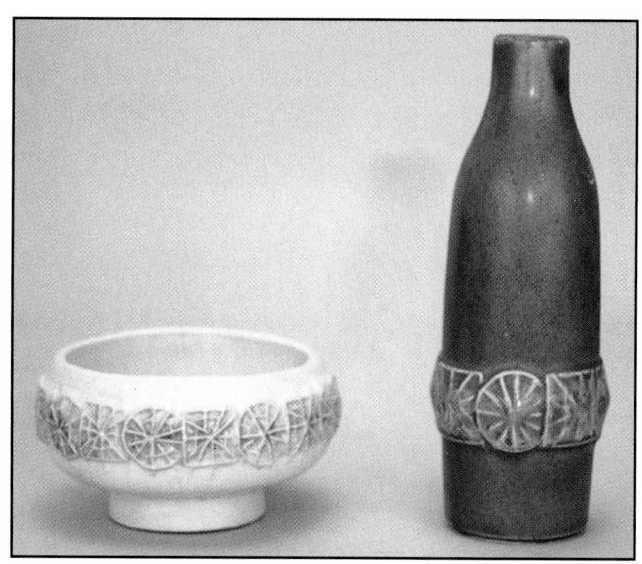

Footed Planter. Marked U.S.A. $20.00 – 25.00.
Bottle Vase. Marked U.S.A. $20.00 – 25.00.

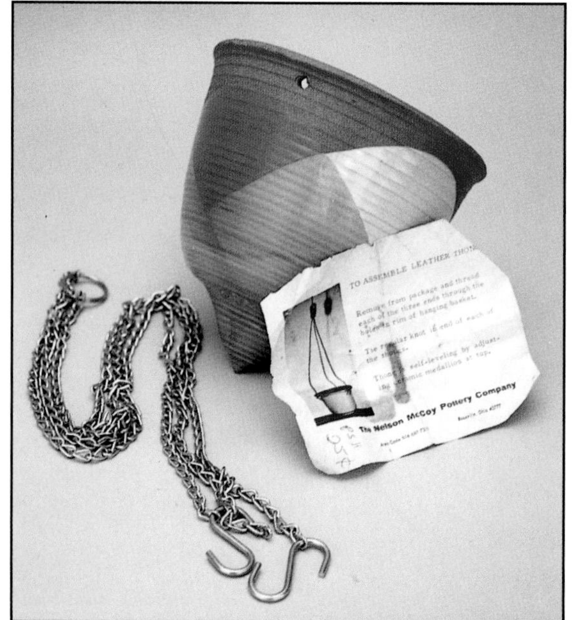

Unusual 1975 Red Clay Hanging Baskets. Example shown with original instructions. $35.00 – 40.00 each.

Hanging Basket with original chain. 1970s. $40.00 – 50.00.

Scandia Line Vase. 1973. Marked McCoy. $20.00 – 30.00.
Pedestal Candle Holder. 1973. $15.00 – 20.00.

Assorted Bell collection. 1970s. $20.00 – 40.00.

Planter 6". 1960s. $15.00 – 25.00.
Planter 7½". 1960s. $20.00 – 25.00.

Green Thumb Hanging Basket. 1975. $40.00 – 50.00.

During the 1970s McCoy Pottery produced many different shapes of steins and mugs. This had to be a wonderful business for McCoy as it seems there is a stein or mug for any occasion. It's too bad they went out of business before the specialty coffee store craze hit — they might still be in business producing their quality steins and mugs.

Pyramid of assorted Model #6395 Beer Mugs. 1975. $15.00 – 25.00.

Tall Beer Stein in the Birchwood glaze. 1972. $30.00 – 35.00.

Model #6036 Advertising Beer Steins. 1973. $20.00 – 25.00.

Advertising Beer Steins. 1970s. $25.00 – 30.00.

Advertising Beer Steins. 1973. $25.00 – 30.00.

Pyramid assortment of Mustache Mugs. Model #9129, 1973. $25.00 – 30.00.

Assorted Advertising Beer Steins. Model #9101. $15.00 – 30.00.

Another assortment of Steins. $15.00 – 30.00.

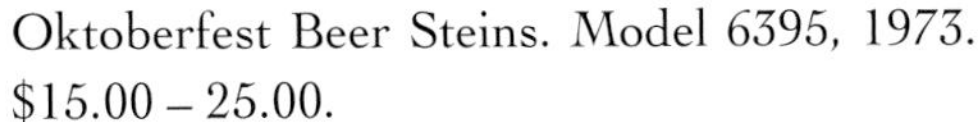

Oktoberfest Beer Steins. Model 6395, 1973. $15.00 – 25.00.

Assorted Advertising Beer Steins #6036.
$15.00 – 30.00.

German Advertising Stein, Mt. Clemens mark. #6029.
$25.00 – 30.00.
Seagram's Benchmark Pitcher. $15.00 – 20.00.

Seagram's Pitcher 7½". $35.00 – 40.00.
Antique Automobile Motif Beer Stein. $20.00 – 30.00.

Schlitz Malt Liquor Stein #6020. 1973.
$25.00 – 35.00.
Schlitz Stein #9132. 1973. $15.00 – 25.00.
Schlitz Stein Bank. $25.00 – 30.00.

Assorted Advertising Coffee Mugs. Late 1960s – early 1970s. Mt. Clemens mark. $10.00 – 20.00.

Clown Coffee Mug. 1977. $10.00 – 20.00.

Advertising Coffee Mugs. $10.00 – 20.00.

Blue Floral Pattern Coffee Mug. $8.00 – 10.00.
Mr. Do Bee Advertising Coffee Mug. $10.00 – 20.00.

Advertising Coffee Mugs. Model 1412. Marked U.S.A. 1970s – 1980s. $10.00 – 20.00.

McCoy employee's Old Timers' Party Souvenir Coffee Mug #1412. $50.00 – 75.00.

Pasta Corner Coffee Mug with original box. 1979. $10.00 – 15.00.

Similac for Ross Coffee Mugs. $10.00 – 20.00.

Declaration of Independence Coffee Mugs. $10.00 – 20.00.

JUST SEND 75¢
FOR EACH MUG YOU ORDER
Use this handy order form and order as many as you like.

TO: MUG OFFER • BOX 384 • MAPLE PLAIN,
MINNESOTA 55359

Please send me__________Campbell's Tomato Soup Mugs. I am enclosing 75¢ for each mug.

NAME__________
Please Print

ADDRESS__________

CITY__________

STATE__________ ZIP__________

Offer expires May 31, 1968 but may be withdrawn earlier. Please allow 3 weeks for delivery. Offer good only in U.S.A. and Puerto Rico. Subject to state and local regulations. Void if taxed, restricted or forbidden by law.

Valley Forge Spirit of 1976 Coffee Mug. $10.00 – 20.00.
Spirit of '76 Jug. $15.00 – 20.00.

Campbell's Soup Advertising Coffee Mugs. Original 1968 order form. $10.00 – 20.00.

Birchwood glazed Coffee Mug. 1970s. $8.00 – 12.00.

Spirit of '76 Coffee Mug. $10.00 – 15.00.

Models 0275 and 0276 Pedestal Coffee Mugs. $10.00 – 15.00.
Right: Model 0278 Pedestal Coffee Mug. $10.00 – 15.00.
Both shapes are from the 1970s Mug Shoppe Line.

Floral Mugs, model 0273. 1970s. $8.00 – 10.00.
Christmas Mug. 1976. $10.00 – 15.00.

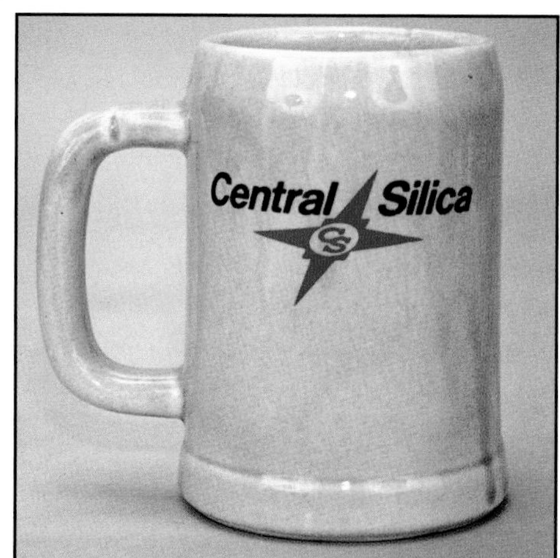

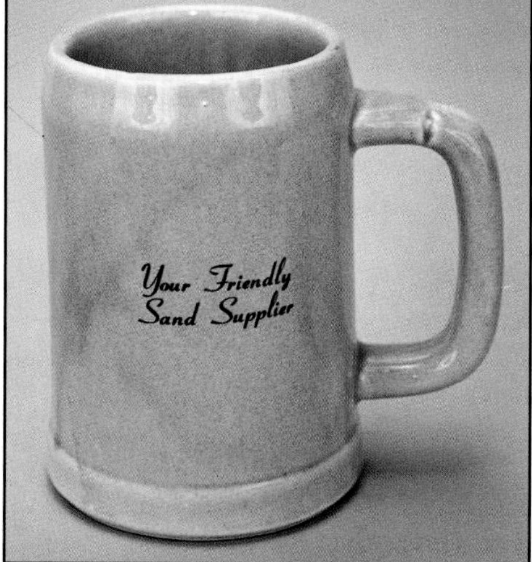

Assortment of 1970s Coffee Mugs. $10.00 – 15.00.

1973 Central Silica Mug, model 6395. Both sides shown. The bottom is marked McCoy and Zane's Trace Pottery. Zane's Trace Pottery applied all the inscriptions. Central Silica supplied sand to McCoy Pottery. $15.00 – 20.00.

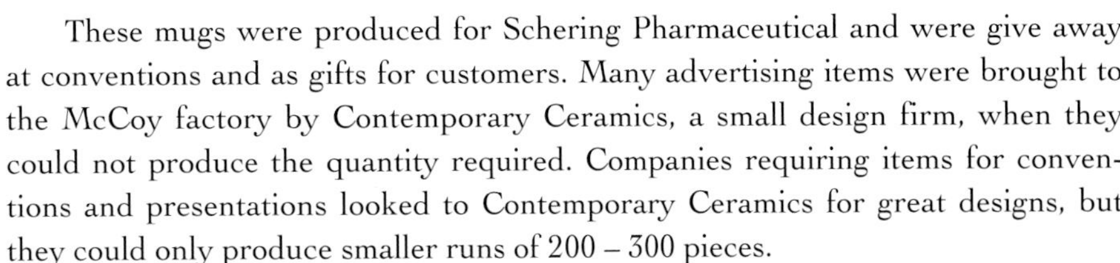

These mugs were produced for Schering Pharmaceutical and were give away at conventions and as gifts for customers. Many advertising items were brought to the McCoy factory by Contemporary Ceramics, a small design firm, when they could not produce the quantity required. Companies requiring items for conventions and presentations looked to Contemporary Ceramics for great designs, but they could only produce smaller runs of 200 – 300 pieces.

Coricidin Coffee Mugs shown in two photos. 1960s. $20.00 – 25.00.

Matte glazed Coffee Mug. 1970s. $10.00 – 15.00.

RhoGAM of Ohio Advertising Mug. $15.00 – 20.00.

Tiara Line Coffee Mugs. 1970s. Pictured with original box, bottom mark shown for reference. $15.00 – 20.00.

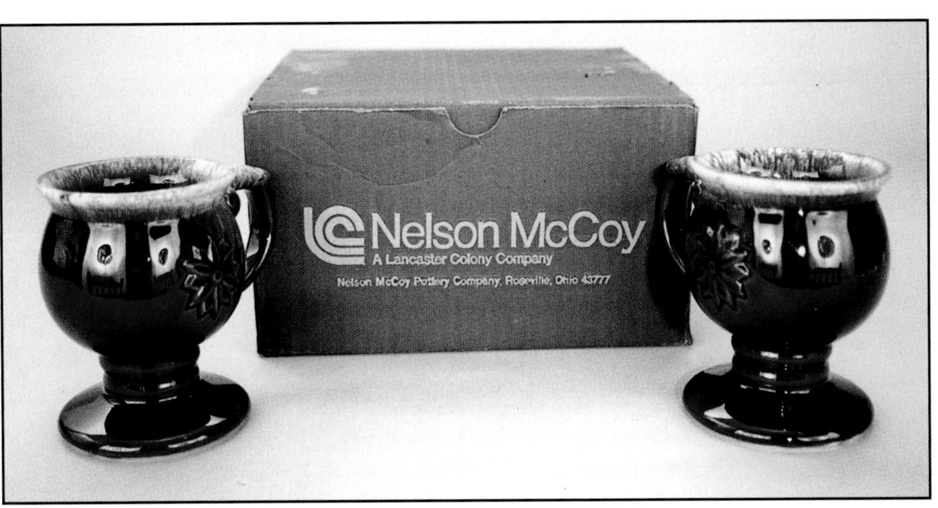

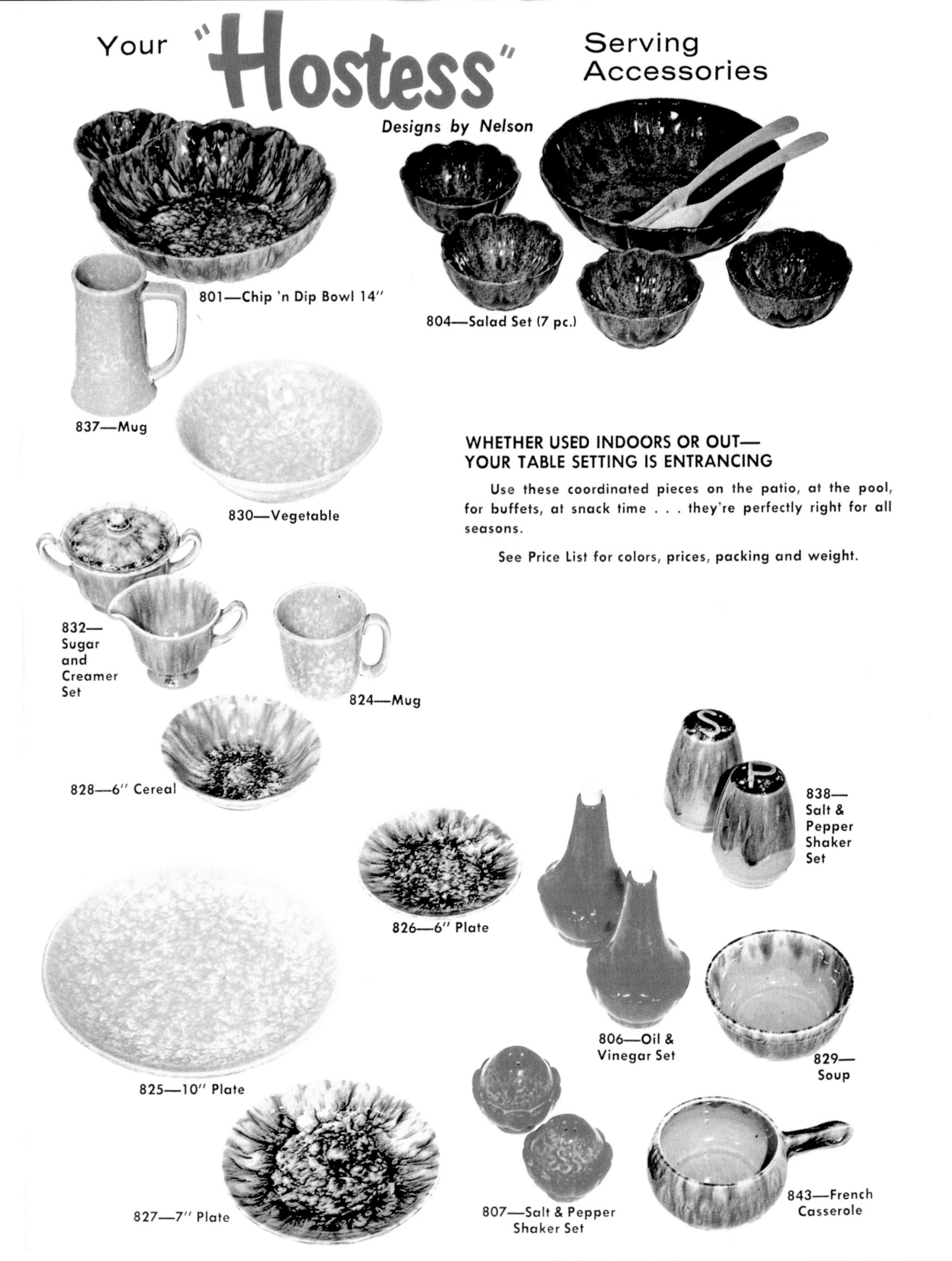
Your "Hostess" Serving Accessories
Designs by Nelson
801—Chip 'n Dip Bowl 14"
804—Salad Set (7 pc.)
837—Mug
830—Vegetable
WHETHER USED INDOORS OR OUT—
YOUR TABLE SETTING IS ENTRANCING
Use these coordinated pieces on the patio, at the pool, for buffets, at snack time . . . they're perfectly right for all seasons.
See Price List for colors, prices, packing and weight.
832—Sugar and Creamer Set
824—Mug
828—6" Cereal
838—Salt & Pepper Shaker Set
826—6" Plate
825—10" Plate
806—Oil & Vinegar Set
829—Soup
827—7" Plate
807—Salt & Pepper Shaker Set
843—French Casserole

Your "Hostess" Serving Accessories
Designs by Nelson
813—Salad Set (3 pc.)
11" Salad Bowl
Wooden Fork & Spoon
808—Quick-Change
All Purpose Server
805—12" Lazy Susan—6 pc.
809—
Condiment Set (7 pc.)
840—Pitcher (80 oz.)
836—Pitcher (32 oz.)
835—Pitcher (16 oz.)
834—Pitcher (6 oz.)
811—
Candle Holde
Set
842—Butter Dish
831—13" Platter
817—
Chip 'n Dip

PASTA CORNER BUYERS GUIDE

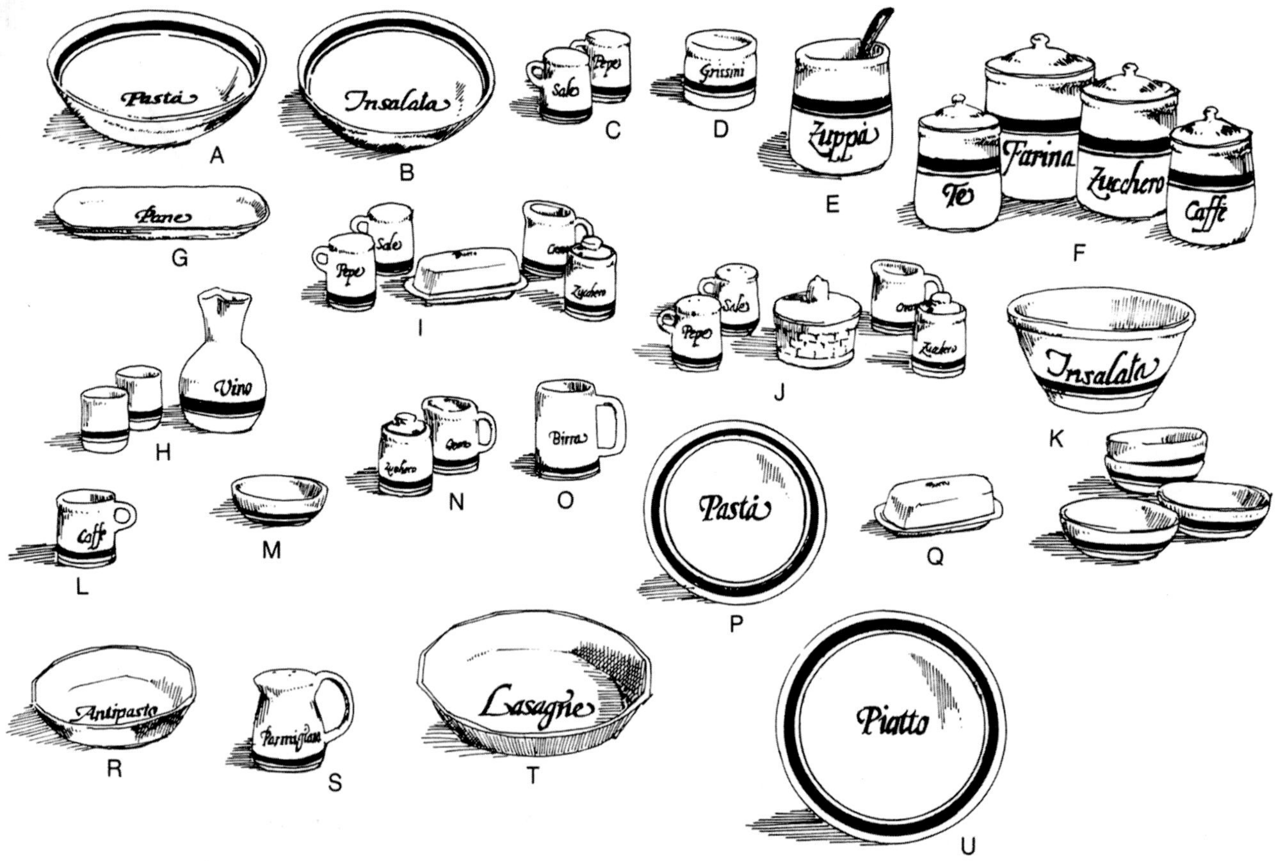

	Item No.	Description	Pack	WT.
A.	0118 1237*	12½" pasta bowl.	6	24
B.	0118 1236*	12½" insalata bowl.	6	24
C.	0127 1237*	Sale and pepe shakers.	6 sets	8
D.	0657 1237*	Grissini, bread stick holder.	6	7
E.	0131 1237*	96 oz. zuppa with brown ladle.	4	22
F.	0134 1237*	4 pc. canister set – Farina, zucchero, caffe and te. Rubber ring seals.	1	19
G.	0658 1237*	Pane, bread/relish tray.	6	12
H.	0661 1237*	Vino set – 1 carafe, 2 tumblers.	4 sets	12
	0659 1200*	6 oz. vino tumbler, set of 2.	6 sets	6
	0660 1237*	1 qt. (1 liter) vino carafe.	4	11
I.	0650 1237*	Center of table set – burro dish, sale and pepe shakers, zucchero and crema set.	6 sets	26
J.	0651 1237*	Center of table set – Margarine dish, sale and pepe shakers, zucchero and crema sets.	6 sets	26
K.	0655 1237*	Insalata set – 1 insalata bowl, 4 individual bowls.	4 sets	32
L.	1412 1237*	10 oz. caffe mug.	24	15
	1412 1299*	10 oz. caffe mugs, 4 pack.	3 sets	15
M.	1413 1200	16 oz. individual insalata bowl.	24	27
	1413 1299*	16 oz. individual insalata bowl, 4 pack.	6 sets	29
N.	1414 1237*	Zucchero and crema set.	6 sets	11
O.	6395 1237	16 oz. birra stein.	24	38
	6395 1299*	16 oz. birra stein, 4 pack.	3 sets	21
P.	7002 1299*	10" pasta plate, 4 pack.	4 sets	34
Q.	7013 1237*	Burro, butter dish.	6	10
R.	7070 1237*	9½" antipasto platto.	6	14
S.	7099 1237*	Parmigiano shaker.	12	15
T.	7072 1237*	12½" lasagne platto.	6	22
U.	7117 1237*	12" piatto.	6	18

*Individually Boxed.

Examples of the Pasta Corner Line can be found on page 294 of Volume I.

CANYON BUYERS GUIDE

		ITEM NO.	DESCRIPTION	PACK	WT.
	A.	1440 0700*	20 pc. starter set.	2 sets	43
		1388 0700*	45 pc. set.	1 set	51
	B.	7002 0790	10" plate.	24	45
	C.	7003 0790	7¼" plate.	24	21
	D.	1413 0700	16 oz. bowl.	24	27
	E.	1412 0700	10 oz. cup.	24	15
		1417 0700	Saucer.	24	15
		1431 0700	10 oz. cup and saucer.	12	16
	F.	1387 0700*	Completer set.	4 sets	32
	G.	1423 0700	32 oz. vegetable dish.	12	18
	H.	7117 0700	12" chop plate.	6	18
	I.	1414 0700*	Sugar and creamer.	6 sets	11
	J.	1418 0700*	6 cup teapot.	6	19
	K.	1426 0700*	4 qt. soup tureen with plate and ladle.	4	29
	L.	1424 0700*	Cookie jar.	4	27
	M.	1422 0700*	2 qt. soup tureen with ladle.	6	31
	N.	1421 0700*	2 qt. casserole.	6	29
	O.	1420 0700*	4 pc. canister set.	1	22
	P.	1717 0700*	Margarine container.	6	10
	Q.	7013 0700*	Butter dish.	6	10
	R.	1425 0700	Oval baking dish.	6	16
	S.	1393 0700*	21 oz. oval gravy boat.	6	13
	T.	1415 0700*	Salt & pepper.	6 sets	8
	U.	7131 0700*	Miniature salt & pepper.	6 sets	5
	V.	7112 0700	12 oz. footed mug.	12	12
	W.	1419 0700*	7 cup coffee server.	6	24
	X.	7050 0700	12 oz. French casserole.	24	28
	Y.	7054 0700	14 oz. French casserole.	12	15
	Z.	7108 0700	12 oz. soup cup with side handles.	12	11
	AA.	1442 0700*	Center of the table set with butter dish.	6 sets	23
	BB.	1443 0700*	Center of the table set with margarine container.	6 sets	23
	CC.	0704 0700*	Candleholders.	6 sets	8
	DD.	1805 0700	6 oz. pedestal mug.	24	20
	EE.	1806 0700	8 oz. pedestal mug.	12	12

*Indicates individual carton with full color litho label.

Nelson McCoy Pottery Company
Roseville, Ohio 43777

Examples of Canyon Dinnerware can be found on page 297 of Volume I and page 193 of Volume II.

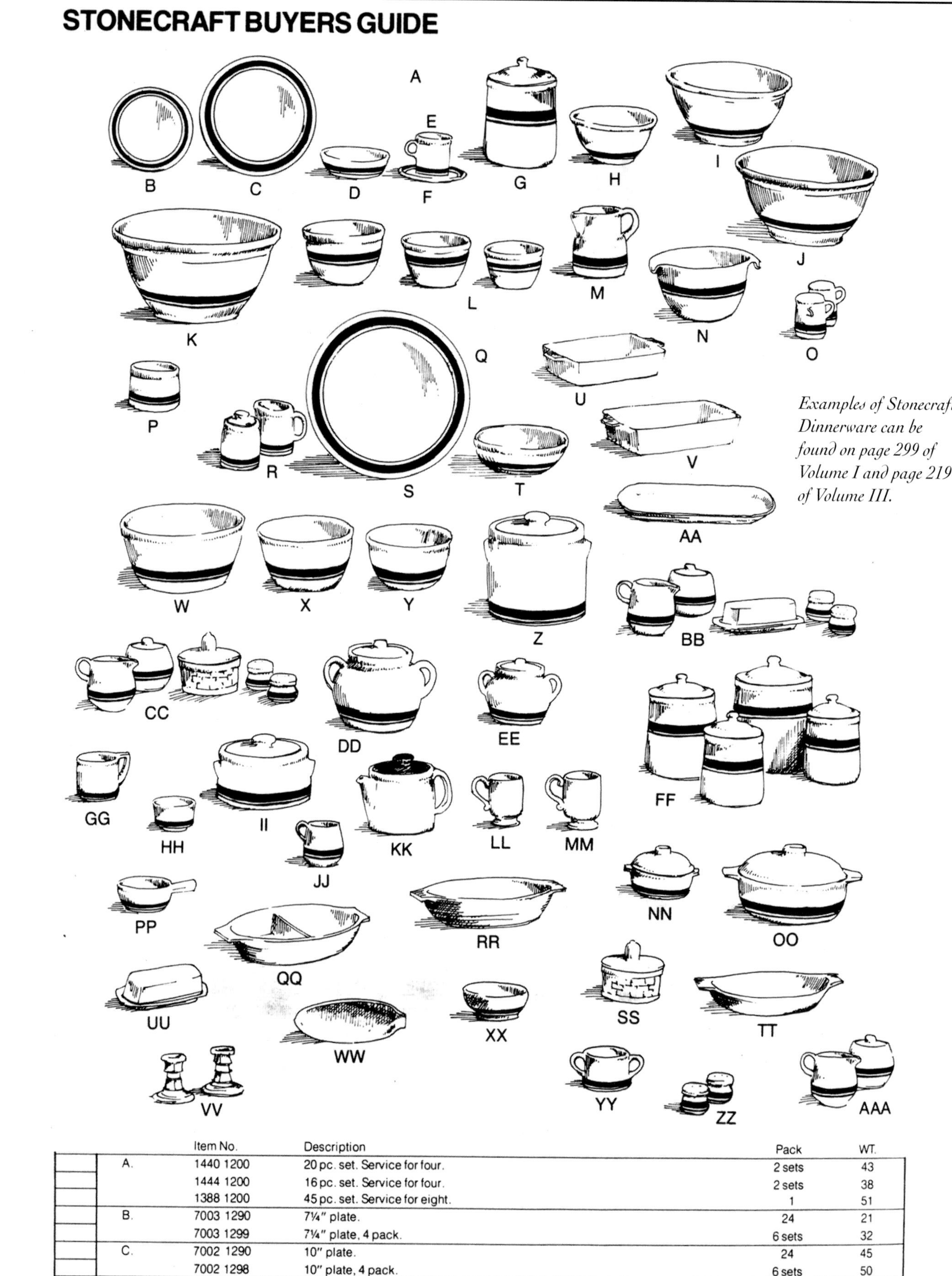

STONECRAFT BUYERS GUIDE

Examples of Stonecraft Dinnerware can be found on page 299 of Volume I and page 219 of Volume III.

		Item No.	Description	Pack	WT.
	A.	1440 1200	20 pc. set. Service for four.	2 sets	43
		1444 1200	16 pc. set. Service for four.	2 sets	38
		1388 1200	45 pc. set. Service for eight.	1	51
	B.	7003 1290	7¼" plate.	24	21
		7003 1299	7¼" plate, 4 pack.	6 sets	32
	C.	7002 1290	10" plate.	24	45
		7002 1298	10" plate, 4 pack.	6 sets	50

1976 Stonecraft
10" Dinner Plate. $10.00 – 15.00.
Pitcher. $25.00 – 35.00.
Creamer. $10.00 – 20.00.
Serving Bowl. $25.00 – 30.00.
Mugs. $6.00 – 10.00.
Salad Plate. $10.00 – 12.00.

Stonecraft Coffee Mugs. 1976. $6.00 – 10.00.
Coffee Server with Bale. $70.00 – 90.00.

Stonecraft Diprolene Creamer. 1976. $15.00 – 20.00.

1976 Stonecraft
Soup Tureen with Ladle. $50.00 – 75.00.
Hurricane Candle Holder. $50.00 – 75.00.
Batter Bowl. $40.00 – 45.00.
Salt and Pepper Shakers. $15.00 – 20.00.
Salt and Pepper with Handles. $15.00 – 25.00.
Spoon Rest. $15.00 – 25.00.
Cereal Bowl. $7.00 – 10.00.
Soup Bowl (handles). $10.00 – 15.00.
Soup Bowl (long handle). $12.00 – 18.00.

SAHARA BUYERS GUIDE

	Item No	Description	Pack	Wt
A.	1440 5100	20 pc set Service for four	2 sets	43
	1444 5100	16 pc set Service for four	2 sets	38
	1451 5100	40 pc set Service for eight	1 set	42
B.	7003 5100	7½" plate	24	21
C.	7002 5100	10" dinner plate	24	45
D.	1413 5100	16 oz bowl	24	27
E.	1412 5100	10 oz mug	24	15
	1412 5198	10 oz mug 4 Pack	6 sets	18
F.	1417 5100	6½" saucer	24	15
G.	0131 5100*	9x6½" cookie jar	4	23
H.	1242 5100*	3 qt bean pot	6	29
I	0196 5199*	7" mixing bowl	12	24
J.	0197 5199*	8" mixing bowl	12	33
K.	0198 5199*	10" mixing bowl	6	29
L.	0134 5100	4 pc canister set	1	19
M.	1415 5100*	Salt and pepper shakers	6 sets	8
N.	1717 5100*	Margarine container	6	10
O.	1803 5100	10 oz mug	24	15
P.	1804 5100	10 oz footed mug	12	12
Q.	7013 4900*	Butter dish	6	10
R.	1387 5100	4 pc completer set	4 sets	32
S.	1423 5100*	32 oz vegetable bowl	6	9
T.	7117 5100	12" chop plate	6	18
U.	1414 5100*	Creamer and sugar	6 sets	11
V.	1835 5199*	11x8" divided vegetable dish	6	24
W.	7050 5100	12 oz individual French casserole	24	28
	7050 5199	12 oz individual French casserole 4 Pack	3 sets	16
X.	1809 5199*	9" rectangular baker	6	17
Y.	1810 5199*	10" rectangular baker	6	18
Z.	1811 5199*	11" rectangular baker	6	22
AA.	1820 5199*	2 qt casserole	6	36
BB.	1821 5199*	28 oz casserole	6	20
CC.	1822 5199*	10 oz casserole	12	23
DD.	1832 5199*	11x8" oval baker	6	26
EE.	1833 5199*	10x6" oval baker	6	17
FF.	7016 5100	12 oz. soup ice cream bowl	36	31

* Indicates individual carton with full color litho label

Nelson McCoy Pottery Company
Roseville, Ohio 43777

STRAWBERRY COUNTRY BUYERS GUIDE

	ITEM NO.	DESCRIPTION	PACK	WT.
A.	0134 3239*	4 pc. canister set.	1	19
B.	0135 3239*	Utensil holder.	6	24
C.	7129 3239*	2 cup teapot.	6	12
D.	0286 3239*	6 oz. tea/coffee cups, set of two.	6 sets	9
E.	1951 3239*	3 pc. candy jar canister.	1	14
F.	0704 3200*	Candle holder, set of 2.	6 sets	8
G.	1418 3239*	6 cup teapot.	6	19
H.	1432 3239*	4 qt. soup tureen with ladle.	4	27
I.	1421 3239*	2 qt. casserole.	6	29
J.	1952 3239*	3 pc. mini canister set.	1	10
K.	0658 3239*	Bread/relish tray.	6	12
L.	1415 3239*	Salt & pepper.	6 sets	8
M.	0268 3239*	8½ x 9½" cookie candy jar.	4	24
N.	7108 3239*	12 oz. soup mug with side handles, 4 pack.	6	24
O.	1950 3239*	6¾ x 4¼" candy jar.	4	14
P.	0621 3239*	6" tube planter with white rope.	6	20
Q.	0622 3239*	7" tube planter.	6	24
R.	0390 3239*	6½" pot and saucer.	6	26
S.	0392 3239*	7½" pot and saucer.	6	36
T.	1725 3239*	Center of the table set with butter dish.	6 sets	23
U.	1429 3239*	32 oz. pitcher.	6	12
V.	0657 3239*	Bread stick holder.	6	7
W.	1726 3239*	Center of the table set with margarine container.	6 sets	23
X.	0165 3299*	13 oz. ice cream mug. set of 2.	6	14
Y.	7010 3239*	6 oz. custard cup, 4 pack.	6 sets	15
Z.	7527 3239*	10 x 11" pitcher and bowl.	2	18
AA.	1414 3239*	Cream and sugar set.	6 sets	11
BB.	7013 3239*	Butter dish.	6	10
CC.	1717 3200*	Margarine container.	6	10
DD.	7528 3239*	5½ x 8" pitcher and bowl.	6	21

*Indicates individual carton with full color litho label.

Examples of Strawberry Country can be found in Volume II on pages 188 through 190.

SANDSTONE BUYERS GUIDE

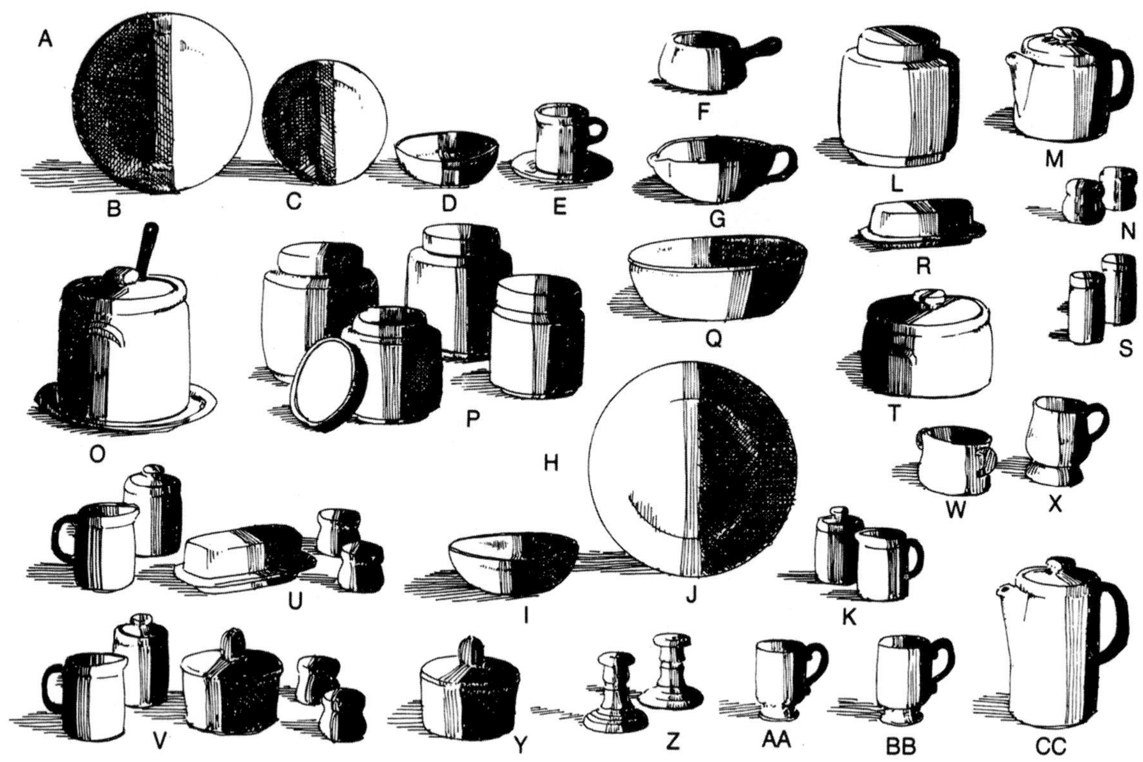

	ITEM NO.	DESCRIPTION	PACK	WT.
A.	1440 5500*	20 pc. starter set.	2 sets	43
	1388 5500*	45 pc. set.	1 set	51
B.	7002 5590	10″ plate.	24	45
C.	7003 5590	7¼″ plate.	24	21
D.	1413 5500	16 oz. bowl.	24	27
E.	1412 5500	10 oz. cup.	24	15
	1417 5500	Saucer.	24	15
	1431 5500	10 oz. cup and saucer.	12	16
F.	7054 5500	14 oz. French casserole.	12	15
G.	1393 5500*	21 oz. Oval gravy boat.	6	11
H.	1387 5500*	Completer set.	4 sets	32
I.	1423 5500	32 oz. vegetable dish.	12	18
J.	7117 5500	12″ chop plate.	6	18
K.	1414 5500*	Sugar and creamer.	6 sets	11
L.	0212 5500*	Cookie jar.	4	20
M.	1418 5500*	6 cup teapot.	6	19
N.	7131 5500*	Miniature Salt & pepper.	6 sets	5
O.	1426 5500*	4 qt. soup tureen with plate and ladle.	4	29
P.	0214 5500*	4 pc. canister set.	1	17
Q.	1425 5500	Oval baking dish.	6	16
R.	7013 5500*	Butter dish.	6	10
S.	1415 5500*	Salt & pepper.	6 sets	8
T.	1421 5500*	2 qt. casserole.	6	29
U.	1442 5500*	Center of the table set with butter dish.	6 sets	23
V.	1443 5500*	Center of the table set with margarine container.	6 sets	23
W.	7108 5500	12 oz. soup cup with side handles.	12	11
X.	7112 5500	12 oz. footed mug.	12	12
Y.	1717 5500*	Margarine container.	6	10
Z.	0704 5500*	Candleholders. Set of 2	6 sets	8
AA.	1805 5500	6 oz. pedestal mug.	24	20
BB.	1806 5500	8 oz. pedestal mug.	12	12
CC.	1419 5500*	7 cup coffee server.	6	24

*Indicates individual carton with full color litho label.

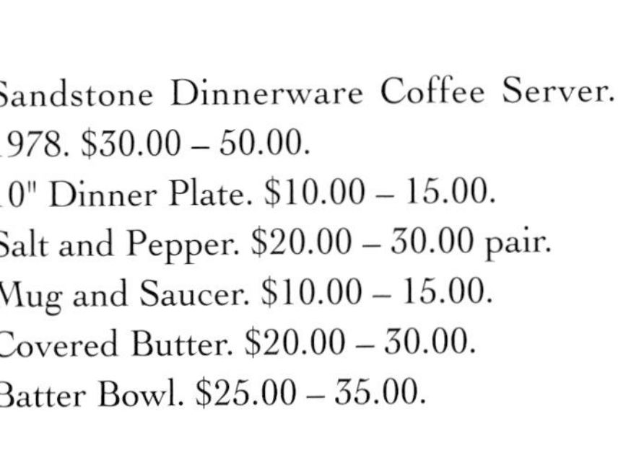

Sandstone Dinnerware Coffee Server.
1978. $30.00 – 50.00.
10" Dinner Plate. $10.00 – 15.00.
Salt and Pepper. $20.00 – 30.00 pair.
Mug and Saucer. $10.00 – 15.00.
Covered Butter. $20.00 – 30.00.
Batter Bowl. $25.00 – 35.00.

Sandstone Dinnerware Covered Canister.
1978. $35.00 – 40.00.

Sandstone Dinnerware Coffee Mug. 1978. $ 8.00 – 12.00.
Square Dinner Plate. $15.00 – 20.00.

BROWN DRIP BUYERS GUIDE

A B C D E F G H I J K L
M N O P Q R S T
U V W X Y Z
AA BB CC DD EE FF GG HH
II JJ KK LL MM NN OO
PP QQ RR SS TT UU VV WW
XX YY ZZ AAA BBB CCC
DDD EEE FFF GGG HHH III JJJ KKK

12 oz. Soup/Ice Cream Bowl.

Examples of the Brown Drip Dinnerware can be found on page 296 of Volume I and pages 196 and 197 of Volume II.

GRAYSTONE BUYERS GUIDE

	ITEM NO.	DESCRIPTION	PACK	WT.
A.	1095 5800*	16 pc. starter set.	2 sets	39
	1058 5800*	45 pc. set.	1 set	51
B.	7002 5800	10" plate only.	24	45
C.	7003 5800	7¼" plate only.	24	21
D.	7004 5800	Soup/cereal bowl.	24	27
E.	7112 5800	12 oz. footed mug only.	12	12
F.	1412 5800	10 oz. cup.	24	15
G.	1417 5800	6¼" saucer.	24	15
H.	1094 5800*	Completer set.	4 sets	32
I.	1423 5800	32 oz. vegetable bowl.	12	18
J.	7117 5800	12" chop plate.	6	18
K.	7020 5800*	Sugar and creamer.	6 sets	12
L.	0135 5800	Utensil holder.	6	24
M.	0125 5800*	3 pc. utility bowl set.	6 sets	35
N.	7013 5800*	Butter dish.	6	10
O.	1717 5800*	Margarine container.	6	10
P.	0132 5800*	32 oz. pitcher.	12	23
Q.	0134 5800*	4 pc. canister set.	1	19
R.	1421 5800*	2 qt. casserole.	6	29
S.	0789 5800*	2 qt. souffle.	6	15
T.	0788 5800*	Set of two individual souffles.	12 sets	15
U.	1393 5800*	21 oz. oval gravy boat.	6	11
V.	0131 5800*	Cookie jar with rubber ring seal.	4	23
W.	1418 5800*	6 cup teapot.	6	19
X.	7131 5800*	Miniature salt and pepper.	6 sets	5
Y.	1415 5800*	Salt and pepper.	6 sets	8
Z.	7050 5800	12 oz. French casserole.	24	28
AA.	0112 5800	6 qt. mixing bowl.	6	37
BB.	0110 5800	3½ qt. mixing bowl.	6	24
CC.	0108 5800	1½ qt. mixing bowl.	12	30
DD.	7080 5800*	Center of the table set with butter dish.	6 sets	27
EE.	7081 5800*	Center of the table set with margarine container.	6 sets	27
FF.	0704 5800*	Candleholders.	6 sets	8

*Indicates individual carton with full color litho label.

Examples of Graystone Dinnerware can be found on page 297 of Volume I.

MEDITERRANEAN BUYERS GUIDE

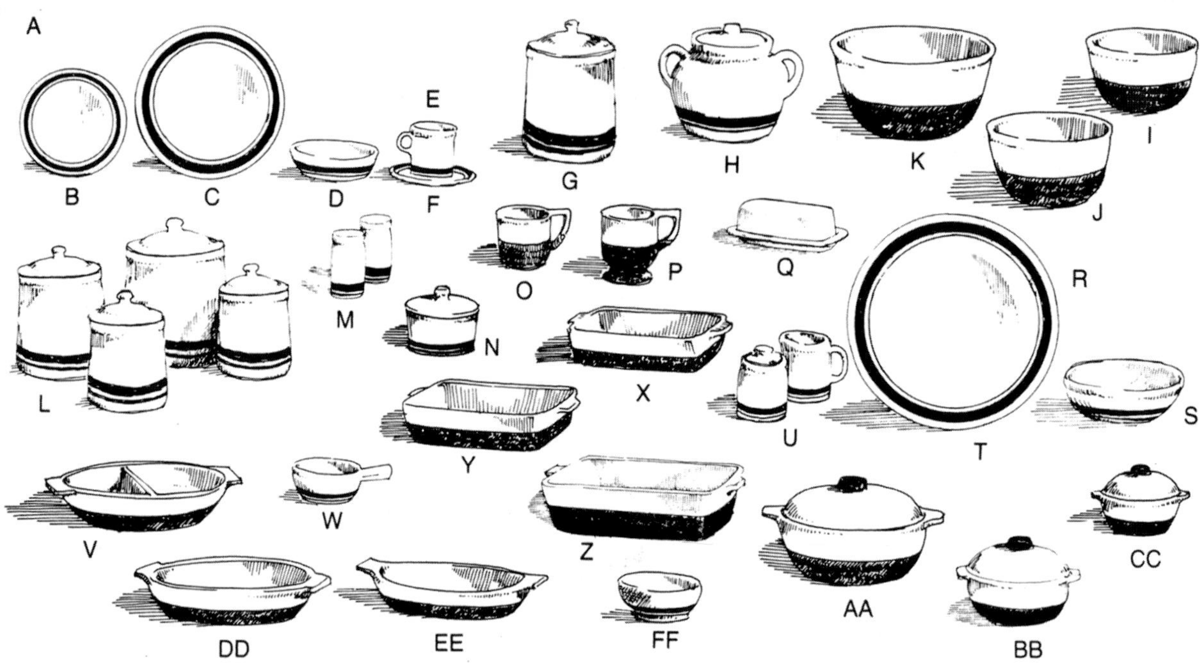

	Item No.	Description	Pack	Wt.
A.	1440 5200	20 pc. set. Service for four	2 sets	43
	1444 5200	16 pc. set. Service for four	2 sets	38
	1451 5200	40 pc. set. Service for eight	1 set	42
B.	7003 5200	7¼" plate	24	21
C.	7002 5200	10" dinner plate	24	45
D.	1413 5200	16 oz. bowl	24	27
E.	1412 5200	10 oz. mug	24	15
	1412 5298	10 oz. mug, 4 Pack	6 sets	18
F.	1417 5200	6¼" saucer	24	15
G.	0131 5200*	9x6½" cookie jar	4	23
H.	1242 5200*	3 qt. bean pot	6	29
I.	0196 5299*	7" mixing bowl	12	24
J.	0197 5299*	8" mixing bowl	12	33
K.	0198 5299*	10" mixing bowl	6	29
L.	0134 5200	4 pc. canister set	1	19
M.	1415 5200*	Salt and pepper shakers	6 sets	8
N.	1717 5200*	Margarine container	6	10
O.	1803 5200	10 oz. mug	24	15
P.	1804 5200	10 oz. footed mug	12	12
Q.	7013 4900*	Butter dish	6	10
R.	1387 5200	4 pc. completer set	4 sets	32
S.	1423 5200*	32 oz. vegetable bowl	6	9
T.	7117 5200	12" chop plate	6	18
U.	1414 5200*	Creamer and sugar	6 sets	11
V.	1835 5299*	11x8" divided vegetable dish	6	24
W.	7050 5200	12 oz. individual French casserole	24	28
	7050 5299	12 oz. individual French casserole, 4 Pack	3 sets	16
X.	1809 5299*	9" rectangular baker	6	17
Y.	1810 5299*	10" rectangular baker	6	18
Z.	1811 5299*	11" rectangular baker	6	22
AA.	1820 5299*	2 qt. casserole	6	36
BB.	1821 5299*	28 oz. casserole	6	20
CC.	1822 5299*	10 oz. casserole	12	23
DD.	1832 5299*	11x8" oval baker	6	26
EE.	1833 5299*	10x6" oval baker	6	17
FF.	7016 5200	12 oz. soup/ice cream bowl	36	31

* Indicates individual carton with full color litho label.

The 1980 Mediterranean Dinnerware line must have not been too popular with consumers as it is hard to find. You can recognize Mediterranean by a wide dark blue line next to a thin blue line under the matte glaze. See page 227.

Surburbia Line pieces.
Model 649. Two-cup Teapots. 1964. $30.00 – 40.00.
Model 646. Pitcher, 22 oz. 1964. $25.00 – 35.00.
Model 645 Pitcher 1½ qt. 1964. $40.00 – 50.00.
Model 647. Creamer. 1964. $15.00 – 20.00.

Model 641. Individual Salad Bowl, 5". 1964. $12.00 – 15.00.
Model 654. Salad Bowl, 10". 1964. $30.00 – 40.00.
Model 653. French Casserole, 10 oz. 1964. $20.00 – 25.00.

Mediterranean Line Creamer. 1980. $12.00 – 15.00.

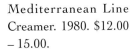

Bluefield Line Salt and Pepper Shakers. 1977. $20.00 – 25.00.

Nice assortment of the 1964 Suburbia Line Ovenproof Cookware.
Coffee Mugs, 8 oz. Model 644. $8.00 – 12.00.
Covered Casserole, 2 qt. Model 652. $25.00 – 35.00.
Plate, 6½". Model 643. $5.00 – 10.00.
Plate, 10". Model 642. $15.00 – 20.00.
Bean Pot, 2 qt. Model 651. $25.00 – 35.00.
Creamer. Model 647. $15.00 – 20.00.
Coffee Server, 5-cup. Model 655. $40.00 – 50.00.
Sugar with cover. Model 648. $20.00 – 25.00.

Gourmet Parisianne Line Ragout Set. 2½ qt. Ragout, Cover, Stand, and Sterno. Model 1073. $50.00 – 65.00.

Brown Oval Serving Platter. $20.00 – 25.00.
Two-Tiered Serving Tray. $20.00 – 25.00.

Gourmet Parisianne Line.
Above: Fondue Plate, 10½". Model 1055. $15.00 – 25.00.
Right: Teapot, 8 cup. Model 1075. $35.00 – 45.00.
Mugs, 9 oz. Model 1051. $10.00 – 15.00

Gold painted McCoy Coffee Mug advertising Roseville Floraline. $20.00 – 30.00. Pictured with our favorite coffee.

Roseville Floraline was introduced in June 1960 for the sole purpose of selling to the retail florist industry. Earl Reynolds, sales merchandise consultant from Columbus, Ohio, was contacted for advice on ways to merchandise and sell this line. This move was taken after several McCoy employees suggested that selling exclusive pieces of pottery direct to the florist trade might be a good idea. After Mr. Reynolds gave his suggestions, advertising agencies were contacted to help with the promotion. In the following pages you will note examples of the fine quality advertising done for this product line.

Named Roseville Floraline, the line became very successful, selling to the most important retail florists in the country. Large customers such as Teleflora, FTD, and Smith Bottle of Atlanta were great supporters of the Floraline program. The designers kept the molds for the product lines simple, and the pieces were mostly glazed in green or white to keep the costs down. Roseville Floraline was a very profitable product for McCoy. The simplicity of the products made them very profitable with outstanding sales reaching $1,000,000.

Most pieces are marked Floraline with a model number. In 1967 after Mount Clemens Pottery purchased the Nelson McCoy Pottery Company, they reused some of the old model numbers for their new shapes. The same is true when Lancaster Colony purchased the company in 1974. This makes identifying the different pieces very difficult by model number because there may be two different shapes with the same model number. We have listed the products by ascending numbers, beginning with model 400. To help identify the different shapes by model number, we have added information after the model number.

The letter L following the model number designates Lancaster Colony. The letter M designates Mount Clemens Pottery and the letters FF distinguish the Fineforms model numbers. These letters are not part of the factory model number, but have been added by the authors to eliminate confusion.

Roseville Floraline was produced for over 24 years and was still in production when the company closed their doors for the last time. Collectors have been drawn to the line in recent years because of the relatively low price and the fact that it is American made pottery. American pottery has become very popular with collectors during this past decade. Being relatively inexpensive and still very available, Roseville Floraline makes a beautiful decorative collection of American pottery.

Top:
Flower Vase, 9⅜". Model 401L. $15.00 – 20.00.
Tall Rose Vase, 11". Model 402. $20.00 – 30.00.
Flower Vase, 8 13/16". Model 402L. $12.00 – 15.00.
Bottom:
Flower Vase, 9 5/16". Three different glazes shown. $10.00 – 15.00.

Roseville
Floraline
1977
A GOLDEN WEDDING
ANNIVERSARY WISH
FOR A
Special
Couple

Top:
Jardiniere 4⅜"x 4¼". Model 404. Two glazes shown. $15.00 – 20.00.
Bud Vase 8¾" x 2½". Two glazes shown. Model 403. $15.00 – 20.00.
Bottom:
Jardiniere 5 5/16" x 5". Model 406 . Three different glazes shown. $15.00 – 20.00.

Ribbed Pedestal Vase 6½"x 3¾". Model 407. $15.00 – 20.00.

Three sizes of the Coal Bucket Jardiniere.
Large, 10" high x 11" across top (Fergie inside). Model 481. $50.00 – 60.00.
Medium, 7¾" high x 8" across top. Model 480. $35.00 – 40.00.
Small size, 6½" high x 6" across top. Model 405. $35.00 – 40.00.

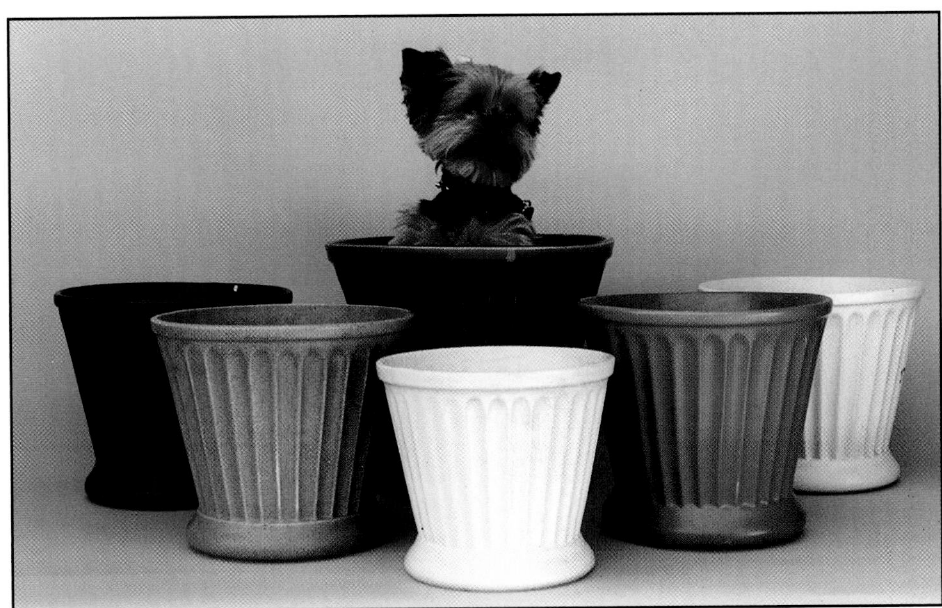

Top:
Swirl planter 4¼". Model 410L. $15.00 – 20.00.
Bottom:
Planters 4" x 10½". Model 410. $20.00 – 25.00.

Top:
Pedestal Arrangement Plate 3½"x 6¾". Model 408. Shown in two glazes. $20.00 – 25.00.
Twist Vase 9". Model 407L. $15.00 – 20.00.
Bottom:
Versatile Bouquet Bowl, 15½" x 5". Model 409. $20.00 – 25.00.

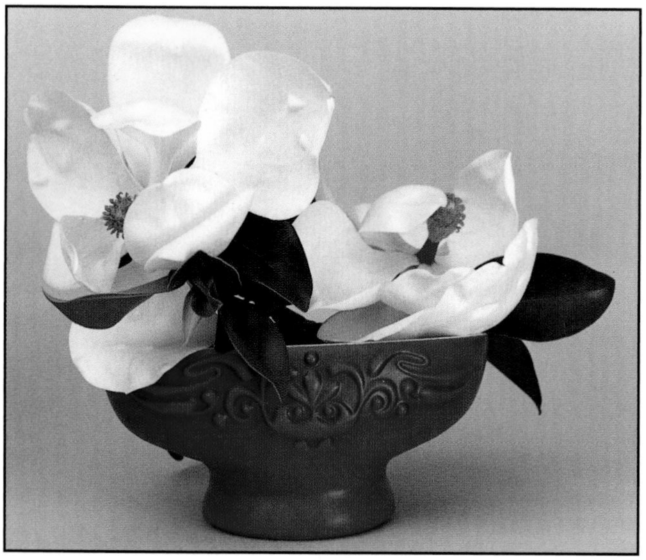

Flourished Oval Pedestal Bowl, 4⁵⁄₁₆" x 5⅜" x 8¾". Model 419. $20.00 – 25.00.

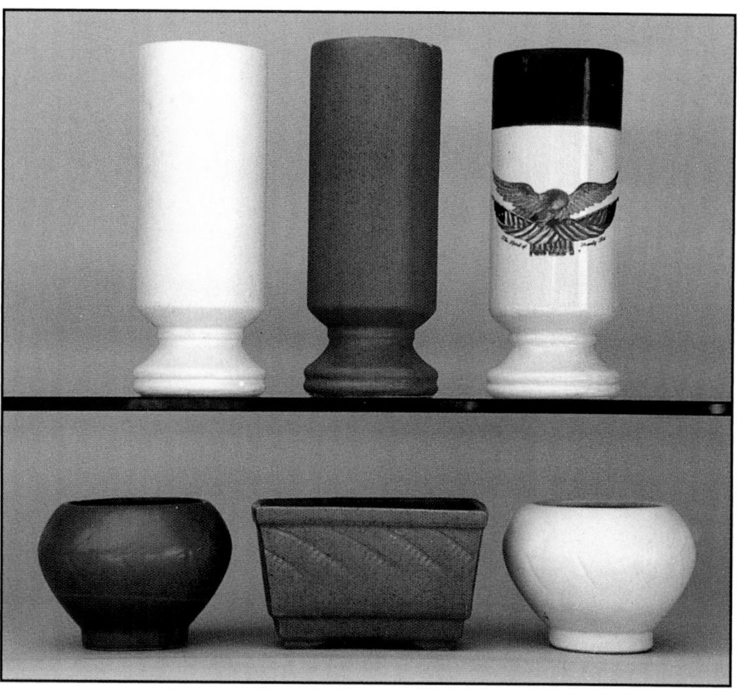

Top: Round Rose Vase 9¼" x 3". Model 412. $15.00 – 25.00. Three glaze colors shown including the Sprit of '76 model.
Bottom: Jardiniere 4". Model 415. Shown in two glaze colors. $10.00 – 15.00.
Rectangular Planter 4" x 6¼" x 3½". Model 411. $15.00 – 20.00.

Jardiniere. Model 415. Same as above right. Shown in rare glaze color. $40.00 – 50.00.

Top: Footed Planter 4" x 8". Model 418. Two glaze colors shown. $12.00 – 18.00.
Bottom: Small Hexagon Bowl 6¼"x 3". Model 420L. Two glaze colors shown. $10.00 – 15.00.

Jardiniere, shown in two glaze colors. Model 420. $40.00 – 50.00.

Top: Stock Vase 10". Model 421. $50.00 – 65.00.
Stock Vase 14". Model 424. $75.00 – 100.00.
Not shown, Stock Vase, 12". Model 422. $60.00 – 75.00.
Bottom: Octagon Bowl 3" x 4¾". Model 426. $10.00 – 15.00.
Octagon Bowl 3¾" x 6¼". Model 422. $10.00 – 15.00.
Octagon Bowl 4½" x 7½". Model 423. $12.00 – 18.00.

Top: Vase 9½". Shown in variety of glazes. Model 413. $20.00 – 25.00.
Large Goblet Planter 8". Model 414L. $25.00 – 30.00.
Bottom: Caterpillar Planter 13½". Model 416L. $30.00 – 45.00.
Planter 3". Model 417L. $12.00 – 15.00.

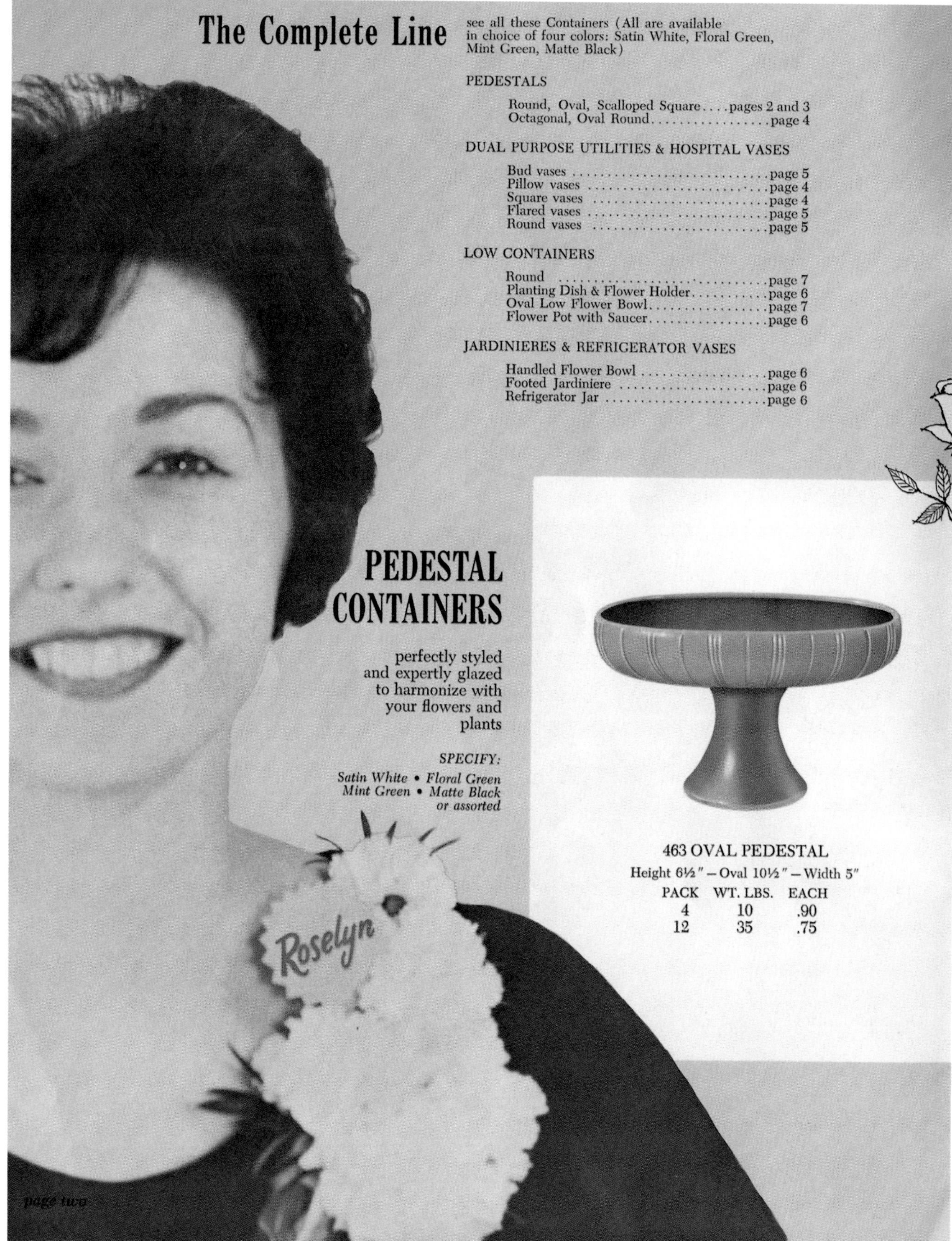

The Complete Line
see all these Containers (All are available in choice of four colors: Satin White, Floral Green, Mint Green, Matte Black)
PEDESTALS
Round, Oval, Scalloped Square....pages 2 and 3
Octagonal, Oval Round..................page 4
DUAL PURPOSE UTILITIES & HOSPITAL VASES
Bud vases..............................page 5
Pillow vases...........................page 4
Square vases...........................page 4
Flared vases...........................page 5
Round vases............................page 5
LOW CONTAINERS
Round..................................page 7
Planting Dish & Flower Holder..........page 6
Oval Low Flower Bowl...................page 7
Flower Pot with Saucer.................page 6
JARDINIERES & REFRIGERATOR VASES
Handled Flower Bowl....................page 6
Footed Jardiniere......................page 6
Refrigerator Jar.......................page 6
PEDESTAL CONTAINERS
perfectly styled and expertly glazed to harmonize with your flowers and plants
SPECIFY:
Satin White • Floral Green
Mint Green • Matte Black
or assorted
Roselyn
463 OVAL PEDESTAL
Height 6½" – Oval 10½" – Width 5"
PACK WT. LBS. EACH
4 10 .90
12 35 .75
page two

1960s Roseville Floraline catalog page.

Early reaction to Roseville Floraline Containers has been electrifying

Inquiries and suggestions are always welcomed

Produced Exclusively for Florists by

ROSEVILLE FLORALINE

Box 594 • Roseville, Ohio

Read these typical comments we hear daily

•

"Glad to see you have a 30¢ Hospital Vase."

•

"Containers in a choice of 4 colors appeal to us."

•

"72 hour delivery lets us keep our inventory in line."

•

"We find your ware free of the usual imperfections."

•

"Large openings let us arrange our flowers artistically."

•

"Buying from the Pottery saves us money we find."

•

"Your price helps our profit picture look lots better."

•

"Our flowers and plants seem to have been grown in your Containers—they are just made for each other."

•

"Important to us is the fact you won't see Floraline Containers in any of the chain stores."

•

"We like to order direct from the manufacturer where our orders can be filled without delay."

•

"Floraline is a complete line from end to end—that makes ordering easier and quicker."

•

"Your unqualified guarantee sold us—that proves you have confidence in your product and will stand back of it."

•

1960s Roseville Floraline catalog page.

Left: Jardiniere 9". Model 425L. \$35.00 – 45.00.
Center: Vase 9". Model 428L. \$15.00 – 20.00.
Right: Planter 8". Model 414L. \$30.00 – 35.00.
(Model 429L, same shape as 414L, but 5" high was also produced. \$15.00 – 20.00.)

Happy Face Jardiniere 5$\frac{5}{16}$". Model 418. \$30.00 – 45.00.

Top: Pedestal Bowl 4$\frac{3}{4}$" x 6". Model 430. \$18.00 – 22.00.
Bottom: Arrangement Mug 5$\frac{3}{4}$" x 2$\frac{1}{2}$". Model 427. \$12.00 – 15.00.

Left: Jardiniere 6½" x 8½". Model 431L. $25.00 – 35.00.
Right: Jardiniere 7¾" x 10½". Model 432L. $35.00 – 45.00.

Jardiniere with original hang-up yarn. Model 431L. $35.00 – 45.00.

Top: Ribbed Jardiniere 4⅞" x 5¼" x 7". Model 424L, several colors. $15.00 – 20.00.
Bud Vase 5¾" x 1½". Model 405. $12.00 – 15.00.
Bottom: Octagon Flower Bowl 3½" x 6⅞". Model 421L. $10.00 – 15.00.

Left: Flower Tray 7" x 4½". Model 432. $10.00 – 18.00.
Right: Flower Tray 11" x 7". Model 431. $10.00 – 18.00.

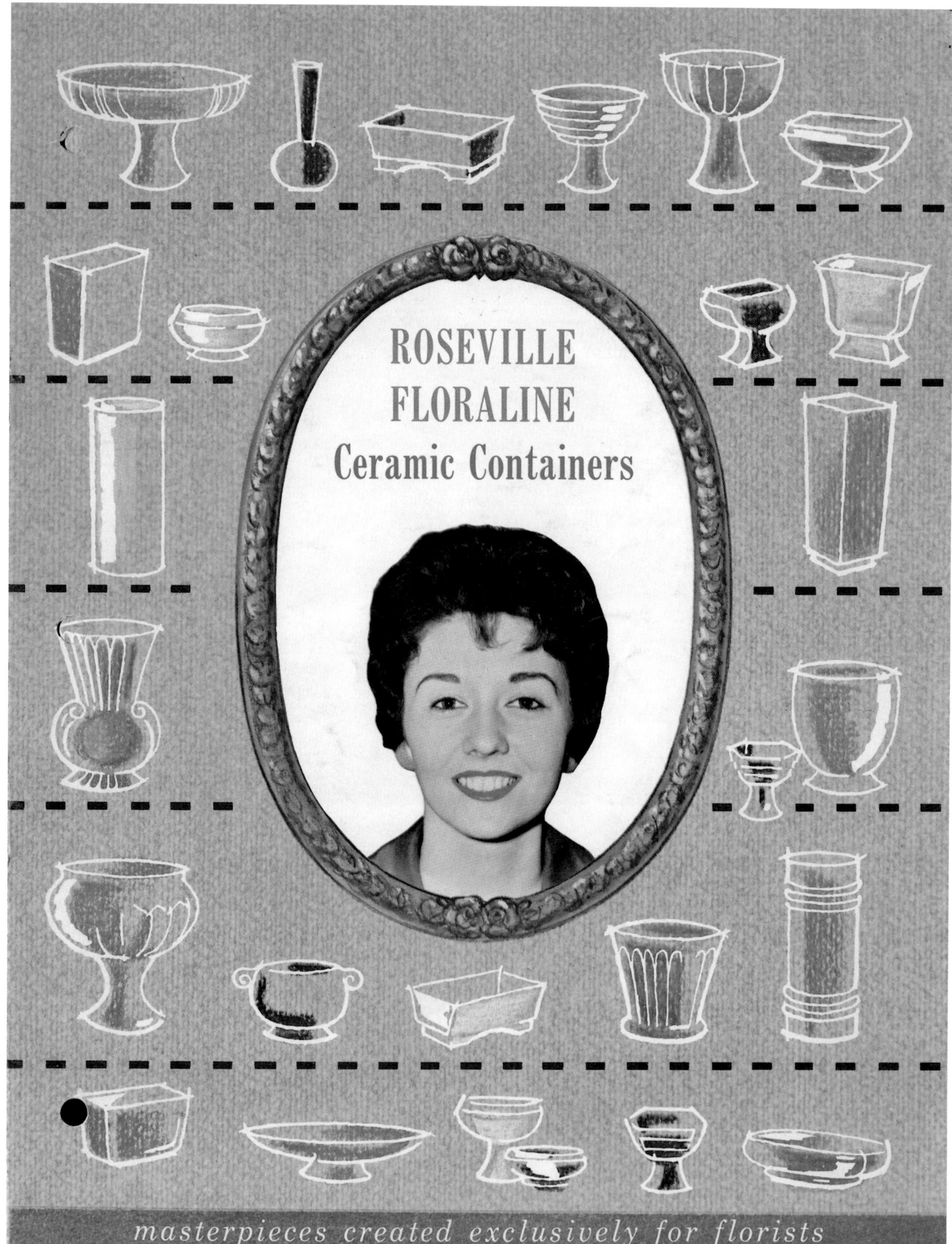
ROSEVILLE
FLORALINE
Ceramic Containers
masterpieces created exclusively for florists

✓*Satin White*
✓*Spec Green*
✓*Olive Green Bronze*
✓*Matte Black*

pedestal containers . . . . . . *perfectly styled and expertly glazed to*

460 SQUARE PEDESTAL CONTAINER
Height 5½" – Opening 4¾"

PACK	WT. LBS.	EACH
6	11	.50
12	20	.45

464 ROUND SCALLOPED PEDESTAL CONTAINER
Height 7½" – Opening 6"

PACK	WT. LBS.	EACH
4	12	.90
12	34	.75

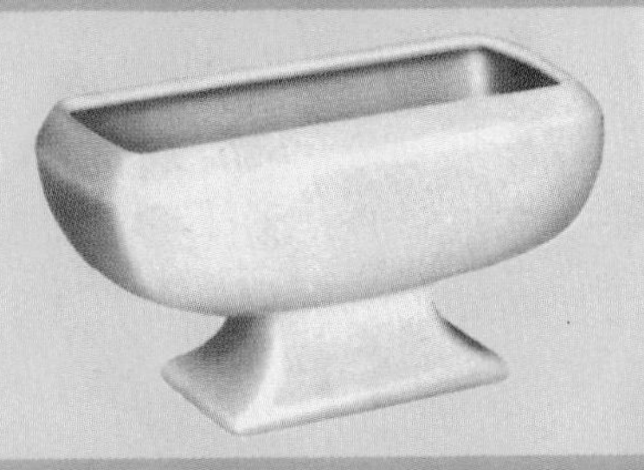

465 PEDESTAL CONTAINER
Height 4½" – Opening 7¼" x 3¾"

PACK	WT. LBS.	EACH
4	10	.65
12	27	.55

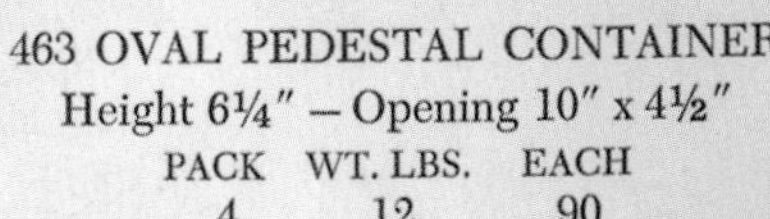

463 OVAL PEDESTAL CONTAINER
Height 6¼" – Opening 10" x 4½"

PACK	WT. LBS.	EACH
4	12	.90
12	34	.75

No. 463–This vase is recommended for inverted "T" or many variations of the crescent design as well as mass bouquets. *(Arrangement by Bill Hixson)*

ROSEVILLE FLORALINE

Produced for

page two

1960s Roseville Floraline catalog page.

harmonize with your flowers and plants ..... **pedestal containers**

✓ *Satin White*
✓ *Spec Green*
✓ *Olive Green Bronze*
✓ *Matte Black*

462 OVAL PEDESTAL CONTAINER
Height 4¾" – Opening 5" x 3¾"

PACK	WT. LBS.	EACH
6	7	.40
24	26	.35

To see this No. 462 as professionally arranged, turn to illustration on Back Cover

CONTENTS

459 OCTAGONAL PEDESTAL CONTAINER
Height 5" – Opening 5¼" x 3½" – Depth 2¼"

PACK	WT. LBS.	EACH
6	7	.40
24	28	.35

461 ROUND PEDESTAL CONTAINER
Height 5" – Opening 4¾"

PACK	WT. LBS.	EACH
6	6	.45
24	27	.40

483 15" TWO-PIECE PEDESTAL BOWL
Height 15" – Opening 13" – Depth 8"

PACK	WT. LBS.	EACH
1 only	25	5.00

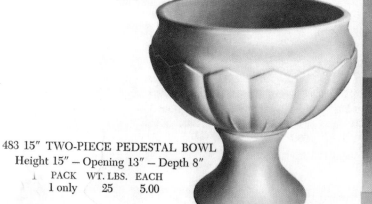

Visualize your flowers artfully arranged in Roseville Floraline's 461 Ceramic Container. You'll agree they are made for each other.

CERAMIC CONTAINERS

Florists Exclusively

page three

1960s Roseville Floraline catalog page.

MASTERPIECES in floral arrangements

using Roseville Floraline Ceramic Containers

It's sheer magic how these Containers, filled with your artfully arranged flowers, become almost miracles of beauty adding special excitement to special occasions. And there is special profit excitement for you, Mr. Florist, in this well-designed line—for all of these newest and most wanted styles are yours at prices 20% or more below competitive items. When you think of Containers, remember how much more you get from Roseville Floraline—so why take less?

ROSEVILLE FLORALINE Box 594 • Roseville, Ohio

Representatives in Principal Cities

(Floral arrangements on this page are by Bill Hixson)

PTD USA

Back page of 1960s Roseville Floraline catalog.

Model 433 pictured in silver glaze. \$30.00 – 40.00.

Top:
Arrangement Vase 7⁵⁄₁₆" x 4¹³⁄₁₆". Model 433. Three glaze colors pictured. \$20.00 – 25.00.
Bottom:
Pedestal Bowl 3¹¹⁄₁₆" x 11½". Model 434. Two glaze colors pictured. \$20.00 – 25.00.

Top:
Pedestal Boat Container 8+" x 3⅝" x 7". Model 436. \$25.00 – 35.00.
Pedestal Boat Container 7" x 5¼" x 11". Model 437. \$25.00 – 35.00.
Bottom:
Pedestal Bowl 5½" x 5". Two glaze colors shown. Model 435. \$15.00 – 20.00.

Left: Pedestal Vase 7" high. Model 440. \$20.00 – 30.00.
Right: Pedestal Vase 7½" high. Model 440L. \$25.00 – 30.00.

Top: Pedestal Flower Bowl 6" Pictured in three glazes. Model 439. $20.00 – 25.00.
Bottom: Boat Centerpiece 3¾" x 4½" x 10½". Pictured in three glaze colors. Model 438. $20.00 – 30.00.

Top: Pedestal Flower Bowl 5" x 8⅜" x 5 3/16". Model 441. $25.00 – 35.00.
Pedestal Flower Bowl 6" x 8⅜" x 5". Model 441L. $20.00 – 25.00.
Bottom: Jardiniere 4⅞" x 6¾". Model 442. $35.00 – 45.00.
Jardiniere 5½" x 6¾". Model 442L. $30.00 – 40.00.

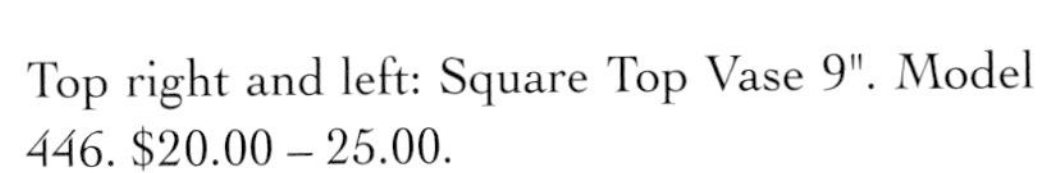

Top right and left: Square Top Vase 9". Model 446. $20.00 – 25.00.
Top middle: Square Top Vase 10½". Model 449. $20.00 – 25.00.
Bottom: Square Top Vase 7". Model 447. $10.00 – 15.00.
Square Top Vase 8½". Model 448, two colors. $12.00 – 18.00.

Model 460 Square Pedestal Containers in eight glaze colors. 5" x 5½". $15.00 – 20.00.

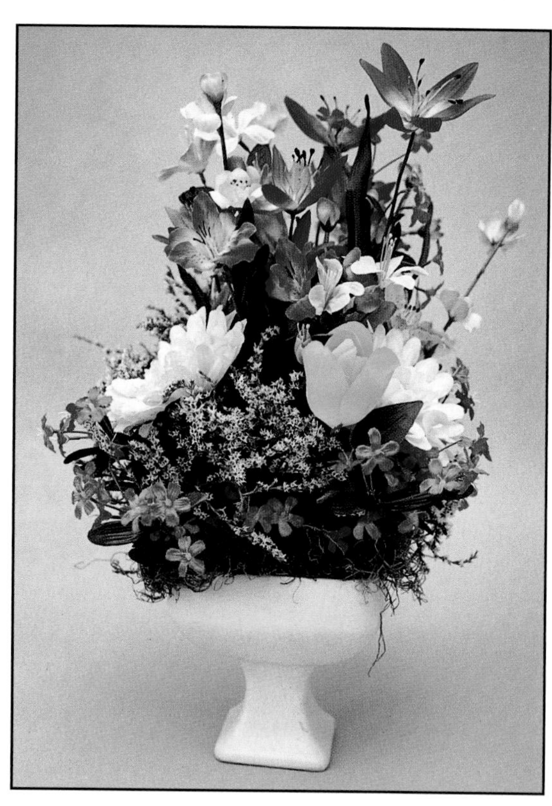

Model 460 Square Pedestal with a lovely bouquet as sold by many florists nationwide during the Floraline production years.

Floraline model 458 Bud Vase shown in two glazes. 6". $12.00 – 18.00.

Top left and right: Jardiniere 5½" x 9". Model 457. Two glaze colors shown. $18.00 – 22.00.

Top middle and bottom: Flared Vase 6½" x 7½". Model 453. Four glazes shown. $15.00 – 18.00.

Floraline model 445 Double Planter in two glaze colors. 5½" x 13½". $35.00 – 45.00.

Round Vase 9". Model 450L. $20.00 – 25.00.
Urn Vase 10½". Model 454. $50.00 – 65.00.
Square Vase 9". Model 451. $15.00 – 25.00.

Top left and right: Round Pedestal Bowl 5" x 5½". Model 461. Shown in two glazes. $12.00 – 15.00.
Top middle: Pedestal Arrangement Bowl 5" x 5½". Model 459. $15.00 – 20.00.
Bottom:
Round Pedestal Bowl 5" x 5½". Model 462. Three glaze colors shown. $15.00 – 20.00.

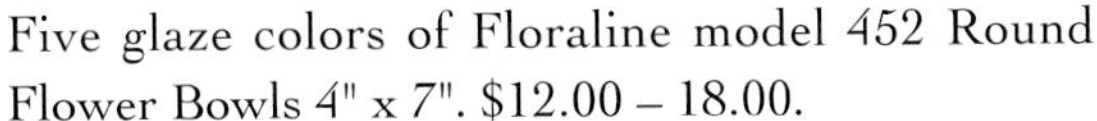

Five glaze colors of Floraline model 452 Round Flower Bowls 4" x 7". $12.00 – 18.00.

Floraline model 450 Pedestal Urn in three glaze colors. 9" x 7½". $25.00 – 35.00.

Top: Pedestal Bowls in three glazes. 7¼" x 7¼". Model 464. $20.00 – 25.00.
Bottom: Pedestal Bowls in two glazes. 6" x 11". Model 463. $20.00 – 25.00.

Top:
Lower Bowl in three glazes, 3" x 6". Model 466-6. $10.00 – 15.00.
Bottom:
Pedestal Planter in three glazes. 4½" x 8½". Model 465. $12.00 – 18.00.

Top left and right:
Pedestal Cup 4" x 4". Model 470. Shown in two glazes. $10.00 – 15.00.
Middle: Rectangular Planter 8½" x 3". Model 468-8.5. $15.00 – 20.00.
Bottom: Planter in three glazes, 6½"x 3". Model 468-6.5. $12.00 – 18.00.

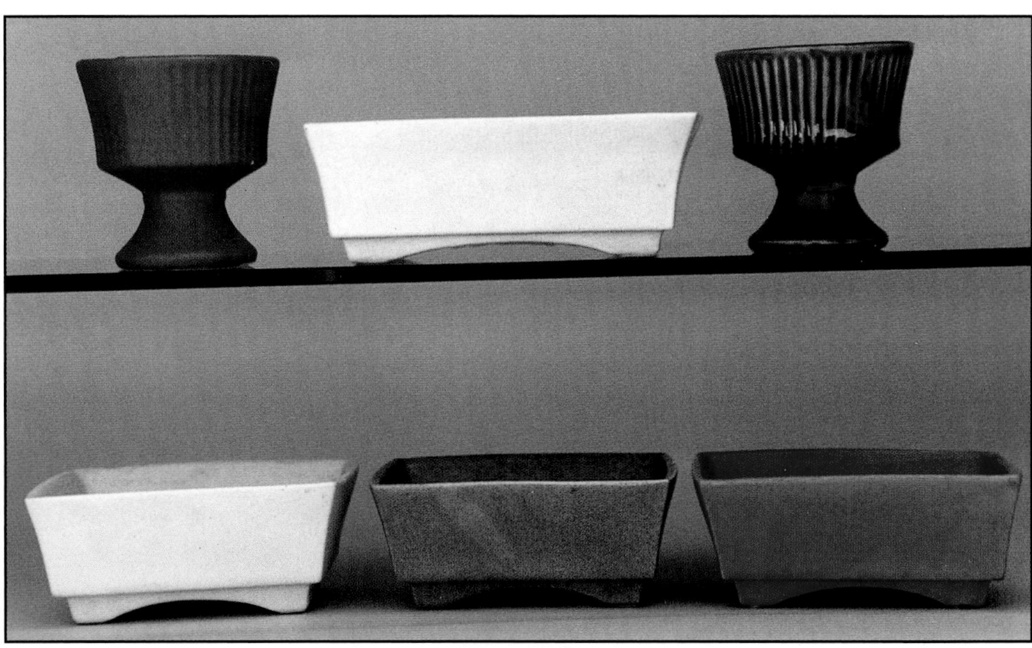

Top row shows three glaze colors of Floraline model 473 Pedestal Planters. 6"x 5". $12.00 – 15.00.
Bottom row shows four glaze colors of model 474 Pedestal Planter. 7" x 5". $15.00 – 20.00.

Pedestal Jardiniere 7¾" x 6½". Model 471-7. $35.00 – 45.00.
Pedestal Jardiniere 8¾" x 7". Model 471-8. $40.00 – 50.00.

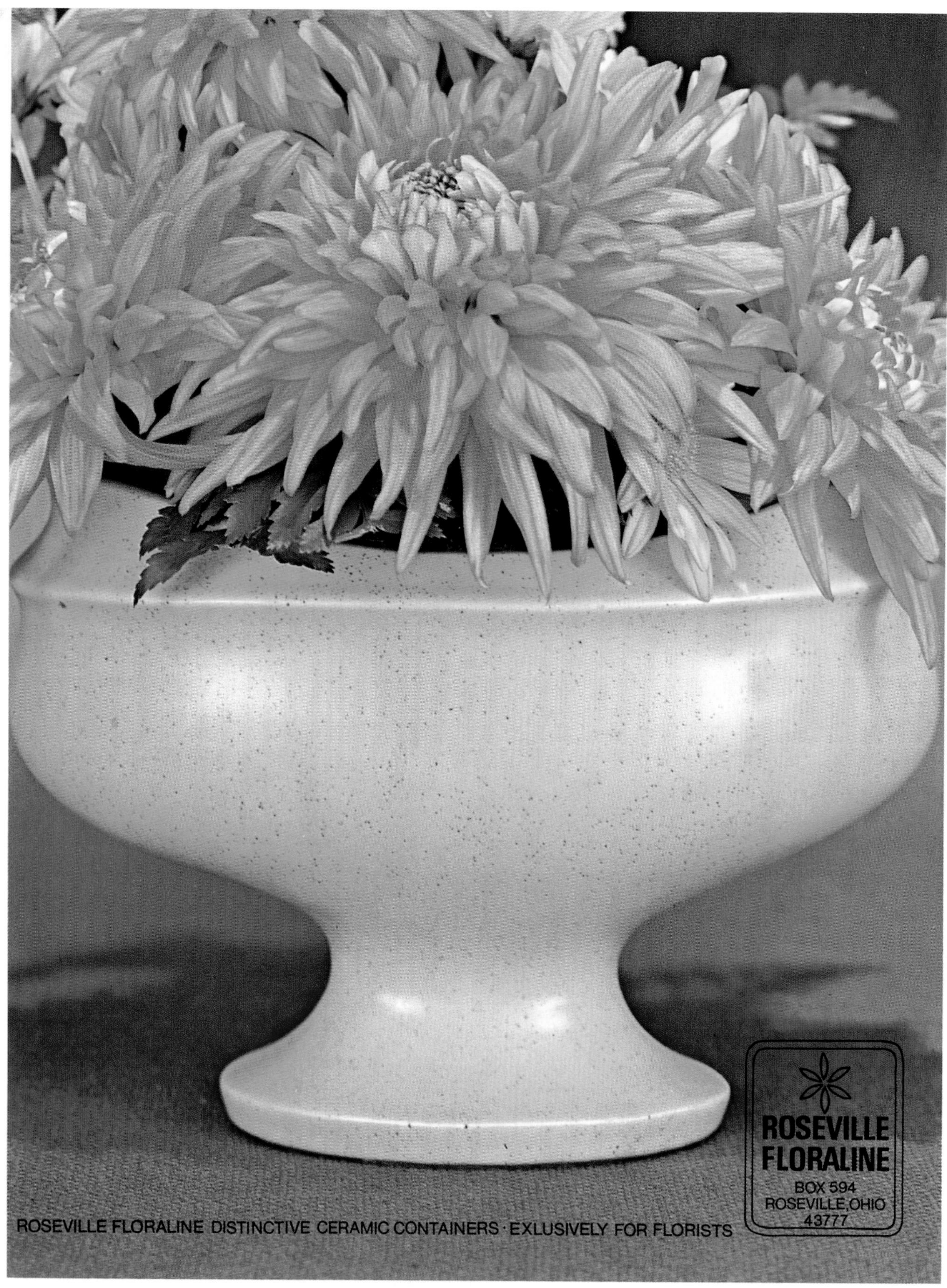

Cover page of 1960s Roseville Floraline catalog.

No. 570—70 pc. "New Look Assortment"

Consists of: 4 only No. 401
6 each No. 402, 403, 436, 437, 438, 439, 440, 441, 442
12 only No. 435

SEE PRICE LIST FOR ASSORTMENTS 2

1960s Roseville Floraline catalog.

NO. 407 RIBBED PEDESTAL VASE
Height: 6½" Opening: 3¾" circle
Packed: 12 (29 lbs.)

NO. 408 PEDESTAL ARRANGEMENT PLATE
Height: 3½" Diameter: 6¾"
Packed: 12 (23 lbs.)

NO. 427 ARRANGEMENT MUG
Height: 6" Opening: 2½" circle
Packed: 24 (24 lbs.)

NO. 430 CLASSIC PEDESTAL BOWL
Height: 5" Opening: 6" circle
Packed:12 (27 lbs.)

NO. 433 ARRANGEMENT VASE
Height: 7½" Opening: 5" circle
Packed: 12 (30 lbs.)

NO. 435 PEDESTAL BOWL
Height: 5¾" Opening: 6"
Packed: 12 (23 lbs.)

NO. 437 PEDESTAL BOAT CONTAINER
Height: 7" Width: 5¼" Length: 11"
Opening: 9¼" x 4"
Packed: 6 (21 lbs.)

NO. 439 PEDESTAL FLOWER BOWL
Height: 6½" Width: 5" Length: 7½"
Opening: 6" x 3½"
Packed: 12 (33 lbs.)

NO. 440 PEDESTAL VASE
Height: 7" Dia.: 5½" Opening: 4"
Packed: 12 (24 lbs.)

NO. 441 OVAL PEDESTAL CONTAINER
Height: 6" Width: 5¾" Length: 8"
Opening: 7" x 4½"
Packed: 12 (33 lbs.)

NO. 450 LARGE PEDESTAL URN
Height: 9½" Opening: 6½" circle
Packed: 6 (32 lbs.)

NO. 460 SQUARE PEDESTAL CONTAINER
Height: 5½" Opening: 4¾" x 4¾"
Packed: 12 (20 lbs.)

NO. 461 ROUND PEDESTAL CONTAINER
Height: 5" Opening: 4¾" circle
Packed: 24 (27 lbs.)

NO. 464 ROUND SCALLOPED PEDESTAL
Height: 7½" Opening: 6" circle
Packed: 12 (34 lbs.)

NO. 465 OBLONG PEDESTAL PLANTER
Height: 4½" Opening: 7¼" x 3¾"
Packed: 12 (27 lbs.)

NO. 470 SMALL RIBBED PEDESTAL VASE
Height: 4½" Opening: 4" circle
Packed: 24 (29 lbs.)

NO. 473 SHORT RIBBED URN
Height: 6" Opening: 4½" circle
Packed: 12 (21 lbs.)

NO. 474 RIBBED URN
Height: 7" Opening: 5" circle
Packed: 12 (25 lbs.)

NO. 477 LARGE RIBBED PEDESTAL VASE
Height: 6¼" Opening: 6" circle
Packed: 12 (29 lbs.)

NO. 499 FLUTED PEDESTAL CONTAINER OR PLANTER
Height: 7" Opening: 8" circle
Packed: 6 (16 lbs.)

NO. 504 MINIATURE ARRANGEMENT PEDESTAL
Height: 3¾" Opening: 3¼" circle
Packed: 36 (19 lbs.)

NO. 505 MINIATURE PEDESTAL CONTAINER
Height: 3½" Opening: 3½" circle
Packed: 36 (19 lbs.)

SEE PRICE LIST FOR ASSORTMENTS 3

1960s Roseville Floraline catalog.

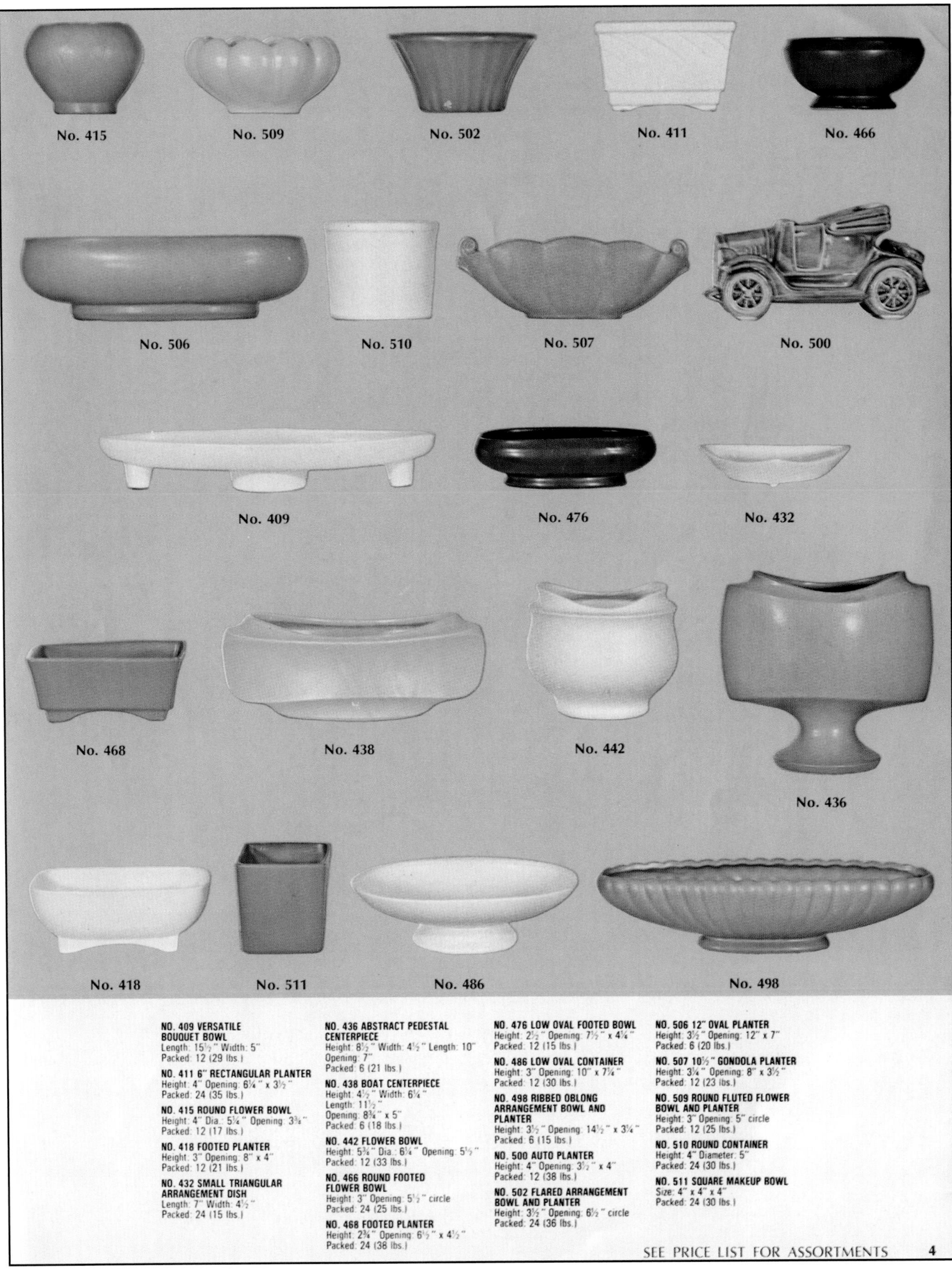

NO. 409 VERSATILE BOUQUET BOWL
Length: 15½" Width: 5"
Packed: 12 (29 lbs.)

NO. 411 6" RECTANGULAR PLANTER
Height: 4" Opening: 6¼" x 3½"
Packed: 24 (35 lbs.)

NO. 415 ROUND FLOWER BOWL
Height: 4" Dia.: 5¼" Opening: 3¾"
Packed: 12 (17 lbs.)

NO. 418 FOOTED PLANTER
Height: 3" Opening: 8" x 4"
Packed: 12 (21 lbs.)

NO. 432 SMALL TRIANGULAR ARRANGEMENT DISH
Length: 7" Width: 4½"
Packed: 24 (15 lbs.)

NO. 436 ABSTRACT PEDESTAL CENTERPIECE
Height: 8½" Width: 4½" Length: 10"
Opening: 7"
Packed: 6 (21 lbs.)

NO. 438 BOAT CENTERPIECE
Height: 4½" Width: 6¼"
Length: 11½"
Opening: 8¾" x 5"
Packed: 6 (18 lbs.)

NO. 442 FLOWER BOWL
Height: 5¾" Dia.: 6¼" Opening: 5½"
Packed: 12 (33 lbs.)

NO. 466 ROUND FOOTED FLOWER BOWL
Height: 3" Opening: 5½" circle
Packed: 24 (25 lbs.)

NO. 468 FOOTED PLANTER
Height: 2¾" Opening: 6½" x 4½"
Packed: 24 (38 lbs.)

NO. 476 LOW OVAL FOOTED BOWL
Height: 2½" Opening: 7½" x 4¼"
Packed: 12 (15 lbs.)

NO. 486 LOW OVAL CONTAINER
Height: 3" Opening: 10" x 7¼"
Packed: 12 (30 lbs.)

NO. 498 RIBBED OBLONG ARRANGEMENT BOWL AND PLANTER
Height: 3½" Opening: 14½" x 3¼"
Packed: 6 (15 lbs.)

NO. 500 AUTO PLANTER
Height: 4" Opening: 3½" x 4"
Packed: 12 (38 lbs.)

NO. 502 FLARED ARRANGEMENT BOWL AND PLANTER
Height: 3½" Opening: 6½" circle
Packed: 24 (36 lbs.)

NO. 506 12" OVAL PLANTER
Height: 3½" Opening: 12" x 7"
Packed: 6 (20 lbs.)

NO. 507 10½" GONDOLA PLANTER
Height: 3¼" Opening: 8" x 3½"
Packed: 12 (23 lbs.)

NO. 509 ROUND FLUTED FLOWER BOWL AND PLANTER
Height: 3" Opening: 5" circle
Packed: 12 (25 lbs.)

NO. 510 ROUND CONTAINER
Height: 4" Diameter: 5"
Packed: 24 (30 lbs.)

NO. 511 SQUARE MAKEUP BOWL
Size: 4" x 4" x 4"
Packed: 24 (30 lbs.)

SEE PRICE LIST FOR ASSORTMENTS 4

1960s Roseville Floraline catalog.

No. 413 No. 403 No. 412 No. 401 No. 458 No. 453

No. 455 No. 456 No. 448 No. 446 No. 449

No. 402 No. 482 No. 424 No. 422 No. 421

NO. 401 DOZEN ROSE VASE
Height: 9½" Opening: 4¼"
Packed: 12 (25 lbs.)

NO. 402 TALL ROSE VASE
Height: 11" Opening: 4¼"
Packed: 6 (18 lbs.)

NO. 403 BUD VASE
Height: 8¾" Opening: 2¼"
Packed: 24 (30 lbs.)

NO. 412 ROUND FOOTED VASE
Height: 9¼" Opening: 3¾"
Packed: 12 (26 lbs.)

NO. 413 DOZEN ROSE VASE
Height: 9¼" Width: 4⅝"
Packed: 12 (22 lbs.)

NO. 421 10" STOCK VASE
Height: 10½" Opening: 6" circle
Packed: 6 (29 lbs.)

NO. 422 12" STOCK VASE
Height: 12½" Opening: 7" circle
Packed: 4 (30 lbs.)

NO. 424 14" STOCK VASE
Height: 14½" Opening: 7" circle
Packed: 4 (35 lbs.)

NO. 446 9" SQUARED CYLINDRICAL VASE
Height: 9¼" Opening: 3¼" x 3¼"
Packed: 12 (35 lbs.)

NO. 448 8" SQUARED CYLINDRICAL VASE
Height: 8¼" Opening: 3" x 3"
Packed: 12 (29 lbs.)

NO. 449 10" SQUARED CYLINDRICAL VASE
Height: 10¼" Opening: 3¼" x 3¼"
Packed: 12 (41 lbs.)

NO. 453 FLARED VASE
Height: 6¼" Opening: 7" x 3½"
Packed: 24 (56 lbs.)

NO. 455 SMALL PILLOW VASE
Height: 4½" Opening: 5¼" x 3¼"
Packed: 24 (37 lbs.)

NO. 456 LARGE PILLOW VASE
Height: 6½" Opening: 5½" x 3½"
Packed: 24 (63 lbs.)

NO. 458 BUD VASE
Height: 6¼" Opening: 1" circle
Packed: 24 (13 lbs.)

NO. 482 TALL BOUQUET VASE
Height: 11½" Opening: 5" circle
Packed: 6 (26 lbs.)

SEE PRICE LIST FOR ASSORTMENTS 5

1960s Roseville Floraline catalog.

NO. 404 SMALL FLOWER BOWL
Height: 4" Dia.: 6½" Opening: 4½"
Packed: 12 (26 lbs.)

NO. 406 LARGE FLOWER BOWL
Height: 5" Dia.: 7½" Opening: 5¾"
Packed: 12 (35 lbs.)

NO. 445 DOUBLE PLANT JARDINIERE
(Holds 2 clay pots)
Height: 5½" Length: 13½"
Opening: 2 – 6" circles
Packed: 6 (32 lbs.)

NO. 452 SMALL HANDLED BOWL
Height: 4" Dia.: 6" Opening: 4"
Packed: 12 (18 lbs.)

NO. 480 8" JARDINIERE
(Holds 6" standard clay pot)
Height: 7¾" Opening: 8" circle
Packed: 6 (35 lbs.)

NO. 481 10" JARDINIERE
(Holds 8" standard clay pot)
Height: 10" Opening: 11" circle
Packed: 4 (45 lbs.)

NO. 501 SMALL JARDINIERE
(Holds 4" standard clay pot)
Height: 5¼" Opening: 5½"
Packed: 24 (50 lbs.)

NO. 503 AZALEA JARDINIERE
(Holds 6" azalea clay pot)
Height: 5½" Opening: 8"
Packed: 12 (35 lbs.)

NO. 2025 8" ROMANESQUE SWIRL VASE
Height: 8" Opening: 5½" circle
Packed: 6 (13 lbs.)

NO. 2026 7" ROMANESQUE SWIRL VASE
Height: 7" Opening: 5" circle
Packed: 6 (12 lbs.)

NO. 2029 8" ROMANESQUE PLANTER
Height: 4" Opening: 8" x 3½"
Packed: 6 (12 lbs.)

NO. 2030 7" ROMANESQUE PLANTER
Height: 3¾" Opening: 7" x 3½
Packed: 6 (7 lbs.)

NO. 2032 6" ROMANESQUE SWIRL FOOTED CONTAINER
Height: 5" Opening: 6" circle
Packed: 6 (13 lbs.)

NO. 2033 5" ROMANESQUE SWIRL FOOTED CONTAINER
Height: 4½" Opening: 5" circle
Packed: 6 (8 lbs.)

NO. 2060 5½" ROMANESQUE FILIGREE VASE
Height: 5½" Opening: 4" circle
Packed: 6 (10 lbs.)

NO. 2061 6½" ROMANESQUE FILIGREE VASE
Height: 6½" Opening: 5" circle
Packed: 6 (15 lbs.)

NO. 2082 8" ROMANESQUE FILIGREE VASE
Height: 8" Opening: 5½" circle
Packed: 6 (16 lbs.)

SEE PRICE LIST FOR ASSORTMENTS 6

1960s Roseville Floraline catalog.

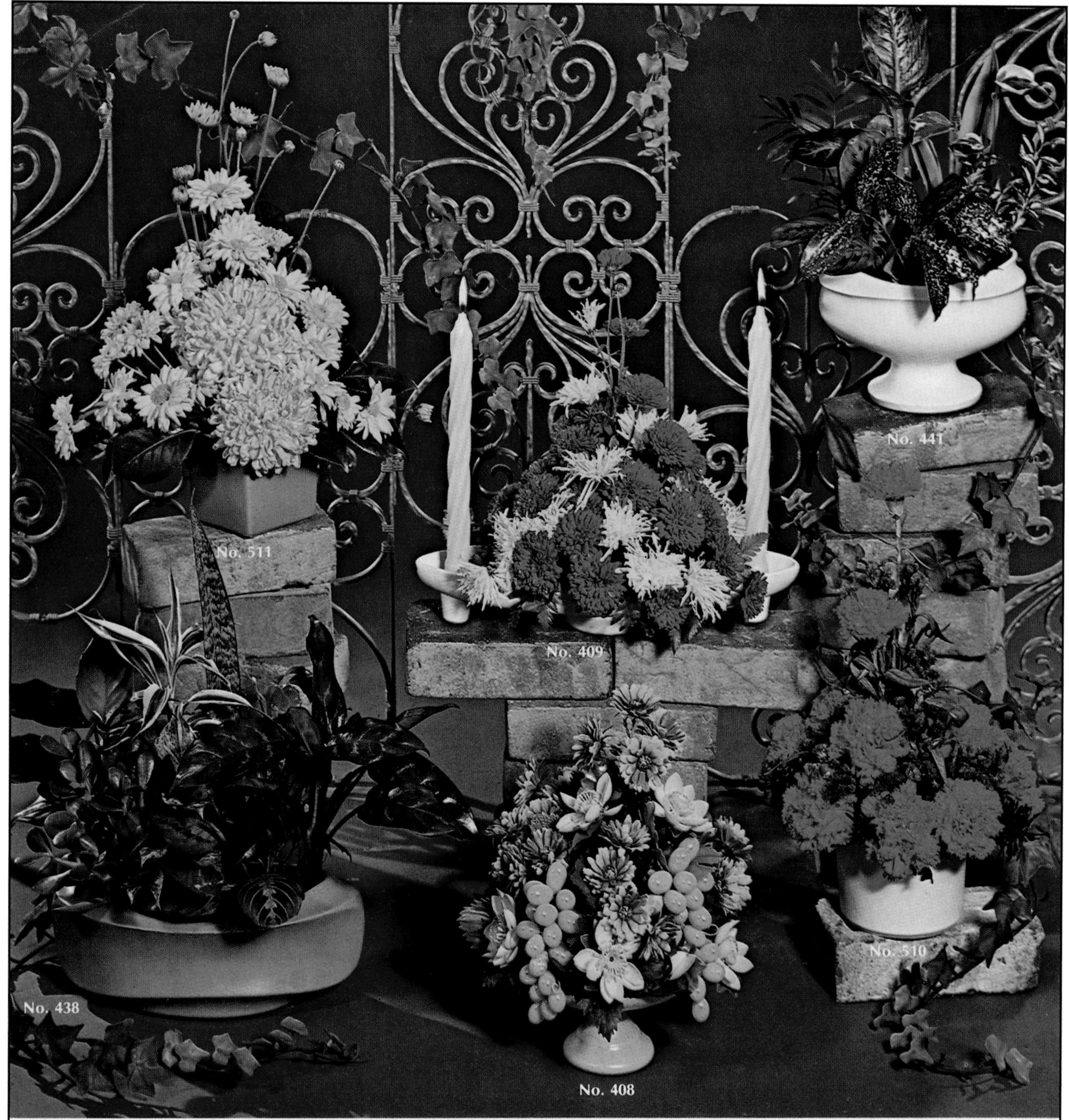

No guess work with these profitable, easy-to-use Roseville Floraline arrangement containers

Whether your order calls for an impressive opening arrangement, a low design of permanents, a candle-lit centerpiece or an old-fashioned bouquet of mixed flowers, these inexpensive, easy-to-use Roseville Floraline containers guarantee profitable, customer-pleasing arrangements every time. Order today!

For description of items No. 408 and No. 441 see page 3.
For description of items No. 409, 438, 510 and 511 see page 4.

SEE PRICE LIST FOR ASSORTMENTS 7

1960s Roseville Floraline catalog.

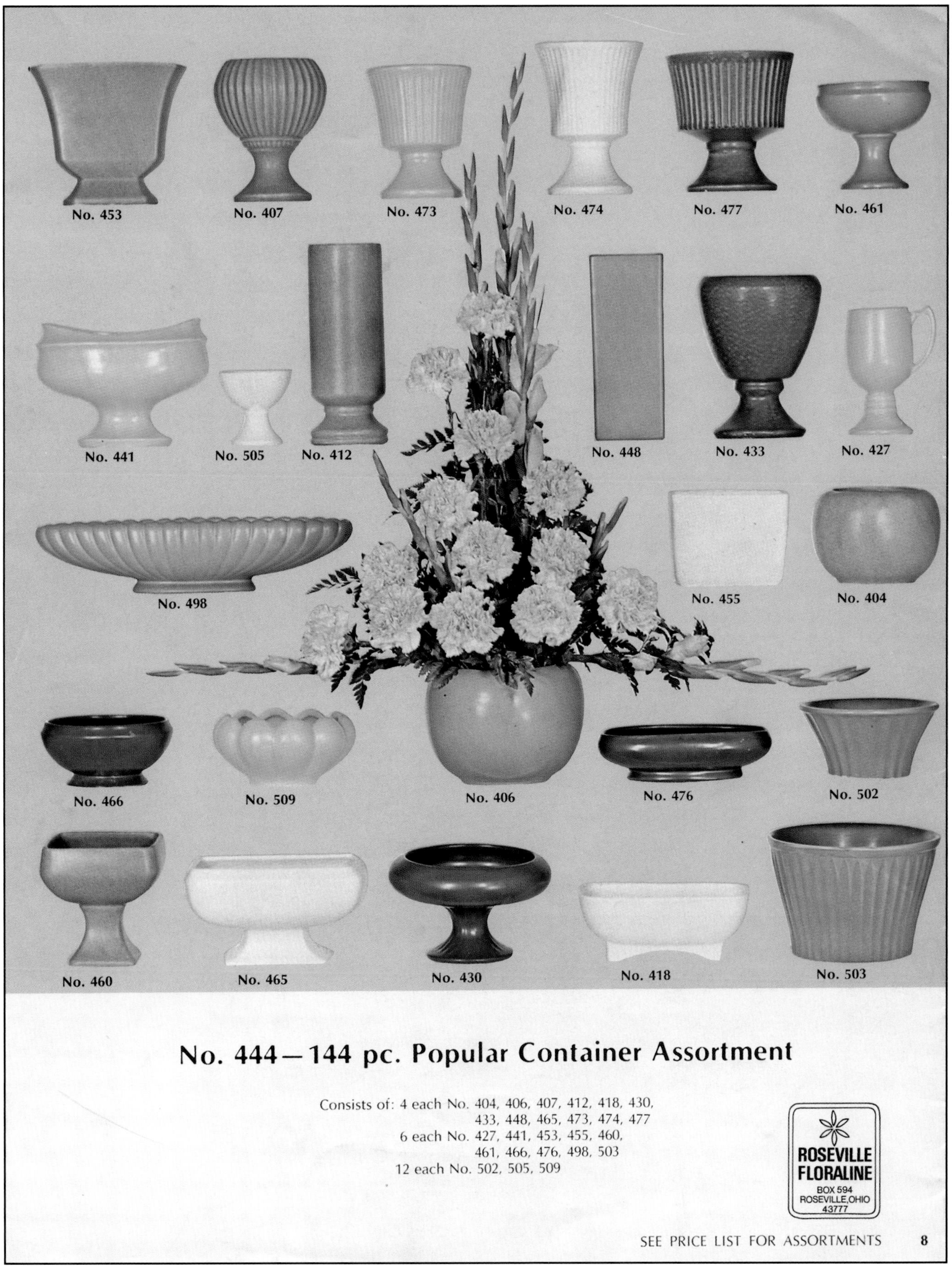
No. 453
No. 407
No. 473
No. 474
No. 477
No. 461
No. 441
No. 505
No. 412
No. 448
No. 433
No. 427
No. 498
No. 455
No. 404
No. 466
No. 509
No. 406
No. 476
No. 502
No. 460
No. 465
No. 430
No. 418
No. 503
No. 444—144 pc. Popular Container Assortment
Consists of: 4 each No. 404, 406, 407, 412, 418, 430, 433, 448, 465, 473, 474, 477
6 each No. 427, 441, 453, 455, 460, 461, 466, 476, 498, 503
12 each No. 502, 505, 509
ROSEVILLE FLORALINE
BOX 594
ROSEVILLE, OHIO
43777
SEE PRICE LIST FOR ASSORTMENTS
8

1960s Roseville Floraline catalog.

Left: Round Utility Vase shown in four glazes. 10" x 4". Model 475-10. $40.00 – 50.00.
This vase was also available in 12" and 14" sizes.
Model 475-14 (14" vase shown on cover). $50.00 – 65.00.

Top right and left: Pedestal Cup 3½" x 4". Shown in two glazes. Model 505. $12.00 – 15.00.
Top middle: Pedestal Bowl 7½" x 8½". Model 499. $30.00 – 40.00.
Bottom: Silver Ribbed Tray 3" x 15". Model 498. $20.00 – 25.00.

Top: Low Oval Bowl 2" x 8". Five glaze colors shown. Model 476-8. $12.00 – 18.00.

Bottom: Low Oval Bowl 3" x 12". Two glaze colors shown. Model 476-12. $15.00 – 20.00.

Top left and right:
Pedestal Planter 6" x 6". Shown in two glazes. Model 477. $12.00. - $18.00.
Footed Planter 3½"x 7½". Model 489. $12.00 – 18.00.
Bottom left and right:
Jardiniere 3½" x 5½". Shown in two glazes. Model 490. $12.00 – 18.00.
Low Oval Bowl 10" x 7¼". Model 486. $15.00 – 20.00.

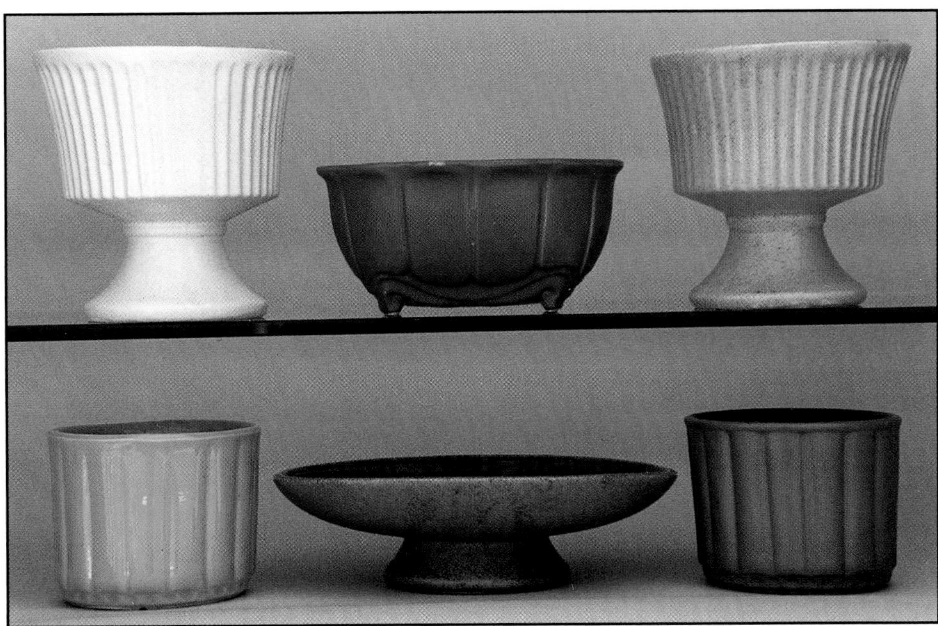

Two glaze colors of model 482 Tall Bouquet Vase. 11½" x 5". $25.00 – 35.00.

Top:
Model 495L. Bouquet Vase 9" high. Two different glazes shown. $20.00 – 25.00.
Model 494. Pedestal Planter 3½" x 7", $12.00 – 18.00.
Bottom left and right:
Pedestal Bowl 5½" x 5½". Two different glazes shown. Model 491L. $12.00 – 18.00.
Pedestal Bowl 6" x 6½". Model 492. $12.00 – 18.00.

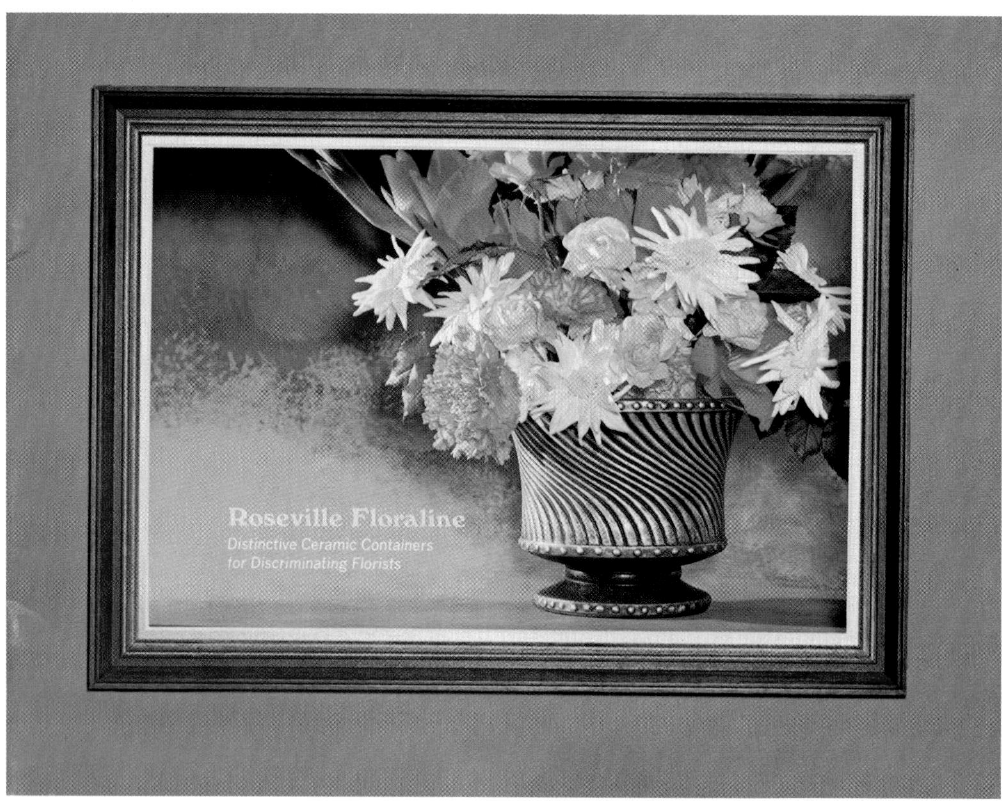

1969 Roseville Floraline catalog page.

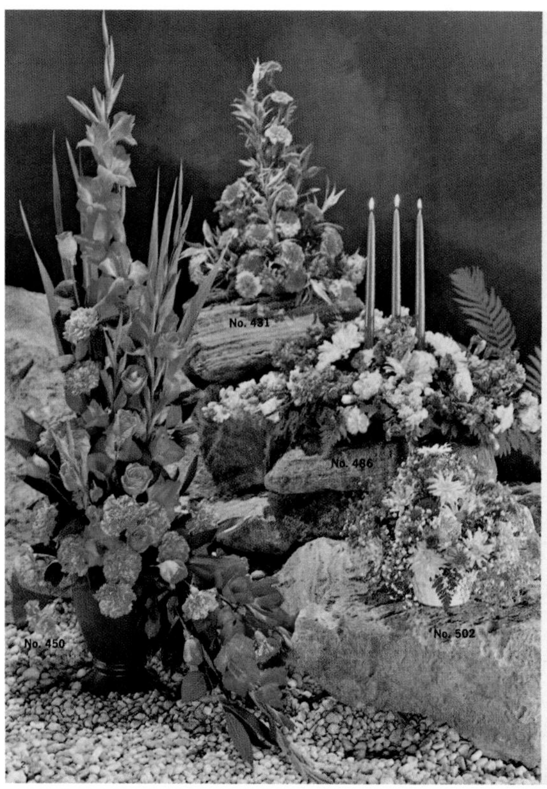

No guess work with these profitable, easy-to-use Roseville Floraline arrangement containers

Whether your order calls for an impressive opening arrangement, a low design of permanents, a candle-lit centerpiece or an old-fashioned bouquet of mixed flowers, these inexpensive, easy-to-use Roseville Floraline containers guarantee profitable, customer-pleasing arrangements every time. Check your inventory and order today.

No. 404—Small Flower Bowl
Height: 4" Dia.: 6½" Opening: 4½"
Packed: 12 (26 lbs.) ......60¢ ea.
Packed: 4 (11 lbs.) ......70¢ ea.

No. 406—Large Flower Bowl
Height: 5" Dia.: 7½" Opening: 5¾"
Packed: 12 (35 lbs.) ......75¢ ea.
Packed: 4 (15 lbs.) ......85¢ ea.

No. 409—Versatile Bouquet Bowl
Length: 15½" Width: 5"
Packed: 12 (29 lbs.) ......80¢ ea.
Packed: 4 (17 lbs.) ......90¢ ea.

No. 415—Round Flower Bowl
Height: 4" Dia.: 5¼" Opening: 3¾"
Packed: 12 (17 lbs.) ......45¢ ea.
Packed: 6 (11 lbs.) ......55¢ ea.

No. 431—
Large Triangular Arrangement Dish
Length: 11" Width: 7"
Packed: 12 (17 lbs.) ......65¢ ea.
Packed: 4 (6 lbs.) ......75¢ ea.

No. 432—
Small Triangular Arrangement Dish
Length: 7" Width: 4½"
Packed: 24 (15 lbs.) ......35¢ ea.
Packed: 6 (8 lbs.) ......45¢ ea.

No. 433—Arrangement Vase
Height: 7½" Opening: 5" circle
Packed: 12 (30 lbs.) ......80¢ ea.
Packed: 4 (10 lbs.) ......90¢ ea.

No. 434—
Scouped Low Arrangement Bowl
Height: 3½" Opening: 7½" x 6½"
Packed: 12 (21 lbs.) ......50¢ ea.
Packed: 4 (9 lbs.) ......60¢ ea.

No. 450—Large Pedestal Urn
Height: 9½" Opening: 6½" circle
Packed: 6 (32 lbs.) .....$1.40 ea.

No. 452—Small Handled Bowl
Height: 4" Dia.: 6" Opening: 4"
Packed: 12 (18 lbs.) ......50¢ ea.
Packed: 6 (11 lbs.) ......60¢ ea.

No. 453—Flared Vase
Height: 6¼" Opening: 7" x 3½"
Packed: 24 (56 lbs.) ......55¢ ea.
Packed: 6 (14 lbs.) ......65¢ ea.

No. 457—Large Handled Bowl
Height: 5½" Dia.: 7¼" Opening: 5¼"
Packed: 12 (36 lbs.) ......75¢ ea.
Packed: 6 (20 lbs.) ......85¢ ea.

No. 486—Low Oval Container
Height: 3" Opening: 10" x 7¼"
Packed: 12 (30 lbs.) ......85¢ ea.
Packed: 6 (15 lbs.) ......95¢ ea.

No. 502—
Flared Arrangement Bowl and Planter
Height: 3½" Opening: 6½" circle
Packed: 24 (36 lbs.) ......35¢ ea.
Packed: 12 (18 lbs.) ......45¢ ea.
(White, Moss Green and Olive Green Bronze only)

Unless specified above, containers available in White, Moss Green, Olive Green Bronze and Slate

1969 Roseville Floraline catalog page.

1969 Roseville Floraline catalog page.

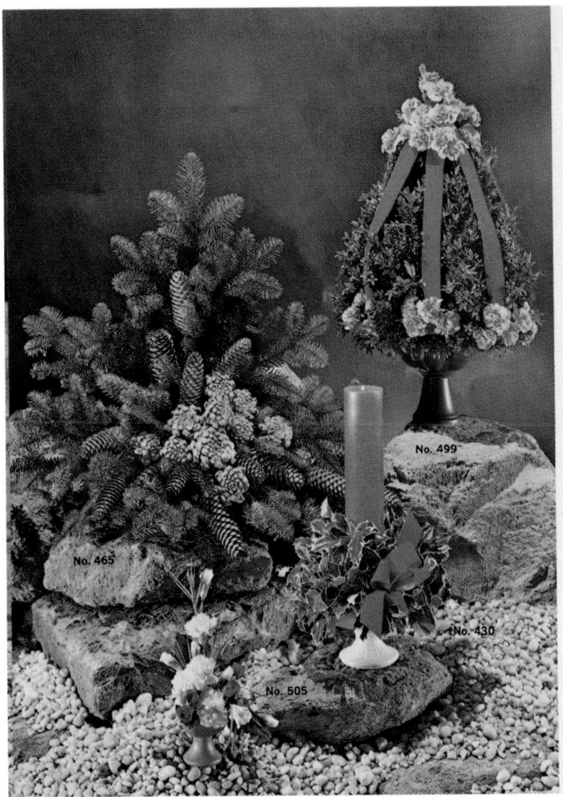

Use these popular Roseville Floraline pedestals to keep your customers coming back for more

Here are containers so practical and so profitable that you cannot afford to be without them. They're convenient to use and enable your designers to put out more work. The perfect solution for Christmas, Valentine's Day, Easter and Mother's Day featured arrangements. And even more important, these reasonably-priced pedestals are sure profit makers for every day of the year! Order a money-making assortment today.

No. 407—Ribbed Pedestal Vase
Height: 6½" Opening: 3¾" circle
Packed: 12 (29 lbs.) ......65¢ ea.
Packed: 4 (13 lbs.) ......75¢ ea.

No. 408—
Pedestal Arrangement Plate
Height: 3½" Diameter: 6¾"
Packed: 12 (23 lbs.) ......55¢ ea.
Packed: 4 (11 lbs.) ......65¢ ea.

No. 430—Classic Pedestal Bowl
Height: 5" Opening: 6" circle
Packed: 12 (27 lbs.) ......70¢ ea.
Packed: 4 (9 lbs.) ......80¢ ea.

No. 460—
Square Pedestal Container
Height: 5½" Opening: 4¾" x 4¾"
Packed: 12 (20 lbs.) ......55¢ ea.
Packed: 6 (11 lbs.) ......65¢ ea.

No. 461—Round Pedestal Container
Height: 5" Opening: 4¾" circle
Packed: 24 (27 lbs.) ......50¢ ea.
Packed: 6 (6 lbs.) ......60¢ ea.

No. 462—
Small Oval Pedestal Container
Height: 4¾" Opening: 5" x 3¾"
Packed: 24 (26 lbs.) ......45¢ ea.
Packed: 6 (7 lbs.) ......55¢ ea.

No. 463—Oval Pedestal Container
Height: 6¼" Opening: 5"x10"x4½"
Packed: 12 (34 lbs.) ......90¢ ea.
Packed: 4 (12 lbs.) ....$1.00 ea.

No. 464—Round Scalloped Pedestal
Height: 7½" Opening: 6" circle
Packed: 12 (34 lbs.) ......90¢ ea.
Packed: 4 (12 lbs.) ....$1.00 ea.

No. 465—Oblong Pedestal Planter
Height: 4½" Opening: 7¼" x 3¾"
Packed: 12 (27 lbs.) ......65¢ ea.
Packed: 4 (10 lbs.) ......75¢ ea.

No. 470—
Small Ribbed Pedestal Vase
Height: 4½" Opening: 4" circle
Packed: 24 (29 lbs.) ......45¢ ea.
Packed: 4 (11 lbs.) ......55¢ ea.

No. 473—Short Ribbed Urn
Height: 6" Opening: 4½" circle
Packed: 12 (21 lbs.) ......55¢ ea.
Packed: 4 (6 lbs.) ......65¢ ea.

No. 474—Ribbed Urn
Height: 7" Opening: 5" circle
Packed: 12 (25 lbs.) ......65¢ ea.
Packed: 4 (10 lbs.) ......75¢ ea.

No. 477—
Large Ribbed Pedestal Vase
Height: 6¼" Opening: 6" circle
Packed: 12 (29 lbs.) ......70¢ ea.
Packed: 4 (9 lbs.) ......80¢ ea.

No. 499—
Fluted Pedestal Container or Planter
Height: 7" Opening: 8" circle
Packed: 6 (16 lbs.) $1.10

No. 504—
Miniature arrangement pedestal
Height: 3¾" Opening: 3¼" circle
Packed: 36 (19 lbs.) ......35¢ ea.
Packed: 12 (7 lbs.) ......40¢ ea.
(White, Moss Green and Olive Green Bronze only)

No. 505—
Miniature pedestal container
Height: 3½" Opening: 3½" circle
Packed: 36 (19 lbs.) ......35¢ ea.
Packed: 12 (7 lbs.) ......40¢ ea.
(White, Moss Green and Olive Green Bronze only)

Unless specified above, containers available in White, Moss Green, Olive Green Bronze and Slate

1969 Roseville Floraline catalog page.

1969 Roseville Floraline catalog page.

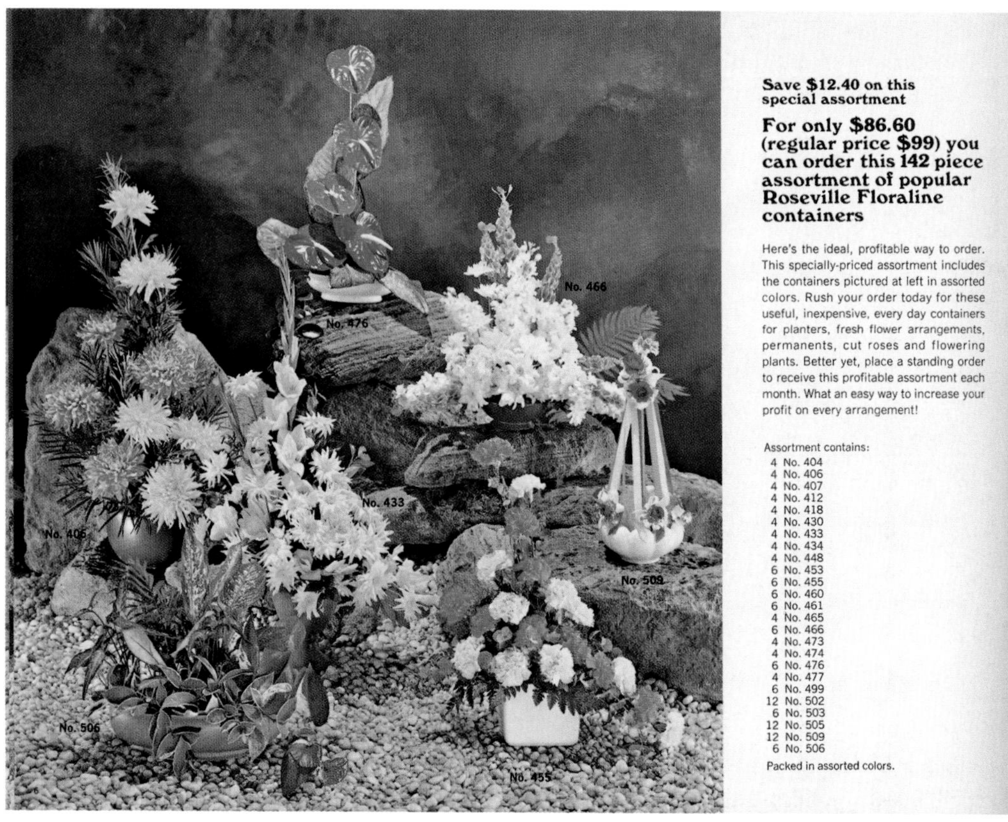

No. 466
No. 476
No. 433
No. 406
No. 509
No. 506
No. 455
Save $12.40 on this special assortment
For only $86.60 (regular price $99) you can order this 142 piece assortment of popular Roseville Floraline containers
Here's the ideal, profitable way to order. This specially-priced assortment includes the containers pictured at left in assorted colors. Rush your order today for these useful, inexpensive, every day containers for planters, fresh flower arrangements, permanents, cut roses and flowering plants. Better yet, place a standing order to receive this profitable assortment each month. What an easy way to increase your profit on every arrangement!
Assortment contains:
4 No. 404
4 No. 406
4 No. 407
4 No. 412
4 No. 418
4 No. 430
4 No. 433
4 No. 434
4 No. 448
6 No. 453
6 No. 455
6 No. 460
6 No. 461
4 No. 465
6 No. 466
4 No. 473
4 No. 474
6 No. 476
4 No. 477
6 No. 499
12 No. 502
6 No. 503
12 No. 505
12 No. 509
6 No. 506
Packed in assorted colors.

1969 Roseville Floraline catalog page.

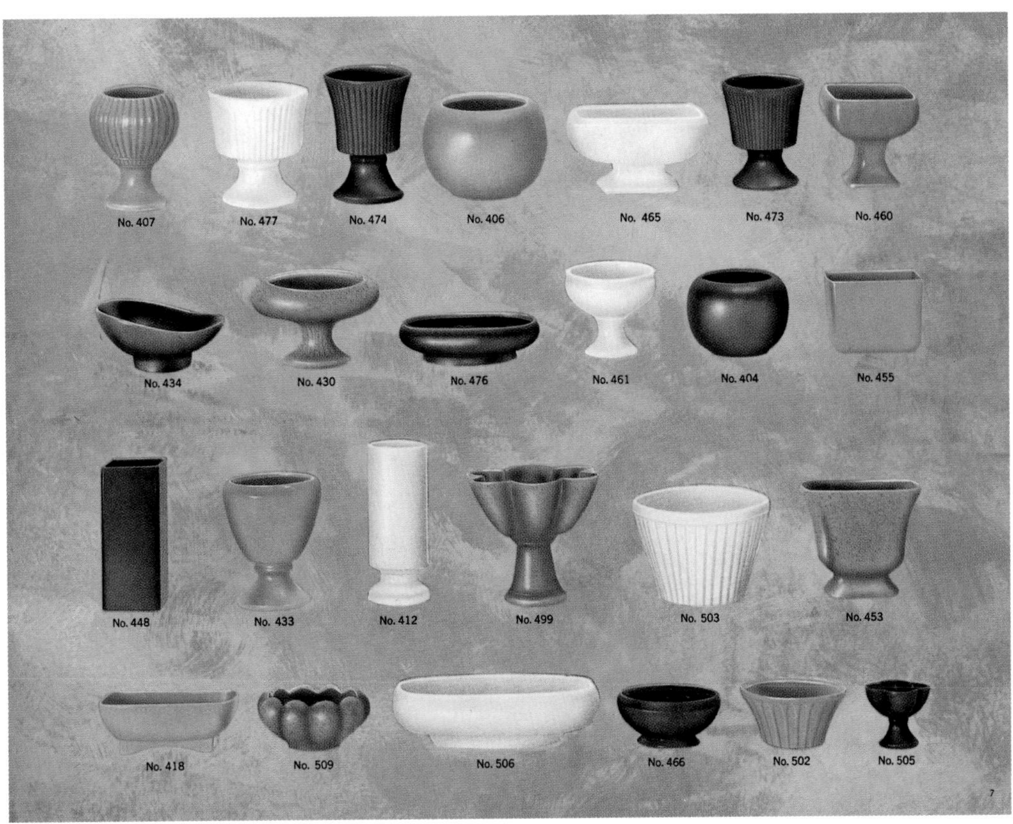

1969 Roseville Floraline catalog page.

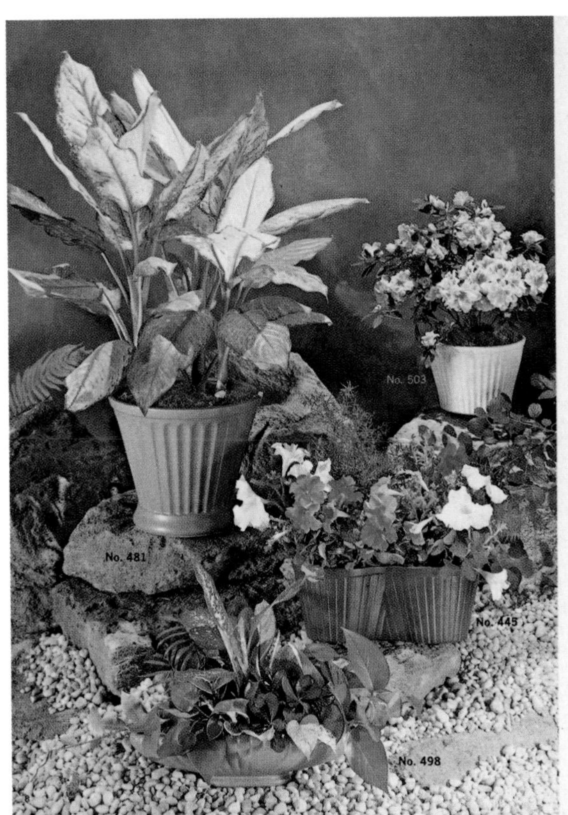

Increase your sales and profits with these economical Roseville Floraline planters and jardinieres

Put your best foot forward! Style your plants in these attractive containers and deliver your foliage and flowering plants in these good-looking jardinieres. You'll be the most talked-about florist in town. Roseville Floraline specially designed these containers to keep plants healthy and growing so your customers will be pleased and your sales and profits will keep growing!

No. 411—6" Rectangular Planter
Height: 4" Opening: 6¼" x 3½"
Packed: 24 (35 lbs.) ......45¢ ea.
Packed: 6 (13 lbs.) ......55¢ ea.

No. 418—Footed Planter
Height: 3" Opening: 8"x4"
Packed: 12 (21 lbs.) ......45¢ ea.
Packed: 4 (6 lbs.) ......55¢ ea.

No. 445—Double Plant Jardiniere
(Holds 2 clay pots)
Height: 5½" Length: 13½"
Openings: Two 6" circles
Packed: 6 (32 lbs.) .....$1.40 ea.

No. 466—
Round Footed Flower Bowl
Height: 3" Opening: 5½" circle
Packed: 24 (25 lbs.) ......50¢ ea.
Packed: 6 (7 lbs.) ......60¢ ea.

No. 468—Footed Planter
Height: 2¾" Opening: 6½" x 4½"
Packed: 24 (38 lbs.) ......45¢ ea.
Packed: 6 (10 lbs.) ......55¢ ea.

No. 476—Low Oval Footed Bowl
Height: 2½" Opening: 7½" x 4¼"
Packed: 12 (15 lbs.) ......55¢ ea.
Packed: 6 (10 lbs.) ......65¢ ea.

No. 480—8" Jardiniere
(Holds 6" standard clay pot)
Height: 7¾" Opening: 8" circle
Packed: 6 (35 lbs.) .....$1.25 ea.

No. 481—10" Jardiniere
(Holds 8" standard clay pot))
Height: 10" Opening: 11" circle
Packed: 4 (45 lbs.) ....$1.85 ea.

No. 498—Ribbed Oblong
Arrangement Bowl and Planter
Height: 3½" Opening: 14½" x 3¼"
Packed: 6 (15 lbs.) .....$1.10 ea.

No. 501—Small Jardiniere
(Holds 4" standard clay pot)
Height: 5¼" Opening: 5½"
Packed: 24 (50 lbs.) ......40¢ ea.
Packed: 12 (25 lbs.) ......50¢ ea.
(White, Moss Green and Olive Green Bronze only)

No. 503—Azalea Jardiniere
(Holds 6" azalea clay pot)
Height: 5½" Opening: 8"
Packed: 12 (35 lbs.) ......80¢ ea.
Packed: 6 (8 lbs.) ......90¢ ea.
(White, Moss Green and Olive Green Bronze only)

No. 506—12" Oval Planter
Height: 3½" Opening: 12"x7"
Packed: 6 (20 lbs.) .....$1.50 ea.
(White, Moss Green and Olive Green Bronze only)

No. 507—10½" Gondola Planter
Height: 3¼" Opening: 8" x 3½"
Packed: 12 (23 lbs.) ......65¢ ea.
Packed: 6 (12 lbs.) ......75¢ ea.
(White, Moss Green and Olive Green Bronze only)

No. 508—14½" Gondola Planter
Height: 4" Opening: 12" x 4½"
Packed: 4 (17 lbs.) .....$1.50 ea.
(White, Moss Green and Olive Green Bronze only)

No. 509—Round
Fluted Flower Bowl and Planter
Height: 3" Opening: 5" circle
Packed: 12 (25 lbs.) ......50¢ ea.
Packed: 6 (13 lbs.) ......60¢ ea.
(White, Moss Green and Olive Green Bronze only)

Unless specified above, containers available in White, Moss Green, Olive Green Bronze and Slate

1969 Roseville Floraline catalog page.

1969 Roseville Floraline catalog page.

Versatile Roseville Floraline containers speak highly of your reputation

These useful containers serve many profitable purposes. Flowers properly displayed are easier to sell—and Roseville's utility containers make your flowers look their very best! For exquisite tall arrangements, and graceful bouquets of roses, Roseville's tall containers are superb! And the progressive, promotional-minded florist selects Roseville's auto and arrangement mug for sure sales winners! Keep a complete selection of these profitable containers in stock at all times.

No. 400—Rose Vase
Height: 8¾" Opening: 3½" circle
Packed: 12 (23 lbs.) ......65¢ ea.
Packed: 4 (11 lbs.) ......75¢ ea.

No. 412—Round Footed Vase
Height: 9¼" Opening: 3¾"
Packed: 12 (26 lbs.) ......65¢ ea.
Packed: 4 (16 lbs.) ......75¢ ea.

No. 421—10" Stock Vase
Height: 10½" Opening: 6" circle
Packed: 6 (29 lbs.) ....$1.35 ea.

No. 422—12" Stock Vase
Height: 12½" Opening: 7" circle
Packed: 4 (30 lbs.) ....$1.85 ea.

No. 424—14" Stock Vase
Height: 14½" Opening: 7" circle
Packed: 4 (35 lbs.) ....$2.10 ea.

No. 427—Arrangement Mug
Height: 6" Opening: 2½" circle
Packed: 24 (24 lbs.) ......55¢ ea.
Packed: 6 (4 lbs.) ......65¢ ea.

**No. 446—
9" Squared Cylindrical Vase**
Height: 9¼" Opening: 3¼" x 3¼"
Packed: 12 (35 lbs.) ......70¢ ea.
Packed: 4 (15 lbs.) ......80¢ ea.

**No. 447—
7" Squared Cylindrical Vase**
Height: 7¼" Opening: 2¾" x 2¾"
Packed: 12 (23 lbs.) ......60¢ ea.
Packed: 4 (11 lbs.) ......70¢ ea.

**No. 448—
8" Squared Cylindrical Vase**
Height: 8¼" Opening: 3" x 3"
Packed: 12 (29 lbs.) ......65¢ ea.
Packed: 4 (13 lbs.) ......75¢ ea.

**No. 449—
10" Squared Cylindrical Vase**
Height: 10¼" Opening: 3¼" x 3¼"
Packed: 12 (41 lbs.) ......80¢ ea.
Packed: 4 (17 lbs.) ......90¢ ea.

No. 455—Small Pillow Vase
Height: 4½" Opening: 5¼" x 3¼"
Packed: 24 (37 lbs.) ......45¢ ea.
Packed: 6 (10 lbs.) ......55¢ ea.

No. 456—Large Pillow Vase
Height: 6½" Opening: 5½" x 3½"
Packed: 24 (63 lbs.) ......60¢ ea.
Packed: 6 (16 lbs.) ......70¢ ea.

No. 458—Bud Vase
Height: 6¼" Opening: 1" circle
Packed: 24 (13 lbs.) ......45¢ ea.
Packed: 6 (4 lbs.) ......55¢ ea.

No. 482—Tall Bouquet Vase
Height: 11½" Opening: 5" circle
Packed: 6 (26 lbs.) ....$1.25 ea.

No. 500—Auto Planter
Height: 4" Opening: 3½" x 4"
Packed: 12 (38 lbs.) ....$1.10 ea.
Packed: 6 (19 lbs.) ....$1.20 ea.
(Birchwood with hand decoration only)

Unless specified above, containers available in White, Moss Green, Olive Green Bronze and Slate

1969 Roseville Floraline catalog page.

1969 Roseville Floraline catalog page.

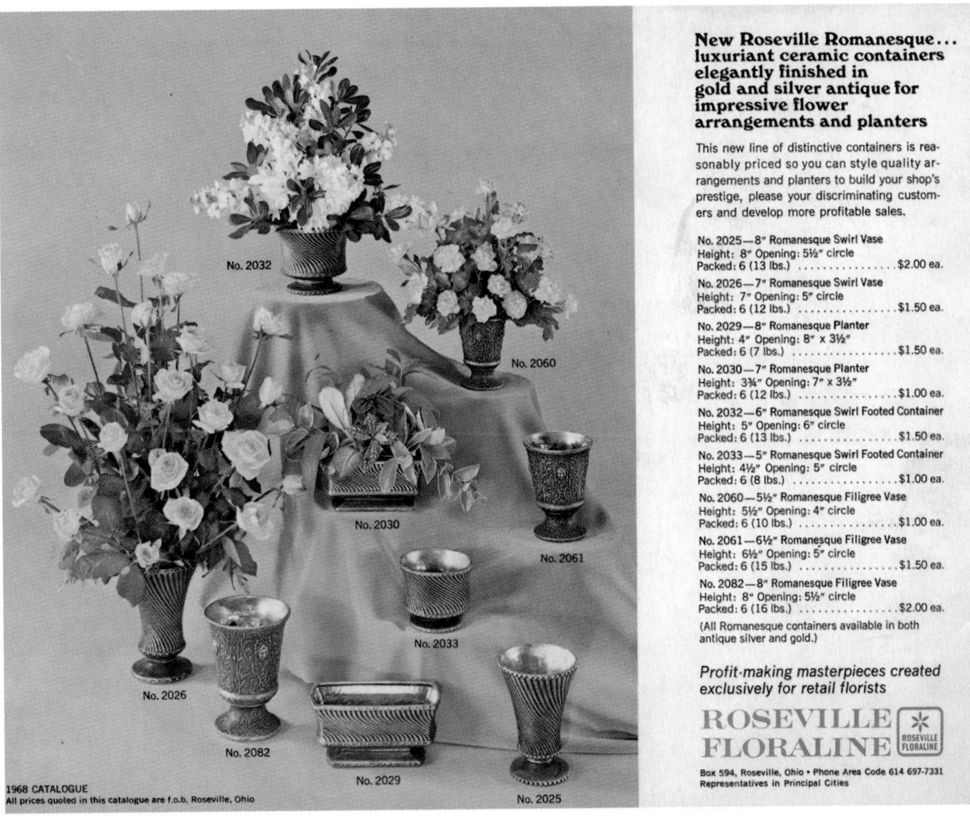

No. 2032
No. 2060
No. 2030
No. 2061
No. 2033
No. 2026
No. 2082
No. 2029
No. 2025

1968 CATALOGUE
All prices quoted in this catalogue are f.o.b. Roseville, Ohio

New Roseville Romanesque... luxuriant ceramic containers elegantly finished in gold and silver antique for impressive flower arrangements and planters

This new line of distinctive containers is reasonably priced so you can style quality arrangements and planters to build your shop's prestige, please your discriminating customers and develop more profitable sales.

No. 2025—8" Romanesque Swirl Vase
Height: 8" Opening: 5½" circle
Packed: 6 (13 lbs.) .... $2.00 ea.

No. 2026—7" Romanesque Swirl Vase
Height: 7" Opening: 5" circle
Packed: 6 (12 lbs.) .... $1.50 ea.

No. 2029—8" Romanesque Planter
Height: 4" Opening: 8" x 3½"
Packed: 6 (7 lbs.) .... $1.50 ea.

No. 2030—7" Romanesque Planter
Height: 3¾" Opening: 7" x 3½"
Packed: 6 (12 lbs.) .... $1.00 ea.

No. 2032—6" Romanesque Swirl Footed Container
Height: 5" Opening: 6" circle
Packed: 6 (13 lbs.) .... $1.50 ea.

No. 2033—5" Romanesque Swirl Footed Container
Height: 4½" Opening: 5" circle
Packed: 6 (8 lbs.) .... $1.00 ea.

No. 2060—5½" Romanesque Filigree Vase
Height: 5½" Opening: 4" circle
Packed: 6 (10 lbs.) .... $1.00 ea.

No. 2061—6½" Romanesque Filigree Vase
Height: 6½" Opening: 5" circle
Packed: 6 (15 lbs.) .... $1.50 ea.

No. 2082—8" Romanesque Filigree Vase
Height: 8" Opening: 5½" circle
Packed: 6 (16 lbs.) .... $2.00 ea.

(All Romanesque containers available in both antique silver and gold.)

Profit-making masterpieces created exclusively for retail florists

ROSEVILLE FLORALINE
ROSEVILLE FLORALINE

Box 594, Roseville, Ohio • Phone Area Code 614 697-7331
Representatives in Principal Cities

1969 Roseville Floraline catalog page.

Top left and right:
Pedestal Cup 3½" x 3½". Model 504. $12.00 – 18.00.
Model 506 Utility Bowl 3½" wide. $15.00 – 20.00.
Bottom:
Flower Bowl, 3+" x 6". Shown in three glazes. Model 506L. $12.00 – 15.00.

White Shoe Planter 3" x 8½". Model 530. $18.00 – 25.00.
Pedestal Arrangement Plate 3½" x 6¾". Model 408. $18.00 – 25.00.

Large Octagon Bowls 4½" x 7½". Model 423L. Shown in two glazes. $15.00 – 20.00.

Top:
Shoe Planter 3" x 8½". Model 530. $18.00 – 25.00.
Round Flower Pot 4" x 5". Model 510. $10.00 – 15.00.
Scalloped Bowl 3" x 6". Model 509. $10.00 – 15.00.
Bottom:
Square Block Planter 4" x 4". Model 511. $10.00 – 15.00.
Round Planter 3½" x 7". Model 522. $12.00 – 18.00.
Round Bowl 3" x 5". Model 518. $10.00 – 15.00.

Outstanding Cradle Planter 4" x 6" x 3¼". Model 491. $65.00 – 95.00.

Top:
Baby Planter 3¼" x 5½" x 2½". Model 590L. $15.00 – 25.00.
Cradle Planter 4½" x 3¾" x 3". Model 592L. $20.00 – 30.00.
Baby Block Planter 4¼" x 3¼" x 3¼". Model 591L. $20.00 – 25.00.
Bottom:
Baby Cradle Planter 4⅛" x 3⅞" x 6". Model 547. $25.00 – 35.00.
Baby Shoe Planter 4" x 3½". Model 549. $25.00 – 35.00.

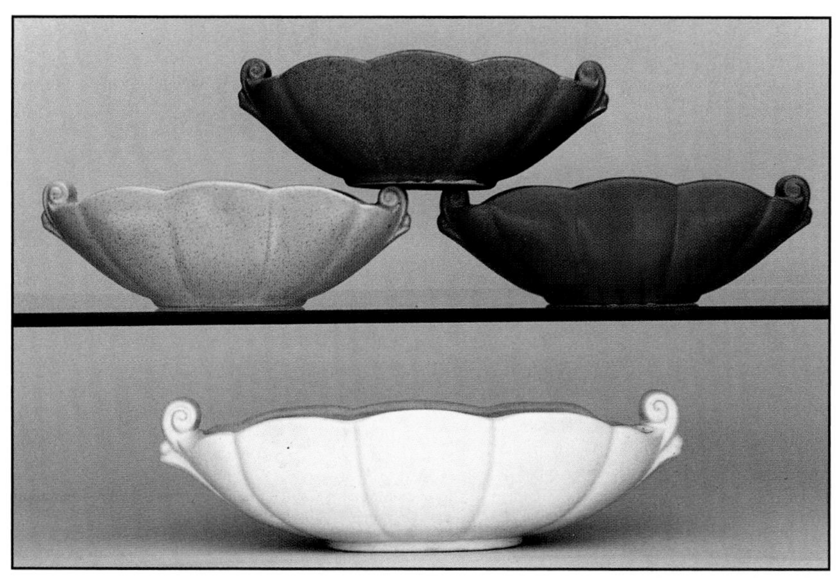

Top:
Model 507 Gondola Planter 10½" x 3¼". $20.00 – 25.00.
Bottom:
Model 508 Gondola Planter 14½" x 4½". $25.00 – 35.00.

Top:
Oasis Arrangement Dish 3½" x 10½". Model 520. $20.00 – 25.00.
Oasis Arrangement Dish 3½" x 7½". Model 521. $18.00 – 25.00.
Bottom:
Flared Oasis Dish 4½" x 5½". Shown in two glazes. Model 526. $15.00 – 20.00.
Flared Oasis Dish 5½"x 8". Model 525. $15.00 – 25.00.

50-0454-82 108 pc. Popular Container Assortment
Consists of: 6 50-0404, 50-0427, 50-0455, 50-0461, 50-0466, 50-0476, 50-0502, 50-0509, 50-0510
4 50-0407, 50-0412, 50-0430, 50-0453, 50-0460, 50-0465, 50-0473, 50-0474, 50-0477
3 50-0401, 50-0406, 50-0418, 50-0433, 50-0448, 50-0503
50-474
50-0412
50-427
50-0460
50-401
50-448
50-0510
50-0453
50-433
50-0473
50-0477
50-0503
50-0502
50-455
50-0461
50-6407
50-406
50-0430
50-0466
50-0404
50-0509
50-0465
50-0418
50-0476
Roseville Floraline
P. O. BOX 594 • ROSEVILLE, OHIO 43777
A/C 614 697-7331

Cover page of 1971 Roseville Floraline catalog.

1971 Roseville Floraline catalog.

1971 Roseville Floraline catalog.

No. 50-0401
Dozen Rose Vase
Height 9½"
Opening 4¼"

No. 50-0482
Tall Bouquet Vase
Height 11½"
Opening 5"

No. 50-0402
Tall Rose Vase
Height 11"
Opening 4¼"

No. 50-0480
Jardiniere
(holds 6" standard clay pot)
7¾"x8"
Opening 8"

No. 50-0456
Large Pillow Vase
Opening 5½"x3½" Height 6½"

No. 50-0413
Dozen Rose Vase
9¼"x4⅝"

No. 50-0503
Azalea Jardiniere
(holds 6" Azalea clay pot)
Height 5½"
Opening 8"

(Disc.)
No. 50-0547-00
Cradle Planter
4¼"x7¼"
Opening 4"x6"

No. 50-0500-06
Auto Planter
Height 4"
Opening 3½"x4"

No. 50-0546-00
Donkey Planter
10¼"x8"x4½"
Opening 4"x4¾"

No. 50-0412
Round Footed Vase
Height 9¼"
Opening 3¾"

No. 50-0448
Square Vase
Height 8¼"
Opening
3"x3"

No. 50-0403
Bud Vase
Height 8¾"
Opening 2¼"

(Disc.)
No. 50-0553-03
Kiddie Planter
4"x5"

No. 50-0458
Bud Vase
Height 6¼"
Opening 1"

No. 50-0551-84
Turtle Planter
7¾"x4¾"x3½"
Opening 2½"x4½"

(Disc.)
No. 50-0549-00
Shoe Planter
4"x7¼"x4½"
Opening 3"x3¼"

No. 50-0446
Square Vase
Height 9¼"
Opening 3¼"x3¼"

No. 50-0481
Jardiniere
(holds 8" standard clay pot)
Height 10"
Opening 11"

No. 50-0455
Small Pillow Vase
Height 4½"
Opening 5¼"x3¼"

No. 50-0453
Flared Vase
Height 6¼"
Opening 7"x3½"

No. 50-0552-84
Frog Planter
5"x7¾"x5¾"
Opening 2¼"x4"

1972

JANUARY — S M T W T F S — 1 / 2 3 4 5 6 7 8 / 9 10 11 12 13 14 15 / 16 17 18 19 20 21 22 / 23 24 25 26 27 28 29 / 30 31
FEBRUARY — S M T W T F S — 1 2 3 4 5 / 6 7 8 9 10 11 12 / 13 14 15 16 17 18 19 / 20 21 22 23 24 25 26 / 27 28 29
MARCH — S M T W T F S — 1 2 3 4 / 5 6 7 8 9 10 11 / 12 13 14 15 16 17 18 / 19 20 21 22 23 24 25 / 26 27 28 29 30 31
APRIL — S M T W T F S — 1 / 2 3 4 5 6 7 8 / 9 10 11 12 13 14 15 / 16 17 18 19 20 21 22 / 23 24 25 26 27 28 29 / 30
MAY — S M T W T F S — 1 2 3 4 5 6 / 7 8 9 10 11 12 13 / 14 15 16 17 18 19 20 / 21 22 23 24 25 26 27 / 28 29 30 31
JUNE — S M T W T F S — 1 2 3 / 4 5 6 7 8 9 10 / 11 12 13 14 15 16 17 / 18 19 20 21 22 23 24 / 25 26 27 28 29 30
JULY — S M T W T F S — 1 / 2 3 4 5 6 7 8 / 9 10 11 12 13 14 15 / 16 17 18 19 20 21 22 / 23 24 25 26 27 28 29 / 30 31
AUGUST — S M T W T F S — 1 2 3 4 5 / 6 7 8 9 10 11 12 / 13 14 15 16 17 18 19 / 20 21 22 23 24 25 26 / 27 28 29 30 31
SEPTEMBER — S M T W T F S — 1 2 / 3 4 5 6 7 8 9 / 10 11 12 13 14 15 16 / 17 18 19 20 21 22 23 / 24 25 26 27 28 29 30
OCTOBER — S M T W T F S — 1 2 3 4 5 6 7 / 8 9 10 11 12 13 14 / 15 16 17 18 19 20 21 / 22 23 24 25 26 27 28 / 29 30 31
NOVEMBER — S M T W T F S — 1 2 3 4 / 5 6 7 8 9 10 11 / 12 13 14 15 16 17 18 / 19 20 21 22 23 24 25 / 26 27 28 29 30
DECEMBER — S M T W T F S — 1 2 / 3 4 5 6 7 8 9 / 10 11 12 13 14 15 16 / 17 18 19 20 21 22 23 / 24 25 26 27 28 29 30 / 31

1971 Roseville Floraline catalog.

50-0439
50-0435
50-0437
50-402
50-0441
50-401
50-0438
50-0436
50-0440
50-0403
50-0442

Refer to price list for correct assortment descriptions

50-0451-81
92 pc. Utility Assortment

Consists of:
12 ea. 50-0502, 50-0510
6 ea. 50-0461, 50-0466, 50-0473
50-0476, 50-0485, 50-0509
50-0521, 50-0526
4 ea. 50-0401
50-0455
50-0500
50-0511
50-0522

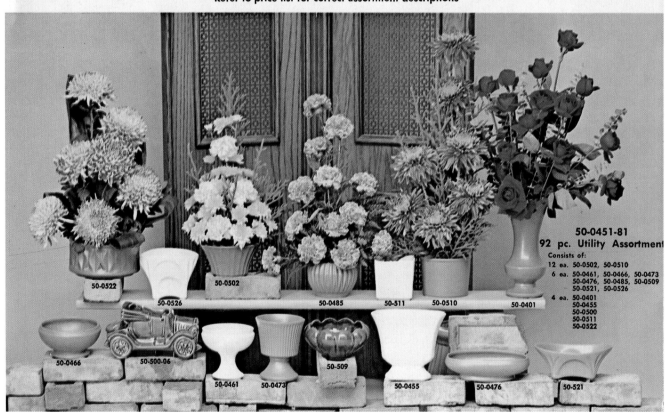

50-0522
50-0526
50-0502
50-0485
50-511
50-0510
50-0401
50-0466
50-500-06
50-509
50-0461
50-0473
50-0455
50-0476
50-521

1971 Roseville Floraline catalog.

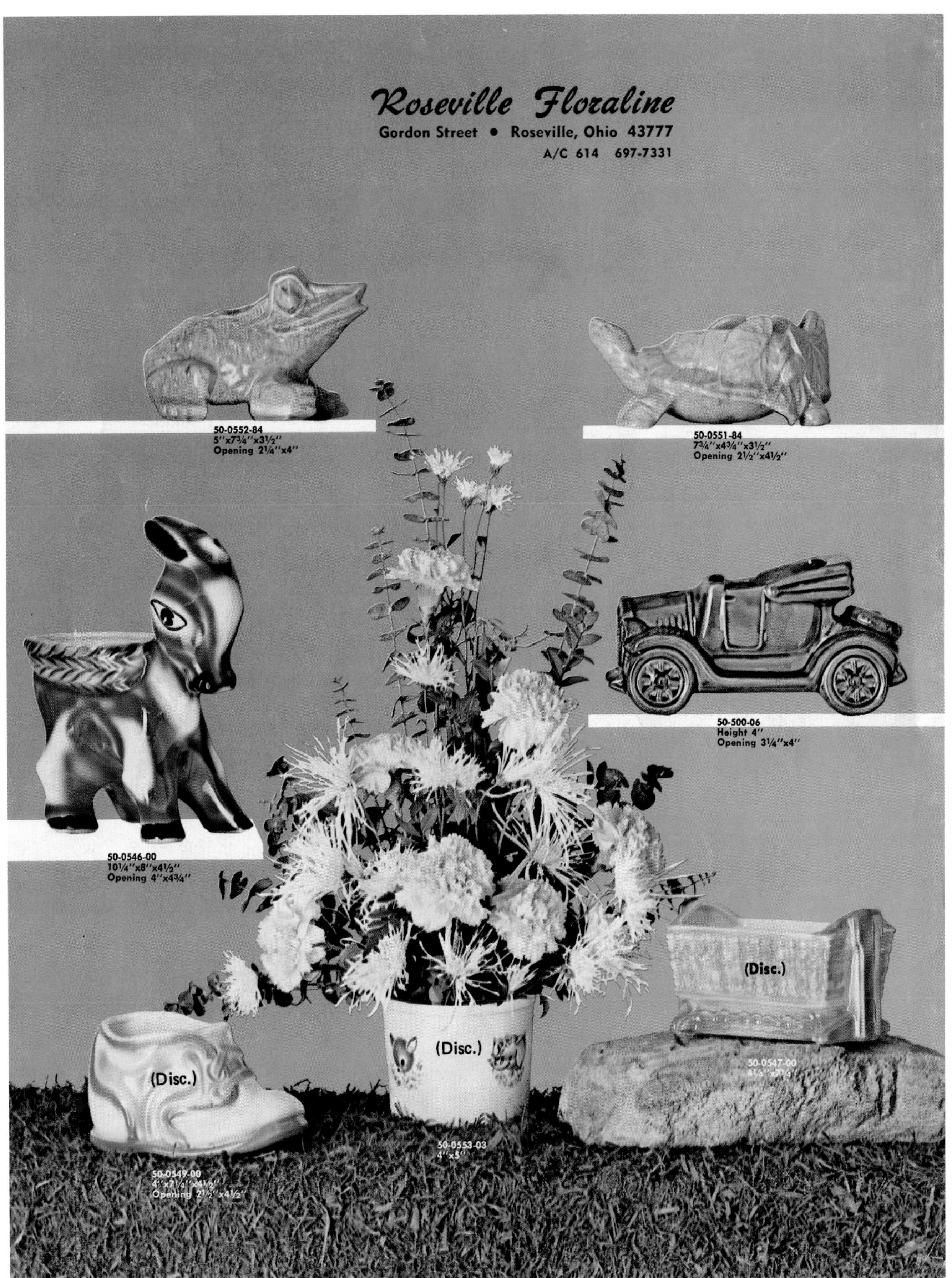

1971 Roseville Floraline catalog page.

Leaves Planters 9⅛" x 3½" x 9". Model 545. $50.00 – 75.00.

Spiral Bud Vase 6½" x 1¼". Shown in three glaze colors. Model 542L. $10.00 – 15.00.
Leaves Planter. Model 545. $50.00 – 75.00.

Top:
Auto Planter 3½"x 8". Model 532L. $10.00 – 20.00.
Bottom:
Turtle Planter 2" x 5". $12.00 – 18.00.
Bear Planter 2" x 5". Model 482L. $18.00 – 25.00.
Horse Planter 3¾" x 5". Model 483L. $18.00 – 25.00.
Dog Planter 2" x 4¾". Model 481L. $18.00 – 25.00.

This beautiful array of Floraline is named Handkerchief, and Billie McCoy is said to be responsible for its design.

Large Jardiniere 5¾" x 7½". Model 538L. $20.00 – 30.00.
Large Vase 8¾" x 6". Model 533L. $35.00 – 40.00.
Small Pedestal Container 5" x 4½". Model 537L. $20.00 – 25.00.
Bud Vase 8¾" x 1¾". Model 534L. $20.00 – 25.00.
Small Jardiniere 3¾" x 4¾". Model 535L. $20.00 – 25.00.

Top:
Wild Waves Planter 3½"x 11". Model 548L. $15.00 – 20.00.
Wild Waves Planter 3" x 9". Model 547L. $15.00 – 20.00.
Bottom:
Large Wild Waves Planter 4½" x 13". Model 549L. $20.00 – 25.00.

Top left and right:
Rock Planter 3¾" x 9". Shown in two glazes. Model 553L. $15.00 – 20.00.
Center: Fancy Vase 6" x 5". Model 535L. $18.00 – 22.00.
Bottom left and right:
Flower Bowl 3½" x 7". Shown in two glazes. Model 550L. $15.00 – 20.00.
Center: Round Flower Bowl 3" x 4½". Model 540L. $10.00 – 15.00.

Top:
Basket Planter 7" x 7½". Model 561L. $25.00 – 35.00.
Bird Vase 8½" x 6". Model 563L. $25.00 – 35.00.
Bottom:
Wheat Theme Vase 4" x 6". Model 571L. $15.00 – 20.00.
Checker Flowerpot 3½" x 6". Model 572L. $12.00 – 18.00.
Apple Tree Jardiniere 4" x 4". Model 570L. $25.00 – $35.00.

Checker Flowerpot without saucer 3½" x 6". Model 572L. $12.00 – 18.00.
Checker Flowerpot with attached Saucer. Model 589L. $25.00 – 30.00.

Top:
Pedestal Bowl 5¾" x 5". Model 574L. $15.00 – 20.00.
Tall Silver Vase 8" x 4". Model 568L. $15.00 – 20.00.
Bottom:
Jardiniere 5" x 5". Model 573L. $18.00 – 22.00.
Pedestal Bowl 4½" x 5". Model 584L. $18.00 – 22.00.
Low Pedestal Bowl 4" x 6". Model 576L. $18.00 – 22.00.

Top:
Pedestal Bowl 6" x 6½". Model 575L. $20.00 – 25.00.
Jardiniere 3½" x 7". Model 582L. $20.00 – 25.00.
Bottom:
Basket Weave Planter 3" x 9". Model 585L. $12.00 – 18.00.
Large Basket Weave Planter 3½" x 11". Model 586L. $18.00 – 22.00.

Top:
Heavy Vase 9" x 6". Model 593L. $25.00 – 35.00.
Beautiful Bud Vase 8" x 3". Model 588L. $15.00 – 20.00.
Bottom:
Small Ribbed Flower Bowl 3¾" x 6". Model 579L. $20.00 – 25.00.
Large Ribbed Flower Bowl 5" x 7". Model 580L. $20.00 – 25.00.

Top:
Large Romanesque Vase 8" x 6". Model 2025M. $20.00 – 25.00.
Small Romanesque Vase 7" x 5". Model 2026M. $15.00 – 20.00.
Romanesque Planter 4" x 8". Model 2030M. $15.00 – 20.00.
Bottom:
Matte Swirl Planter 4" x 8". Model 2029M. $15.00 – 20.00.
Romanesque Jardiniere 4" x 5". Model 2033M. $15.00 – 20.00.
Romanesque Jardiniere 5" x 6". Model 2032. $15.00 – 25.00.

Roseville Floraline 1975

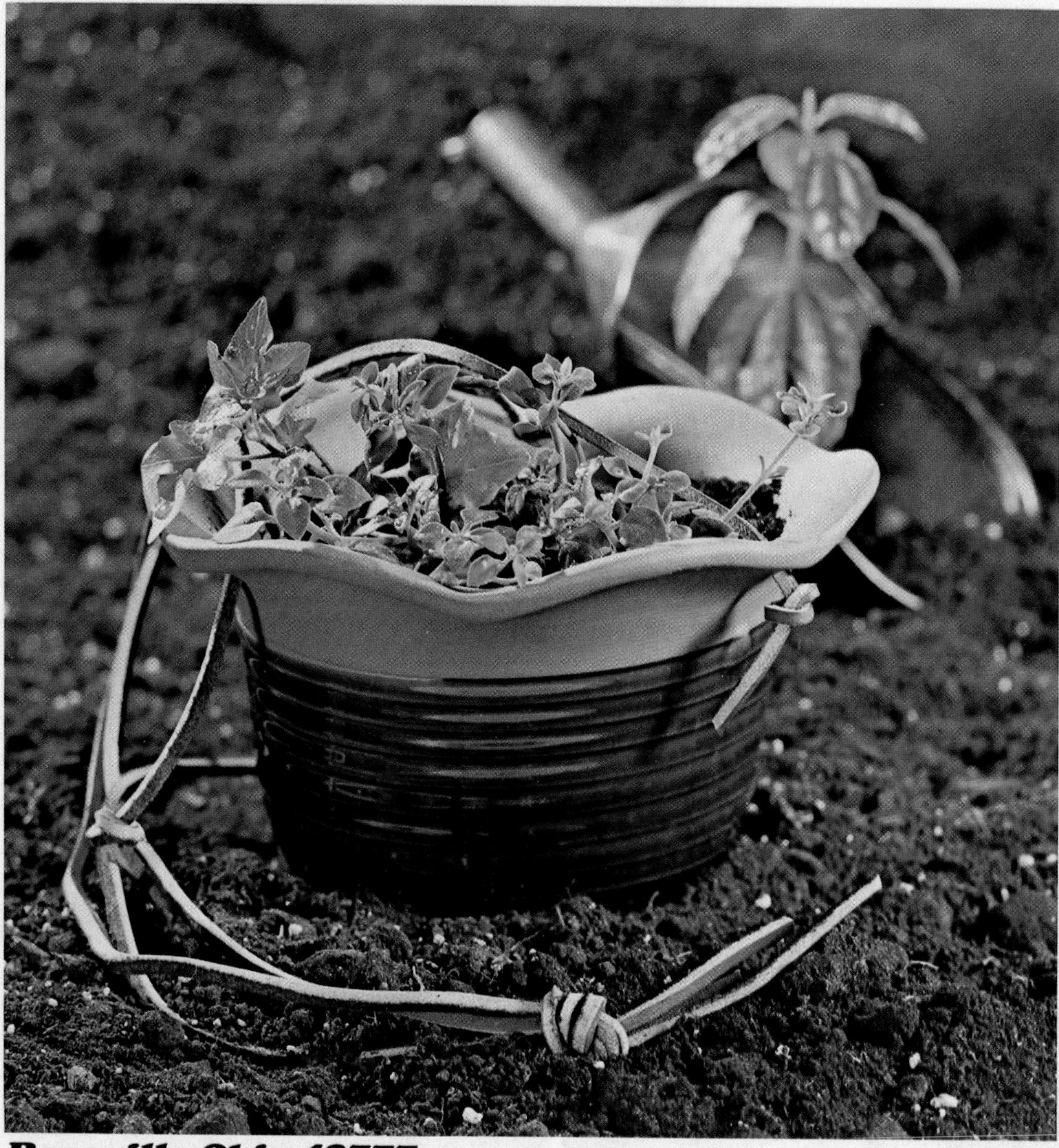

Roseville, Ohio 43777

1975 Roseville Floraline catalog cover.

Page 2

50-0429-01 Goblet Planter
Height 5", Opening 4"
Pack 12, 23 lbs.

50-0431-01 Jardiniere
Height 6½", Diameter 9"
Opening 8½"
Pack 4, 23 lbs.

50-0432-01 Jardiniere
Height 7¾", Diameter 10¾"
Opening 10½"
Pack 4, 28 lbs.

50-0553-01 Rock Planter
Height 3½", Opening 7½" x 4"
Pack 12, 23 lbs.

50-0554-01 Hanging Basket
Height 2¾", Opening 4"
Pack 6, 8 lbs.

50-0555-01 Hanging Basket
Height 3¾", Opening 5½"
Pack 6, 15 lbs.

50-0561-01 Double Hanging Basket
Large Bowl 5 x 7½", Opening 5¾"
Small Bowl 4 x 6½", Opening 4½"
Pack 6, 31 lbs.
Complete with double
rope hanging basket.

Page 3

50-0407-17 Ribbed Ped. Vase
Height 6½", Opening 3¾"
Pack 12, 29 lbs.

50-0410 Ped. Container
Height 4¼", Opening 5¼"
Pack 24, 38 lbs.

50-0424-01 Ribbed Ped. Bowl
Height 5", Opening 4¾"
Pack 12, 28 lbs.

50-0430-06 Classic Ped. Bowl
Height 5", Opening 6"
Pack 12, 27 lbs.

50-0433 Arrangement Vase
Height 7½", Opening 5"
Pack 12, 30 lbs.

50-0450 Large Ped. Urn
Height 9½", Opening 6½"
Pack 6, 32 lbs.

50-0453-01 Flared Vase
Height 6¼", Opening 7" x 3½"
Pack 12, 29 lbs.

50-0460
Square Pedestal Container
Height 5½", Opening 4¾" x 4¾"
Pack 12, 20 lbs.

50-0461 Round Ped. Container
Height 5", Opening 4¾"
Pack 12, 14 lbs.

50-0470
Small Ribbed Pedestal Vase
Height 4½", Opening 4"
Pack 24, 29 lbs.

50-0555-01

50-0554-01

50-0561-01

50-0429-01

50-0431-01
50-0432-01

50-0553-01

**New... from
Roseville Floraline.**

1975 Roseville Floraline catalog page.

1975 Roseville Floraline catalog page.

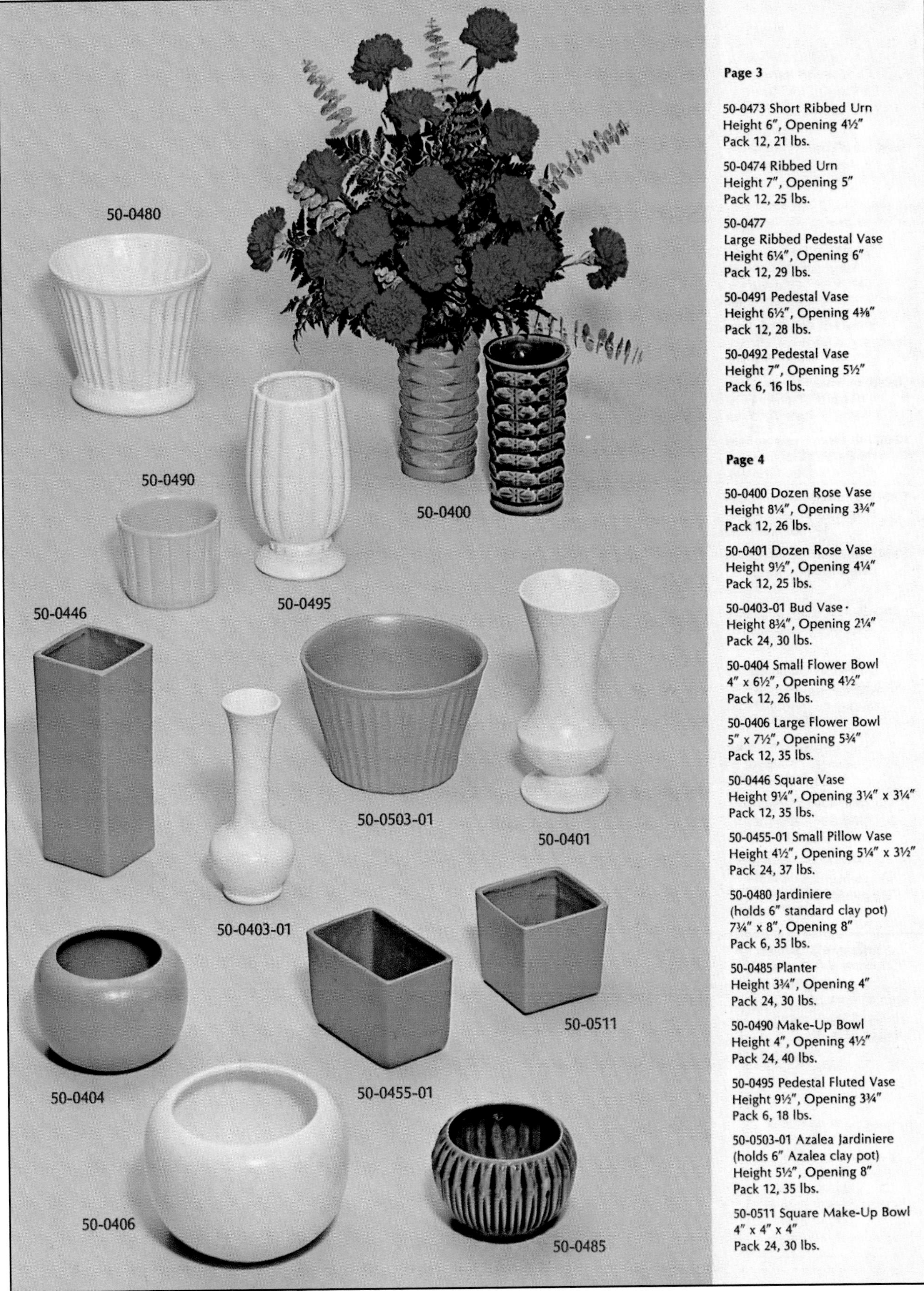

Page 3

50-0473 Short Ribbed Urn
Height 6", Opening 4½"
Pack 12, 21 lbs.

50-0474 Ribbed Urn
Height 7", Opening 5"
Pack 12, 25 lbs.

50-0477
Large Ribbed Pedestal Vase
Height 6¼", Opening 6"
Pack 12, 29 lbs.

50-0491 Pedestal Vase
Height 6½", Opening 4⅜"
Pack 12, 28 lbs.

50-0492 Pedestal Vase
Height 7", Opening 5½"
Pack 6, 16 lbs.

Page 4

50-0400 Dozen Rose Vase
Height 8¼", Opening 3¾"
Pack 12, 26 lbs.

50-0401 Dozen Rose Vase
Height 9½", Opening 4¼"
Pack 12, 25 lbs.

50-0403-01 Bud Vase ·
Height 8¾", Opening 2¼"
Pack 24, 30 lbs.

50-0404 Small Flower Bowl
4" x 6½", Opening 4½"
Pack 12, 26 lbs.

50-0406 Large Flower Bowl
5" x 7½", Opening 5¾"
Pack 12, 35 lbs.

50-0446 Square Vase
Height 9¼", Opening 3¼" x 3¼"
Pack 12, 35 lbs.

50-0455-01 Small Pillow Vase
Height 4½", Opening 5¼" x 3½"
Pack 24, 37 lbs.

50-0480 Jardiniere
(holds 6" standard clay pot)
7¾" x 8", Opening 8"
Pack 6, 35 lbs.

50-0485 Planter
Height 3¾", Opening 4"
Pack 24, 30 lbs.

50-0490 Make-Up Bowl
Height 4", Opening 4½"
Pack 24, 40 lbs.

50-0495 Pedestal Fluted Vase
Height 9½", Opening 3¾"
Pack 6, 18 lbs.

50-0503-01 Azalea Jardiniere
(holds 6" Azalea clay pot)
Height 5½", Opening 8"
Pack 12, 35 lbs.

50-0511 Square Make-Up Bowl
4" x 4" x 4"
Pack 24, 30 lbs.

1975 Roseville Floraline catalog page.

Page 5

50-0417-01 Hexagon Bowl
Height 3", 5" Diameter
Opening 4½"
Pack 12, 18 lbs.

50-0419-01 Oval Ped. Bowl
Height 4¼", Opening 8¾" x 5½"
Pack 12, 27 lbs.

50-0420-01 Small Hexagon Bowl
Height 3", Opening 6¼"
Pack 12, 27 lbs.

50-0421-01 Large Hexagon Bowl
Height 3½", Opening 7¾"
Pack 12, 27 lbs.

50-0422-01 Small Octagon Bowl
Height 3¾", Opening 6¼"
Pack 12, 22 lbs.

50-0423-01 Large Octagon Bowl
Height 4½", Opening 7½"
Pack 12, 28 lbs.

50-0425-01 Pedestal Jardiniere
Height 9", Opening 8½"
Pack 6, 27 lbs.

50-0426-01 Octagon Bowl
Height 3", Diameter 4¼"
Opening 4½"
Pack 12, 18 lbs.

50-0428-01 9" Vase
Opening 4"
Pack 6, 20 lbs.

50-0529-08 Smile Planter
Height 3⅝", Opening 2½"
Pack 24, 23 lbs.

50-0532-06 Auto Planter
Length 8¼"
Opening 4¾" x 3⅞"
Pack 12, 24 lbs.

50-0536-11 Planter
Height 3¾", Diameter 4½"
Opening 4¼" (Speck White)
Pack 12, 14 lbs.

50-0536-75 Planter
Height 3¾", Diameter 4½"
Opening 4¼" (Brown/White)
Pack 12, 14 lbs.

1975 Roseville Floraline catalog page.

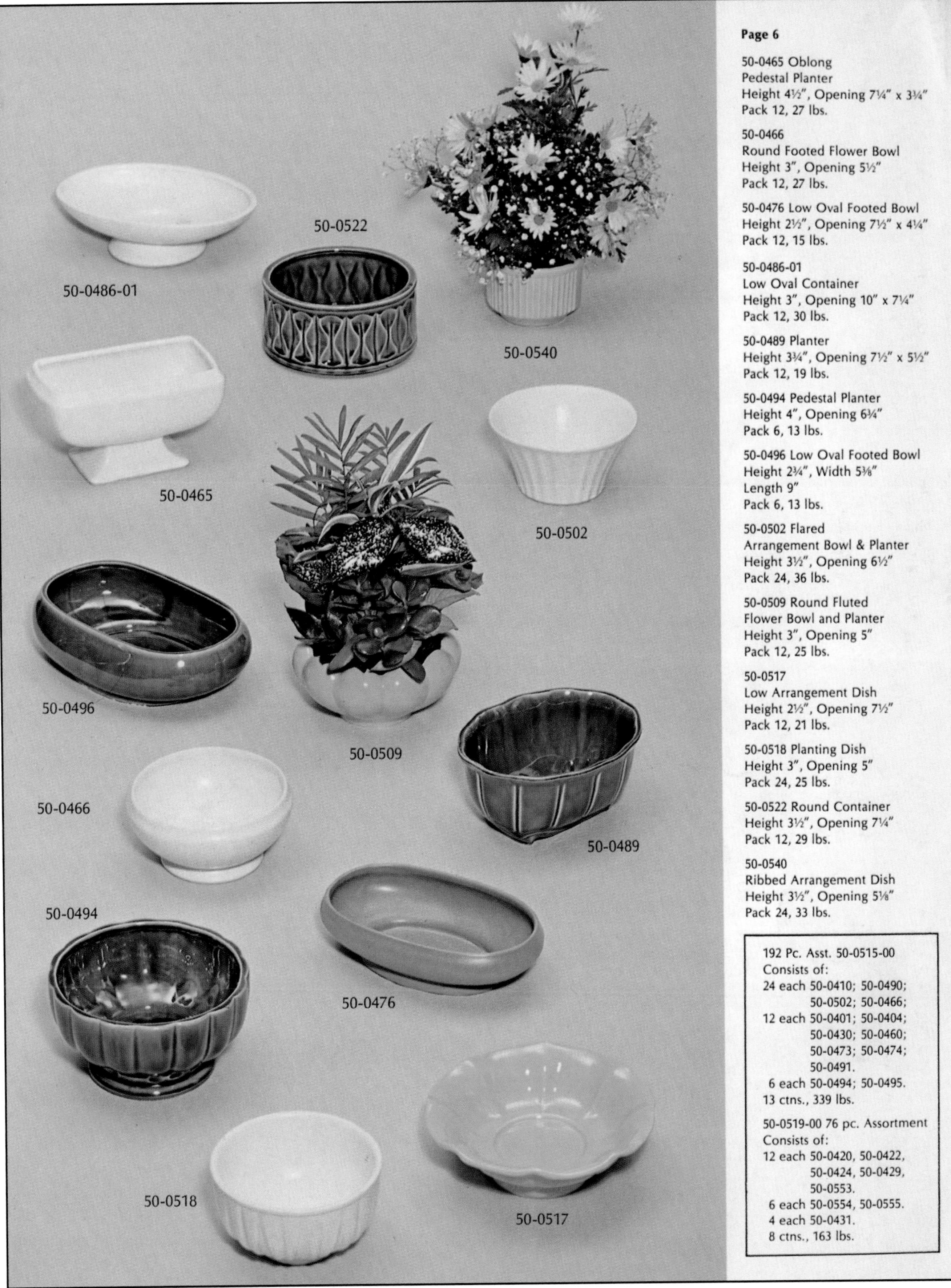

Page 6

50-0465 Oblong
Pedestal Planter
Height 4½", Opening 7¼" x 3¾"
Pack 12, 27 lbs.

50-0466
Round Footed Flower Bowl
Height 3", Opening 5½"
Pack 12, 27 lbs.

50-0476 Low Oval Footed Bowl
Height 2½", Opening 7½" x 4¼"
Pack 12, 15 lbs.

50-0486-01
Low Oval Container
Height 3", Opening 10" x 7¼"
Pack 12, 30 lbs.

50-0489 Planter
Height 3¾", Opening 7½" x 5½"
Pack 12, 19 lbs.

50-0494 Pedestal Planter
Height 4", Opening 6¾"
Pack 6, 13 lbs.

50-0496 Low Oval Footed Bowl
Height 2¾", Width 5⅜"
Length 9"
Pack 6, 13 lbs.

50-0502 Flared
Arrangement Bowl & Planter
Height 3½", Opening 6½"
Pack 24, 36 lbs.

50-0509 Round Fluted
Flower Bowl and Planter
Height 3", Opening 5"
Pack 12, 25 lbs.

50-0517
Low Arrangement Dish
Height 2½", Opening 7½"
Pack 12, 21 lbs.

50-0518 Planting Dish
Height 3", Opening 5"
Pack 24, 25 lbs.

50-0522 Round Container
Height 3½", Opening 7¼"
Pack 12, 29 lbs.

50-0540
Ribbed Arrangement Dish
Height 3½", Opening 5⅛"
Pack 24, 33 lbs.

192 Pc. Asst. 50-0515-00
Consists of:
24 each 50-0410; 50-0490;
50-0502; 50-0466;
12 each 50-0401; 50-0404;
50-0430; 50-0460;
50-0473; 50-0474;
50-0491.
6 each 50-0494; 50-0495.
13 ctns., 339 lbs.

50-0519-00 76 pc. Assortment
Consists of:
12 each 50-0420, 50-0422,
50-0424, 50-0429,
50-0553.
6 each 50-0554, 50-0555.
4 each 50-0431.
8 ctns., 163 lbs.

1975 Roseville Floraline catalog page.

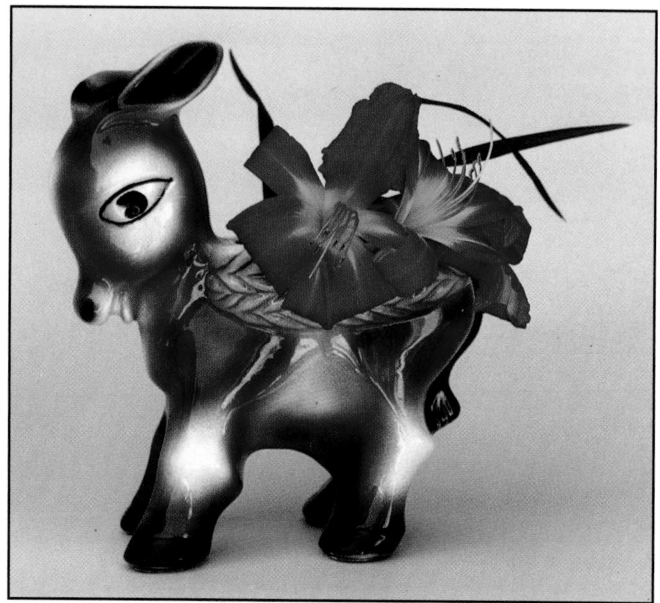

Donkey Planter 10¼" x 8" x 4½". Marked U.S.A. Model 546. $35.00 – 45.00.

Romanesque Filigree Covered Container 6¾". No mark. No model number. $40.00 – 50.00.
Because this is a covered container, it was probably produced as McCoy, not Floraline.

Romanesque Filigree Pedestal Vase 8" x 6". Shown in silver/black and brown. Model 2082M. $30.00 – 35.00.
Romanesque Filigree Pedestal Vase 6½" x 5". Model 2061M. $25.00 – 30.00.

Left:
Hanging Basket 3¾" x 5½". Model 555L. $20.00 – 25.00.

Right:
Hanging Basket to show the use of red clay. As a rule, McCoy did not use red clay.

Silver Swan Planter 5½" x 3". Model 531. $20.00 – 25.00.

These two Roseville Floraline are part of our Finders Keepers section. They are the most desirable and most difficult Floraline pieces to find.
Kneeling Madonna Planter, 7" high with a 6¼" x 3¼" opening. Model 492. $200.00 – 250.00.
Panda Bear Planter 4¾" high with a 5½" x 3" opening. Model 490. $80.00 – 110.00.

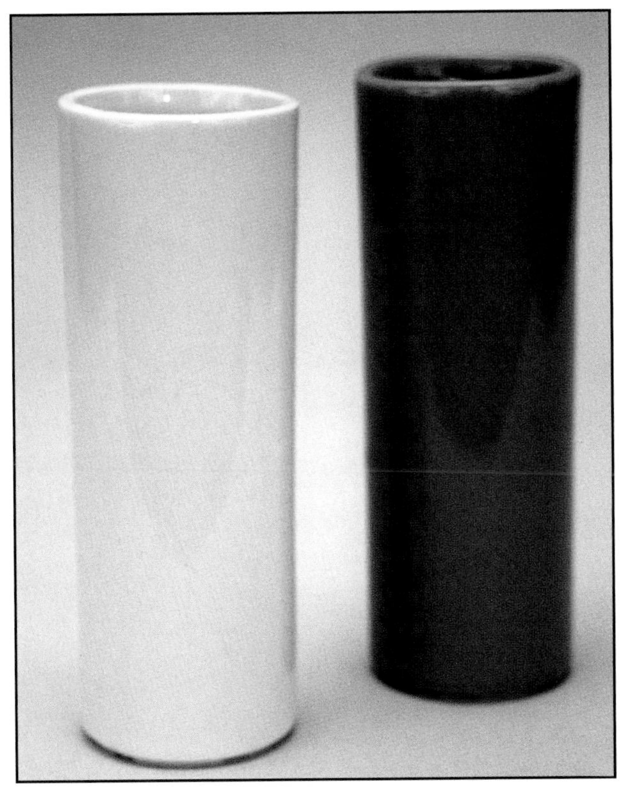

Round Rose Vase 9" x 3½". Shown in two glaze colors. Model 450. $20.00 – 25.00.

Nice display of Planters, 3⅝" x 3⅞". Model 485. $10.00 – 15.00 each.

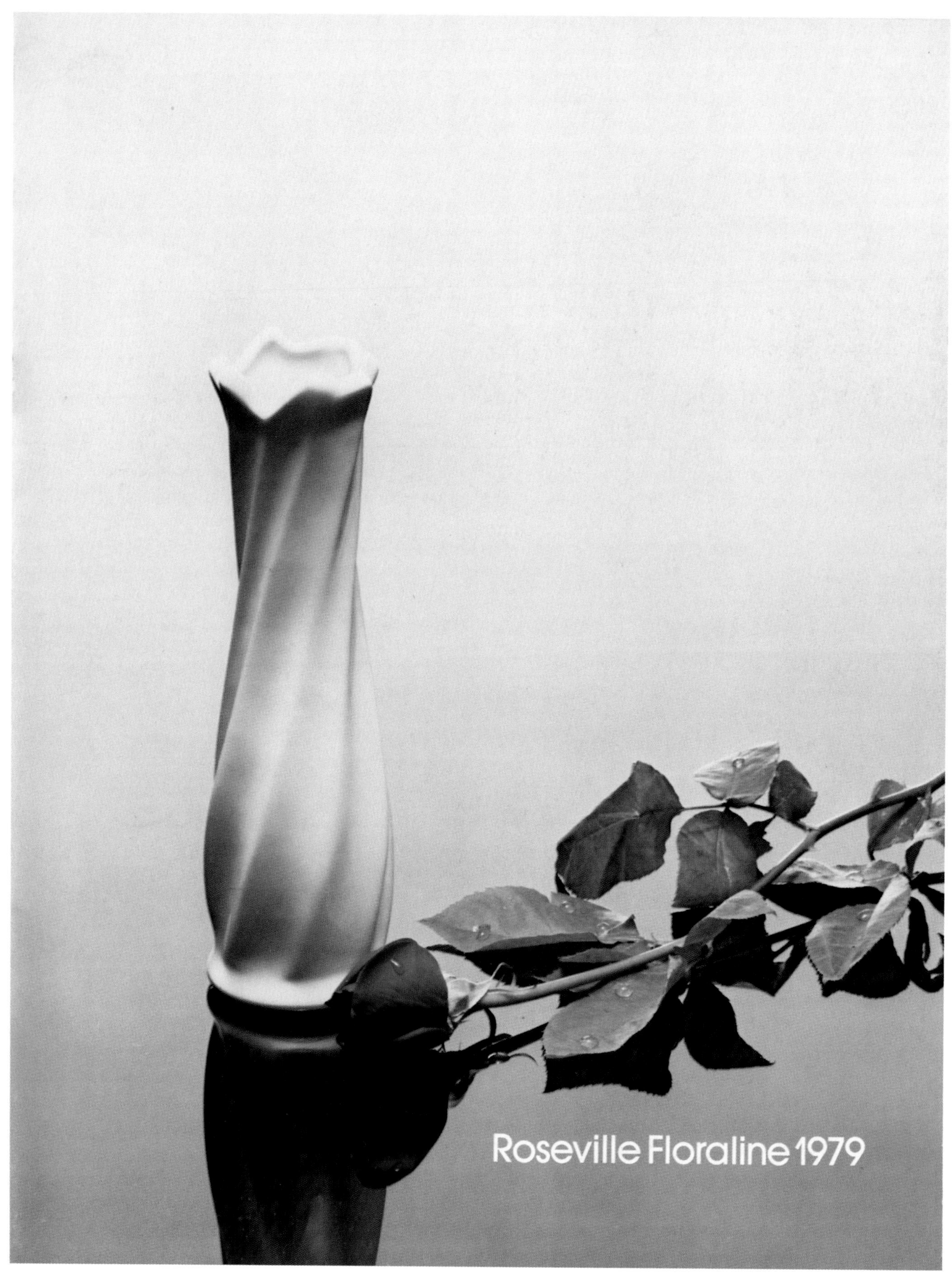

1979 Roseville Floraline catalog cover.

1979 Roseville Floraline catalog page.

0165 0100
Assorted Porcelain White, Green and Buttercup
Ice Cream Mug
Height 5¼", Opening 3"
Pack 12, 12 lbs.

0400 0100
Assorted Porcelain White and
Emerald Green
Dozen Rose Vase
Height 8¼", Opening 3¾"
Pack 12, 26 lbs.

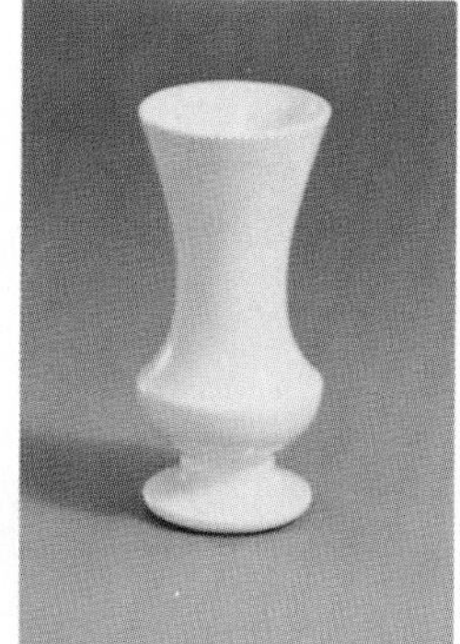

0401 0100
Assorted Porcelain White and
Emerald Green
Dozen Rose Vase
Height 9½", Opening 4¼"
Pack 12, 25 lbs.

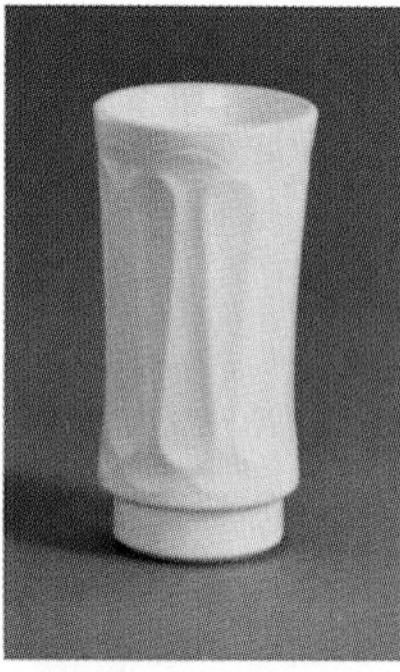

0402 0100 Assorted Matt
White and Moss Green
0402 0300 Matt White
0402 2100 Moss Green
Vase
Height 9", Opening 4"
Pack 12, 29 lbs.

0403 0100
Assorted Matt White
and Moss Green
Bud Vase
Height 8¾", Opening 2¼"
Pack 24, 30 lbs.

0405 0100
Assorted Porcelain
White and Emerald
Green
Small Bud Vase
Height 6"
Pack 24, 18 lbs.

0407 0100
Assorted Porcelain White and
Emerald Green
Large Spiral Vase
Height 9¼", Opening 3¼"
Pack 12, 32 lbs.

0410 0100 Assorted Sand
and Emerald Green
0410 2000 Buttercup
Pedestal Container
Height 4¼", Opening 5¼"
Pack 24, 38 lbs.

0411 0100
Assorted Porcelain White and Emerald
Green
Low Oval Centerpiece
Height 3½", Opening 10" x 7"
Pack 12, 23 lbs.

0421 3901 Assorted as
follows: 4 Antique Olive
4 Antique
Snow White
4 Antique Gold
Large Hexagon Bowl
Height 3½", Opening 7¾"
Pack 12, 27 lbs.

0420 3901 Assorted as
follows: 4 Antique Olive
4 Antique
Snow White
4 Antique Gold
Medium Hexagon Bowl
Height 3", Opening 6¼"
Pack 12, 27 lbs.

0417 3901 Assorted as
follows: 4 Antique Olive
4 Antique
Snow White
4 Antique Gold
Small Hexagon Bowl
Height 3", Opening 4½"
Pack 12, 18 lbs.

3

1979 Roseville Floraline catalog page.

0419 3901 Assorted as follows: 4 Antique Olive
4 Antique Snow White
4 Antique Gold
Oval Pedestal Bowl
Height 4¾", Opening 8¾" x 5½"
Pack 12, 27 lbs.

0423 3901 Assorted as follows: 4 Antique Olive
4 Antique Snow White
4 Antique Gold
Large Octagon Bowl
Height 4½", Opening 7½"
Pack 12, 28 lbs.

0422 3901 Assorted as follows: 4 Antique Olive
4 Antique Snow White
4 Antique Gold
Medium Octagon Bowl
Height 3¾", Opening 6½"
Pack 12, 22 lbs.

0426 3901 Assorted as follows: 4 Antique Olive
4 Antique Snow White
4 Antique Gold
Small Octagon Bowl
Height 3", Opening 4½"
Pack 12, 18 lbs.

0424 0100
Assorted Sand, Emerald Green and Textured Tan
Ribbed Pedestal Bowl
Height 5", Opening 4¾"
Pack 12, 28 lbs.

0432 3901 Assorted as follows: 2 Antique Olive
1 Antique Snow White
1 Antique Gold
Jardiniere
Height 7¾", Opening 10½"
Pack 4, 28 lbs.

0431 3901 Assorted as follows: 2 Antique Olive
1 Antique Snow White
1 Antique Gold
Jardiniere
Height 6½", Opening 8½"
Pack 4, 23 lbs.

0445 0300 Matt White
0445 2100 Moss Green
Double Mum Pot
Height 5½", Length 13½"
Pack 6, 32 lbs.

0450 0300 Matt White
0450 2100 Moss Green
Large Pedestal Urn
Height 9½", Opening 6½"
Pack 6, 32 lbs.

0433 0300 Matt White
0433 2100 Moss Green
Arrangement Vase
Height 7½", Opening 5"
Pack 12, 30 lbs.

0453 0100
Assorted Sand and Emerald Green
Flared Vase
Height 6¼", Opening 7" x 3½"
Pack 12, 29 lbs.

0455 0100
Porcelain White and Emerald Green
Small Pillow Vase
Height 4½", Opening 5¼" x 3½"
Pack 24, 37 lbs.

4

Roseville Floraline catalog page.

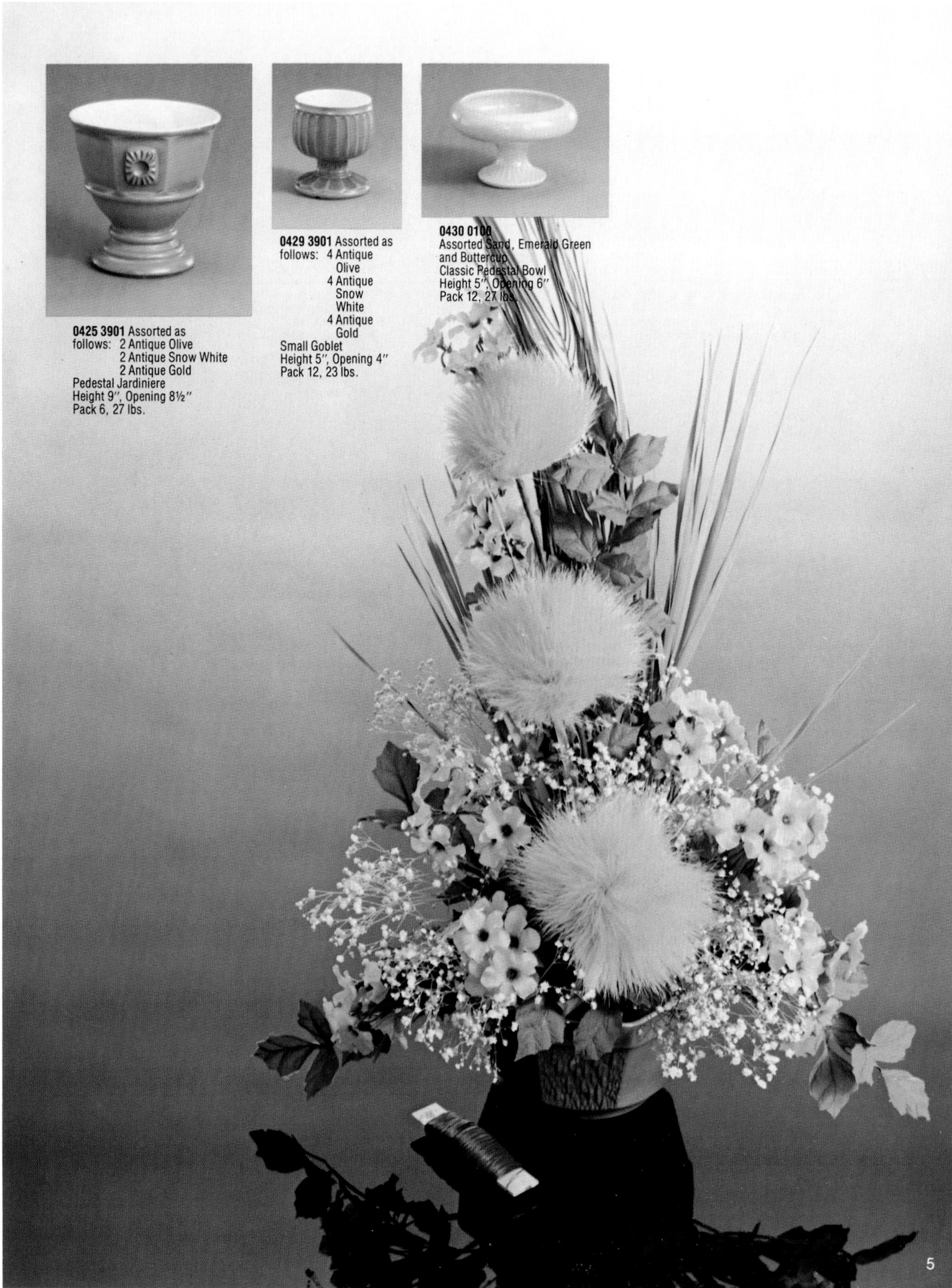
0425 3901 Assorted as
follows: 2 Antique Olive
2 Antique Snow White
2 Antique Gold
Pedestal Jardiniere
Height 9", Opening 8½"
Pack 6, 27 lbs.
0429 3901 Assorted as
follows: 4 Antique
Olive
4 Antique
Snow
White
4 Antique
Gold
Small Goblet
Height 5", Opening 4"
Pack 12, 23 lbs.
0430 0100
Assorted Sand, Emerald Green
and Buttercup
Classic Pedestal Bowl
Height 5", Opening 6"
Pack 12, 27 lbs.
5

Roseville Floraline catalog page.

0460 0100
Assorted Porcelain White and Emerald Green
Square Pedestal Container
Height 5½", Opening 4¾" x 4¾"
Pack 12, 20 lbs.

0464 0100
Assorted Sand, Textured Tan and Emerald Green
Round Scalloped Pedestal
Height 5", Opening 4¾"
Pack 6, 17 lbs.

6

Roseville Floraline catalog page.

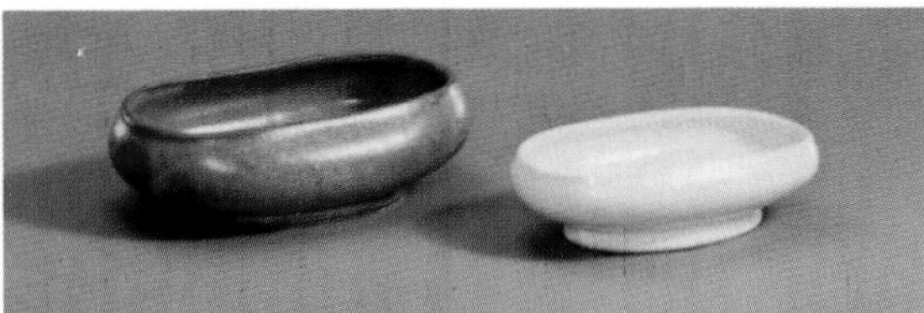

0496 0100
Assorted Sand and Textured Tan
Low Oval Footed Bowl
Height 2¾", Width 5⅜", Length 9"
Pack 6, 13 lbs.

0476 0100
Assorted Sand, Emerald Green and Textured Tan
Low oval Footed Bowl
Height 2½", Opening 7½" x 4¼"
Pack 12, 15 lbs.

0485 0100
Assorted Porcelain White, Emerald Green and Flo-Glo Brown
Miniature Dog, Horse, Turtle and Bear
Height 2¼", Length 5", Opening 1½" to 2¼" (Approx.)
Pack 24, 13 lbs.

0489 0100
Assorted Porcelain White, Emerald Green and Textured Tan
Planter
Height 3¾", Opening 7½" x 5½"
Pack 12, 19 lbs.

0491 0100
Assorted Porcelain White, Emerald Green and Textured Tan
Pedestal Vase
Height 6½", Opening 4⅜"
Pack 12, 28 lbs.

0494 0100
Assorted Porcelain White, Emerald Green and Textured Tan
Pedestal Planter
Height 4", Opening 6¾"
Pack 12, 26 lbs.

0506 0100
Assorted Sand and Emerald Green
0506 2000 Buttercup
Utility Container
Height 3½", Opening 6"
Pack 24, 35 lbs.

0509 0100
Assorted Porcelain White, Emerald Green and Buttercup
Round Fluted Flower Bowl and Planter
Height 3", Opening 5"
Pack 12, 25 lbs.

0511 0100
Assorted Porcelain White and Emerald Green
Square Make-Up Bowl
4" x 4" x 4"
Pack 24, 30 lbs.

0518 0100
Assorted Porcelain White and Emerald Green
Planting Dish
Height 3", Opening 5"
Pack 24, 25 lbs.

0522 0100
Assorted Sand, Emerald Green and Textured Tan
Round Container
Height 3½", Opening 7¼"
Pack 12, 29 lbs.

0533 3200
Porcelain White
"Handkerchief" Vase
Height 8¾", Opening 6"
Pack 6, 16 lbs.

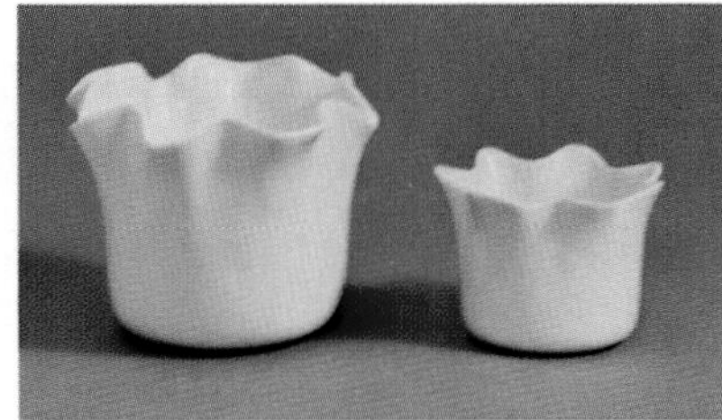

0535 3200
Porcelain White
"Handkerchief" Large Jardiniere
Height 5¾", Opening 7½"
Pack 6, 14 lbs.

0534 3200
Porcelain White
"Handkerchief" Small Jardiniere
Height 3¾", Opening 4¾"
Pack 12, 15 lbs.

0536 7500
Brown and White
Planter
Height 3¾", Opening 4¼"
Pack 12, 14 lbs.

7

Roseville Floraline catalog page.

0537 3200
Porcelain White
"Handkerchief" Small
Pedestal Container
Height 5", Opening 4½"
Pack 12, 9 lbs.

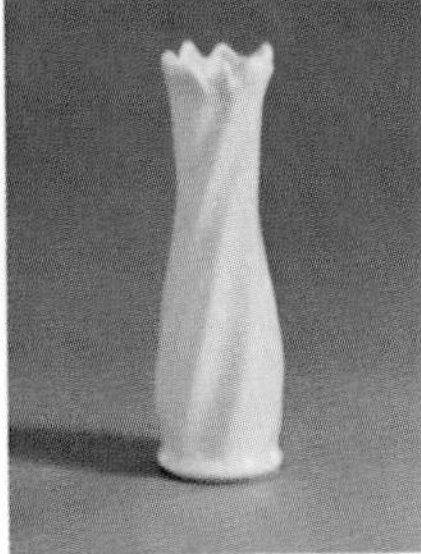

0538 3200
Porcelain White
"Handkerchief" Bud Vase
Height 8¾", Opening 1¾"
Pack 24, 20 lbs.

0540 0100
Assorted Porcelain
White, Emerald Green
and Buttercup
Ribbed Arrangement
Dish
Height 3½", Opening
5⅛"
Pack 24, 33 lbs.

0542 0100
Assorted Porcelain
White and Emerald
Green
Spiral Bud Vase
Height 6½", Opening 1¼"
Pack 24, 14 lbs.

0550 0100
Assorted Emerald Green and
Textured Tan
Versatile Arrangement Container
Height 3½", Width 7", Length 7"
Pack 12, 20 lbs.

0561 0100
Assorted Porcelain White
and Brown
Basket With Handle
Height 7", Opening 8¼"
x 4¼"
Pack 6, 11 lbs.

0570 0100
Assorted Porcelain White,
Emerald Green and
Buttercup
Small Planter or Flower
Bowl
Height 4", Opening 4¼"
Pack 24, 27 lbs.

0571 0100 Assorted Sand
and Emerald Green
0571 2000 Buttercup
Utility Bowl
Height 3¾", Opening 6"
Pack 24, 39 lbs.

0572 0100 Assorted Sand
and Emerald Green
0572 2000 Buttercup
Utility Bowl
Height 4", Opening 6"
Pack 24, 39 lbs.

0575 0100
Assorted Porcelain
White, Emerald Green
and Buttercup
Large Pedestal
Container
Height 6", Opening 6¼"
Pack 12, 33 lbs.

0574 0100
Assorted Porcelain
White, Emerald Green
and Buttercup
Medium Pedestal
Container
Height 5¾", Opening 4½"
Pack 12, 21 lbs.

0578 0100
Assorted Porcelain
White, Emerald Green
and Buttercup
Small Pedestal
Container
Height 4½", Opening 4"
Pack 24, 27 lbs.

0576 0100
Assorted Porcelain White,
Emerald Green and Buttercup
Footed Planter/Flower Bowl
Height 4½", Opening 5¾"
Pack 12, 24 lbs.

0577 0100
Assorted Porcelain White,
Emerald Green and Buttercup
Classic Pedestal Container
Height 5", Width 7½", Opening 6¼"
Pack 6, 19 lbs.

8

Roseville Floraline catalog page.

0553 0100
Assorted Textured Tan and Sand
Rock Planter
Height 3½", Opening 7½" x 4"
Pack 12, 23 lbs.

9

Roseville Floraline catalog page.

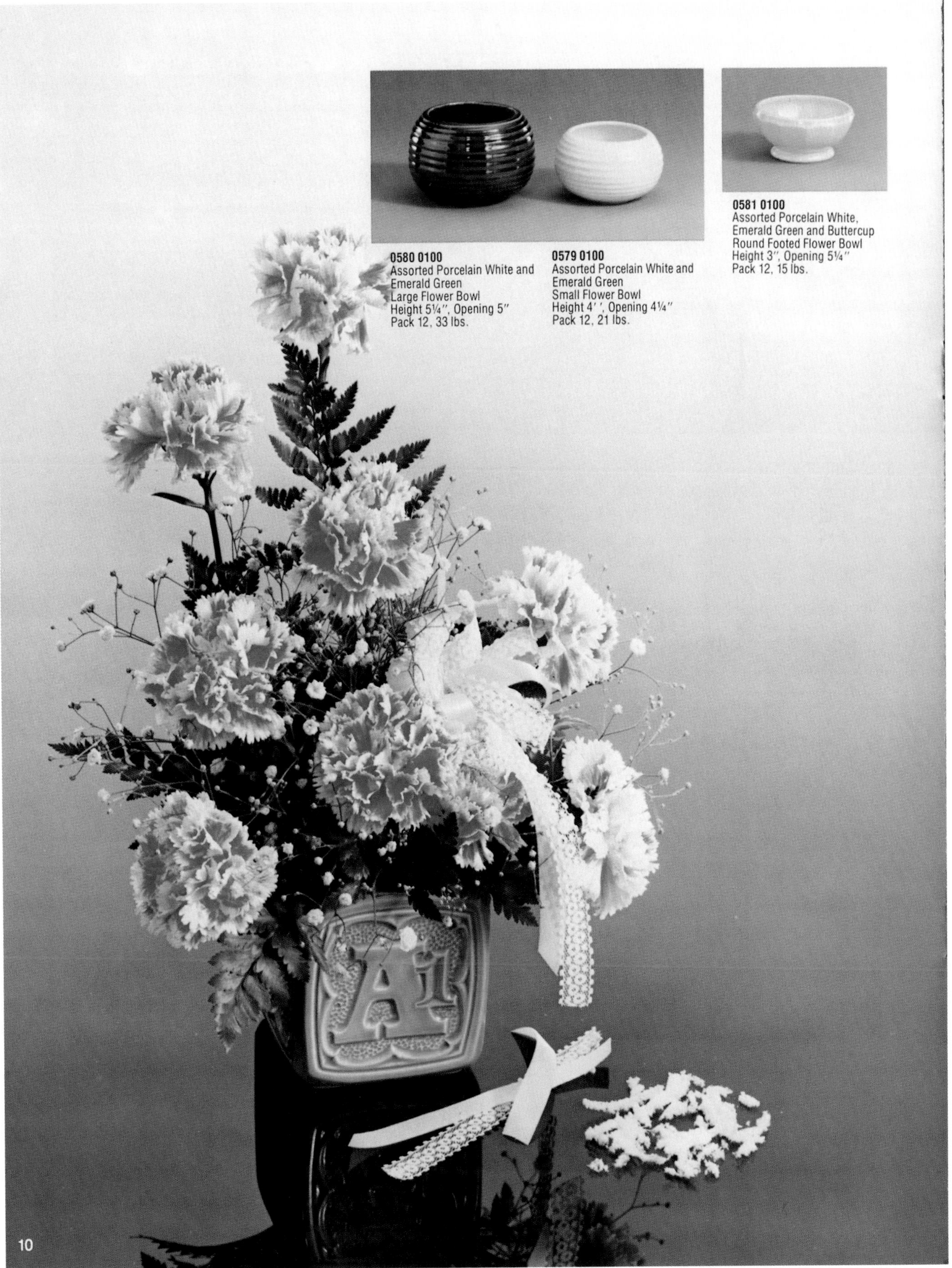
0580 0100
Assorted Porcelain White and
Emerald Green
Large Flower Bowl
Height 5¼", Opening 5"
Pack 12, 33 lbs.
0579 0100
Assorted Porcelain White and
Emerald Green
Small Flower Bowl
Height 4' ', Opening 4¼"
Pack 12, 21 lbs.
0581 0100
Assorted Porcelain White,
Emerald Green and Buttercup
Round Footed Flower Bowl
Height 3", Opening 5¼"
Pack 12, 15 lbs.
10

Roseville Floraline catalog page.

This beautiful line of vases was introduced during the final years of Lancaster Colony ownership and was sold to McCoy dealers as well as to the florist trade. Designer Accents purchased the Nelson McCoy Pottery in 1985/1986 and merged it into their company as Nelson McCoy Ceramics, closing in 1990. They continued to sell the Fineforms Line for awhile after purchasing the company.

Two beautiful Fineforms Vases.
12" high, 4" opening. Peach glaze. Model 0458FF. $50.00 – 75.00.
12" high, 4" opening. Heritage Blue glaze. Model 0476FF. $50.00 – 75.00.

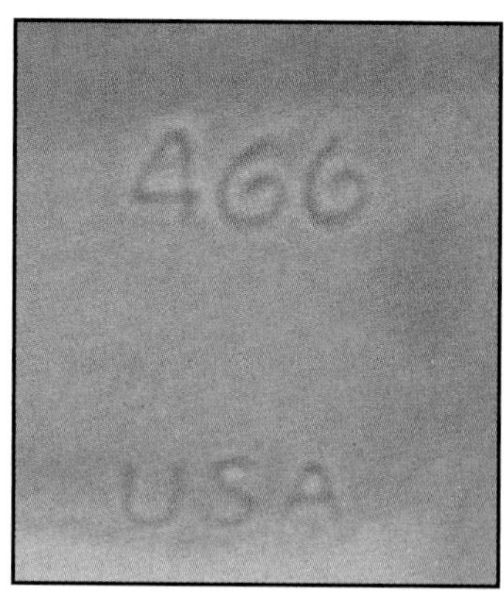

Bottom of Model 0466FF in a gray glaze showing typical bottom designs of the Fineforms Line.

Dark Mauve Fineforms Vase 12½" x 9". No mark. Model 0488FF. $50.00 – 75.00.
Heritage Blue Fineforms Vase 7¾" high x 12" wide. Model 0444. $50.00 – 75.00.

Bijou Fineforms Vase 11" x 10" x 4½". Model 0466FF. $50.00 – 75.00.

Roseville Floraline

A.

F•I•N•E•F•O•R•M•S

THE SPIRIT OF DECO COMES ALIVE. IN COLOR. SHAPE. AND ATTITUDE.
THE LEGENDARY STYLE OF ELEGANCE AND PIZZAZ IS THE "RIGHT ON" LOOK FOR NOW.
FINEFORMS, A BEAUTIFUL COLLECTION.
VASES TO ACCENT AND UPLIFT EVERY ROOM SETTING.

The Beautiful Roseville Floraline Vase on this catalog cover page is Crown, 9⅝" high with 2" opening. Model 452.

"BIJOU"

I. Globe–#0459
10⅛" H. 6" Opening
Pack 4
Wt. 26. Cube 2.38

J. Tall Neck–#0457
12" H. 1½" Opening
Pack 4
Wt.22. Cube 1.47

K. Tall Oval–#0458
12" H. 4" Opening
Pack 4
Wt. 22. Cube 2.77

All Fineform vases are available in these colors. When ordering, use style number plus color code.

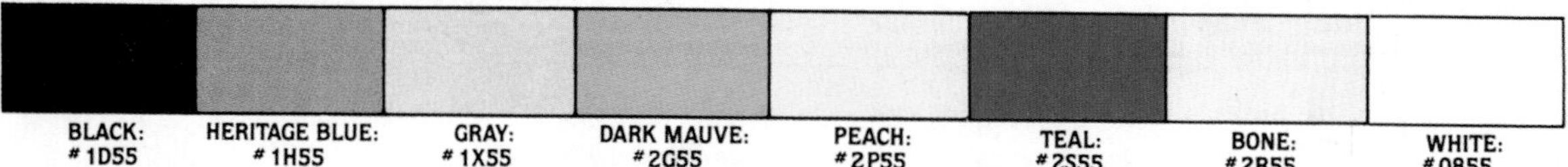

IT SELLS ITSELF.

MADE IN THE UNITED STATES OF AMERICA.

ROSEVILLE FLORALINE, P.O. BOX 130, LANCASTER, OHIO 43130, 800/848-9801, IN OHIO, 614/653-0620

Roseville Floraline Fineforms catalog page.

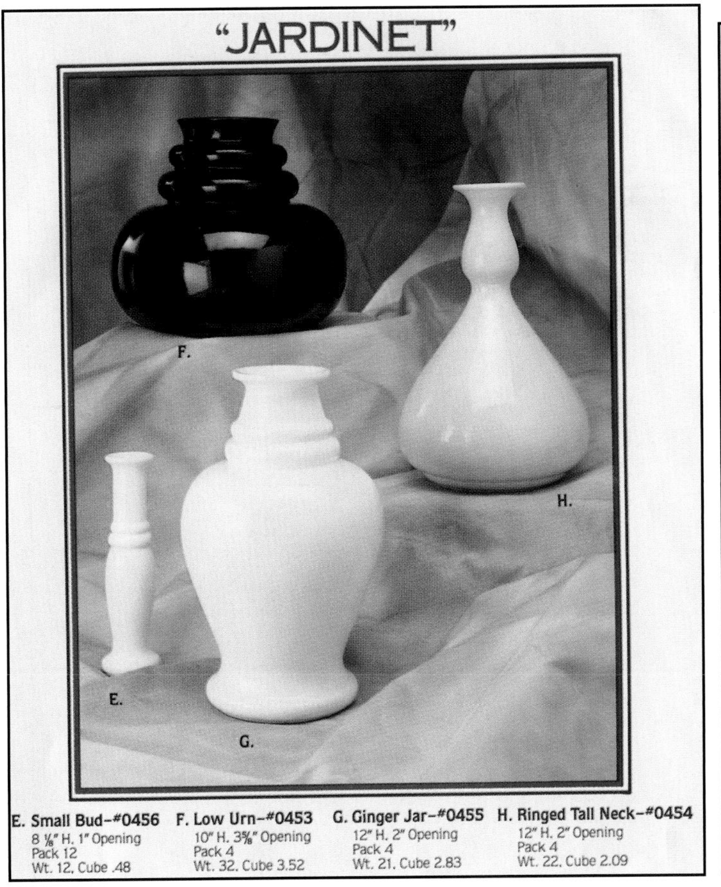

"JARDINET"
F.
H.
E.
G.
E. Small Bud–#0456
8 ⅛" H. 1" Opening
Pack 12
Wt. 12, Cube .48
F. Low Urn–#0453
10" H. 3⅝" Opening
Pack 4
Wt. 32, Cube 3.52
G. Ginger Jar–#0455
12" H. 2" Opening
Pack 4
Wt. 21, Cube 2.83
H. Ringed Tall Neck–#0454
12" H. 2" Opening
Pack 4
Wt. 22, Cube 2.09

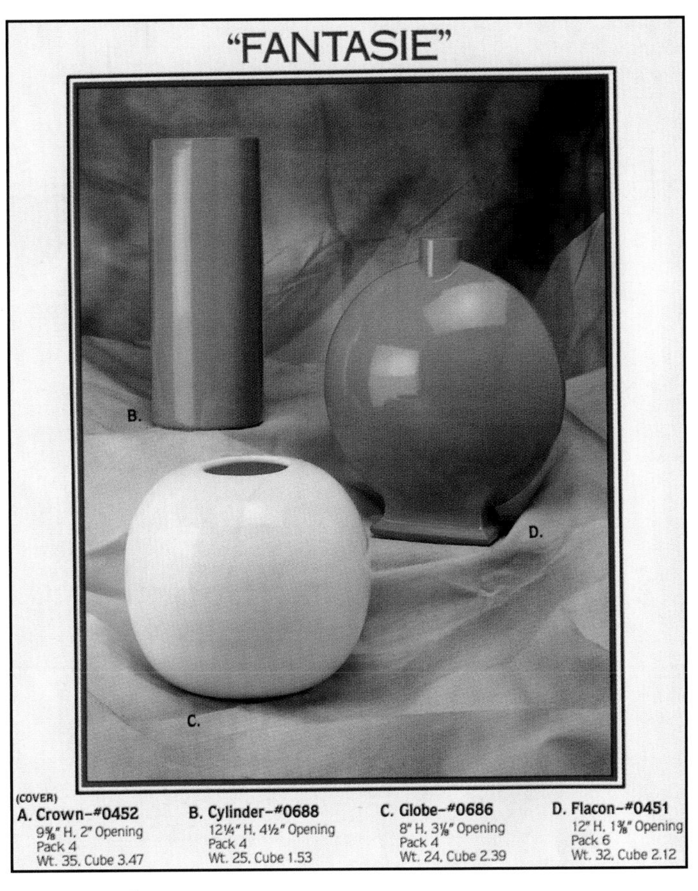

"FANTASIE"
B.
D.
C.
(COVER)
A. Crown–#0452
9⅝" H. 2" Opening
Pack 4
Wt. 35, Cube 3.47
B. Cylinder–#0688
12¼" H. 4½" Opening
Pack 4
Wt. 25, Cube 1.53
C. Globe–#0686
8" H. 3⅛" Opening
Pack 4
Wt. 24, Cube 2.39
D. Flacon–#0451
12" H. 1⅜" Opening
Pack 6
Wt. 32, Cube 2.12

Roseville Floraline Fineforms catalog page.

Ritz Fineforms pieces:
Oval Vase 7½" x 12½". Model 0469FF.
Heart-Shaped Vase 11" x 7". Model 0467FF.
Temple-Shaped Vase 12" x 4". Model 0468FF.

Additional Fineforms shapes (listed by catalog names):
Bauhaus, 12" high with 4" opening. Model 0475FF. Similar in shape to Model 0476, shown on page 296.
Globe, 10½" high with 6" opening. Model 0459FF. Similar design pattern as in Model 0458 shown on page 298.
Bouquet, 8¼" high x 4" diameter. Model 0445FF.
Urn, 8¼" high x 6¼" diameter. Model 0446FF.
Temple, 8¼" high x 5⅞" diameter. Model 0447FF.
Ginger, 8¼" high x 6¼" diameter. Model 0448FF.
Oval, 8¼" high x 6¼" diameter. Model 0449FF.
$50.00 – 75.00 each.

Index

Description	Era	Size	Volume I	Volume II	Volume III
Flower Bowl, Sunburst Gold	50s	5½"		103	
Flower Box	50s	6½", 9", 12"			60
Flower Dish	60s	7"	283		
Flower Dish, Artificial	60s	5"	259		
Flower Dish, Artificial	60s	7"	283		
Flower Dish, Artificial	60s	10"	152, 283"		
Flower Dish, Winged – Grecian	50s	9"	193		
Flower Holder – Hands of Friendship	40s	4"	88	45, 47, 135	
Flower Holder – Cornucopia	40s	4"	91, 197		
Flower Holder (Little Trough)	40s	5"		55	
Flower Holder, Bird – in – Flight				200	
Flower Holder, Butterfly	40s	4"			147
Flower Holder, Fish	40s	4¼"	86	47, 135	
Flower Holder, Pigeon	40s	4"	89	135	
Flower Holder, Pitcher	40s	4"	87, 197	45	
Flower Holder, Swan	40s	4¾"	90, 197	135	
Flower Holder, Turtle	40s	4¼"	89	135	
Flower Holder, Vase	40s	3½"	87	45	
Flower Pot	50s	4½", 5½"		100	
Flower Pot	50s	7½", 8½"		100	
Flower Pot	40s	3¾"	137	53	
Flower Pot	40s	5"		53	42
Flower Pot	20s, 30s	3"	35, 135		37
Flower Pot	40s	3½"	67		
Flower Pot	50s	6½"	243		
Flower Pot	50s	4"	263		
Flower Pot with bird/fence detail		4"		201	
Flower Pot with Saucer	50s	3½", 4½"		95	
Flower Pot with Saucer	50s	5½", 6½"		95	147
Flower Pot with Saucer	20s, 30s	4", 7"			37
Flower Pot with Saucer	40s	3½", 6½"			41
Flower Pot with Saucer	40s	5"			42
Flower Pot with Saucer	70s	4", 5", 6"			201
Flower Pot with Saucer with Flower Pattern	40s	3¾, 5", 6"	135	54	
Flower Pot with Saucer; Unusual Detail	50s	5"			57
Flower Pot with Saucer – Decorative Decal	70s	4, 6"			194
Flower Pot, Garden Club	50s	6½"		96	
Flower Pot, Leaves with Saucer	20s, 30s	4", 5½", 6"	39		
Flower Pot – Basketweave	40s	3½", 5"	73	44	41
Flower Pot – McCoy spelling	50s	4½"	241	80	
Flower Pot – McCoy spelling	50s	6"		80	
Food Warmer, Chuckwagon El Rancho Line	60s	3 qt.	309	156	202
Foot Warmer	Early				15
Frame, Picture		6" x 7"			161
Frog	40s	3½"	93	200	
Funnel, Islander Collection	70s	4"		191	
Garden Dish	40s	8½"	63		
Garden Dish	40s	5½"	81		
Garden Dish	40s	7¾"	81	48	
Garden Dish, Jagged Edge	40s	9½"	67		
GOLD TRIM PIECE SECTION – Starting page			180	114	130
Gondola Candy Boat, Sunburst Gold	50s	11½"	197		
Grape Cuspidor	20s, 30s	5¼"	13		
Grass Growing Gleep	70s	8"	219		
Grater Holder, Islander Collection	70s		298	191	
Hand Planter	40s	7¾"	79		
Hand Vase	40s	7"	60	136	
Hand Vase	40s	8¼"	79	52	
Hand Vase	40s	6½"	78		116
Hand Vase with Glove	40s	8¼"	80		118
Hanging Basket	20s, 30s	6"	45		
Hanging Basket, Basketweave	40s	7½"	73		
Hanging Basket, Burlap Bag	70s			178	
Hanging Basket, Fish	70s	10½"	293		
Hanging Basket, Leaves, Berries	20s, 30s	5", 6"	43, 45		
Hanging Basket, Red Clay	70s	5", 6"			204
Hanging Basket, Vesta Line	60s	6½"		101	
Hanging Planter, Bird or Owl	70s	9"		190	
Hanging Planter, Laughing Face	70s	4½"			194
Hanging Planter, Open Design	70s	7"			200
Hanging Pot	70s	6¼"		171	
Hanging Pot, Basket Line	50s	6½"	257		
Hobnail V Vase	40s	9"	77	137	
Hobnail Castlegate Vase	40s	6"	76	136	
Hobnail Fernery	40s	5½", 8¼"	75, 76		
Hobnail Flower Pot w/ saucer – Leaves Decoration	40s	4"	77	56	

Description	Era	Size	Volume I	Volume II	Volume III
Pitcher, Blades, Vine Detail					150
Pitcher, Cascade	60s	9"	212		
Pitcher, Cow	40s				149
Pitcher, Doe, Fawn Brown	20s, 30s	8½"		18	
Pitcher, Donkey	40s	7"	72	54	118
Pitcher, Duck Head Design					150
Pitcher, Duck Neck Handle	20s, 30s		50		
Pitcher, Elephant	40s	7"	72	51	118
Pitcher, Fish	50s	7"	200	78, 205	121
Pitcher, Fish	20s, 30s	6½"	13		
Pitcher, Fish Handle	20s, 30s	5½", 7"	14		
Pitcher, Floral Country	80s				93
Pitcher, Floral Decal	70s	8"		171	
Pitcher, Grape	50s	9"	163		
Pitcher, Happy Face	70s	7"			192
Pitcher, Happytime	70s	5½"	291		
Pitcher, Happytime Line	70s				94
Pitcher, Hummingbird	20s, 30s	5"	13		
Pitcher, Johnny Walker	70s	7"		186	
Pitcher, Large Spirit of '76 Line	70s	8"	289		
Pitcher, Milk Canyon	70s	7¼"	297		
Pitcher, Nassau County GOP	70s	6¼"	319		
Pitcher, Old Crow Distillery	70s	7"	319		
Pitcher, Parading Ducks	20s, 30s		50	26	
Pitcher, Pig	40s	5"		51	
Pitcher, Pig Archer	40s	9"			149
Pitcher, Rum – Bacardi	60s	5½"	315		
Pitcher, Small Spirit of '76 Line	70s	5½"	289		
Pitcher, Spice Delight	70s	5"	280		
Pitcher, Stone Craft	70s	5¾"	299		
Pitcher, Strawberry Country	70s	32 oz.		190	
Pitcher, VAT 69	60s	5½"	315		
Pitcher, W.C.Fields	60s	7¾"	315		
Pitcher, Welch's		10"		184	
Pitcher – Western Ware	70s	9"			190
Place Setting – Four Piece; Futura	70s			181	
Planter	50s	8¼"		102	
Planter	40s	5"	67		
Planter	40s, 50s	6"	67, 243		
Planter	60s	6"	277		
Planter	60s	6", 8", 9"			63
Planter	60s	14"			94
Planter	40s	7"	55		
Planter	50s	7½"			54
Planter	70s	4½"			204
Planter	70s	6, 7"			205
Planter (NM mark)	40s	8"		51	
Planter Bowl, Brocade	50s	5½"	225		
Planter Bowl, Garden Club	50s	5½", 6½", 7½"			85
Planter Bowl, Pedestal Line	50s	5", 6"	257		
Planter or Ashtray		7"			157
Planter Vase, Harmony	60s	7"	265	93	
Planter with Applied Birds	40s	8"			155
Planter with Bow Decoration					157
Planter with Leaf Design	50s	7"			60
Planter with Stand – Classic Line	60s	6"			95
Planter, Y Bridge		3"			159
Planter, Alligator	50s	10"	237		
Planter, American Eagle	40s	10"			147
Planter, Anvil	50s	9"	249		
Planter, Applied Butterfly	50s	7½"	218	154	
Planter, Applied Butterfly	50s	6", 8½"		154	
Planter, Applied Dragonfly	50s	7½", 5½"	218	154	55
Planter, Artisan	60s	7½"			58
Planter, Auto	Floraline	8"	271	110	274
Planter, Auto with Hardtop	50s	9½"	246	82	
Planter, Baa Baa Black Sheep	40s	4½"	69		41
Planter, Baby Crib	50s	6½"	155	88	
Planter, Baby Rattle or Baby Scale	50s	5½"	155		119
Planter, Baby Shoe	Floraline	8"		111	267
Planter, Backward Bird	40s	4"	72	132	
Planter, Ball Shape	40s	3½"	55	49	
Planter, Banana Boat	50s	11"	219	150	
Planter, Barrel (Calypso)	50s	7½"	219	150	
Planter, Baseball Glove	50s	6"	179		
Planter, Basket	50s	9"	159		

Description	Era	Size	Volume I	Volume II	Volume III
Planter, Basket Line	50s	6½"	257		
Planter, Basket with Oak Leaf, Acorn Décor	50s			78	
Planter, Basketweave	50s	7½"	151		
Planter, Bear	50s	7"	154	75, 147	
Planter, Bear	Floraline	5"	270	111	274
Planter, Bird	40s	4½", 7"	140, 141		
Planter, Bird Dog	50s	12½"	203	87, 149	
Planter, Bird Dog	50s	7¾"	205	149	
Planter, Birds in Nest	50s	5"	159		
Planter, Black Stove	70s	4"	276		
Planter, Bowling	50s	6½"	178, 179		
Planter, Boxing Gloves	50s	6½"	179		
Planter, Brocade	50s	5½", 9¾"	225		
Planter, Brown Shoe	70s	5"	276		
Planter, Brown Square	70s	3"	276		
Planter, Bunny		8"			158
Planter, Capri	60s	5"			56
Planter, Carriage with Umbrella	50s	9"	234	153	
Planter, Cart Basket Line	50s	10"	257		
Planter, Cat	50s	7"	157		
Planter, Cat Face	70s	6"	294		
Planter, Child's	70s	5"	316		
Planter, Chinese	50s	5½"	238		
Planter, Chinese with Wheelbarrow	50s	5½"	238		
Planter, Cleopatra's Boat		12"			161
Planter, Clown Riding Pig – Ears Up or Down	50s	8½"	149	202	153
Planter, Coal Bucket	70s	10"	285	176	
Planter, Cobbler's Bench	50s	8¾"	249		
Planter, Conch Shell	50s	7"	247		
Planter, Convertible	50s	9½"	179, 246	82	
Planter, Convertible with Wire Windshield	50s	9½"	246		
Planter, Cope Monkey		5½"	146	69, 140	157
Planter, Corinthian	60s	9"			92
Planter, Corinthian Garden Line	60s	4½"	274		
Planter, Cornucopia	40s	4"	63		
Planter, Cowboy Hat	50s	8"	249, 250		
Planter, Crestwood	60s	13"			90
Planter, Crouching Cat NM Mark	40s			205	
Planter, Davy Crocket				203	
Planter, Deco Style	40s	5"		39	120
Planter, Deer	70s	6¾"	292	173	
Planter, Doe, Fawn	40s	7"	82		
Planter, Doe and Fawn	50s	7"	204		
Planter, Dog	Floraline	4½"	270, 271"	111	274
Planter, Dog	70s	7½"	292		198
Planter, Dog	40s	7"			149
Planter, Dog with Cart	50s	8½"	161		44
Planter, Dog with Holder	40s	7"	70		
Planter, Donkey	Floraline	10½"		112	284
Planter, Donkey	40s	7"	66, 69		
Planter, Double Basketweave	50s	8¼"	243		
Planter, Double Ducks with Eggs	40s	6"	135	86	
Planter, Driftwood	50s	8½"	159		
Planter, Duck with Egg	40s	7"	135, 156		
Planter, Duck with Egg	50s	6"	158		
Planter, Duck with Umbrella	50s	7½"	234	153	
Planter, Dutch Shoe	40s	7½"	227	69	
Planter, Early American	60s	7½"		103	
Planter, Fawn	50s	12"	203	87, 149	
Planter, Fawn	50s	5"	204		
Planter, Fish	50s	12"	200, 201, 229	79, 146	
Planter, Fisherman	50s	6"	179	82, 147	
Planter, Flying Ducks	50s	10¾"	202	148	
Planter, Football	50s	7"	178, 179		159
Planter, Footed – Sunburst Gold	50s	6"			62
Planter, Footed – Crestwood	60s	4½"		172	
Planter, Frog	50s	7½", 8"	235		
Planter, Frog	50s	5"	237		
Planter, Frog	60s	6"	235		
Planter, Frog with lotus	40s	5"	237	47	40
Planter, Frog with Umbrella	50s	7½"	234, 235	153	
Planter, Fruit – Apple or Bananas	50s	6½"	129	141	
Planter, Fruit – Grapes	50s	6½"	128		123
Planter, Fruit – Lemon or Pear	50s	6½"	129	141	
Planter, Fruit – Orange	50s	6½"	129	80, 141	
Planter, Fruit – Pomegranate	50s	6½"	129		123

Description	Era	Size	Volume I	Volume II	Volume III
Planter, Garden Club	50s	5¾", 7½"		96	
Planter, Garden Club	50s	11½"			84
Planter, Goat		6"			156
Planter, Golf	50s	6"	179	147	
Planter, Goose with Cart	40s	8"	141	67	
Planter, Hand with Bowl	40s	6"			146
Planter, Hanging Iron Basket	70s	6½"	280		
Planter, Happy Face	70s	4½"	279		
Planter, Harmony	60s	9¼"	265	93	
Planter, Harmony	60s	8½"		93	
Planter, Hat	40s	4"	142	51	
Planter, Hobby Horse	50s	8"			158
Planter, Horse	Floraline	5"	270	111	274
Planter, Horse with Holder	40s	7"	70	133	
Planter, Jagged Edge	50s	9½"			95
Planter, Jeweled	50s	8½"	218		
Planter, Keats					149
Planter, Kettle with Stand	50s	5½"		176	
Planter, Kitten	40s	6"	69		
Planter, Kitten with Ball of Yarn	50s			200	
Planter, Kitten with Ball of Yarn	70s	7"	292	157	198
Planter, Lamb	50s	5"	155		
Planter, Lamb	50s	8½"	157, 158, 159		
Planter, Lamb		7"			153
Planter, Lamb (Marked NM)	40s	6"		42	
Planter, Large Harmony	60s	12"	264, 265	93	
Planter, Large Mama Duck		10"		199	
Planter, Large Scandia Line	70s	10¾"	301		
Planter, Large Starburst	70s	9"	281		
Planter, Leaves, Berries	20s, 30s	6"	23		
Planter, Liberty Bell	50s	10"	199, 233	83, 147	
Planter, Lily Bud – Banana	40s	8½"	80, 81		
Planter, Lily Bud – Cross	40s	7½"	81		
Planter, Lily Bud – Double Divided	40s	11½"	83		
Planter, Lily Bud – Heart, Oval	40s	6½"	81		
Planter, Log	50s	12¼"	249		
Planter, Log – Chocolate Bisque	50s	8¾"			63
Planter, Low	70s	10"	263		
Planter, Low Centerpiece	60s	8½"	147		
Planter, Madonna	Floraline	7"	268	110	125, 285
Planter, Madonna	50s	6"	140		
Planter, Noel	40s				155
Planter, North Pole	50s			199	
Planter, Novelty	50s	7"			60
Planter, Old Mill	50s	7½"	231		
Planter, Pail, Birds		6"			156
Planter, Panda, Crib	50s	6"	157		
Planter, Panther	50s	16"	226	102	
Planter, Pebble Small	60s	6"	259		
Planter, Pedestal – Z Design	50s	9"		89	
Planter, Pedestal – Early American Line	60s	7"			90
Planter, Pelican	40s	7¾"	135		
Planter, Pelican with Cart	40s	8¼"	141		
Planter, Pheasant	50s	7½"	205		
Planter, Piano	50s	6"	148	145	
Planter, Pig	40s	6"	149		
Planter, Pine Cone Decoration	40s	9", 10½"			154
Planter, Plowboy	50s	8"		83, 148	
Planter, Poodle	50s	7½"	161	88	
Planter, Puppy	50s	6¼"	157		
Planter, Pussy at the Well	50s	7"	231	154	
Planter, Quail	50s	9"	205		
Planter, Rabbit	50s	7¼"	156, 157		
Planter, Rabbit, Stump	50s	5½"	154	88	158
Planter, Raggedy Ann Block	50s	5¼"	155		
Planter, Rectangle – Tonecraft	60s	10½"			95
Planter, Rhinoceros	40s			200	148
Planter, Ribbed	20s, 30s	4", 5", 5½", 6"	36		
Planter, Robin Hood				203	153
Planter, Rocking Chair	50s	8½"	242, 243		
Planter, Rodeo Cowboy	50s	7¾"	248	82, 155	
Planter, Rolling Pin with Boy Blue	50s	7½"		81	
Planter, Rooster	40s, 50s	7"	244		
Planter, Round Harmony	60s	6"	265	93	
Planter, Round Springwood	60s	6½"	261		
Planter, Saddle		7¼"			156

Description	Era	Size	Volume I	Volume II	Volume III
Planter, Scoop with Mammy	50s	7½"	230	150	
Planter, Shell	50s	5"	229	81	
Planter, Small Fawn	50s	5"	159		
Planter, Snail	70s	10"		190	
Planter, Snowman	40s	6"	134, 135	81	
Planter, Spinning Wheel	50s	7¼"	233	87	
Planter, Spinning Wheel with Cat		7"		203	156
Planter, Sprinkling Can – Antique Rose	50s	7"		91	
Planter, Square – Capri	60s	5"			56
Planter, Square Grecian	50s	3½"	193		
Planter, Squirrel	50s	5"	159	102	
Planter, Stained Glass	50s	7"			154
Planter, Starburst	70s	6"	281		
Planter, Stone	50s	6¾"	243		
Planter, Stork	40s	7"	68		
Planter, Stork	50s	7½"	160, 161		
Planter, Strap Design	50s	8"		88	
Planter, Stump	50s	5"	229		
Planter, Sunburst Gold	50s	9¼"			62
Planter, Swan	40s	7½"	149		
Planter, Swan – Sunburst Gold	50s	6"	196		
Planter, Swan Antique Rose	50s	7½"	247	90, 91	
Planter, Swan with Decal	50s	7½"			86
Planter, Teddy Bear	Floraline	5"	272		124, 285
Planter, Tierra Line	60s	5", 8"	282, 283		
Planter, Triple Pot	50s	12½"	169	143	
Planter, Trivet	50s	8¾"	242		
Planter, Trolley Car	50s	7"	242		
Planter, Turtle	70s	9"		190	
Planter, Turtle	50s	8"	237	187	
Planter, Turtle	50s	12½"	229	146	
Planter, Turtle	Floraline	5¼"	270, 271	111	274
Planter, Turtle	60s	7"	237		
Planter, Turtle	70s	9½"	293		
Planter, Turtle Green Thumb Line	70s	8"	290		
Planter, Twin Shoes	40s	4½"	135		
Planter, Twin Swans	50s	8½"		87	
Planter, Uncle Sam with Eagle	40s	9"			146
Planter, Village Smithy	50s	7½"	233		
Planter, Vine design	50s	8½"	218		
Planter, Wagon Wheel	50s	8"	249		
Planter, Wheelbarrow w/ Rooster	50s	10½"	141	75, 147	
Planter, Wild Rose	50s	8"	176, 177		
Planter, Wishing Well	50s	6¾", 7¾"	242, 243	87	
Planter, Zebra	50s	8½"	211	150	30
Planting Dish	50s, 60s	9"		165	54, 55
Planting Dish	40s	9"	149		
Planting Dish	40s	7"	263		
Planting Dish	40s, 50s	8"	149, 277		
Planting Dish	40s, 50s	6½"	241, 277		
Planting Dish	50s	9", 9½", 10½", 12"			56, 57, 59
Planting Dish	50s	10", 14"			63
Planting Dish	50s, 60s	7", 7½"	277		
Planting Dish	60s	5"	263		
Planting Dish	60s	14"			65
Planting Dish with Bud	50s	11"	171		
Planting Dish with handles	50s	10"			61
Planting Dish with Icing Design	50s	10", 14"			65
Planting Dish, Love	70s	6"	293		
Planting Dish, Antique Rose	50s	12"		91	
Planting Dish, Antique Rose	50s	8", 15"			86
Planting Dish, Basket Line	50s	9½", 11½"	257		
Planting Dish, Blossomtime	40s	8"	175		
Planting Dish, Brocade	50s	7¾", 14¼"	225		
Planting Dish, Capri	60s	7"	245		
Planting Dish, Capri	60s	11", 14½"			56
Planting Dish, Decal	50s	8 "			87
Planting Dish, Fan	50s	9"	240		
Planting Dish, Filigree	50s	8¾"	244		59
Planting Dish, Footed	50s	8", 10"		77	
Planting Dish, Garden Club	50s	8", 10"	255		
Planting Dish, Garden Club	50s	8"	255		85
Planting Dish, Long	60s	10"	263		
Planting Dish, Long Grecian	50s	12"	193		
Planting Dish, Low Scandia Line	70s	"5¼"	301		
Planting Dish, Pedestal Line	50s	7", 11"	257		

Description	Era	Size	Volume I	Volume II	Volume III
Sand Jar	50s	14"	152, 153	151	
Sand Jar with Handles	20s, 30s	18"	33		116
Sand Jar, Sphinx	20s, 30s	16"	41		114
Seahorse	40s	6"	92		
Seal Figural	40s	6½"	134		
Serving Bowl, Canyon	70s	8"	297		
Serving Bowl, Shell Morano Line	60s		296		
Serving Dish, Chip, Dip	70s	9"			195
Serving Dish, Tiered	70s	9"			195
Shaker, Parmesan Pasta Corner Line	70s	5"	295		
Shell	40s	6"			45
Shell Planter	40s	7½"	74		
Shoe Planter – Mary Ann	40s	5"	68, 69		
Sign, Clemson				204	
Sign, Pottery Shop	80s	5"	292	157	320
Single Cache Planter	50s	9"	171	79	
Skillet	40s, 50s	10"			60
Slow Cooker/electric	70s	10"			203
Snack Bowl	70s	8"	291		
Snack Bowl, Western Line	70s	4"	286		
Snack Dish, three piece	40s	11"	215		
Snack Tray (Kidney or Rectangular) with Cup	60s	10"		173	
Snowman Figural		6"			157
Soap Dish, Rustic	40s	4½", 4¼"	217		
Sombrero Serve All, El Rancho Line	60s	13"	308	156	
Soup Bowl Cup with Decal	70s	5"		179	
Soup Kettle with Cover	70s	7"	291		
Soup Pot with Ladle Pasta Corner Line	70s	7"	295		
Soup Pots	70s	4"	291		
Specialty Piece, Maimonides	70s	5"	319		
Specialty Piece, Secundum Artem	70s	5"	319		
Specialty Piece, USP 150th Anniversary	70s	5"	319		
Spittoon	40s				146
Spoonrest	70s	4"		179	201
Spoonrest, Butterfly	50s	7½"	139	150	
Spoonrest, Penguin	50s	7"	139		121
Stein, Beer 68 oz.	70s	8¾"	287		
Stein, Beer – Old Milwaukee			318		
Stein, Beer – Primo	70s	6½"	315		
Stein, Beer – Vintage Auto Decal	70s	5½"	319		
Stein, Beer 7 – League Boot	70s	7"	284, 285		
Stein, Decorative	70s	70 oz.		178	
Stein, German Theme	70s	8¾"	284, 285, 287		
Stein, Miller Brewing – 1977	70s	6¾"	315		
Strawberry Jar	70s	9"		175	
Strawberry Jar	50s	7, 8"	220, 233		
Stretch Dog	40s	7¼"	85	135	
Stretch Goat (Standing)	40s	5¼"	84, 85		
Stretch Hound (Dachshund)	40s	8¼"	85	135	
Stretch Lion	40s	5¼, 7½"	85	46	
Stretch Pony (Horse)	40s	5⅜"	85		
Stretch Ramming (Butting) Goat	40s	5½"	84, 85	135	
Sugar Bowl, Covered Grecian	50s	4½"	195		
Sugar Dish, Covered – Sunburst Gold	50s	5"	197		
Sugar Dish, Lost Glaze	50s		198		
Sugar, Avocado	50s	8 oz.			122
Sugar, Cook Serve Line	50s				89
Sugar, Covered	50s	4½"	239	86	
Sugar, Covered	60s	12 oz.			89
Sugar, Covered – Canyon	70s			193	
Sugar, Covered – Elmer	70s	3½"			199
Sugar, Covered – Esmond	60s	5"		94	
Sugar, Covered – Floral Decal	70s			184	
Sugar, Covered – Islander Collection	70s	5"		191	
Sugar, Covered – Strawberry Country	70s			190	
Sugar, Covered Brocade	50s		222		
Sugar, Covered Stone Craft	70s	4"	299		
Sugar, Daisy	40s	8 oz.	143		
Sugar, Ivy	50s	8 oz.	145		
Sugar, Leaves, Berries	20s, 30s	5"		27	
Sugar, Pine Cone	40s		228		
Table, Onyx	20s, 30s	20"	48	10	
Tankard, Barrel	20s, 30s	8½"	13		24
Tankard, Buccaneer, Cross or Grapes Detail	20s, 30s	8½"	14		22
Tankard, Floral Motif	20s, 30s	8½"			24
Tankard, Grapes Detail	20s, 30s	7½", 9½"			22

Description	Era	Size	Volume I	Volume II	Volume III
Vase with Low Bud Design	40s	6, 8"	53		
Vase with Low Bud Design	40s	10"	53, 106		
Vase with small Handles	20s, 30s	6, 8"	27	30	34
Vase with small Handles	20s, 30s	9"		30	
Vase with uneven Handles	40s	8"	63		
Vase, Arrowhead	40s	8"		57	
Vase, With Love	70s	7¼"	293		
Vase, Antiqua	70s	9"	275		
Vase, Antique Rose	50s	10"		91	
Vase, Antique Rose	50s	9"			86
Vase, Antique Rose	50s	5", 7', 8"			87
Vase, Arcature	50s	6¼", 8", 9"	220, 221		
Vase, Arrangement	60s	6"		99	
Vase, Atrisan	60s	7½", 9½"	252, 253		
Vase, Atrisan	60s	10"			58
Vase, Ball Footed Design	50s	6½", 9½"			90
Vase, Basket	50s	9"	242	145	
Vase, Basket Line	50s	8"		103	
Vase, Basketweave	40s	5½", 6", 8", 12"	73	44	
Vase, Basketweave	50s	4¼", 6½"	265		
Vase, Blossomtime	40s	8"	174		
Vase, Boots Western Line	70s	7"	286		
Vase, Brocade	50s	8", 9½"	223, 225		
Vase, Bud	60s	6¼"		99	
Vase, Bud	70s	6"	277		204
Vase, Bud	50s	6½"	226		
Vase, Bud	40s	6"			151
Vase, Bud – Classic Line	60s	6"			93
Vase, Bud – Gold Finish	50s	7¼"			59
Vase, Bud – Leaves, Berries	30s, 40s	8"		37	
Vase, Bud – Sunburst Gold	50s	6¼"	197		
Vase, Bud Brocade	50s	7¼"	225		
Vase, Bud Capri	60s	7"	245		56
Vase, Bud Cascade	60s	6¼"	213		
Vase, Bud Garden Club	50s	6½"	255, 256	47	
Vase, Bud Golden Brocade	70s	6"	304		
Vase, Bud Grecian	50s	4"	193		
Vase, Bud Pottery Shop Collection	70s	6"	300		
Vase, Bud – Vesta Line	60s	8"			88
Vase, Bud with Birds	50s	8"		81	44
Vase, Bud with Decoration	40s	5"		47	121
Vase, Bulbous	70s	5"			203
Vase, Capri	60s	8¼"			56
Vase, Cat	60s	14"		97	123
Vase, Chrysanthemum	50s	8"	165		
Vase, Classic Line	60s	8", 12"			95
Vase, Column	20s, 30s	8½"	21	14	
Vase, Column Decorated	20s, 30s	10½"	20	14	
Vase, Corinthian	60s	11"		176	
Vase, Cornucopia	50s	6"		165	
Vase, Cornucopia	20s, 30s	6", 8", 10"	29	28	
Vase, Cornucopia	20s, 30s	5"		28	
Vase, Cornucopia	40s	8"	137		
Vase, Cornucopia	50s	7"	149		
Vase, Cowboy Boots	50s	7"	249, 250		
Vase, Crestwood	60s	14½"			90
Vase, Disc Design	40s	6¾"	66	44	119
Vase, Divided Handle Blossomtime	40s	7"	175	139	
Vase, Double Handled	50s	9"		66	
Vase, Double Ringed Handles	40s	6"		42	
Vase, Double Tulip	40s – 50s – 60s	8"	166, 167 "	70	
Vase, Early American	60s	9"		103	
Vase, Early American	60s	8"	283		
Vase, Embossed	40s	7"	147		
Vase, Fan	40s	12"			148
Vase, Fan	50s	6"	144	39	153
Vase, Fan	50s	10½"	147		
Vase, Fan – Garden Club	50s	7½"		96	85
Vase, Fancy	50s	9"	227		
Vase, Fancy – Brocade or Sunburst Gold	50s	6½"		103	
Vase, Fawn	50s	9"	240	155	
Vase, Feather	50s	8½"		67	
Vase, Finger Antique Curio	60s	8"	266, 267	100	
Vase, Floor Scandia Line	70s	14½"	301		
Vase, Floral	40s	9"	170		
Vase, Floral Theme		6", 8"		202	

Hanson, Bob, Craig Nissen, and Margaret Hanson. *McCoy Pottery Collector's Reference and Value Guide, Volume I.* Collector Books. 1996.
Hanson, Bob, Craig Nissen, and Margaret Hanson. *McCoy Pottery Collector's Reference and Value Guide, Volume II.* Collector Books. 1999.
Huxford, Sharon & Bob. *Collector's Encyclopedia of McCoy Pottery.* Collector Books. 1978.
Sanford, Steve & Martha. *Guide to McCoy Pottery*. Adelmore Press. 1997.
NM Express, monthly McCoy newsletter. 1994 – present.
Our McCoy Matters, monthly McCoy newsletter. 1988 – 1994.

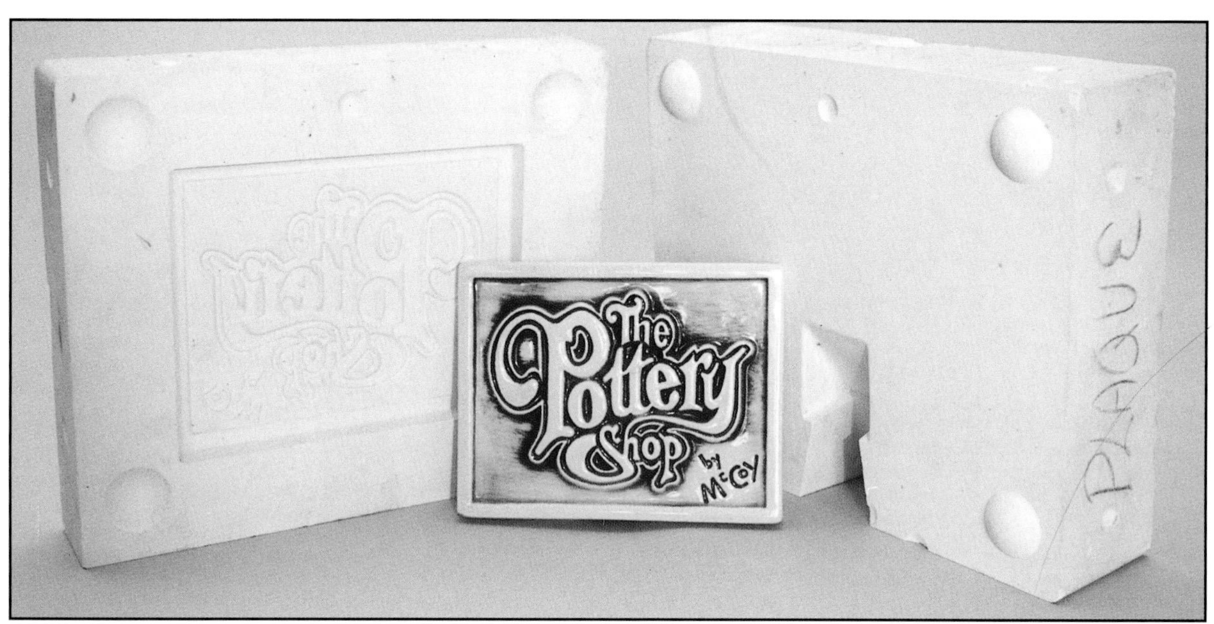

Pictured with its original mold, the Pottery Shop Sign 4" x 5". Early 1980s. Made for a promotion for J.C. Penney Co., but the account was lost and the signs were never shipped. It is estimated that there were 125 – 150 made. $350.00 – 500.00.

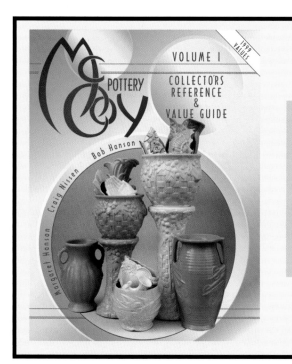

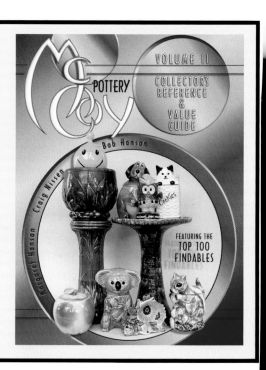